THE RESEARCH CRAFT

AN INTRODUCTION TO
SOCIAL SCIENCE METHODS

THE RESEARCH CRAFT

AN INTRODUCTION TO SOCIAL SCIENCE METHODS

John B. Williamson, *Boston College*
David A. Karp, *Boston College*
John R. Dalphin, *Merrimack College*

in collaboration with

Richard S. Dorr, *Boston College*
Stephen T. Barry, *Boston State College*
Victoria H. Raveis, *Columbia University*

Little, Brown and Company
BOSTON   TORONTO

Library of Congress Catalog Card No.: 76-45932

ISBN 0-316-943592

12   11   10   9   8   7   6   5

HAL

*Published simultaneously in Canada
by Little, Brown & Company (Canada) Limited*

Printed in the United States of America

The authors acknowledge permission to use material from the following sources:

Table 2.1 (page 51): Adapted from *Analyzing Social Settings* by John Lofland. © 1971 by Wadsworth Publishing Company, Inc., Belmont, California, 94002. Reprinted by permission of the publisher.

Table 2.2 (page 52) and *Table 2.3* (page 53): Reprinted with permission of Macmillan Publishing Co., Inc. from *The Language of Social Research* by P. Lazarsfeld and M. Rosenberg, pp. 41, 45: Copyright 1955 by The Free Press.

Figure 2.1 (page 54), *Figure 15.9* (page 436), and *Figure 15.10* (page 437): Adapted from P. Blau and O. D. Duncan, *The American Occupational Structure,* 1967, p. 170. Reprinted by permission of John Wiley & Sons, Inc.

Table 5.1 (page 120): From *Survey Research* by Charles H. Backstrom and Gerald D. Hursh, 1963, p. 33. Reprinted by permission of The Northwestern University Press, Evanston, Illinois.

Figure 13.1 (page 350): From *Handbook of Social Psychology, Second Edition,* 1968, Vol. 2, p. 695, by Gardner Lindzey and Elliot Aronson, (eds.). Reprinted by permission of Addison-Wesley Publishing Co., Inc., Reading, Massachusetts.

Preface

This book is designed for use in the first course on social research methods, particularly in departments of sociology, political science, social psychology, social work, and education. One distinctive feature of this text is the comprehensiveness in coverage of alternative research methods. Whereas most texts focus on a few of the most common alternatives, our goal is to expose the reader to the full range of methods available to the social researcher. Another distinctive feature is the emphasis given to obtaining some "hands on" experience with each of the methods considered.

The book is divided into two parts. In Part One we discuss the central issues (such as measurement, objectivity, sampling, and ethical considerations) which come up as problems in all social research regardless of the specific approach selected. Our aim is to acquaint the reader with the nature and complexities of the research process. We seek to convey an understanding of social research as both a science and a craft. The material presented in Part One prepares the reader to better understand the individual methods described in Part Two of the book. For the first course in research methods Part One is a must; for a more advanced course it provides a comprehensive review of the basic issues.

In Part Two we devote a separate chapter to each of nine research methods. An effort has been made to provide even-handed treatment of both qualitative and quantitative methods, perspectives, and research styles. Here our goals are understanding of the types of research problems for which the method is applicable, familiarity with some of the specific mechanics of using the method, and an appreciation of the method's distinctive advantages and limitations.

Our text offers the instructor considerable flexibility. Each of the chapters in Part Two can stand alone. The instructor may choose freely those chapters to be included as well as those to be passed over. The chapters may be assigned in any order. It is likely, for example, that instructors who prefer a more quantitative focus in their course will select Chapters 6, 9, 12, 14, and 15 for emphasis. Similarly, those who favor a more qualitative approach might emphasize Chapters 7, 8, 10, and 11. While we remain committed to a comprehensive approach which would emphasize both qualitative and quantitative perspectives, the book lends itself equally well to use by those who do not share this committment. We suggest that all courses start with the material in Part One and then go on to cover between five and ten of the chapters in Part Two, depending on the length of the course and the desired focus.

For those who choose to focus on a small number of research methods in detail, the annotated references at the end of each chapter should prove valuable. Note that we include one set of suggested readings *about the method* and a second set of studies *using the method*. The readings about the method will be particularly useful to those who plan to undertake a major study using that method.

The experience of actually using a method, even if only on a modest scale, provides knowledge which cannot be obtained by simply reading about the method. For this reason we have prepared for each of the methods a set of exercises designed to provide first hand experience with the method. Some are designed to be carried out individually, others to be done in small groups. For each method there is at least one exercise that calls for a replication on a small scale of some aspect of one of the studies mentioned in the suggested readings about the method. We have tried to keep these exercises brief enough so that students can be reasonably expected to complete them as part of a weekly assignment.

Chapter 15 provides an overview of quantitative data analysis methods. It does not assume any prior background in statistics, but some of the material toward the end of the chapter will be somewhat advanced for students who have had no prior background in statistics. This chapter has been included for those situations in which there is no separate course on statistical methods. It may be skipped when such a course does exist. However, many will find the chapter a useful review even if they have had a first course in statistics.

ACKNOWLEDGMENTS

Each chapter of this book went through numerous drafts. In many instances several persons contributed in a significant way to the final product. We choose to consider all those involved as co-authors of the final chapter. The chapters are co-authored as follows: John Williamson,

Chapters 1-7, 9, 12-15; David Karp, Chapters 1-3, 8-12; John Dalphin, Chapters 4-6, 13, 14; Richard Dorr, Chapters 2, 5-7, 9, 11; Stephen Barry, Chapters 3, 8, 15; Victoria Raveis, Chapters 10, 13, 15; Michael Fusco, Chapters 2, 15; Winifred Allen, Chapter 14; Leo Barrille, Chapter 11; and Nancy Wohl, Chapter 12.

Many people have given us useful suggestions and have helped us in other ways. We are particularly grateful to: Daniel Baer, Lorraine Bone, Donnah Canavan-Gumpert, Alice Close, Sharlene Hesse, Everett Hughes, Bette Johnson, Darleen Karp, Michael Sacks, Shirley Urban, and Allen Wakstein. We owe a special debt to Franklin Graham, Tina Samaha, Jane Lovinger, and Sandra Rigney of Little, Brown for their encouragement and assistance. We wish also to thank our reviewers for their suggestions, many of which proved to be most useful; we particularly want to thank Alex Inkeles, Larry Beckhouse, Robert Bilby, Loren Cobb, Gerry Hendershot, Albert Higgins, David Knoke, Howard Nixon, James O'Connor, and Alvin Rudoff.

Contents

Foundations of Social Research

PART ONE

The Research Process

A popular sociology textbook of the early 1960s (Berger, 1963:1) began with the observation that there are very few jokes about sociologists. More than a decade later it is still true that sociologists are unlikely to be the object of Johnny Carson's nightly wit, but the role of the sociologist has in recent years become more visible to the public. Politicians increasingly cite the findings of sociological research to formulate and justify certain of their policy positions. Citizens and government policy makers who are seeking better ways to deal with racial conflict, crime, drug addiction, and poverty make use of the wealth of sociological data gathered on these issues. Often a sociologist is part of a research team commissioned to evaluate the effectiveness of a social program such as Head Start. Such research has the potential to affect social policy and is probably most responsible for the public's growing awareness of the sociologist.

What motivates social research? For some, it is curiosity about people different from themselves. For others, a specific social group or phenomenon seems to require detailed description; still others feel compelled to analyze and explain what has been recorded. One group of sociologists view their research as a form of social criticism; their goal is to mobilize opinion in support of a change in the status quo. Still others may make the distinction between basic and applied research, indicating that their concerns are more theoretical than practical. Even among these persons there are differences in focus because some are committed to testing the validity of existing theories and others to the creation of new theories.

3

The various research goals mentioned — social policy creation, program evaluation, social criticism, verification of theory, discovery of theory, description of phenomena, explanation of phenomena, and understanding for its own sake — are not, of course, mutually exclusive. Researchers may have a combination of goals in mind as they begin work, and the goals may change as the work progresses.

Some critics have asserted that social research will not be meaningful until consensus is reached on research goals, appropriate problems for investigation, theoretical models to explain social phenomena, and methodologies with which to acquire data about these phenomena. Faced with this criticism, many social scientists have been defensive about their inability to develop any such consensus. The authors of this book wish to begin without adopting an apologetic stance. Rather, they want to suggest that the multiplicity of goals, methodologies, problems for investigation, and theoretical models presently in use is necessary and sensible, given the complexity of the social world. Social knowledge is not a monolithic entity. Social scientists never will be and never should be committed to producing a single body of knowledge.

LEVELS OF SOCIAL RESEARCH

Much of sociology is concerned with describing the patterned relationships that exist among the different units of a society. The most basic and frequently used unit is the *individual.* A more inclusive unit is the collectivity of individuals constituting a social *group.* The group may be small, as in a study of work groups in an industrial setting, or large, as in a study which compares racial groups on a national basis with respect to unemployment rates or average earnings. Sociologists often study an *institution.* The institution may be small, as in a study of a specific school, or large, as in a study of the political system of a nation. The most comprehensive unit of analysis is the *society*. A society too may be small (e.g., a small African tribe) or large (e.g., China or India). Knowing these units, we can now specify the different levels on which the sociologist can carry out an investigation. The following are three possible alternatives. The reader should be able to figure out some other alternatives and examples of each.

INDIVIDUAL/INDIVIDUAL — Some researchers whose major interest is with detailing the basic dimensions of social interaction may attempt to analyze the basis for social organization in relatively small social systems. The simplest social system imaginable would be just two individuals in interaction with one another. Sociologists have referred to this simple social system as a social dyad.

INDIVIDUAL/GROUP — The next larger system for analysis involves inquiry into the ways in which individual behavior is influenced by group membership. This level of analysis has been a major concern of much social psychological investigation. A typical interest of researchers working on this level might be to examine the basis for individual conformity in social groups.

GROUP/GROUP — As the label would imply, it is often the concern of social scientists to study the relationships between various groups in a society. The field of race relations offers many examples of research carried on at this level as social scientists have sought to detail the nature of contact, conflict, and accommodation between various racial groups.

The point of this exposition is simply to alert the reader to the idea that as the level of research shifts so also will the problems faced by the researcher change. Research techniques applicable at one level may not be applicable at another. A researcher setting out to investigate patterns of interaction in a relatively small social system may find direct observation of behavior a wholly appropriate method for acquiring data. But it would certainly be more difficult to use observational techniques when investigating the interrelations between the major social institutions in a society. It is also true that the nature of the knowledge acquired is inextricably related to the level on which the research has been conducted. Each of the levels we have considered represents, in fact, a distinct feature of social reality.

The aspects of social life a researcher seeks to investigate and the goals he selects are influenced by a number of factors. One is the researcher's personal experience, particularly graduate school training and expertise obtained from prior research projects. Also important is the researcher's theoretical orientation. Another factor is the source of employment: a certain type of research may be expected at each university and agency. The priorities of the federal agencies which provide much of the social research funding also influence the goals and levels selected.

THE CONDUCT OF RESEARCH

Methods textbooks frequently mislead students who are trying to learn how to do research. Research is often discussed as though it occurred trouble free. The reader assumes that once a researcher has defined the problem and chosen a methodology appropriate for dealing with that problem, her research flows forth unproblematically. This image is enhanced for students who also read research reports. What they typically see is the finished product. In that finished product they might read a statement of the problem to be investigated, a tight theoretical exposition, a discussion of the methodology used, a presentation of the data, and some discussion of the data. The student has no way of knowing the subtle ways in which the problem might have changed as the research proceeded. Nor has he any way of knowing the numerous judgments that the researcher had to make as difficulties arose during the course of the research.

These limitations mean that a methods textbook can carry students only so far. It can outline typical procedures and present the likely process through which the researcher will go. Ultimately, however, a student learns the vagaries, difficulties, and the joys in doing research only by doing it. Each piece of research is to some degree idiosyncratic because each presents special difficulties for the researcher. It is quite common for the research process to take a number of unanticipated turns and twists, pushing the researcher in directions that could not have been anticipated at the outset of the study.

As research progresses the investigator may come to see that new theoretical models are called for or that additional problems are important. It often happens that she must reformulate, reassess, and continually reinterpret her focus. As new issues arise, she may see the need for collecting certain types of data not anticipated at the outset, and she may then see the need for using methodological techniques quite different from those with which she started.

A researcher may begin by investigating phenomena at one societal level, say the individual/individual level. Soon she may see that certain issues cannot be analyzed only at that level. She may begin to think, for example, about the conditions under which persons misinterpret each other's communications and may find it necessary to examine their social values. Such a theoretical consideration may lead her to examine the group affiliations of those being studied. She might, then, find herself shifting from one level of analysis to another as the research progresses.

When a researcher begins a project, she can rarely anticipate all of the procedural data-gathering problems that will arise: she may experience difficulty in gaining access to those she wants to study; she may come to realize that her questionnaire items are not providing her with the kind of knowledge that she seeks; she may see the necessity of doing some in-depth interviews with a selected sample of individuals, and so on.

The researcher must be willing to change her focus, her methodology, or her theory as the research situation demands. Sometimes the end product of a research project is very different from what had been envisioned at the outset. This is just as it should be. If a researcher could clearly determine what her findings would be at the outset of a project, there would not be much reason for carrying out the investigation. The student must avoid the idea that once he masters certain techniques, the research will proceed smoothly. He must realize that a list of the general steps in a research process is not to be treated too literally.

A general procedure of survey research will move the researcher through the following progression of steps.

1. Formulation of the problem.
2. Development of a theoretical framework for explaining phenomena associated with the problem.
3. Formulation of a set of hypotheses that can be tested.
4. Identification of the major variables in these hypotheses.
5. Provision of a set of criteria for measuring these variables.
6. Development of a questionnaire for collecting the data.
7. Selection of the sample of persons to be interviewed.
8. Gathering the data from the persons in the sample.
9. Coding, keypunching, and otherwise organizing the data for statistical analysis.
10. Analyzing the data and formulating conclusions.
11. Reporting the findings of the study.

Virtually all methods textbooks have some such statement of the steps in survey research. While the authors do not wish to understate the heuristic importance of such steps in outlining the procedure of research, they feel that a list of steps can not fully alert the reader to the number of unforeseen contingencies that he may face at each stage. Such a list fails to give a sense of the multiple problems that may cause the researcher to reassess at various points the direction of his research.

The problems of specifying a constant progression of steps or stages is even more difficult where a relatively unstructured technique, such as participant observation, is used. Works attempting to codify the procedures of participant observation have been few because the procedures are rarely systematic, dependent as they are on the particular research setting. Codification of these procedures is especially difficult because participant observation utilizes a variety of methods such as direct observation, informant interviewing, respondent interviewing, and document analysis.

The authors wish the reader to understand that there are no rules they can give which will ensure that a study will be a good study. They can explicate the general differences in styles of research. They can clarify certain criteria that sociologists consensually use in evaluating a piece of research. They can suggest some critical questions to be asked about the work of others — and they will ask them within the context of this book. All these aids to good research and the evaluation of research still bring us back to the same truth about methodology, however: there is no formula for doing insightful, imaginative sociological research.

The sociologist Everett Hughes was once asked what makes a good sociologist. His answer was that whether or not one can become a good sociologist is probably determined by about the age of twelve: by that age, one either has the curiosity and imagination about the social world to do good sociology or one does not. Although Hughes's response contains an element of hyperbole, its underlying message is well taken. No technique or set of methodological procedures will ever replace a keen sociological imagination in producing a good piece of research.

In some ways doing a good piece of research is a bit like painting. The technique is important, but technique alone will not produce a Picasso. We should think about methodologies and styles of research in much the same way. They are indispensable as tools for the collection of data about the world. We can improve our ability to understand and use these tools, but such skills are not enough.

One danger particularly must be avoided. It is absolutely crucial that the reader, a potential researcher, not become enamored with the elegance of tools to the exclusion of important substantive issues.[1] The sociologist Peter Berger (1963:13) puts social science methodology in proper perspective when he writes that "in the social sciences as in love an overemphasis on technique can lead to impotence."

Rather than specifying a particular process of investigation, the authors will describe characteristic styles of research, indicating the commonalities shared by these styles. There is one major commonality to most research in sociology which cuts across all the investigative procedures. This commonality is that *most researchers conceive of themselves as working within a scientific mode of inquiry.* The authors suggested at the outset of the chapter that the overall goal of sociological research is to acquire knowledge, understanding, and explanation of social phenomena. Most researchers, whatever might be the specific techniques used or problems investigated, consider the knowledge, understanding, and explanation that they produce to be scientific.

We must ask what is demanded of researchers who adopt science as their mode of inquiry. What do scientists demand of their techniques? How do scientists evaluate the quality of their theories or their data? Most generally, what does a scientific mode of inquiry demand of researchers before they can safely claim to have understood or explained something? Let us now consider science as a mode of inquiry and ask how well sociology meets the scientific criteria.

SCIENCE AS A MODE OF INQUIRY

Nearly every introductory textbook makes the claim that sociology is the scientific investigation of human behavior. Almost since its inception in the nineteenth century, sociology has modeled itself after the natural sciences. Sociologists have been intent on using the same tools as the natural sciences for investigating human behavior, and they have traditionally been interested in formulating scientific generalizations about the social world. Most sociology textbooks argue that the twin goals of sociological investigation are to *explain* and *predict* human

---

[1] A similar argument can also be made with respect to other aspects of the research process. We should not allow ourselves to become enamored with our theory, our hypotheses, our data collection methods, or our techniques for statistical analysis.

behavior and social processes. These goals are interrelated in that one measure of the quality of an explanation is its utility in successfully predicting other related phenomena.

It is not surprising that sociologists attempted to work in a scientific mode of inquiry. The development of the scientific method during the seventeenth century was a major stimulus to the exploration of the social world. With the growth of the natural sciences and the scientific method, there developed the search for laws, axioms, first principles, and theories about the physical world. Early social thinkers, spurred on by the success of the natural sciences, began to strive for the development of laws, axioms, and generalizations about human behavior as well.

The full significance of scientific development for social science investigation was not to be realized until the nineteenth century. A major turning point was the publication of Charles Darwin's *Origin of the Species* in 1859. Darwin brought together in that work two major strands of thought: the ideas of the natural sciences with the idea of human development (progress). Using Darwin's writings as a model, early social thinkers like Herbert Spencer tried to draw analogies between the development of society and the development of biological organisms as described by Darwin's theory of evolution.

Science was the natural model of inquiry to adopt because it showed itself to have tremendous explanatory and predictive power. There was another good reason, aside from purely intellectual ones, that sociologists naturally adopted science as their model: in American society, science nearly possesses elements of the sacred. In a society with a built-in bias toward pragmatism (Does it work? If not, what good is it?), science, or at least the technology that science has produced, does work. Because of this reverence for science in American society, sociologists, seeking legitimation for their young discipline, tried to convince others that they were engaged in building a cumulative science.

It is not our intention here to trace the development of sociology. This is not, after all, a book on sociological theory. But we should realize that sociologists have since the beginning seen themselves as engaged in a scientific pursuit. However, there are those who argue that despite claims to scientific stature, sociology cannot easily meet the demands of scientific investigation. Let us consider briefly, then, some of the technical demands of science. What distinguishes science as a mode of inquiry from nonscientific modes of inquiry? In the simplest sense, and as a place to begin, one might claim that there are several major canons or criteria of the scientific method, one of which is objectivity.

Objectivity

The canon of objectivity asserts that in the investigation of any phenomenon (in the case of sociology, a social phenomenon) the researcher's own private values must never intrude in determining the findings. In other words, the researcher's race, creed, color, political beliefs, and the like should be of absolutely no significance in determining the outcome of the study. The canon of objectivity asserts that any two researchers who study the same behaviors, processes, or phenomena, should arrive at identical findings.

Many sociologists have serious reservations about the possibility of truly objective social research. The model of the objective researcher essentially sees the researcher as a kind of machine that works the same way in every case — and all researchers as identical machines. There is considerable evidence in the social psychological literature, however, to support the claim that no two persons see the world in the same way. To use the phrase of the philosopher Alfred Schutz (1967), there are "multiple realities." We would agree with Schutz that the way a person sees the world is necessarily influenced by his background, biography, personality, biases, needs, and interests.[2]

If social psychologists are correct in asserting that each person observing a social phenomenon will exercise selective perception and selective memory, we should well expect, by way of example, that a black sociologist and a white sociologist viewing a race riot will likely not see it the same way; even if they did record the same events, they would be unlikely to interpret the events in the same way.

A general issue of particular concern to those who are involved in social policy research is that such research has a rather peculiar place in governmental policy formation. It is often used largely to legitimate a policy position already decided upon by government officials. So, if the research findings agree with the ideological position already taken, the research will be used to show the validity of that position. Alternatively, if the findings are contrary to the ideological position of those making decisions, the research is considered invalid and not worth considering. For example, the Report of the President's Commission on Pornography (1970) seemed to provide evidence that pornography was not only harmless, but potentially beneficial. Such findings implicitly suggested that pornography ought to be legalized. The failure to act on the report was largely a function of the political undesirability of its findings.

The general point here, without belaboring it further, is that human beings cannot be wholly objective. It is silly for sociologists to make any claim to total objectivity. Even in choosing a problem for investigation the sociologist is indicating certain value biases. The sociologist Howard Becker (1967) remarks that it is impossible for the sociologist to keep from taking sides in studying some social phenomenon.

---

[2] As will become evident in later chapters, there are many sources of bias in research that are beyond the control of the researcher. Even if it were possible for the researcher to be completely unbiased, there would still be other sources of bias at work (e.g., those who intentionally or unintentionally provide an interviewer with false information).

If, for example, sociologists are studying worker behavior in a factory, it is virtually impossible to see the situation equally from the point of view of workers and from the point of view of management.

Martin Nicolaus (1969) argues that most sociological research has served the vested interests of those in positions of power in society. He describes sociologists as those who "have their hands up and their eyes down," meaning that sociologists have typically obtained grant money from persons in power positions and then have studied those at the bottom of the stratification system. Such information, he argues, has been used to keep those at the bottom in their place.

There are some who argue that sociologists ought to clearly take a value position and present evidence for some point of view with little or no effort to present opposing points of view. This movement has been labeled *forensic sociology*. Most sociologists, including the authors, cannot agree with that outlook. They feel that, while sociologists cannot be perfectly objective and should try, therefore, to make as clear as possible their own biases and assumptions, they should strive to minimize those sources of bias over which they have some control. If, for example, a sociologist has a theory and is trying to test that theory, the logic of scientific inquiry demands that he or she seek out evidence that might lead to a rejection of the theory as well as the evidence which supports it. Science progresses by disproving theories rather than by proving them. The sociological researcher can maintain a degree of objectivity by carefully putting theories to rigorous tests and by continually looking for evidence that might abrogate these theories.

Replication

The criterion of replication is another canon of the scientific method. It decrees that research conducted in such a way as to preclude replication cannot be considered scientific, regardless of how objectively the research has been conducted. It must be possible for those who question the outcome of a study to do it over again and get the same results. In the physical sciences it is possible to replicate a previous study under conditions virtually identical to the original study. In social research it is often difficult to recreate the original conditions. Thus, in a duplication of a study, any difference in results could be due to the difference in conditions rather than to a lack of objectivity in the original study.

Precision in Measurement

Another objective of scientific inquiry is precision in measurement. The problems of measurement are among the most challenging problems the social researcher faces. Sociologists are typically interested in measuring complex, abstract variables such as happiness, alienation, anomie, cohesion, and morale. As will be documented, sociologists have a great deal of difficulty in agreeing how best to measure such concepts. It is frequently unclear what kinds of observable behaviors can be taken as evidence of the presence, or degree of presence, of such abstract factors as alienation. It is sometimes argued that sociologists will never be able to agree on how to measure a variable such as alienation because the meaning of the concept varies with the social context. The nature of the alienation suffered by ghetto dwellers is different from that suffered by whitecollar workers. Clearly, the meaning of many sociological variables cannot be separated from the social situation being studied. The situational nature of sociological variables importantly distinguishes them from the kinds of variables most usually dealt with by natural scientists. The measurement of such variables as height, density, distance, and pressure does not vary from situation to situation; all natural scientists will agree how to measure such variables.

In many ways the social world is more complex than the physical world. One can analyze a piece of paper blown about by the wind in terms of such variables as velocity, weight, gravity, and the like. It is obviously more difficult to understand how persons are swept along by crowd emotion. The complexity of the social world accounts, in part, for the difficulties faced by the social scientist in measuring specific phenomena. While such difficulties are often unavoidable, sociologists do have means available for checking on the quality of their measures. So, while we could no more make the claim to perfect measurement than we could to perfect objectivity, we must again consider the problem to be one of degree.

We find the criteria of objectivity, replication, and precision useful in forming a definitional baseline for evaluating the scientific status of social research. Like any purely definitional criteria, however, they do not fully enough characterize the quality of scientific work. We must broaden our image by conceiving of scientific investigation as the reflection of a particular attitude held by the researcher.

Attitude of Researcher

Scientists are continually bothered by the quality of the knowledge they produce. They adopt a *critical* attitude which forces them to question the status of the data being collected. The scientist continually asks "Is my data valid and reliable? What are the potential errors that might be intruding into my findings? What kinds of data will cause me to reevaluate my theoretical ideas?" The stress that we see on data is important because one of the hallmarks of scientific work is that it is empirical. One's understanding, knowledge about, and explanation of some aspect of the social world must be grounded in clear evidence from the world itself. Theoretical speculation without the acquisition of data is a nonscientific way of proceeding. When we speak of social "scientists" as being empirical we mean that they allow the object of inquiry — the social world — to speak back. Scientists should never become so committed to a set of theoretical ideas that they are unwilling to modify their ideas in the face of conflicting empirical evidence (Merton, 1949).

A second feature of the scientific attitude is the researcher's attempt to be conceptual or *analytical* about the object of his inquiry. Scientists are rarely concerned with the simple description of the phenomena being studied. Rather they seek to understand the underlying dimensions represented by the empirical observations. One aspect of the scientific inquiry, then, is the use of concepts to facilitate efficient organization of complex phenomena and to direct attention to the underlying elements of those phenomena. These categories cannot, of course, be arbitrarily imposed on a passive world. The real world acts and reacts continuously, causing social scientists to modify their assessments frequently.

Quantitative Data

One final point deserves clarification. Students frequently make the mistake of assuming that in order for research to be classified as scientific it must be presented in quantitative, mathematical terms. The criteria that we have offered contradict this image. We would certainly be willing to bestow the label scientific on much of the work of such persons as Karl Marx and Charles Darwin.

What conclusions can we draw at this point concerning the scientific status of sociology? It seems fruitless to look at the issue of science in either/or terms. The issue is not whether sociology is or is not a science. We perhaps do best to think of science in terms of a continuum ranging from those attempts to deal with the world which are wholly nonscientific to those that are highly scientific. We might for example, place physics at the highly scientific end of the continuum and theology at the highly nonscientific end of the continuum. Sociology would clearly fall in between. Since there is great diversity in sociological research in the extent to which the criteria of scientific research are met, it would not be meaningful to classify all sociological research as falling at any specific point along the continuum. This diversity also makes it foolish to attempt to classify the various social sciences relative to one another along this continuum.

We have seen that researchers may approach the acquisition of knowledge from a number of different methodological and theoretical perspectives and still be judged to be conforming to the logic of scientific inquiry. The production of scientific work does not depend on any one research process; we can identify characteristic research styles, but so far we have considered this argument largely in the abstract. Now we should look at some explicit details of a few of these possible variations in research style and process.

Believing that all knowledge rests on careful comparison of aspects of the phenomena under investigation, the authors have chosen to contrast two broad research styles or approaches in the pages that follow. They choose this strategy as a convenient way to highlight some of the generic differences that distinguish research efforts in the social sciences. More directly, they want to compare *structured* and *unstructured* methodological techniques, with the intent of detailing variations in the research process generated by each.

We will consider the questionnaire interview as the prototype of structured data-gathering techniques in the social sciences. As an example of a relatively unstructured methodology, we will focus on participant observation. We must keep in mind, though, that the broad distinctions we are about to draw do not fully encompass or describe all the possible differences in research style and process existent as part of the sociological enterprise!

STRUCTURED AND UNSTRUCTURED TECHNIQUES: VARIATIONS IN THE RESEARCH PROCESS

Broadly speaking, it is possible to distinguish between two major philosophical orientations held by researchers about the nature of the social world. One assumes that the nature of social reality is enormously problematic. The social world and the reality it embodies are not independent of human conception or human definition and redefinition. For those who hold this view, the way human actors assign meaning to the objects, events, or situations that they daily confront must be the major concern of the investigation. The preferred methodological technique for those who share this world view is direct participant observation. Researchers should whenever possible closely observe and directly participate in the behavior that they are trying to understand. Most usually, those who engage in participant observation do not produce studies where data is presented in quantitative terms. Rather data is typically presented in the form of qualitative descriptions of events and statements from the individuals involved. Direct participant observation is the first of the two methodological procedures we will consider.

There are other sociologists who do not view social reality as so enormously problematic. They are willing to assume that at least for certain issues it is possible to get a reasonably objective picture of people's attitudes, beliefs, and values by asking them. They are also willing to assume that for certain issues people will give reasonably accurate reports of past behavior and intended future behavior. Sociologists who share this perspective view the social world as an objective entity that can be approached, described, and understood with the use of structured techniques. They have traditionally been concerned with using procedures that ultimately allow for a quantitative rendering of social phenomena. Such researchers frequently use survey research based on questionnaire interviews, which they administer to a representative and reasonably large cross-section of the population of interest. We shall consider this type of research as a second methodological procedure.

We may now try to determine how the research processes demanded by each of these methodologies or styles of research differ. The first distinction between the two involves the issue of whether the primary goal of the research is to test a theory that we formulate at the outset of the research or to come up with a new theory during the course of the investigation. The first alternative is often referred to as *theory testing* or *verification;* the second is referred to as *theory construction* or *discovery.*

Discovery Versus Verification

The conventional wisdom of scientific research is that the researcher does not begin a piece of research without first defining the problem and one or more hypotheses to be tested. This is often done on the basis of the empirical findings of previous studies and the theories which have been proposed to account for these findings. Typically the researcher has identified the major variables and specified procedures for measuring these variables at the outset. Such research can be termed a *priori* research. It should be clear that those who use the questionnaire as their major data gathering device are often involved in a *priori* research. The construction of the questionnaire typically occurs prior to the collection of any data; and once constructed, the questionnaire itself limits the nature and type of data that will be collected. The major emphasis in much research that utilizes the questionnaire format is to verify (or, more accurately, to empirically test) a number of hypotheses or theoretical notions specified at the outset of the research.

Alternatively, as Glaser and Strauss (1967) point out, the emphasis of qualitative research is with *discovery* of substantive theory. Participant observation is normally not guided by an a *priori* development of hypotheses, concepts, and measurement procedures. Rather, the emphasis is on having the problem emerge as a result of the researcher's direct confrontation with a set of behaviors. As a matter of fact, the field process of discovery may lead researchers to a problem after they have been in the field for some time. The research focus, the development of theory, and the production of an analysis may emerge at any point in the research process, even towards the very end of that process.

Another way to state this difference in approach and process is to distinguish between *inductive* and *deductive* modes of inquiry. The process of discovery in observational research is an inductive process. An inductive approach is one in which the acquisition of knowledge or the process of the research works out from actual data to the development of theoretical models. In other words, theoretical statements are built up out of the data that the researcher has collected. A deductive approach, on the other hand, begins with broad abstract theoretical statements generated independently of the data.[3] These interrelated propositions, which are designed to explain some set of events, are then tested by acquiring data to see if the data fit the theoretical propositions.

Consider the general process through which Charles Darwin generated his theory of evolution. The process was, in effect, to make wide-ranging observations of physical differences between organisms and, on the basis of these observations, to construct some logical system of explanation relative to the development of these physiological differences. An inductive approach begins with observations of the empirical world, from which a theoretical model is constructed to explain them.

Consider, alternatively, the way that a natural scientist might approach the phenomenon of gravity. Here again, the research process must begin with some kind of empirical observation. In this case, let us assume that the observation is that apples fall from trees. The research may then attempt to construct some kind of theoretical model, a model composed of interrelated propositions designed ultimately to explain the empirical event of apples falling from trees. In this case, a wide range of observations is not called for. One simply begins with the class of events to be explained — objects falling from heights. The researcher may then go on to construct a theory, taking into account such things as acceleration, pressure, distance, and the like; his goal is for his theory to permit predictions about the behavior of falling bodies. At this point the researcher armed with a theory will begin to collect data in a systematic way that will help either to confirm or disprove the original theoretical ideas. Using the new theory, the researcher may construct a set of predictions about the way different objects fall in a vacuum. If these predictions are realized, the researcher can be said to have verified the deductive theory *at least for the time being.* To use Glaser and Strauss's term, deductive theory is not "grounded" in the data; it does not emerge from the data. In a deductive approach the function of data is to verify the researcher's theory.

In reality, despite the distinction we have just made, the development of theory is necessarily both inductive and deductive. We often begin with a deductive theory and try to test it with actual data and

---

[3] These theories are often obtained from the published literature on the topic. Some of this literature is purely theoretical and some is generally empirical. Thus what we are calling deductive research is *not* independent of all data, rather it is independent of the data in the present study.

then may find that the theory does not predict well. At that point we may choose to modify our theory in terms of the data which have been collected. When we see that the data dictate further theoretical development we are beginning to engage in an inductive process. In general, however, for qualitative research the emphasis is on inductive processes of theoretical development, and for quantitative research a more deductive approach is emphasized.

The argument is frequently made by field researchers (investigators who do participant observation) that those who set out only to test preestablished theoretical ideas may be unnecessarily imposing their own meanings as researchers onto the social world. Their argument is that survey research does an injustice to the complexity of social reality because the reality that is brought back is in many ways predetermined. This is so because the variables, concepts, and events for study have been preestablished.

The authors do not wish to dismiss the importance of this argument, but they must point out that those who do participant observation research (field work) also have their predetermined conceptualizations which unavoidably influence the social reality they bring back. Any researcher must begin with some set of assumptions, hypotheses, and theoretical ideas. The distinction to be made is in the flexibility that is built into the two alternative approaches. The issue here is whether the methodology allows for a continual reevaluation of initial assumptions and concepts. Field research, by its very nature, demands such continual reconceptualization; therefore, the claim that the field work process is one of discovery is a reasonable claim.

One of the strengths of participant observation implied by our discussion is that the researcher utilizing that approach may continuously integrate the processes of data collection and data analysis. In the case of research using questionnaire devices, analysis of the data typically cannot take place until the very end of the research process. This is so because the researcher normally does not see the data until it has all been collected.[4]

Related to theory construction and the point at which it occurs in the research process is a second distinction between the two methodological approaches that we have chosen to compare. We now turn to a discussion of attempts at *generalization* from social science data.

Empirical and Analytical Generalization

Like other scientists, sociologists seek through their research to make general statements about the world. As a discipline, sociology seeks after generalization. If, for example, a group of researchers are

---

[4] An exception to this generalization is the investigator who is carrying out a small-scale survey research project and doing all the interviewing personally.

interested in finding out how poverty affects family life style, they must surely find some other source of information than a study of every poor family in the United States. Given only limited time and resources, these investigators will be able to study only a sampling of poor families (and possibly a comparative sample of families who are better off financially). While we cannot at this point get into the complexities of sampling procedures, let us acknowledge at least that researchers wish the results of the study on a limited study of poor persons to be applicable to the poor more generally.

Another example perhaps better illustrates the point. If we are interested in how well Americans feel the President is doing his job, we must acknowledge at the outset that we cannot question every American on that issue. But if we very carefully select a sample of, say, 1500 persons, we will be able to generalize about the attitudes of Americans as a whole, knowing that the error in our estimate is small and within tolerable limits. In many studies the researcher wants to generalize from a sample of the population to the entire population.[5] In order to facilitate our discussion from this point on, we will refer to the type of generalization in which the researcher estimates the characteristics of a known population of persons by interviewing a sample from that population as *empirical generalization*. We may now consider the elements necessary in order to produce solid empirical generalization in sociological research. We can do that by turning once again to a specific hypothetical example.

Suppose we have in mind the theoretical idea that there is a relationship between the size of an organization and the morale of workers in that organization. In this case, for all intents and purposes, the population is all organizations and all workers in those organizations. Suppose further that we have theoretical reasons to believe that the larger the organization the poorer the morale among workers; this is the proposition which we wish to test.

If we look at one large organization and find that the morale of workers is low, would we have satisfactorily verified the proposition relating organization size to morale? Obviously not. We would want also to look at a small organization and measure the morale of workers there. If we do this and find that the morale of workers is high, we begin to have some faith in the empirical generalization we are seeking to verify. Finally, if we add to this sample a large number of organizations varying in size and show that the postulated relationship between size and morale holds up, we will have even greater faith in the validity of the original proposition. From this example we should be able to infer some important elements necessary for a convincing empirical generalization.

Solid empirical generalization depends upon the collection of systematic data from a relatively large sample. This is one of the great

---

[5] Sometimes the total population of persons to which the researcher wants to generalize is referred to as the *universe*.

strengths of survey research as a methodological approach. Since all persons in the sample are answering the same questions, we are provided with systematic data. With this approach we can generally reach a reasonably large sample of persons from the population of interest to us. We may now say that one of the great advantages of the structured questionnaire, and one of the major reasons that proponents of the approach are willing to give up the flexibility of unstructured approaches such as participant observation, is that it allows for empirical generalization. Such generalization is, as we have seen, a major goal of any science.

Let us consider the second methodological procedure of concern here — participant observation. Keeping in mind the criteria just named for strong empirical generalization, we must decide how we are to evaluate the generalizing prospects of data gathered through participant observation.

Typically in the case of participant observation, the researcher can observe only a limited number of persons and situations. In our hypothetical study of the relationship between organization size and worker morale, a participant observer would find it difficult, if not impossible, to catalogue the behavior of the hundreds of workers who might well have been interviewed using the survey research method. More typically the participant observer would focus on an in-depth understanding of the workers in one or two organizations. Instead of having a large number of cases for analysis, the participant observer is more likely to be involved in a single case analysis. Most participant observation involves what has been termed *case study*. The implications of this mode of research for empirical generalization should be clear.

Because the participant observer can observe only a limited number of persons, situations, or events, the possibility of what we are calling empirical generalization is severely limited. It should come as no surprise, therefore, that a major complaint lodged against participant observation is that as a methodological procedure it does not allow for adequate generalization.

This criticism is frequently leveled at what has been called the "community study," in which a sociologist has studied one community over an extended period of time. Floyd Hunter (1953), for example, studied the power structure of Atlanta, Georgia some years ago. The question that is frequently raised about studies such as Hunter's is whether the community studied is in any way a representative community. Might it be that Atlanta is not at all typical of most communities? And if this is so, then what possible kinds of generalizations can be made by studying this one community? Many critics claim that case studies done through participant observation have limited scientific value.

At the beginning of this chapter we suggested that the goals of research are quite varied. In terms of the criticisms leveled at participant observation studies, it might be useful to distinguish between *exploratory* studies and *explanatory* studies.

When sociologists speak of exploratory studies they essentially mean studies that are primarily concerned with *generating* ideas or hypotheses rather than actually *testing* them in any way. The purpose of exploratory studies is to uncover tentative ideas that can be more rigorously tested in a later study. Alternatively, the study in which the theories are actually put to the test are termed explanatory studies; in these studies, the researcher's explanations are either accepted or rejected on the basis of the collected data. When a survey research study is conducted with the idea of verifying a set of hypotheses, we would classify the study explanatory in nature.[6]

In the case of participant observation, it is frequently claimed that hypotheses are not really being tested since one has not begun with any hypotheses. Many would claim that since the possibility of empirical generalization is low in the types of case studies conducted by participant observers, such studies should not appropriately be thought of as explanatory studies. In short, the argument is frequently made that participant observation studies can be most useful as a first step in research. The purpose of participant observation studies, some say, is to generate ideas, hypotheses, theories, or concepts that can later be employed in a survey research study designed to test these ideas more systematically.

Qualitative studies can and do frequently perform this useful, preliminary research function of uncovering issues for systematic investigation. Suppose we are interested in how teachers' attitudes and behaviors affect students' performance. One research strategy would be to begin with some in-depth observation of a few classrooms. We might begin by looking at what actually transpires behaviorally between teachers and students, hoping as we watch to cultivate some ideas about the main relationship of concern — that between teachers' behavior and students' performance.

Let us assume that through this preliminary observational work we come to feel that teachers display three general types of teaching style. The first is an *authoritarian* teaching style, in which teachers are fairly rigid in their treatment of students. Students are allowed to talk only when the teacher specifies that they may ask questions, everyone must wait to be called on, and students never have any voice about what will be covered in class. Other teachers are much more *democratic* in their attitude and behavior toward students. Some teachers still represent the major source of power and authority in the classroom, but students are allowed much greater input in terms of what is covered in class. Finally, there is a third teaching style which can be termed *laissez-faire*. Here students stand on a basis of nearly full equality with the teacher. The

[6] Not all survey research studies are conducted with the goal of testing an explicit hypothesis. Often the goal is to obtain some descriptive information that will subsequently be used in formulating a set of hypotheses. Such use of survey research would be classified as exploratory.

students are pretty much allowed to pursue whatever interests they have.

Having uncovered this typology of teaching style through observational techniques, a typology that might never have occurred to us had we not done this "exploratory" qualitative research, we are in a position to gather through questionnaires rather extensive data relating these teaching styles to student performance. We might now choose to sample a large number of teachers and students using a standardized questionnaire. Having done a preliminary investigation, we are led to include questions in the questionnaire which allow us to discriminate between teachers in terms of their teaching styles. These styles become the basis for our comparative analysis and are related to various performance measures for a large sample of students. In the questionnaire phase of the research we are able to collect systematic data on a large number of persons. We are now in a position to test the relationship between style and performance; that is, we are in a position to test the explanatory value of the typology generated through participant observation.

Examples such as the preceding, which shows the possible integration of structured and unstructured techniques, could be multiplied many times over. We might add here that despite the obvious strength of combining observational and more structured techniques, it is very rarely done in the social sciences — for many reasons. One is that many researchers are unwilling to invest the large amount of time and money that would be demanded by the kind of preliminary observational work suggested here. Good observational work sometimes takes several months or more. Therefore, despite the suggestion often made in methods textbooks that qualitative and quantitative techniques be merged, it is a technique seldom used.

At this point, therefore, the authors are willing to concede that one major function of participant observation is exploration. At the same time, they stress that this is not the only function of qualitative research. We have seen that one goal of scientific research is the production of empirical generalization. We can alternatively speak of a kind of conceptual or *analytical* generalizability. The authors suggest that case studies of the sort produced by participant observers can have greater utility than that which is often acknowledged for them. One important function of participant observation is to produce a comprehensive analysis that might be applicable in a variety of social contexts. Everett Hughes begins to point out the importance of analytical generalization when he says that "each social situation is a laboratory where some aspect of social life can best be studied because there it is best illuminated." Let us weigh the significance of Hughes's statement and the kinds of generalization that are producible from qualitative case studies. In order to more fully explain what we mean by conceptual or analytical generalization we must turn to the distinction that can be made between the *content* of social life and the *form* of social life.

One obvious task of scientific work, following from our earlier discussion, is to understand the underlying dimensions of the phenomena being studied. Consider once more the case of apples falling from trees. It had from the beginning of time been obvious to everyone that apples fell from trees. As an empirical event by itself, the falling of apples from trees is not terribly important scientifically. What is important from the scientific point of view was the conceptual breakthrough that allowed us to understand the laws of gravity. Once discovered, we were able to see the phenomenon of gravity as an underlying form, a generic feature of the physical world. In some ways, then, the fact of apples falling from trees, as an empirical event, becomes incidental and unimportant once the underlying forms represented by that empirical event are discovered. Once the notion of gravity was understood, a large number of empirical events became explicable: any falling object could be explained in terms of the same laws. The content of the empirical events examined could range quite widely, but the form would remain constant. We are asserting here that important forms can be discovered by examining initially only *one* case. This being so, we must reassess the value of the qualitative case study.

Good social science also seeks to uncover generic forms of phenomena that may vary in empirical content — underlying forms of social life. We can assert that human behavior presents itself in constant behavioral forms that differ only in content. If we accept the notion that specific analytical generalizations can be made, and that these generalizations cut across contexts varying in empirical content, we begin to see the importance of the case study. One task of sociological analysis is to reveal universal social forms that display themselves in a variety of empirical contexts. Let us consider a concrete example of this abstract distinction between form and content.

Suppose that we are interested in the phenomenon of religious devotion. As a form of social life, religious devotion expresses itself in quite different empirical contexts. So, we would claim that churches are only one context among many where this phenomenon might be investigated. In order to understand religious devotion as a form of social life, one could analyze such diverse empirical areas as football games, rock concerts, and people's behavior on national holidays. While the content of each of these cases is quite different, those different contents or behavioral variations might be commonly understood as forms of religious devotion; it is possible to abstract from empirically different phenomena some commonalities or similarities in form. Science must do more than simply estimate the parameters of some known universe through a sampling of that universe, as is the case when we make empirical generalizations. Science must also discover the forms of life about which we have been speaking.

If we accept this second task as a legitimate one, we see that the claim of many that case studies are scientifically useless must be questioned. To say that what goes on in one community, say Atlanta, Georgia, may not be exactly what goes on in another misses the point. Of course the content may be different, but the forms may be the same!

What all this implies is that, to some degree, the actual context of investigation for the participant observer is not important *per se*. It is only important to the extent that it provides the researcher with the opportunity to produce an analysis that has some greater universal significance. One way to speak of a good analysis produced from case studies is to say that it has carried us beyond the specific case being investigated. In this regard, the case studied by the participant observer is important only as a useful vehicle for producing an analysis.

In 1943, William F. Whyte published a study of some streetcorner boys in the North End of Boston. What is the worth of such a study to us today? After all, Whyte studied only a few persons in a quite distinctive community over thirty years ago. The fact is that Whyte's study remains important because he was able to see a number of overriding themes in his data. Among other things Whyte was able to show that there is a relationship between a boy's status in the corner gang and his behavior. That relationship between status and behavior is a form of social life that will help us to explain behavior in *any* group. Whyte also caused us to see that one cannot define an area of the city as a slum only in terms of its physical state. One must also consider the internal, social dynamics of the area. Such an observation has obvious implications for social planning in virtually any community.

In 1963 Howard Becker published a study on marihuana smokers. He tried to show in that study the stages through which persons became involved in a marihuana subculture. The authors have frequently assigned his work in their classes. Often the response of students is to question the significance of Becker's work in the 1970s. After all, they say, the smoking of marihuana is now quite a common event. It is no longer seen as the kind of criminal act that it was in 1963, and so on. In making these amendments they are quite right. Unfortunately, however, by focusing on changes in content over time, they miss the significance of the analytical generalizations produced from this study.

Becker argues that one of the important elements in becoming a committed marihuana smoker is one's being *labeled* by others as a smoker. What students fail to see sometimes is that it is the discovery of the labeling process that is the significant contribution of the work. Once the phenomenon of labeling is discovered, the specific case of marihuana smokers, just as the specific case of apples falling from trees, becomes relatively unimportant. The notion of labeling as an important feature of the process through which one becomes committed to a "deviant career" can now be applied to a number of empirically different deviances. Labeling will help us to understand the careers of such diverse groups as the mentally ill, homosexuals, and drug addicts, to mention only a few.

In the last few pages we have sought to distinguish between two types of generalizations in the social sciences. Survey research is typically directed at producing empirical generalizations. Participant observation, with its stress on discovery, aims more frequently at the production of conceptual or analytical generalizations. Both are quite important goals of any scientific endeavor and are often intertwined with each other. Also, within the broader context of our discussion, the authors have meant to take issue with the frequent claim that participant observation research can be useful only as an exploratory venture. While the authors quite agree that one viable function of qualitative research is frequently to generate ideas for more systematic study, their notion of analytical generalization leads them to see much qualitative research as having significant explanatory power in its own right.

Finally, there is one last point of comparison between structured and unstructured processes of research to consider. To talk about a research process implies some discussion of the specific role of the researcher in that process. Our comparison between survey research and participant observation has afforded us the opportunity to indicate that there is no one role for the researcher. As the problems of investigation change, as the appropriate methodologies change, as the process of the research therefore changes, so also will the specific role of the researcher change.

THE ROLE OF THE RESEARCHER
IN THE DATA COLLECTION PROCESS

In the case of research utilizing structured questionnaires the researcher's role is a relatively passive one. The researcher, the interviewer, ideally acts as a receptacle for information. In some ways the interviewer is expected to behave much like a tape recorder. Indeed, in those situations where several interviewers are employed in the collection of data, they are systematically "trained" so that they will administer the questionnaire in a uniform fashion. Decisions concerning the proper behavior of research personnel are clearly delineated prior to the data collection process. In that regard, the options open to the researcher during the data collection phase of the research are quite limited. Like the problem for investigation and the ways that variables will be measured, the role of the interviewer is determined in an a priori fashion.

The participant observer, on the other hand, must make some crucial decisions about the role to be assumed in the field. As a matter of fact, consonant with our earlier description of the way qualitative research proceeds, the decision cannot be made in advance of data collection. Herbert Gans (1968), for example, distinguishes between the field worker as total participant, as a researcher participant, and as a total researcher. The total participant tries to think and write about the situation of research analytically only after completely withdrawing from the situation. The researcher participant tries to remain detached enough from the situation so as to be able to function as an analyst during the time of involvement. The total researcher, as the label would imply, is the investigator who never becomes personally involved in the situation being studied. Other writers have made similar distinctions.

Even these roles, once chosen, are not static. The sociologist's role may change at different times during the course of the study depending upon the kind of data sought, the nature of the research context, and the receptivity of those being investigated. Often, the field researcher will find it necessary to shuttle back and forth between different research roles as the situation demands. Along these same lines, the reader should see that the more active, participatory role of the qualitative researcher increases the likelihood that *personal introspection* will play a large part in the inquiry.

By personal introspection we mean the researcher's making use of and analyzing the quality of personal experience. That is to say, in the case of participant observation research, researchers are often their own best data source; their personal feelings and behaviors constitute relevant data. The researcher's own experience may importantly and continually direct the course of future data collection. It is not uncommon to find as data in qualitative studies statements reflecting the researcher's own introspection. In trying, for example, to relate the quality of experience of persons participating in the purchase and consumption of pornography, Karp (1973:435) presents the following kind of qualitative data:

> I can on the basis of my own experience substantiate, at least in part, the reality of impression-management problems for persons involved in the Times Square sexual scene. I have been frequenting pornographic bookstores and movie theatres for some nine months. Moreover, unlike most persons similarly engaged I have available a legitimating rationale for such participation: "I am the sociologist documenting others' behaviors in this setting." Despite my relatively long experience and academic status I have not been able to overcome my uneasiness during activity in these contexts. I feel, for example, nervous at the prospect of entering a theatre. This nervousness, indeed, expresses itself physiologically in increased heartbeat. I consciously wait until few persons are in the vicinity before entering; I take my money out well in advance of entering; I feel reticent to engage the female ticket seller in even the briefest eye contact; I am suspicious of and avoid fellow patrons. . . .

We can make one further extension of our distinction between an active and passive data collection role. It is that the problems of bias and error will differ significantly as the methodology that we employ changes. While selective perception and selective memory will be potentially great problems in participant observation, they are minimized using a questionnaire that highly structures the data to be collected. The problems of bias and error, which affect the general problems of reliability and validity in the various methods, is an important enough topic to be treated separately in later chapters.

It may seem that the role of the investigator in a survey research study is both passive and unimaginative. This is not at all the case. We have been discussing data collection, which is only one phase of the research process. In survey research the actual data collection does tend to be quite mechanical. However, prior to the actual data collection, the researcher must play a creative and active role in the formulation of the research problem, in specifying key variables, in constructing the survey instrument (questionnaire), in training the interviewers, and in drawing up the sampling procedures. And after the data has been collected, the researcher must play an active role in the often elaborate statistical analysis of the data and in writing up the findings of the study.

CONCLUSION

The idea that all endings should provide the basis for new beginnings seems especially appropriate as a guideline in concluding this first chapter. Let us briefly reflect on some of the salient points we have considered.

We have worked to make plain the various types of knowledge that social researchers quite legitimately pursue. In this context we have given particular emphasis to the alternative goals for social research and the various levels of social reality that may be considered. We have characterized the social scientist as striving for objectivity, precise measurement, and the replication of research findings.

In the second half of the chapter we have, through the comparison of two distinctive research styles, looked at a number of additional questions about the conduct of social research. We find that in survey research the emphasis is on theory testing; in contrast, the focus in observational research is on theory construction. Survey research is particularly well suited to what we refer to as empirical generalization, whereas with observational research, analytical generalization is more appropriate. In observational research the investigator tends to play a very active role during the data collection phase of the research; in survey research the investigator plays the most active role in the phases of the research that precede and follow the actual data collection.

In the course of this chapter we have considered some of the major problems faced by those who wish to investigate what we now know to be a very complex social reality. We can freely recognize that knowledge is not acquired in a wholly predictable, unproblematic fashion, and we should probably conclude that this makes it all the more interesting. Were we able to predict the outcome of our work at its inception, we would be engaged, to be sure, in a dull task. We would have foregone the art of sociology in favor of a ritualized technicism. To the reader who welcomes the challenges of research, this first chapter is truly a beginning.

EXERCISES

1. Using the ideas developed on pp. 4–5 of this chapter, choose three or four research studies conducted at different "levels of reality." For each of these studies answer the following questions:
   a. On which of the levels named in the chapter is the study conducted?
   b. What seem to be the goals of the study?
   c. Briefly describe the methodological procedure used to collect the data.
   d. If the procedure used was an unstructured procedure, could the study have been done using a structured procedure, and vice versa?

2. Imagine that you are about to embark on a study of the behavior of college students in their dormitories. Without specifying in any great detail what you would study, write a short essay on the difficulties you might expect to face in meeting the three canons of the scientific method — *objectivity, precision,* and *replication.*

3. We have suggested that "religious devotion" is a *form* of social life that might be investigated in a number of diverse empirical contexts. Try to list as many different settings or contexts as possible where you could conceivably do a *case study* of *alienation.*

4. In this chapter we have referred to sociological investigation as being both a *science* and an *art.* Do you see any contradiction in the use of these two descriptions of sociological work? Justify whichever position you take.

SUGGESTED READINGS

Adams, Richard N., and Jack D. Preiss, eds.
1960   *Human Organization Research: Field Relations and Techniques.* Homewood, Illinois: Dorsey.

This is a first-rate compendium of articles covering virtually every phase of qualitative field research.

Bruyn, Severyn
1966   *The Human Perspective in Sociology: The Methodology of Participant Observation.* Englewood Cliffs, N.J.: Prentice-Hall.

Bruyn's book is one of the more sophisticated treatments of field work techniques. It is particularly useful because of its careful attention to the philosophical roots of that methodology.

Cole, Stephen
1972   *The Sociological Method.* Chicago: Rand McNally (Markham).

An easy-to-understand introduction to social research with an emphasis on quantitative methods.

Denzin, Norman K.
1970   *The Research Act.* Chicago: Aldine.

An introduction to social research methods written from a symbolic interactionist perspective.

Filstead, William J., ed.
1970   *Qualitative Methodology.* Chicago: Markham.

A useful anthology of articles on qualitative methodology.

Gouldner, Alvin
1962   "Anti-minotaur: the myth of a value-free sociology." *Social Problems* 9 (winter):199–213.

A sharp, literate critique of sociological attempts at objectivity.

Hammond, Phillip
1964   *Sociologists At Work.* New York: Basic Books.

This book is made up of articles by famous sociologists on how they did their work. It is one of the few attempts to give a "real" picture of the research process.

Lundberg, George
1955   "The natural science trend in sociology." *American Journal of Sociology* 61 (November):191–202.

Lundberg is one of the most outspoken advocates for the necessity of a highly quantitative, scientific sociology. This article reflects his bias for continuing scientific development in the social sciences.

Robinson, W. S.
1951   "The logical structure of analytic induction." *American Sociological Review* 16 (December):812–818.

A clear presentation of the strengths of analytic induction as a model of reference.

Sanders, William B., ed.
1974   *The Sociologist as Detective.* New York: Praeger.

An anthology for the introductory student which attempts to draw a parallel between social research and the research of a detective.

REFERENCES

Becker, Howard S.
1963   *Outsiders: Studies in the Sociology of Deviance.* New York: Free Press.
1967   "Whose side are we on?" *Social Problems* 14 (winter):239–248.

Berger, Peter
1963   *Invitation to Sociology.* New York: Doubleday.

Gans, Herbert
1968   "The participant observer as a human being: observations on the per-
        sonal aspects of field work." In *Institutions and the Person,* ed. Howard
        Becker. Chicago: Aldine.

Glaser, Barney, and Anselm Strauss
1967   *The Discovery of Grounded Theory.* Chicago: Aldine.

Hunter, Floyd
1953   *Community Power Structure.* Chapel Hill: University of North Carolina
        Press.

Karp, David A.
1973   "Hiding in pornographic bookstores: a reconsideration of the nature of
        urban anonymity." *Urban Life and Culture* (January):427–453.

Merton, Robert
1949   *Social Theory and Social Structure.* Glencoe, Ill.: Free Press.

Nicolaus, Martin
1969   "Remarks at ASA convention." *American Sociologist* (May):154–156.

Schutz, Alfred
1967   *The Phenomenology of the Social World.* Chicago: Northwestern Univer-
        sity Press.

Whyte, William Foote
1943   *Street Corner Society.* Chicago: University of Chicago Press.

Generating and Testing Ideas

CHAPTER TWO

One of the questions students ask most is: "What is a proper problem to write about in my term paper?" Even graduate students undertaking a doctoral dissertation are often perplexed in trying to choose a topic for investigation. Behind this general question are a number of other related questions: What kind of research constitutes an important contribution to the field? Is it legitimate to write a paper that is wholly descriptive? Must I make some kind of theoretical contribution in my work? How much data will I need to substantiate my arguments? How will my work fit into existing bodies of literature? If I choose a particular problem, will I have the resources to employ the methodologies which might be demanded? We wish to make clear that these kinds of questions precede *any* piece of research in the social sciences, whether undertaken by students or by professional researchers.

While there are no facile answers to such questions, we might begin by calling attention to a major theme of the previous chapter — that there are a multitude of problems that are wholly legitimate in the social sciences. We argued that both the levels (e.g., individual, group, society) and goals (e.g., social policy, theory testing, social criticism) of social research vary considerably. Despite this diversity, it is possible to outline some major factors involved in directing research efforts in the social sciences. The question we propose considering in this first section is: "What are some of the factors involved in generating research problems in the social sciences?" Although many of the factors operate simultaneously in effecting the choice of a research topic, we will, for purposes of clarity and organization, treat them separately. The first of these problem-orienting factors is the researcher's own curiosity about some phenomenon, situation, or set of behaviors.

THE ROLE OF CURIOSITY IN PROBLEM FORMATION

We must begin here by noting, once again, that distinctive "styles" of research demand quite different orientations on the part of the researcher; they also affect the methodologies employed, the goals of the research, the types of data acquired, and so on. One of the ways we characterized such unstructured approaches as participant observation was by saying that the goal of the research was the discovery of substantive theory. This emphasis on discovery means that the researcher does not begin with a well-delineated problem, a rigorously worked-out theoretical apparatus, or a set of explicit hypotheses to be tested. Typically, those who do qualitative research begin with a set of loosely structured, guiding questions. Very often the qualitative researcher begins to investigate some setting or phenomena for little reason other than being intrigued by, curious about, or perplexed by a set of behaviors. It seems reasonable to say that if there is something occurring that we simply do not understand, some set of behaviors that is so foreign to us that we cannot grasp the actors' motives, those same behaviors are probably worthy of study. The history of all sciences is one of researchers grappling with mystery.

To say it yet another way, it is frequently the context, setting, or phenomenon that is initially of interest rather than a specific empirical problem or a set of theoretical ideas. One need only look through studies accomplished using observational techniques to find examples of research generated out of pure interest on the part of the researcher. An example follows.

Several years ago researchers led by Leon Festinger (1953) chose to study through participant observation a small group of religious zealots who were vociferously claiming that the end of the world was at hand. Of course the researchers did have some questions, largely springing from personal curiosity, which led them to that group: What kinds of persons would want to join such a group? What was the internal organization of the group? And so on. As they began to learn about the group, they found that one question kept reasserting itself: How did the members of this group maintain their faith in the dictums of the group leaders when the world failed to come to an end? How did persons continually reaffirm their faith in the face of the failed prophesy? The result of this study, which initial curiosity itself could not have allowed the researchers to predict, was that they developed a major theoretical notion in social psychology — cognitive dissonance[1] — to explain what seemed irrational behavior from the perspective of an outsider. Consistent with the general aims of participant observation research, the major focus or problem for investigation emerged only after the researchers had been in the field for some time.

The number of research studies motivated largely by curiosity could fill many pages of text. Researchers have embarked on the investigation of such diverse groups or phenomena as pool hustling (Polsky, 1967), nudist colonies (Weinberg, 1968), homosexuals meeting in public bathrooms (Humphreys, 1970), behavior in pornographic movie theatres (Karp, 1971), asylums (Goffman, 1961a), and the like, simply because there existed groups of persons or sets of behaviors which were intriguing to the researcher. We should carefully note that while curiosity is often a chief motivating factor, the worth of a piece of research so motivated is to be, in part, measured by the researcher's capacity to show the sociological significance of the collected data. The analysis produced from such studies should help in some way to explain some underlying dimensions of social life.

The kind of research we have just described begins with few, if any, theoretical ideas. In the last chapter, we also considered a *priori* research which, in contrast, often begins with well-delineated theoretical ideas. Thus, a second major factor involved in generating a research idea may be the quest for a way to make a contribution to existing theories in the field.

THE ROLE OF EXISTING THEORY IN THE DEVELOPMENT OF RESEARCH IDEAS

In a widely read and discussed book called *The Structure of Scientific Revolutions,* Thomas Kuhn (1967) argues that one way science develops is through the continual testing of already existent theoretical ideas. Much social science research is dedicated to showing the worth of some theory by testing the explanatory value of that theory in new ways or in new settings. Often the result of such work is to specify, amend, or importantly qualify the existing theory. In some cases, the result of such research is to cause us to thoroughly reject an existing theory and to generate in its place a new theory of our own. This process of continually trying to test the validity of existing theory is crucial to the development of science. The scientific attitude, which we considered in

---

[1] According to the theory of cognitive dissonance, people strive for consistency in their beliefs (cognitions). The existence of dissonance (inconsistency) among beliefs produces psychological discomfort which motivates people to change some of these beliefs in a direction that reduces this dissonance.

the last chapter, demands that researchers never fully accept a theory; rather, the task of science is to continually try to show ways in which a theory may be inadequate.

Each time a theory is proposed it generates a number of possible empirical contexts where the whole theory or some segment of the theory may be put to the test. We may, for example, turn our attention briefly to the extraordinary number of research studies generated from the works of one sociologist, Talcott Parsons. Parsons (1959) is generally regarded as the major American contributor to a theoretical school of thought in sociology labeled structural-functionalism. The essential elements of the theory are as follows: every element of a society that exists over a period of time serves some distinctive function relative to the maintenance of the social system. The most appropriate analogy here is that society is much like any living organism. So, the argument made by Parsons is that if there is a change in any one social institution, there will be corresponding changes in other elements of the system. Any change, for example, in the economic system of a society will cause corresponding changes in the political, religious, and educational spheres of the system. Functionalists argue that any social system is always moving toward a state of equilibrium. To the functionalist, society is much like a flexible rubber ball that may on occasion be pushed out of shape but is always striving to return to its original shape. The insistent question for functional analysis, therefore, is: What function is performed by this or that social element and what would be the consequences for the social system as a whole if it were absent?

Although it is not our concern to critique this particular global theory of society, we should mention that there are those who argue that functional theory does not adequately deal with social change in a society, that it does not adequately explain conflict or deviance in a society. Beyond that, there are those who find fault with functionalism because they see it as an inherently "conservative" theory of society, a theory which too strongly supports the status quo.

The importance of the theory of structural-functionalism in terms of generating research problems for investigation has been considerable. The research that has been generated has been actually of two types. First, there have been studies which have applied functional theory to show its utility in explaining a large number of empirical phenomena. Some notable examples of such work would include Kingsley Davis's (1961) argument that prostitution serves a distinctively useful function in any society by operating as a kind of "safety valve"; that is, it provides the opportunity for persons to act out certain sexual behaviors that might be considered illegitimate within the context of family life. Davis thus makes the interesting argument that prostitution works to preserve the family system. Other spin-offs from the general theory of functionalism have been studies of the functional significance of specific elements in the society. Kingsley Davis and Wilbert Moore (1945) have developed, for example, a functional theory of stratification systems. These researchers argue that a system of institutionalized inequality is necessary to motivate persons to carry out the more important tasks in a society. On a more empirical level, researchers starting off armed with functional theories have investigated large-scale organizations, schools, and the military.

On the other hand, much research has been generated out of what investigators see to be the limitations of functional theory. These researchers often begin with a deductive theory that stands in opposition to functionalism and seek then to show how their new theory might more adequately explain certain phenomena. In short, many research problems are generated by an investigator specifying a fresh theory in response to felt gaps or omissions in old theories. We have seen that in qualitative research, the theory often emerges from the investigator's involvement in a particular setting; but in the case of research generated from already existing theoretical constructs, the choice of setting is often dictated by the theory itself. The researcher asks what setting or which behaviors will be best for him to use in assessing the explanatory power of his theory. Here again, there are many examples of specific problems or empirical areas that have been investigated where the choice of the setting or phenomenon was determined by its appropriateness for testing one or another theory.

One example of an ingenious choice of a research context in response to a particular theoretical problem is to be found in a study done by Oscar Grusky (1963). One of the major theoretical issues that had been unresolved in the literature on large-scale organizations concerned the influence of managerial succession. Grusky wanted specifically to know whether a new manager in a large-scale organization increased or decreased the productivity and efficiency of workers. He asked himself what context would best facilitate his gathering solid evidence to help resolve this theoretical bone of contention. While his choice in retrospect seems an obviously good one, it took some imagination on Grusky's part to realize that this specific theoretical issue could be investigated by choosing a context where two elements existed: (1) a context where there was frequent succession of managers, and (2) a context where productivity and efficiency could easily be measured. Holding in mind these two criteria, criteria generated out of a theoretical issue, Grusky chose to study the effects of managerial succession on the efficiency of major league baseball teams. This choice of a context for investigation was not one that sprung initially from Grusky's curiosity. Rather it was an eminently rational choice relative to an already existing set of theoretical ideas.

Another good example is afforded by the research endeavors stimulated by Howard Becker's (1963) original formulation of labeling theory. Becker argued that a major factor influencing an individual's involvement in a deviant career was the public labeling of that person by others as deviant. Such labeling, proponents of the theory argue, strongly affects one's self-concept. More explicitly, one major effect of labeling is that those so labeled deal with the derogatory label by even further involving themselves in the deviant behavior. For those wishing to verify or discard labeling theory, the choice of contexts for further research seemed clear: the choice was to turn to those institutions or settings where one might expect that just such labeling was occurring. It comes as no surprise, therefore, that researchers attempted to test the labeling effect in such contexts as prisons, juvenile homes, the court system, and schools.

One of the factors that allows a researcher to generate a meaningful problem for investigation is knowledge of the theoretical and empirical literature in the field. It seems clear that the more one understands the kinds of theoretical debates going on in the field, the better he will be equipped to choose a research topic. This probably yields little comfort for the student first embarking on the field of sociology, whose knowledge of the literature is scant or lacking altogether. Perhaps, though, we can be a bit more helpful by indicating the way in which sociological literature itself ought to be read if one is intent on formulating a problem for research.

THE ROLE OF THE LITERATURE IN PROBLEM FORMATION

We have already mentioned that much research is developed with the purpose of trying to resolve theoretical arguments, discrepancies, conflicts, and the like. A student need not be fully knowledgeable about the complexities of professional theory debate in order to see contradictions in the literature. Let us suppose that as one requirement of the course in which this book is assigned, a student must formulate some kind of problem and carry out a piece of empirical research around that problem. He begins by thinking about the traditional areas of sociological concern that interest him most. Let us still further suppose, for purposes of continuing our example, that this student was a juvenile delinquent in his earlier years and decides that now he would like to fashion a research project around that issue. The task is to work towards specifying the problem so that it becomes reasonably manageable in the course of one semester.

A first step in specifying a problem for research is to immerse oneself as far as possible in the literature on the subject of juvenile delinquency. What are some of the questions one might ask as one reads this literature? For the student curious about delinquency, some reasonable questions might be: What are the various theories offered to explain delinquency? Do the theories ever seem to contradict one another, and if so, in what ways? Which of the theories seems most plausible to me?

What difficulties do I find with the theories mentioned in the literature? Do the authors themselves call attention to unresolved issues? (It is not uncommon for authors to make the pointblank assertion that little research has been done on this or that particular problem.) As problems begin to emerge through such a critical reading of the literature, the reader must continually consider what kinds of data and what methodological technique would be called for to adequately deal with each of the potential problems generated out of the literature.

We could go on with this analysis of how problems emerge from a reading of the literature, but we have taken it far enough to emphasize the importance of a close, careful reading of the salient research already done in the field.

There are many other sources of research problems. Among the most important are those which relate to the desire to do research that will in some way foster social change. One example is the social research carried out by Ralph Nader's public interest research groups. Another is the empirical research of Marxist and other radical sociologists. However, the most common form of social change research is what we call social policy research, particularly a form of social policy research referred to as evaluation research.

THE GOAL OF SOCIAL CHANGE AND PROBLEM FORMATION

The goal of *social policy research* is to come up with results that will be of use in the formulation of public policy on such issues as welfare, education, criminal justice, mental health, housing, and drug abuse. For some researchers the objective is to uncover inadequacies in existing policies. For others, it is to use the knowledge of the inadequacies to permit proposal of modifications in these policies. *Evaluation research* is a form of social policy research in which the goal is to assess the effectiveness of a social program or agency. The scope of evaluation research ranges from an effort to evaluate the quality of the services provided by one local social service agency to an effort to evaluate a major federal social service program on a national scale.

With increasing frequency the federal government is requiring that an evaluation of program effectiveness be built into social service programs receiving federal funds. Much such research starts with the overall problem defined by the requirements of a federal agency. Typically the research does not have any direct relevance to theoretical issues in the sociological literature and is not a product of the social researcher's curiosity. However, it is sometimes possible for the researcher to explore some issues of more general theoretical relevance as part of such a research effort.

At one point the Nixon administration was backing the Family Assistance Plan, which is a form of what is referred to as a negative income tax. That is, the federal income tax system would be used to make payments to those with low wages, including those with no other source of income. One component of the Family Assistance Plan and of any negative income tax plan is a guaranteed income. In the late 1960s an experiment was begun to assess the impact of a guaranteed income on work incentives, family stability, and other such behavior. A major objective of the study was to obtain information which could be used to assess the viability of the proposed Family Assistance Plan. As part of this experiment several hundred families were issued a guaranteed income over a period of three years. The researchers found that the guaranteed income had little impact on work effort for men, but it did have a modest impact on the labor force participation of married women (Rees, 1974). This experimental study was one of the most ambitious examples of social policy research to date. In this study, as in much social policy research, the work began with an already well-defined problem.

Another form of social change research is muckraking sociology (Marx, 1972). A major goal of such research is social criticism (Bottomore, 1974). While the case can be made that much muckraking sociology is just another form of social policy research, there tends to be a difference in the tone with which the results are presented and in the intended audience. The primary audience for much social policy research is the government agency which has commissioned the work; in contrast, the primary audience for much muckraking sociology is the general public. This difference is also reflected in the tone of the writing; muckraking sociology gives much more attention to the expression of moral outrage. It seeks to document the ways in which various institutions (such as the welfare system, the educational system, and the criminal justice system, to name only a few) function at variance with our basic values, such as respect for fairness, justice, and human dignity. Among the issues considered by those doing this type of social research have been sexual assaults in prisons (Davis, 1972), the mechanisms for tax avoidance and evasion used by the wealthy (Stern, 1972), the part played by the drug industry in contributing to the drug problem (Bernstein and Lennard, 1973), and the adverse effects of tracking in schools on those in the lower tracks (Rosenbaum, 1975). Such research seeks to uncover facts which dramatically call attention to gross injustice in one of our major institutions in the hope that such attention will act as a source of pressure on those in positions of power to remedy the situation or to reform the institution involved.

One of the most widely cited examples of muckraking sociology is Piven and Cloward's (1971) study, *Regulating the Poor*. Their research is based on a series of historical case studies from as far back as the sixteenth century. They cite case after case from sixteenth-century Europe to mid-twentieth-century America, documenting their thesis that social welfare has throughout the ages been used as a mechanism of social control. They argue it is used to regulate the political and economic activity of the poor. In periods of severe economic depression it is used to control civil disorder, lest the poor expropriate the property of the rich and in other ways upset the status quo of power and property relationships in society. When economic conditions improve, the relief rolls are cut back in response to pressure from those who employ the poor so as to ensure an adequate supply of low-wage labor. This view of the functioning of the welfare system is clearly at odds with the view that welfare is simply a humanitarian effort by the rest of society to help the poor in times of need. The goal as seen by Piven and Cloward is rather to help the poor a little, so that they will not help themselves to a great deal more.

As a final category of social change research we consider the work of Marxists and other radical sociologists. There is some overlap between the work done by Marxist sociologists and those who do muckraking sociology. In both cases there is a heavy component of social criticism and exposé as well as a desire to bring to the attention of the general public ways in which people are being oppressed by those in control of our major social institutions. A major source of difference is that many who would classify themselves as muckraking sociologists are relatively optimistic about the possibility of remedy for the adverse situation through social reform within the context of the existing political and economic structure; in contrast, the Marxist sociologist is more likely to be pessimistic about the possibility of any real improvement in the situation without a fundamental restructuring of society along socialist lines. Thus the research of the radical sociologist is undertaken not so much as a mechanism for a specific reform as it is a means to call to the attention of all who can be reached the exploitative nature of the existing structure in the hope that eventually the dissatisfaction will be sufficient to bring about the fundamental social restructuring called for. Among the problems of particular interest to the Marxists and other radical sociologists are American militarism and imperialism, the power and behavior of multinational corporations, the concentration of wealth and power in American society, and the nature of monopoly capitalism.

An example of radical social research is *The Power Elite* by C. Wright Mills (1956). The author argues that America is controlled by a relatively small group of men who sit at the top of the major business, political, and military institutions. This group tends to be self-perpetuating. They also shift from one institutional sphere to another with relative ease, as when a retired general becomes a member of the board of directors for a major defense contractor, or when a wealthy businessman becomes the nation's vice-president. A Marxist critique of Mills's analysis states that it does not go far enough. That is, Mills does not go on to point out that the leaders of these major institutions are all members of, or employed by, a capitalist class. Both Mills and his Marxist critics are highly critical of the structure of power they find in American society.

We have looked at a number of related sources from which research problems may originate. We have been careful not to settle on any specific or definitive rules for generating research problems in the social sciences because we do not believe such rules exist. Perhaps, as claims the sociologist C. Wright Mills, we do better to think of research problem development as a craft. We turn to Mills's notion of "intellectual craftsmanship" as a way of summarizing some of the points made so far in this chapter.

INTELLECTUAL CRAFTSMANSHIP

In the section on "intellectual craftsmanship" of his book *The Sociological Imagination*, Mills (1959) tells us that ideas and problems for research do not appear spontaneously. Rather, social scientists are continually "playing around" with possible research ideas. It is not uncommon to begin formulating an idea and wait sometimes several years before actually beginning to work on that problem. During the intervening period the problem remains in the back of the mind and each time one reads something or has a personal experience pertaining to that problem, he makes a mental note of it. Part of what Mills calls intellectual craftsmanship involves this continual reflection on ideas over time.

Mills, in fact, advocates that researchers keep a file; a kind of intellectual journal which serves as a repository for accumulating ideas. He argues that entries into this file should continually reflect personal life experiences. As researchers we must never separate our own life experiences from our intellectual work. As the file begins to grow over time — a file at last filled with personal memos, excerpts from books, half-baked theories — we periodically go through our entries trying to create categories of ideas, trying to see which pieces of information seem to have things in common. This periodic rearranging of files itself constitutes an exercise of the "sociological imagination" and frequently generates new ideas. We may find through such a continual reorganization that certain key concepts or ideas emerge and that many of our entries, previously seen as wholly independent and discrete, begin to fit into a larger mosaic.

We might say here that one of the features of such an idea formation process is that we will eventually reach a point where we have generated more ideas than we could likely investigate in a lifetime. We find ourselves necessarily setting priorities among our several ideas. In Mills's own words, "Any working social scientist who is well on his way ought at times to have so many plans, which is to say ideas, that the question is always, which of them am I, ought I, to work on next?" (Mills, 1959:198).

Contrary perhaps to popular conception, a creative imagination is not something that one either possesses or does not. Mills causes us to see that creativity is something to be acquired by an individual. A sociological imagination is something to be acquired through the continual structuring of one's thoughts and ideas. One must work to develop this imagination. It is especially in this sense that the production of important research ideas is a craft. The essence of this craftsmanship is captured in the following statement by Mills:

> In such a file . . . there is joined personal experience and professional activities, studies underway and studies planned. In this file, you, as an intellectual craftsman, will try to get together what you are doing intellectually and what you are experiencing as a person. Here you will not be afraid to use your experience and relate it directly to various work in progress. . . . Your file . . . also encourages you to capture "fringe thoughts": various ideas which may be the byproducts of everyday life, snatches of conversation overheard on the street, or, for that matter, dreams. Once noted, these may lead to more systematic thinking, as well as lend intellectual relevance to more direct experience. (Mills, 1959:196)

Beyond our discussion of intellectual craftsmanship there is another way of summarizing our ideas. Consider the necessary interrelationship between theory and research. Information in this relationship flows in both directions. Typically empirical research is used to test or verify theory, but as Merton (1948) points out, there are a variety of ways in which research influences theory. One example is what he refers to as the *serendipity component* of research, that is, the discovery of an unanticipated anomalous datum (result) that becomes the basis for extending existing theory or for the development of a new theory.

We noted in the last chapter that one of the hallmarks of scientific work is that it is empirical. One's understanding, knowledge about, and explanation of some aspect of the social world must be grounded in clear evidence from the world itself. We suggested quite strongly that theoretical speculation without the acquisition of data is a nonscientific way of proceeding. To complete this triadic relationship we should see that the function of methodology in the social sciences is to ensure that the data we collect is both reliable and valid.

What we mean to imply is that theory, data, and methodology cannot be separated from one another, that the quality of social science knowledge depends on a continuous integration among the three. There exists a fine balance among these elements. A change in theoretical position will likely cause a change in the kind of data to be acquired, and hence a change in the kind of methodology employed. If, on a practical level, we have the resources to use only certain kinds of methodological procedures, it means that we will be able to acquire only certain types of data; and finally this has implications for the kinds of theories that can be tested. If, for example, we have a theory which presumably accounts for attitude change over time, we will be able to test this theory only if we have the resources to utilize methodological techniques that allow us to measure attitude change. Also, as noted in the last chapter, theories will be continually informed by the acquisition of new data.

A good portion of our discussion in Chapter 1 centered around the relationship between method and data. Our comparison between structured and unstructured methodological techniques alerted us to the quite different qualities of data produced by each. In that chapter, the role of theory in the research process largely lurked about the edges of our discussion. Because theory is such a prominent feature of the total process through which knowledge is produced, we really are obliged to treat the idea of theory more rigorously than we have to this point.

As we talk about theory, we must at the same time recognize that the broader, more generic issue at hand involves the nature of explanation. If our mutually understood goal is to explain events, processes, or phenomena, we must now ask what criteria are to be employed in satisfying ourselves that our explanations are sufficient.

THE NATURE OF THEORY

The question of what constitutes a proper theory is a confusing matter — so much so that there is a serious question about the theoretical status of much that social scientists claim to be theory. More to the point, there are those who argue that much of what passes for theory in the social sciences represents little more than elaborate classificatory schemes. In the sociological literature, the issue is further confused by the proliferation of terms applied to the handling of data. We read about *models, paradigms, taxonomies, typologies,* and *conceptual frameworks.* Not infrequently writers will use these terms nearly interchangeably, and sometimes they are used in the same context where "theory" is being discussed. We may offer a couple of examples to illustrate those types of cases where the claim to theory is considered by some to be illegitimate.

The sociologist Erving Goffman (1959, 1961b, 1963a, 1967) has spent his academic life trying to understand the basic processes governing social interaction. In a number of his books, Goffman has generated a picture of role playing which emphasizes the manipulative, sometimes artificial, quality of people's relations with one another. At the very heart of Goffman's presentation, serving as the analytical starting point for his exposition, is Shakespeare's claim "that all the world's a stage and all the men and women merely players." Goffman treats that notion seriously and tries to offer evidence for its correctness. Because of the close analogy of Goffman's description of social life to the events that occur on the stage, his has come to be called the *dramaturgical model* of interaction. The usual response to Goffman's writing is that the categories he develops to organize an enormous variety of data provide striking insights into people's behavior as they relate to each other. But one often hears reference to Goffman's *theory.* Many sociologists stress that to classify Goffman's contribution as theory is inappropriate. Goffman seems to have provided us with a view, a perspective on social life — less rigorous than a theory, perhaps, but equally useful.

Earlier we briefly touched on Talcott Parsons's functional theory. Once again, however, despite the enormous influence Parsons has had on American sociology, there are some who claim that Parsons's writings do not constitute theory. Rather, his work represents, it is said, an enormously elaborate taxonomy — an elaborate, if not elegant, set of categories or pigeon holes into which various phenomena may be classified. What is implied here is that the notion of classificatory scheme or model is to be treated as analytically distinct from a theory. Linnaeus, the great biologist, spent his life classifying various animal species and his classification is still useful today. In fact, Linnaeus's classification has always been lauded as a great contribution to science. It seems clear, therefore, that one important task of science is to *order* complex phenomena. We will consider the value of ordering devices in social science research once we have more thoroughly examined what is meant by theory.

The Nature of Axiomatic Theory

One conception of theory, referred to as axiomatic theory, involves the manipulation of a set of interrelated propositions, using the rules of logic, in an effort to explain some class of empirical phenomena. Such theories take the form: Proposition A logically leads to Proposition B which in turn leads logically to Proposition C, and so on, until some empirical event has allegedly been explained. As we saw in Chapter 1, this form of explanation is deductive. A tentative theory will illustrate the form of explanation that we are here describing. Let us return to our student who is grappling with her term paper on delinquency. Let us assume, further, that she has read through the literature on theories of delinquency and as part of her research effort wishes to specify a theory to explain that empirical phenomenon — juvenile delinquent behavior. If she were to draw heavily on the work of Cloward and Ohlin (1960), she might come up with a theory similar to the following one.

PROPOSITION 1   There is a high cultural value in American society placed on individual achievement.

PROPOSITION 2   There are societally designated legitimate means for achievement which involve movement through the educational system and into the occupational world.

PROPOSITION 3   These means of achievement are not equally open to all persons in American society.

PROPOSITION 4   These means of achievement are closed off to a significant proportion of lower class persons.

PROPOSITION 5   Where the legitimate means for achievement are blocked and persons have internalized the value of achievement, alternative or illegitimate means for achievement will be used.

PROPOSITION 6   Delinquent behavior may be seen as representing one easily accessible means in lower class culture of acquiring the material goods that reflect achievement in American society.

Apart from the truth or falsity of this particular theory, its form should give us some sense of the form that deductive theories take. We have moved from broad, abstract statements about culture to progressively more concrete propositions about the functioning of certain social institutions. The researcher did all of this with an eye toward making sense out of delinquency as an empirical event. The underlying question that motivated the theory in the first instance — why do persons commit delinquent acts — has been tentatively explained. Next, the researcher would proceed by deciding how he might collect data to affirm or discard the theory. Perhaps the researcher will make a series of predictions, based on this theory, about which individuals in which particular social situations would most likely engage in delinquent behaviors. In other words, the researcher could generate a whole series of *hypotheses* that might lend themselves to specific testing. She might decide that her theory enables her to predict that obstacles to achievement will be greatest for individuals who possess specific social attributes. She might propose a series of hypotheses of the following sort.

The greater the number of persons in an individual's family, the greater is the individual's potential for delinquency.

Among those who are blocked off from the legitimate avenues for achievement, the potentiality of becoming deviant will be a function of how deeply the value of achievement has been internalized.

Hypotheses, or statements of predictive relationships between two or more variables,[2] must be set out in such a way that the researcher will clearly be able to measure each of the variables named. So, we may see that the ultimate test of a theory involves the capacity to adequately *measure* the variables in the hypotheses derived from the theory itself. We will spend considerable time in Chapter 3 discussing the difficulties

[2] Sex, education, income, achievement motivation, and delinquency are all variables; that is, they are all characteristics, attitudes, or behaviors which can be measured and which take on two or more values.

involved in such measurement. The greater the number of testable hypotheses that are supported by collected data, the more faith we can have in the correctness of the theory itself.

There are a few sociologists who hold that axiomatic theory is the only legitimate form of social theory, but this view is distinctly a minority position. While it is true that many sociological theories could be recast in the format of axiomatic theory, this is rarely done. Very often a theory takes the form of the final proposition of an axiomatic theory; and there is little or no effort to explicitly specify the preceding propositions, many of which are considered too obvious to warrant mentioning. As we shall see, theories are often presented in the form of typologies or causal models.

Difficulties of Theory Testing

Theories are never proved. We simply provide evidence, through the testing of hypotheses derived from the theory, that the theory is not incorrect. There is always the possibility that our collected data may continually support our hypotheses and that our theory may still be wrong. It may be that our stated hypotheses are supported by the data for reasons simply unknown to us. In a larger sense still, it has been argued by some that social science theories are inherently unprovable since they can all be seen as resting ultimately on unprovable assumptions. Without unnecessary elaboration at this point the authors would ask the reader to accept their assertion that social science theories have been constructed on quite diverse assumptions of the following sort: man is rational and self-serving, man is an approval-seeking animal, man is an aggressive animal, man is motivated by internalized values, or man is motivated by reward. To the extent that these assumptions do not easily submit themselves to empirical verification, one could call into question the whole edifice of theory construction, which has just such assumptions as its foundations.

There are other difficulties with social science theory that in all fairness the authors must briefly mention here. The concepts frequently found in social science theory propositions and ultimately in the hypotheses tested to verify the theory itself do not have constant meanings. If we were, for example, to take a concept such as alienation, we would find that however we chose to measure this concept, some social scientists would disagree with our measurement technique. And perhaps we ought to expect that this would happen since it may be reasonably argued that the meaning of alienation will vary in a society from group to group, from person to person, and over time. While we will look again at this general problem of varying meanings in our chapter on measurement, we should realize at this point that strong deductive explanation depends on each variable, concept, or element in a theoretical argument having a stable, universal meaning. Since this condition does not obtain for most social science theories, we see yet another reason why the empirical verification of deductive social theories remains, at best, an arduous task. Indeed, critics often reject the conclusion of a study on the grounds that the concepts in the theory have been inappropriately measured.

We might add here that the problem we are raising about measurement is often the source of major ideological splits between researchers in the social sciences. In the last chapter we spoke of a philosophical split in the social sciences between those who view the world as an objective entity and those who view the world in more subjective terms. Such a difference in orientation has considerable implications relative to the acceptance or rejection of measurement techniques in the field. Should a researcher conduct a study and measure variables through a given procedure such as survey research, the findings of the study are likely to be accepted by those who see this procedure as fitting into their philosophical conception of the world and rejected by those who hold a contrary view. This is perhaps one of the reasons that we see such a multiplicity of theories, even though the empirical events to be explained may be much the same.

An important characteristic of deductive theory is that the more general theories are capable of explaining the greater number of phenomena. And the more diverse the phenomena covered by the theory, the greater the number of testable hypotheses covered. This characteristic is important because one criterion for evaluating the "correctness" of a theory is whether it allows us to predict *as-yet unobserved events*. If, for example, a scientist is able to generate a deductive theory designed to predict the behavior of falling bodies under natural conditions, it should of course be possible to test this theory under natural conditions for a variety of falling bodies. Beyond that, if the theory is correct, it should be generalizable in such a way that we can explain events not specifically covered by the original theory. The theory should have, in other words, a strength of generalization that will allow the scientist to predict as-yet unobserved events. In this case our faith in the original theory will be greatly increased if the scientist can generalize to correctly predict how objects will fall in a vacuum.

The ability to test a general theory by using that theory to predict as-yet unseen phenomena is one way we may ensure that we have not produced a circular, *tautological theory;* a tautological theory is one that cannot be proved false because of the logic of its construction. We may see the dangers of circularity in theories by looking at an example of a theory some critics have claimed to be circular.

Earlier we spoke of theories derived from Parsons's general conception that every element in a social system serves some distinct function in maintaining equilibrium in the system as a whole. One such theory is the "functional theory of stratification." Some researchers who have begun their inquiry with a Parsonian functional bias assert that every complex society must have some type of well-delineated stratification system so that individuals will be motivated to perform the more important tasks in the society. They argue, for example, that because of the long period of training and general difficulty of becoming a doctor, persons would not be motivated to fill this functionally important position unless they were ultimately rewarded by the society with greater prestige, power, and wealth than most.

We must, however, be careful in our evaluation of this theoretical argument because closer examination shows it to be a wholly circular argument. How so? The functional theory of stratification asserts that elements of a society are differentially rewarded because they are more or less functionally important to the operation of the total system. In turn we may ask, "How do we know that one element is more functionally important than another in a society?" The functionalist's response would necessarily be: "It is obviously more functionally important because it is awarded more power, prestige, status, and wealth than other positions in the society." The logical difficulty here is that the theory, as stated, is true by definition. It is a bit like trying to explain why people smoke by saying that they enjoy smoking; when asked how we measure enjoyment, we must say that enjoyment is measured by the frequency with which persons smoke! If we are to avoid this type of circularity in our theories it seems plain that what we take to be the "causes" of phenomena must *not* be measured in the same way as the presumed "effects" of those causes. The capacity to predict the operation of phenomena other than those that were initially the object of explanation in a theory is a characteristic that assures us we have a workable theory, not a tautology.

The kinds of difficulties we have been considering are especially apparent in those instances in which global theories are involved. Mills (1959) has termed global theories such as that developed by Parsons as "grand theories." While one must applaud the brilliance of those theorists who try to integrate in one theory an enormously large number of phenomena, such grand theory is particularly susceptible to the difficulties that we have discussed. It is unclear in such theories what specific hypotheses will provide an adequate test of the theory. It is unclear how the concepts in grand theories can be measured. In the most general sense there is the danger that a theory which tries to explain everything ends up explaining nothing.

At the other extreme, there are those sociologists so intent on avoiding the logical and methodological problems we have been raising that they have chosen work on theories that are capable of explaining only a very small class of empirical phenomena. If one starts out to explain only a very limited number of events where only a few variables or concepts are involved, where the hypotheses to be tested are few in number, and where reasonably wide agreement can be achieved as to the methodological procedures for testing those hypotheses, lots of problems are avoided. The criticism often raised, however, about the work of these social scientists is that in their zeal to produce tightly developed theories which submit to clear testing, they are forced to work on problems that are simply unimportant.

Cognizant of the difficulties of theory testing and unsatisfied with the products of both grand theory and theories used to explain a few "abstracted empirical" events, the sociologist Robert Merton (1957) has advocated that social scientists work to produce what he calls *theories of the middle range*. Theories of the middle range, as the label implies, focus on such empirical phenomena as deviance, the operation of social groups, processes of social perception, and the like. The task is to circumscribe the phenomena for explanation in such a way that it becomes possible to form clear hypotheses and achieve reasonably wide agreement concerning the appropriate data for testing these hypotheses. Merton's hope is that it will be possible ultimately to merge these discrete theories generated around specific institutional features of the society and to produce some more general theory of society.

There is considerable debate in the field concerning the appropriate level of theory to pursue. Social scientists are much divided on this issue, as some continue to use very specific theories, some have tried to make Merton's suggestion workable, and others strive to produce grand theory. Each of us must decide for himself how satisfying he finds the accounting currently being produced at each of these levels. In making this decision we must realize that there is no substitute for a careful reading of at least a modest amount of theory at each of these levels.

MAKING SENSE OUT OF DATA: TOWARD THE DEVELOPMENT OF THEORY

In the last section we talked primarily about deductive modes of theoretical explanation. In previous discussions we also stressed the idea that theory may emerge inductively. Glaser and Strauss (1967) argue that the essence of qualitative analysis is that any developed theory be grounded in the collected data. Given this point of view, we can agree that many examples of the use of classificatory schemes as an intermediate step in the production of theoretical explanation should come from qualitative research. At the same time, we should acknowledge that researchers using survey research techniques often generate new theoretical ideas after their data has been collected.

Our focus in this section shifts now to describe how data may be used to *generate* theory rather than to *test* theory.

The most fundamental operation involved in inductive theoretical explanation is the attempt to order the collected data in such a way that we can see significant classes, properties, or underlying dimensions in the data. As we examine the data our concern is to discover a general model or overriding pattern that cements together, and efficiently represents, the key features of a large bulk of the data. In the case of qualitative research, the search for such key linkages is normally accomplished through close reading of field notes and the like. Those who have collected systematic survey data tend to rely on statistical techniques to order the data.

One way to think of typologies, taxonomies, or classificatory schemes more generally is that they are all tools that help us to see underlying or basic dimensions in our data. For lack of a better term we will refer to the use of such devices as part of what might be called *typological analysis*.

While typological analysis typically proceeds once we have collected our data, there are many instances where we will develop a preliminary, tentative rendering of the operation which is hypothetical, formulated before the data is gathered. Such preliminary models serve as a kind of orienting device as we begin to collect our data, guiding research questions and containing in their expression the basic ideas which may be later incorporated into the production of theory itself. As a matter of fact, we would be willing to say that any classificatory scheme implies a potential theory. One such frequently used device for thinking about some aspect of the empirical world has been called the *ideal type*.

The Ideal Type

There is nothing particularly mysterious about ideal types. Each of us has undoubtedly, at one time or another, constructed ideal types. Consider the following situation. Several students are sitting around the dorm on Saturday night and begin to talk about the characteristics of the person they would consider an ideal mate. One begins to list a set of physical characteristics considered important. Another begins to list personality dimensions. Another cites the status attributes that the ideal mate should have, and so forth. Each of our hypothetical participants recognizes that there is probably no one in the real world who would meet all the requirements demanded by the characteristics named. The list of characteristics represents a kind of composite and in that sense constitutes an abstract, intellectual invention of sorts. Despite the unreality of this invention it does serve a useful purpose. Holding the produced model in mind, each individual may now compare those they meet to the model. How close does the person approximate the ideal type? The ideal type operates as a kind of yardstick against which certain aspects of the real world may be evaluated. It is an ordering device for thinking about and evaluating what does exist in the real world.

Perhaps the use of ideal types in social research is most closely associated with the work of Max Weber (1947). In a book called *The Theory of Social and Economic Organization,* Weber attempted to analyze the ways in which the trend of Western history was toward greater and greater bureaucratization of social life. In order to produce this analysis, Weber constructed an ideal-type model of bureaucracy. Just as the students indicated the criteria for their ideal mate, Weber proceeded by outlining the criteria of his "ideal-type" bureaucracy. Although the complete set of criteria is not of great import in this context, we can look briefly at what Weber saw as the essence of bureaucracy: that bureaucratic structures are governed by a set of rational-legal rules; that bureaucratic structures are characterized by a clear hierarchical authority structure; that bureaucratic structures are characterized by an extensive division of labor among its members; and so on.

Weber clearly understood that his ideal-type bureaucracy did not exist empirically. In that regard his statement of the ideal-type bureaucracy could not itself constitute the end product of his research. What Weber did, in effect, was to magnify certain features of the social phenomenon that he was investigating; by so doing, by using the ideal type as a heuristic tool, he was able to examine more precisely and analytically the social structures of the West as they actually existed.

Weber's analysis of bureaucratic structure, developed initially with the aid of the ideal type, still remains as the cornerstone of an enormous amount of theory subsequently produced to explain the operation of large-scale organizations. Some of this theory reflects an attempt to show the validity of Weber's seminal idea. Other bodies of theory on large-scale organizations have had the effect of modifying and specifying Weber's original contribution. For example, Weber largely stressed the role of the bureaucracy's *formal structure.* More recent theoretical contributions (e.g., Blau, 1963) have diverged from Weber's original depiction of bureaucratic structure by emphasizing the role of *informal organization* within bureaucracies.

The ideal type has also been used in slightly different but related ways. One frequent variation is its use to describe phenomena as lying somewhere on a continuum. There are many classic examples of this particular use, the most famous of which are to be found in the writings of early European sociologists who were intrigued by the decline of the traditional peasant community and the development of large industrialized cities. The French and Industrial revolutions, which gave birth to a wholly new social order in Europe, provided the intellectual stimulus for a thorough analysis of changing modes of social organization in society.

Many early theorists constructed ideal-type categorizations describing the state of society or community before the French and Industrial revolutions and after them. The French sociologist Emile Durkheim (1947), for example, distinguished between what he termed "mechanically" and "organically" integrated societies. Mechanically integrated societies, constituting one ideal type, were those societies held together because of the essential similarity of individuals. Organically integrated societies, the ideal type at the opposite end of the hypothetical continuum, were held together by a rigorous division of labor, by the specialized and distinctive functions performed by societal members. Much the same kind of analysis is to be found in the writings of Ferdinand Tönnies (1957) who distinguished between two ideal-type forms of social organization at polar ends of a continuum, which he termed *Gemeinschaft* and *Gesellschaft*. Still later, the American anthropologist Robert Redfield (1941) picked up on the kinds of distinctions made by Durkheim, Tönnies, and others and created what he called a "folk-urban continuum."

In all these cases, the continuum was used as a tool for analyzing and producing theoretical explanations of various modes of social organization. The point is that regardless of the issues around which ideal types are constructed, they help the researcher to set out the dimensions of the phenomena being investigated, and constitute, therefore, an important aid in theory building.

The examples we have seen of the ideal type have all been cases where the goal of the research is to deal with macrosociological issues. We have chosen as examples cases where the goal is the production of "grand theory." It might be useful to consider some typological devices employed as a step in producing something less than grand theory. One such device has been called the *property space*.

The Property Space as a Constructed Typology

To illustrate the use of property spaces we will look at a study conducted by John Lofland (1970). Lofland was interested in analyzing proselytizing religious groups. He spent a good deal of time in the field observing the behaviors of members of religious groups, detailing the structure of their religious organizations. As he became more familiar with these groups he began to collect data more specifically related to their proselytizing activities. As he examined his data he realized that members' concerns about contacting prospective converts consistently involved the following themes:

1. Whether or not to impart information and make new contacts in a face-to-face manner or to employ indirect means such as radio or newspaper advertisements.
2. Whether or not to immediately make clear the group's beliefs (in this case, belief in the coming of a new Christ and the imminent end of the world) or to withhold revelation of those beliefs.
3. Whether or not to attempt contact in religious places (churches) or secular places (street corners).

For each of these issues, members of the religious group had to make a dichotomous choice. Lofland began to see that it might be possible to better order his thinking and data on proselytizing activity if he considered all the possible variations of the three dichotomous choices already outlined. Perhaps the best way to speak of a property space is to say that it allows us to see all the possible combinations of the dimensions tentatively uncovered in a study. In Lofland's case, the property space would graphically look like the one shown in Table 2.1. By cross-classifying each of the three dimensions simultaneously Lofland has uncovered eight distinct proselytizing types. For example, proselytizing activity type A would be the case in which the conversion activity was attempted face to face, in which the beliefs of the group are made immediately clear to a potential convert, and in which the proselytizing activity takes place in a religious setting. Similarly, we can figure out the characteristics of each of the remaining seven types.

In constructing this property space Lofland has accomplished a number of important things. First, he has uncovered all the logical types of proselytizing activity implied by the themes in his data. Second, he has put himself in a position to think critically about what separates these various types from one another. He may begin to ask himself about the possible consequences for the religious group if they adopt one or another type. How will it affect the internal organization of the group? How might different types of activity affect the division of labor in the religious group or the need to make explicit the group's ideology? Third, once Lofland begins to ask questions such as these, he may very well be alerted to new theoretical themes. The property space, having helped us to order our thoughts about our data, may be the stimulus to a more general theory. It is in this sense, especially, that typologies, although not themselves constituting theory, may be important theory catalysts.

Lofland (1970) is quick to point out that the procedure of constructing types can easily become a sterile exercise, revealing nothing, if it is not performed within the context of a full, extensive, sensitive

TABLE 2.1 Property-Space of Religious Proselytizing Types*

	Information Imparted			
	Face-to-face		Indirect	
	New Christ Announced		New Christ Announced	
Type of Place	Yes	No	Yes	No
Religious	A	B	C	D
Secular	E	F	G	H

* *Source:* John Lofland, *Analyzing Social Settings* (Belmont, Calif.: Wadsworth Publishing Co., 1970), p. 23.

knowledge of the empirical data collected. Arbitrary box building is something to be avoided. It must be seen in its rightful place as an aid to a more comprehensive understanding of collected materials.

We may briefly continue our descriptive, illustrative discussion by introducing one other variant of typology construction here. There are instances when a researcher has constructed a property space and then sees the need to simplify it, to reduce it to one with even fewer dimensions. The simplification of a constructed property space has been referred to as *substruction*.

Substruction

Substruction refers to the process through which the researcher begins with a property space of the type described in the last section and then attempts to reduce the property space to one with even a fewer number of dimensions.

The reduction of a property space is accomplished by the combining of classes in order to obtain a smaller number of more comprehensive categories. We can illustrate the process by beginning with a simple property space.

In 1952, Allen Barton conducted a study of the national election. On the basis of his data, a person's *political position* was determined to be a function of two major dimensions — *usual party affiliation* (Democrat, Republican, or independent) and *degree of political interest* (high, medium, or low). In terms of these two dimensions, each of which consisted of three categories, Barton constructed a nine-celled property space as indicated in Table 2.2.

After examining the property space that he had constructed, Barton came to feel that somehow a person's political position could be simplified to fewer categories. As a way of reducing his original property space, he decided that perhaps the major distinction in terms of party affiliation was that between persons who identified with either of the two major parties and those who were Independents. On the degree of

TABLE 2.2 A Qualitative Property-Space of Political Position*

| | | *Usual Party Affiliation* | | |
		Republican	Democrat	Independent
Degree of Political Interest	High	A	B	C
	Medium	D	E	F
	Low	G	H	I

* *Source:* Allen Barton, "The Concept of Property-Space in Social Research," in *The Language of Social Research*, ed. P. Lazarsfeld and M. Rosenberg (New York: Free Press, 1955), p. 41.

TABLE 2.3 Reduction of a Property-Space by Simplifying the Dimensions*

		Usual Party Affiliation	
		Republican or Democrat	Independents
Degree of Political Interest	High or Medium	Partisans	Independents
	Low	Habituals	Apathetics

* *Source:* Allen Barton, "The Concept of Property-Space in Social Research," in *The Language of Social Research*, ed. P. Lazarsfeld and M. Rosenberg (New York: Free Press, 1955), p. 45.

political interest dimension, he chose to distinguish between those who had high interest and those who had either medium or low interest. By taking variables originally expressed in terms of three categories and merging them to form only a dichotomy on each, Barton was able to reduce his nine-celled property space to a four-celled space. Having done that, he was able to specify four distinct political types. The new, reduced property space, with the designation of political types, is recreated in Table 2.3. One could imagine these political types as central to the development of a theory of political involvement, political socialization, or patterns of voting behavior, to name only three.

Before we leave this general discussion, we should consider one final point. In the preceding pages we have characterized the ways in which typological constructions may serve as part of an inductive process leading to the development of theoretical ideas. There are, however, many cases in which a constructed model is derived from an a priori theory and descriptively embodies the major elements of that theory. In other words, models are sometimes used to present a theory in a short-hand fashion, calling attention to the relationships between the major variables constituting the theory in its more expanded version. As a matter of fact, it should be possible to construct a model identifying the proposed relationships between variables in *any* theory.

One example of the use of models as just described is to be found in the writings of those who engage in what has been called *causal modeling*. One specific type of causal modeling which may be used as an illustration has been termed *path analysis*.

Causal Modeling with Path Analysis

Blau and Duncan (1967) have made many contributions to the literature on social mobility. One of their models (see Figure 2.1) was constructed with the purpose of isolating the major variables that should

FIGURE 2.1 A Model of the Process of Stratification*

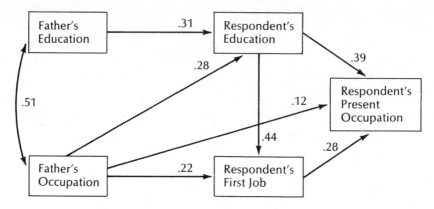

* Adapted from Peter Blau and Otis Dudley Duncan, *The American Oc-cupational Structure* (New York: John Wiley, 1967), p. 170. We have excluded the residual paths.

theoretically be predictive of an individual's occupational status. Their reading of the literature led them to produce a theory that focuses on the following five variables:

1. Father's educational attainment.
2. Father's occupational status.
3. Respondent's educational attainment.
4. Status of respondent's first job.
5. Status of respondent's present occupation.

The arrows in Figure 2.1 indicate the causal relationships the authors are assuming to exist among the five variables in their model. You will note that their model shows no direct effect of the father's education on the respondent's first job, but it does show an indirect effect of the father's education on the respondent's first job through the respondent's education. For this reason we refer to the respondent's education as an *intervening variable*. The numbers along the arrows in the model are referred to as path coefficients. They are statistical esti-mates of the direct effect of one variable on another in the model; the higher the number, the stronger the effect.[3] We see, for example, that an individual's present occupational status is more strongly influenced by his education than by the status of his first job.

---

[3] Our goal is to describe some of the basic elements of path analysis. The path coefficients are statistically estimated, using the appropriate beta weights (partial regres-sion coefficients in standard form). In our model we have not included the residual paths. For a thorough explication of path analysis, see Duncan (1966).

Typically a path analysis is produced in two stages. The first is an *a priori* stage wherein we postulate the causal linkages that we believe exist between the variables being considered. This original formulation of the model is made on the basis of theories proposed by others, previous research findings, and the researcher's intuitive judgments. This theoretical model is used as a guide for both collection and presentation of the data. After the data has been collected and the path coefficients have been computed, we are in a position to assess how well the data fit the original model. If the fit is not good, we move on to a second stage of path analysis which calls for an inductive use of the method. That is, we modify the model in light of the computed path coefficients to produce a revised model that is more consistent with the data.

Suppose that in their preliminary model Blau and Duncan had hypothesized an arrow (direct effect) between father's education and respondent's first job. In that event, they would have computed a path coefficient to estimate the strength of that direct effect. If that path coefficient had been large, the path would have been included in the final model; if it had been very weak, it would have been omitted from the final model, which would then have been the model in Figure 2.1.

Models such as the one produced by Blau and Duncan have a number of clear advantages. The use of path analytic models forces us to specify explicitly the interrelations among all the variables in our theory, and it allows us to compare the relative strengths of all the hypothesized predictors. It should also be clear that the construction of path models forces us to isolate only those variables we believe to be most crucial in producing one or another phenomenon. The result of this constraint is often the expression of theory in a tighter or "cleaner" form than might otherwise be the case.

In terms of future research, the specification of a path model may serve as a starting point for other researchers who, guided by their own theoretical ideas, would argue that additional or different variables be included in an explanation of the phenomenon under investigation. We could well imagine, for example, a researcher investigating mobility patterns among groups who might argue that Blau and Duncan's general model does not adequately show the operation of the variables involved in the mobility patterns of blacks in American society. In trying to show how the causal relations between the variables in the original model operate differently for blacks, the researcher may also demonstrate the necessity of adding certain variables to the model.

In concluding our consideration of path models, we must be alerted once more to an important feature of theory production and testing in the social sciences — nonexclusiveness. In this chapter and elsewhere we have adopted the convention of speaking about inductive and deductive research processes separately. But in fact, most research in the social sciences which works toward some system of coherent explanation employs both inductive and deductive approaches. Most usually, researchers who begin their inquiry with a deductive theoretical model will find that their *a priori* explanations do not fully account for the collected data and will work to reformulate their original theoretical construction. When this happens, the researchers have allowed the empirical world to talk back; thus, they have begun to engage in an inductive explanatory process.

In our discussion of path analysis we have used such expressions as "causal linkages," "direct effects," and other terminology which assume causal relationships among the variables considered. This convention raises the more general question of how to deal with the issue of *causality* in social research. It has been a topic of debate among philosophers of science for a long time. Causality can never be proven with complete certainty in either the social sciences or the natural sciences. However, most social researchers make (or lead their readers to make) inferences about the causal relationships among the variables considered. Many social researchers are willing to infer that A is a cause of B if three criteria are met. These have been referred to as the criteria of association, causal order, and lack of spuriousness (Hirschi and Selvin, 1967:38).

The criterion of *association* requires that A and B be associated. Using the example presented in Figure 2.1, we might compare present occupational level for respondents with high education with that for those with low education. If we were to find no evidence that those with high education have better occupations, we would not want to infer that education has a causal effect on occupation.

The second criterion, *causal order,* requires that A be prior to B. Using the same example, we can argue that father's education is prior to respondent's education. Thus a case can be made for inferring that father's education has a causal effect on respondent's education, but of course it would not be plausible to infer the reverse.

The third criterion, *lack of spuriousness,* demands that the association between A and B cannot be accounted for by other variables prior to both A and B. If we originally find a substantial association between respondent's education and present occupation, but then find that this association disappears when father's education and occupation are taken into consideration, we would decide against inferring a causal effect of respondent's education on his present occupation. We would instead conclude that the association between these two variables is *spurious* because it can be entirely accounted for in terms of the educational and occupational background of the respondent's father. To clarify this point, let us suppose that those who go to college tend to get better jobs, that most middle class children go to college, and that few poor children go to college. Suppose also that we were able to show that the children of the middle class get these same jobs even if they do not go to college and that the children of the poor do not get the better jobs even if they do go to college. Confronted with such results, we would conclude that the association between going to college and getting a good job is spurious because it can be accounted for in terms of social class background, which is causally prior to the choice to go, or not to go, to college. We would conclude that the mistake made by the poor was not the failure to attend college, but rather the failure to be born middle class.

A reasonably strong case can be made for inferring causality on the basis of some kinds of studies (e.g., a carefully executed experimental study), but the nonexperimental studies with which sociologists typically deal are often vulnerable to two criticisms: of not having adequately demonstrated that a causal relationship exists, or of not having accurately assessed the strength of the causal effect of one variable on another. In view of these limitations, many sociologists avoid any use of causal language when describing the results of their studies.

While it is certainly true that our estimates of causal effects are typically crude approximations to the "true" effects, the avoidance of explicit causal language does not really resolve the problem. At least implicit assumptions as to the existence of causal relationships among variables are unavoidable in most social research. For example, suppose we interview a number of people, asking each of them their income and a set of questions which we can use to assess their level of happiness. When writing up the results of our study, we could carefully avoid any explicit use of language which implies a causal relationship between income and happiness, but the reality is that our readers are going to assume a causal relationship (and we are going to want them to do so). We might just as well be more explicit and specify our assumption that income contributes to (has an effect on) happiness. We would probably also want to say something about the accuracy of our estimate of the strength of the causal effect.

CONCLUSION

There is a story told about a group of researchers at a large mental hospital who were trying to inquire into the causes of schizophrenia. One researcher, while doing routine laboratory tests on some of the schizophrenic patients in the hospital, made the startling discovery that the level of caffeine in the stools of the schizophrenic patients was dramatically higher than in "normal" patients. They reported this finding to their colleagues with the result that a number of researchers within the hospital began to verify the same findings.

As evidence of the relationship between caffeine and schizophrenia seemed to grow, a number of the researchers began to work out elaborate theories to explain this consistent finding. They became so enthusiastic that they applied for, and received, a government grant to study this relationship. The researchers began a large-scale investigation of the phenomenon. After several months and several thousands of dollars were spent, one of the researchers was stopped one day in the hallway by a manual worker in the hospital. The worker first apologized for possibly talking out of turn; he emphasized that he understood little about the "scientific methods" that researchers use and that he certainly could not understand the sophisticated analyses they were producing. At the same time, he claimed, there was something about the entire research that bothered him. When urged to continue, he simply asked the researcher: "Did you know that the coffee machine is on the same floor as the schizophrenic ward?"

The moral of this story should be clear. We have carefully studied the necessary relationship between theory and data in the total research process. We have stressed that the end goal virtually all social scientists have in mind as they do their research is to produce explanation of some aspect of the social world. It has been a continuous theme that such explanation can be arrived at through both inductive and deductive approaches. We have determined that there is equal importance for both theory development and theory testing in the social sciences. Our story illustrates, however, that no matter how logical and complete our theoretical explanation, no matter how sophisticated the typological devices and models used to order our data, our proposed understanding of the world may be flawed. We cannot become so enamored with our theories or with the methodological devices available to us that we dismiss *common sense* in formulating our research problems and setting out to test our ideas.

Apart from our recent injunction that we avoid shrouding the obvious with a proliferation of concepts and unnecessarily complex theoretical distinctions, we must adopt a skeptical attitude about *any* explanation we produce, through whatever method. We consider all explanation to be inevitably tentative and provisional. We propose our explanations with the full awareness that they stand only until a better explanation is provided. Such an attitude about the status of our explanation seems only reasonable when we consider the variety of epistemological difficulties faced by the social scientist. We have mentioned some of these difficulties in the course of this chapter. We have tried to show that we cannot count a theory correct just because the hypotheses derived from the theory allow us to clearly predict the events under investigation. We have discussed the difficulty of verifying the basic assumptions on which our theories are built. We have also discussed the dangers of tautological explanation.

Overall, we may see that there is one central issue that must be considered as we try to evaluate the quality of our theoretical explanations in the social sciences. If we are to have any faith in our theories and any hope of testing them, and if we are to avoid circular explanation, we must employ measurement procedures adequate to the task. Scientific theories stand or fall in terms of our ability to make reliable and valid measurements of those elements of the world that are the objects of our inquiry. We devote the next chapter, therefore, to a fuller examination of social science measurement problems.

EXERCISES

1. Choose any three pieces of research in the social sciences that attempt to offer theoretical explanation of some phenomena. For each, indicate whether the theoretical explanation is arrived at through an inductive or deductive process. Indicate as well whether you feel the theories have been adequately verified by collected data.

2. Using the same pieces of research as for exercise 1, try to do the following:

a. Indicate as many as possible of the unstated assumptions you feel underlie the respective theories.

b. If the theory is stated only in verbal terms, try to create a model similar to that used by Blau and Duncan to illustrate the proposed causal connections between the variables in the theory.

3. Using Richard Cloward and Lloyd Ohlin's book *Delinquency and Opportunity* as a basic reference, find at least two competing theories of delinquency. Indicate which you find most reasonable and why. Also try to indicate the type of data that might be necessary to test each of the chosen theories.

4. On the basis of your personal observation, try to construct some kind of classificatory scheme for describing the types of students on your campus.

5. How would you expect Lofland (Table 2.1) to classify a religious group that attempted to proselytize in both religious and secular places? Would it be necessary to modify the property space to handle this situation?

6. Conservatives, liberals, and radicals all have quite different ideas about the causes of poverty. What would be some of the major causes as viewed from each of these ideological perspectives? Are they contradictory? Diagram the relationships among some of these causal factors.

SUGGESTED READINGS

Becker, Howard
1958   "Problems of inference and proof in participant observation." *American Sociological Review* 23 (December):652–659.

A classic statement on the difficulties of idea testing and verification in qualitative research.

Blalock, Hubert
1969   *Theory Construction.* Englewood Cliffs, N.J.: Prentice-Hall.

> This book would be helpful especially to those students with some mathematical sophistication. Blalock's purpose here is to describe the process of moving from verbal theories to more rigorous formulations in terms of mathematical models.

Homans, George
1950   *The Human Group.* New York: Harcourt, Brace & World.

> Homans is one of the leading proponents of deductive theory in the social sciences. In this book he demonstrates the utility of deductive theory in explaining a number of empirical events.

Parsons, Talcott
1950   "The prospects of sociological theory." *American Sociological Review* 15 (February):3–16.

> A statement on the status of sociological theory by a leading "grand theorist."

Wrong, Dennis
1961   "The oversocialized conception of man in modern sociology." *American Sociological Review* 26 (April):183–193.

> A critical statement of contemporary sociological theory with special emphasis on the assumptions underlying functional theory. Wrong argues here that we must examine our assumptions in order not to produce tautological explanations.

Zetterberg, Hans
1965   *On Theory and Verification in Sociology.* Totowa, N.J.: Bedminster Press.

> A useful text informing the reader about the nature and production of axiomatic theory in the social sciences.

REFERENCES

Barton, Allen
1955   "The concept of property-space in social research." In *The Language of Social Research,* ed. Paul Lazarsfeld and Morris Rosenberg. New York: Free Press.

Becker, Howard S.
1963   *Outsiders: Studies in the Sociology of Deviance.* New York: Free Press.

Bernstein, Arnold, and Henry L. Lennard
1973   "Drugs, doctors and junkies." *Society* 10 (May/June):14–25.

Blau, Peter
1963   *The Dynamics of Bureaucracy.* Chicago: University of Chicago Press.

Blau, Peter, and Otis Dudley Duncan
1967   *The American Occupational Structure.* New York: John Wiley.

Bottomore, Thomas B.
1974   *Sociology as Social Criticism.* New York: Random House (Pantheon).

Cloward, Richard, and Lloyd Ohlin
1960   *Delinquency and Opportunity.* New York: Free Press.

Davis, Alan J.
1972   "Sexual assaults in the Philadelphia prison system." In *Muckraking Sociology: Research as Social Criticism,* ed. Gary T. Marx. New York: Dutton.

Davis, Kingsley
1961   "Prostitution." In *Contemporary Social Problems,* ed. Robert Merton and Robert Nisbet. New York: Harcourt, Brace & World.

Davis, Kingsley, and Wilbert Moore
1945   "Some principles of stratification." *American Sociological Review* 10 (April):242–249.

Duncan, Otis Dudley
1966   "Path analysis: sociological examples." *American Journal of Sociology* 72 (July):1–16.

Durkheim, Emile
1947   *The Division of Labor in Society.* Glencoe, Ill.: Free Press.

Festinger, Leon; Henry Riecken; and Stanley Schachter
1953   *When Prophecy Fails.* New York: Harper & Row.

Glaser, Barney, and Anselm Strauss
1967   *The Discovery of Grounded Theory.* Chicago: Aldine.

Goffman, Erving
1959   *The Presentation of Self in Everyday Life.* New York: Doubleday.
1961a   *Asylums.* New York. Doubleday.
1961b   *Encounters.* Indianapolis: Bobbs-Merrill.
1963a   *Behavior in Public Places.* New York: Free Press.
1963b   *Stigma.* Englewood Cliffs, N.J.: Prentice-Hall.
1967   *Interaction Ritual.* Chicago: Aldine.

Gouldner, Alvin
1970   *The Coming Crisis in Western Sociology.* New York: Basic Books.

Grusky, Oscar
1963   "Managerial succession and organizational effectiveness." *American Journal of Sociology* 69 (July):21–31.

Hirschi, Travis, and Hanan C. Selvin
1967   *Delinquency Research.* New York: Free Press.

Humphreys, Laud
1970   *Tearoom Trade.* Chicago: Aldine.

Hunter, Floyd
1953   *Community Power Structure.* Chapel Hill: University of North Carolina Press.

Karp, David A.
1971   *Public Sexuality and Hiding Behavior.* Unpublished Ph.D. dissertation: New York University.

Kuhn, Thomas
1967   *The Structure of Scientific Revolutions.* Chicago: University of Chicago Press.

Lofland, John
1970   *Analyzing Social Settings.* Belmont, Cal.: Wadsworth.

Marx, Gary T., ed.
1972   *Muckraking Sociology: Research as Social Criticism.* New York: Dutton.

Merton, Robert K.
1948   "The bearing of empirical research upon the development of social theory." *American Sociological Review* 13 (October):505–515.
1957   *Social Theory and Social Structure.* Glencoe, Ill.: Free Press.

Mills, C. Wright
1956   *The Power Elite.* New York: Oxford University Press.
1959   *The Sociological Imagination.* New York: Grove Press.

Parsons, Talcott, and Edward Shills
1959   *Toward a General Theory of Action.* Cambridge, Mass.: Harvard University Press.

Piven, Frances Fox, and Richard A. Cloward
1971   *Regulating the Poor: The Functions of Public Welfare.* New York: Random House (Vintage).

Polsky, Ned
1967   *Hustlers, Beats and Others.* Chicago: Aldine.

Redfield, Robert
1941   *The Folk Culture of the Yucatan.* Chicago: University of Chicago Press.

Rees, Albert
1974   "An overview of the labor-supply results." *Journal of Human Resources* 2 (spring):158–180.

Rosenbaum, James E.
1975   "Stratification of socialization processes." *American Sociological Review* 40 (February):48–54.

Stern, Philip
1972   *The Rape of the Taxpayer.* New York: Random House (Vintage).

Tönnies, Ferdinand
1957   *Community and Society.* East Lansing: Michigan State University Press.

Weber, Max
1947   *The Theory of Social and Economic Organization.* New York: Oxford University Press.

Weinberg, Martin
1968   "Sexual modesty, social meanings and the nudist camp." In *Sociology and Everyday Life,* ed. Marcello Truzzi. Englewood Cliffs, N.J.: Prentice-Hall.

Problems of Measurement

It has frequently been argued that precise, reliable, and valid measurement lies at the very heart of any science. Precision in measurement is fundamental to scientific advancement because good measuring devices extend our ability to see, hear, feel, and generally get close to the objects we are studying. The better our measurement, the more critically we can test our ideas about the social world. Our ability to resolve disputes between competing ideas or sets of ideas is in large part contingent on the accuracy of our measurements. Theological idea systems can, for example, compete with one another endlessly without any clear resolution because no one has figured out a way to observe (let alone measure) the divine. If we are committed to a scientific sociology, ideas about the operation of society and individual behavior should be open to testing. At the very least our research should allow us to reject as unsound the theories we have proposed.

If the "correctness" of any theory is to be properly evaluated, it is necessary for the researcher to obtain measures of all the variables contained in the theoretical statement. Let us assume, for example, that a critical proposition in a particular theory is as follows: the higher the level of anxiety among a group's members, the greater will be the degree of cohesion in the group. It seems plain that if we are to have any hope of accepting or rejecting this proposition, we must have precise ways of measuring both anxiety and cohesion. This example is, of course, meant to be just an illustration. The point is that much of sociological investigation is dedicated to showing that a theoretically predicted relationship exists between two or more variables. Sociologists have tried to show, for example, the relationships between social class and rates of mental illness, family organization and rates of juvenile delinquency, and ethnicity and childrearing practices. In all these cases we must be able to measure the variables involved with some degree of precision.

Ideally, when we set out to measure a particular attribute, any differences between those persons we study should reflect "true" differences on that attribute. So, if we were measuring mental health status, all the differences among individuals' scores on our mental health inventory (or on whatever measure of mental health we were using) would be due to actual differences in their mental health. Or, if our concern were with measuring people's intelligence, any measured differences on an IQ test would represent "true" differences in their intelligence. If this could be accomplished, we would have achieved a perfect state of measurement. In a perfect state of measurement, differences between persons would be due entirely to the variable in which we were interested; none of the differences between persons would reflect either "chance" variation or variation due to the effects of factors unknown to the investigator.

Unfortunately, such a state of perfect measurement is not easily within our grasp as sociologists. Our measures are frequently beset by "errors" of various sorts. The task of this chapter is to discuss the distinctive problems faced by social scientists as they attempt to measure social variables and to detail the kinds of potential errors that may intrude on their measurement efforts. Having outlined the difficulties faced in measuring our variables, we should then be in a position of suggesting how sociologists may work to create better measures. Let us look at the following questions, which will be of concern as we move through this chapter:

1. What is the nature of sociological variables and how does it affect measurement procedures?
2. How does the sociologist actually create measures of these variables and what are the kinds of errors that are likely to creep into this measurement process?
3. How does the sociologist assess the quality of these measures?
4. What can be done to improve the quality of social science measurement?

Some variables (or concepts) are, on the face of it, much easier to measure than others. If we wish to know how many men or women, blacks or whites, persons over or under six feet tall, and the like are in a room, researchers are likely to agree on the criteria for discriminating between persons on these dimensions. In the case of the gender, the two categories, male and female, are generally considered *mutually exclusive* and *exhaustive*. No person in the room will fit into more than one of the two categories (the categories are, then, mutually exclusive), and there will be no one in the room who does not fit into one of the two categories (the categories are exhaustive). Even here, however, there could be sources of error in our attempt to discriminate between genders. We can think of cases, for purposes of illustration, where the categories male and female may not be mutually exclusive or exhaustive categories — there may be transsexuals and hermaphrodites in the room. We have used an extreme example to illustrate that even in those cases where measurement would seem to pose no particular problem, there are still potential sources of error. But in general we can see that certain variables can be relatively easily measured. These are variables where there is a one-to-one relationship between the variable and the observations we must make to measure that variable. If these were the only variables with which social scientists had to contend, there would not be much necessity for this book to contain a chapter on the problems of measurement.

In most instances researchers are interested in measuring variables that are considerably more complex than age, sex, and race. Sociologists are usually in the business of trying to measure such concepts as alienation, freedom, happiness, cohesion, morale, leadership, self-image, and the like. These variables, quite obviously, are abstractions and it is not self-evident which observations allow us to note their presence or the degree to which they are present. These are complex *analytical constructs* which bear no obvious one-to-one relationship to things observable. The measurement of such variables must be approached indirectly. As the variables become more complex, more abstract, further removed from direct observation, it becomes much harder for sociologists to reach some consensus as to how they are best measured. As a matter of fact sociologists' attempts to measure such variables are distinguished by a nearly total absence of consensus. This is nicely illustrated in a recent study of measurement consensus.

In 1967 three sociologists (Bonjean, Hill, and McLemore, 1967) inventoried the measurement scales and indices that appeared in four major sociology journals over a period of twelve years. They found 2,080 separate measures, which they could reduce to 78 conceptual categories. This means that on the average each of these concepts has been measured in more than 26 different ways by sociologists. Further, their data indicate that sociologists use concepts in nearly as many different ways as they attempt to measure them. Over all, only 28 percent of the indices were used more than once and only about 2 percent were used five or more times. In fairness, we ought to acknowledge that there were some concepts around which sociologists seem to have generated a degree of consensus. The data from this study indicates substantial agreement regarding the measurement of status, racial and ethnic stereotypes, segregation, and authoritarianism. Some of this agreement is no doubt a function of the investigators' having used measures first developed in pioneer, landmark studies. On the whole, however, there is one inescapable conclusion from this study:

> *Sociologists display wide disagreement as to how to measure key concepts in their field.*

Let's consider in a somewhat more detailed way some of the reasons for this lack of consensus. A chief factor may be that in the case of the social sciences the meaning of concepts may change depending on the situation being studied.

THE SITUATIONAL MEANING OF SOCIOLOGICAL VARIABLES

Most social phenomena are more like liquids than solids. That is, their shape depends on circumstances. Consider, as an example, the field of attitude measurement. Does a person have the same feelings about race when he is among blacks as he has when among whites? Do adolescents have the same attitudes toward sex in a discussion with parents as they have when among their peers? These are tricky issues, but some social psychologists would argue that behavior-related attitudes vary according to an individual's definition of the situation. And so it is with a variety of social phenomena: their shape depends on circumstances, a fact which makes it very difficult to measure their "true" dimensions. The variability of social phenomena, however, goes far beyond the issue of attitude measurement and has profound implications for the development of scientific explanation in sociology, profound implications for the possibility of generating social laws analogous to the kinds of laws possible about the physical world. It is worth considering for a moment the relationship between the variability of social phenomena and scientific theorizing. We can do this by considering first the nature and structure of a scientific explanation of the physical world.

How would we explain the phenomenon of water boiling at lower temperatures on a mountain than at the seashore? We might construct an explanation that looks like this:

1. The air surrounding the earth exerts atmospheric pressure on the surface of the earth.
2. There is a direct relationship between altitude and pressure; the higher the altitude, the less the atmospheric pressure.
3. Water will boil at different temperatures depending on the magnitude of pressure applied to it; the lower the pressure, the lower the temperature at which water will boil.

Hence,

4. Water boils at a lower temperature on the mountain than at the seashore.

The form of the explanation here is deductive. The fact has been explained showing that it can be deduced from assumed premises. This is the model of explanation in the natural sciences; we may want to consider the conditions necessary for the same type of explanation in the social sciences.

The logic of deductive explanation demands that each assertion, each element, each concept, each variable entering into the argument have a stable, universal meaning. In our example, the meaning of such variables as altitude, pressure, and temperature will be understood and measured the same way by all scientists. The meaning of the variables will not change each time the scientist goes to a different mountain or seashore to test the theory. But is this stability true of the variables in a situation in the realm of the social sciences?

Suppose we are interested in explaining why suicide rates are higher in Sweden than in the United States. We might explain it by saying that the welfare state robs a person of initiative, that when persons are robbed of initiative they are likely to get depressed, and that there is a much higher incidence of suicide among depressed persons. We might conclude logically that suicides will be higher in Sweden (a welfare state) than in the United States. This explanation certainly has the *structure* of a deductive explanation and appears strongly analogous to the water boiling explanation. What makes the explanation quite different is the nature of the variables in the two.

To follow on our previous point, the major concepts in the suicide explanation — initiative, depression, and even suicide — do not have constant meanings. There is unlikely to be anything approaching consensus among social scientists as to their meaning, nor can there be consensus. After all, it seems only reasonable that the meaning of a variable such as initiative is going to vary in different situations. Does initiative, for example, mean the same thing for a poverty-stricken person as for a millionaire; will it mean the same thing in the United States as in other countries? The answer is clearly "no." Most sociological concepts allow for a variety of interpretations and meanings.

In sociology, concepts like social disintegration or social disorganization will never achieve any kind of universal applicability. In one study, it seems appropriate to consider a high divorce rate a proper indicator of social disorganization. But are we to assume that the breakup of the extended family indicates the same thing? Or how about the rates of juvenile delinquency, or the dilapidation of buildings in certain areas of the city, or crime rates, or any pathology for that matter? The meaning of a social concept is extremely variable, depending on the situation in which it is applied. In terms of our previous example we would have to say that for the social scientist, no one mountaintop or seashore can be taken as the equivalent of any other mountain or seashore for the purposes of testing a theoretical explanation.

A second factor which reduces measurement consensus lies not in the nature of the social world but rather in the different theoretical and personal biases held by researchers. Whether consciously or unconsciously, we are all equipped with assumptions about human nature and the nature of the social world that necessarily guide the questions we ask about social phenomena, the methods we employ, and ultimately the way we choose to measure the variables of interest to us. Sociological analysis is necessarily reflexive, founded on our personal experience in the world.

THE REFLEXIVE NATURE OF SOCIOLOGICAL INVESTIGATION

Some sociologists will undoubtedly argue that they make no *a priori* assumptions about human nature or society, or that their assumptions are based on empirical evidence. To suggest the former is to deny their own existence and experience as human beings. To suggest the latter is, to some degree, to misunderstand the nature of certain major assumptions that underlie social research; for example, there is no way to *verify empirically* that people either do or do not have free will. Yet it is unavoidable that assumptions about this issue and similar ones underlie both our theoretical and our empirical efforts.

For example, let us consider attempts to measure the amount of deviance in some organization. The construction of such a measure will necessarily be related to the researcher's theoretical and personal conception of what constitutes deviance. From whose point of view is an act deviant? Should we consider the breaking of *any* rule deviant? Perhaps from the perspective of workers it might be considered deviant *not* to break certain management rules. And which rules are we talking about: only the formal written rules of an organization, the informal unwritten rules, or both?

In short, before we can measure anything we must decide what it is we want to measure. Our intention is to suggest that even the definition of what we seek to measure will be, in part, a function of our theoretical and personal dispositions.

Finally, at this point, we might suggest that the measurement of variables will not be independent of the goals of the research.

THE GOALS OF RESEARCH AND THE MEASUREMENT OF VARIABLES

It is, of course, difficult to separate the goals of sociological research from the kinds of issues discussed in the last section, one's own personal experience and theoretical interests. But certainly one can distinguish between two types of research. As we have seen, the goal of one type is to *verify* theories, propositions, or hypotheses that are specified at the very beginning of the research process; the goal of the other type is to *discover* what might be important theories, concepts, or hypotheses. The important point for us is that concepts or variables are treated differently when the goal of the research is verification from how they are treated when the goal is discovery.

The conventional approach in scientific research is that the researcher prepares a relatively well-articulated problem in advance of the inquiry and does not begin a piece of research without having first defined the problem, defined the major variables involved, and set out the procedures for measuring those variables. Participant observation, however, is not typically guided by an *a priori* development of hypotheses, concepts, or measurements. Rather, the emphasis is on having concepts, hypotheses, and theories emerge as a result of the researcher's direct confrontation or involvement with the behaviors or situations being studied. Field researchers speak of the proper use of concepts as sensitizing devices. By sensitizing concepts they mean concepts that are not transformed immediately into operational definitions. (Blumer, 1956).

If, for example, we choose a sensitizing approach to measuring the concept of intelligence, we enter the field and learn the specific meaning of intelligence by the persons we observe. The logic of the sensitizing approach is based on the notion that the meaning of the concept may vary for persons and groups at different points in the social structure. Some argue that we cannot safely decide ahead of time the best way to measure a concept like intelligence for all groups. It may be that for one group intelligence is to be appropriately thought of as the ability to manipulate verbal symbols, but for another group intelligence is better measured by the ability to con the police or talk one's way out of a confrontation.

Ultimately, all concepts must somehow be *operationalized,* must be observed and measured. The sensitizing approach, often used by field researchers, merely delays the point at which operationalization of variables occurs. We can see, therefore, that an additional factor accounts for the lack of measurement consensus among social scientists. Broadly speaking, as the goals and emphasis of the research change, the very same variable is likely to be measured in quite different ways.

In sum, we have argued that there is little consensus among social scientists with regard to the measurement of key concepts in the field, and we have tried to outline some of the reasons this is so. The three related factors mentioned are as follows:

1. Unlike the variables common in natural science explanation, the meaning of social variables may vary from situation to situation.
2. The measurement of social variables is inextricably related to the experiences, biases, assumptions, and theoretical dispositions of the researcher.
3. As the *goals* of social research change so also will the manner in which concepts are measured change.

Thus far, we have discussed some of the reasons that social scientists have difficulty in agreeing on how variables are best measured. If we could assume, for the moment, that such problems could be resolved, we would still have to cope with a variety of errors that inevitably beset our measurement efforts. Early in the chapter we defined a perfect state of measurement as one in which all differences between those studied would be due entirely to the variable in which we were interested. A state of perfect measurement would exist where none of the differences between persons would reflect either chance variation or variation due to the effect of factors unknown to the investigator. In the next section we take it as our task to outline some of the major sources of error that intrude on social science measurements.

OPERATIONALIZING A VARIABLE: THE SOURCES OF MEASUREMENT ERROR

In our discussion of some of the factors that make it difficult for social scientists to agree on how best to measure their variables, we have indirectly suggested what might be some sources of measurement error. In this section we want to consider these error sources more explicitly. One way of beginning to identify the sources of measurement error is to look briefly at the general process through which the social scientist must go in measuring variables. The process of arriving at a measure for a variable is referred to as the *operationalization* process. What, then, is the procedure through which the social scientist takes an abstract concept so that he ultimately arrives at some kind of quantitative rendering of that concept?

For purposes of illustration, assume we are interested in assessing whether some people are happier than others. Let us further assume, in order to strengthen our frame of reference, that we have a large grant and can afford to carry out a survey research study. If our major dependent variable is happiness, we must first figure out some way to operationalize this variable.

When we are confronted with the prospect of operationalizing a complex, abstract variable such as happiness we must begin by considering what might be the *indicators* of that variable. By indicators in this case we mean those measures which we can use as criteria for assessing happiness. To some degree, the delineation of appropriate indicators calls for some guessing on the part of the researcher. Although we may decide, for example, that the ability to function successfully during the day, or a strong sense of self-esteem, or a feeling of general well-being are all reasonable indicators of happiness, we cannot be sure any of these adequately tap happiness. A problem we always face in our efforts to operationalize a complex variable is that we can never be sure that the indicators named adequately reflect the presence or absence of the characteristic we wish to measure. Obviously the number of potential indicators of a variable are many. As we work to detail the indicators of happiness, we come to see that some of these indicators closely cluster together; and it may be possible that we will ultimately choose to distinguish between different types or dimensions of happiness because we begin to think that our indicators belong to different types. Clearly, however, these indicators are themselves still abstract entities and the researcher must operationalize these various indicators of happiness.

The empirical referents of a variable's indicators can potentially take many forms — they might be actual behaviors, they might be written records, they might be expressed attitudes, and so forth. The process of operationalization involves the determination of concrete measurable items that are reflective of the abstract concept with which we begin. Once we can determine these concrete empirical referents, they can be assigned numbers that represent the strength of their presence.

Let us continue by assuming that we have decided to use the responses to a set of attitude questions to operationalize the happiness variable. The form and content of such questions may vary, but anyone who has ever filled out a questionnaire has probably seen questions like those in Table 3.1. After these questions have been answered, we have a score for each question for each respondent which runs from 1 (for those we classify as least happy) to 5 (for those we classify as most happy). For certain purposes we may want to sum the scores to get an overall index (the index score) of happiness.

We have briefly outlined the process of operationalizing a variable, starting with a very abstract concept (happiness) and finally arriving at an operationalized version of this concept in the form of an index score. We have described this process to call to the reader's attention an important point. The process of operationalization is a multistage pro-

TABLE 3.1

We have listed below a number of statements. Could you please circle the number which best describes how you feel about each of these statements. For each of these statements you may *strongly agree* (SA = 1), *agree* (A = 2), *be neutral* (N = 3), *disagree* (D = 4), or *strongly disagree* (SD = 5).

	SA	A	N	D	SD
I often feel depressed during the day.	1	2	3	4	5
Sometimes I wish that I were someone else.	1	2	3	4	5

cess and there is the possibility of error creeping into the measurement at each point along the way. We cannot be sure that our indicators adequately reflect the concept we set out to measure. Nor can we be certain that our operational measures of these indicators are valid.

There are two helpful analogies to use in explaining the nature of the data we ultimately obtain. One explains data as a combination of information and noise. The job of the researcher is to collect information-rich data and somehow separate the true information from the static or noise error so the message can come through clearly. A somewhat more mathematically useful analogy asserts a similar understanding of data but explains it in terms of *variation*. Social science deals with variations between persons, groups, institutions, nations, and the like. The data we collect consists of systematic variation (information) and random variation (noise). The systematic variation is that component of the variation which would be present in the absence of any measurement error; the random variation is that component of the variation attributable to measurement error. In practice it is very difficult to separate these two components of variation; we often have little or no idea as to how much of the variation in our observations is due to true differences and how much is due to error in our measurement procedures. At the end of any statistical analysis we are left with what is called unexplained variation. This is variation due to relevant variables not considered in our analysis and variation due to measurement error, but we generally have no indication of the relative contribution of each to the unexplained variation.

We have already given a good deal of attention to one source of error, the error that results from our effort to measure "intangible constructs" like happiness which demand a complicated multistage process of operationalization. Many judgments must be made as we move through this process, with the final result being that we cannot be certain that our final quantitative scores really bear a direct relationship to the concept with which we began. There are two other major sources of error, particularly threatening when some form of questionnaire is being employed. They are (1) respondent lying and (2) systematic error in respondents' answering of questionnaire items. We can consider them in turn.

Lying as a Source of Measurement Error

Sociologist Derek Phillips (1971) reports the results of a study that compared the age subjects stated on the 1960 census with official birth records. Disagreement between the two sources was found among 27 percent of the white males, 35 percent of the white females, 57 percent of the black males and 66 percent of the black females. Some of these discrepancies were probably due to inaccurate records, but we might reasonably suspect that a large part of it resulted from people either not knowing their true age (not caring, trying to forget) or lying. If we think of disagreements like this just in terms of error, then the discrepancies observed appear to be a pure and simple nuisance factor getting in the way of our intent to analyze the relationship between age and some other socially relevant variable. It is important to note that people do not tell the truth all the time in response to even the simplest questions and there may well be an important pattern to what types of people lie and on which types of issues. It may be quite sociologically relevant to investigate how subjects define the situation and consequently how they respond when a stranger interviewing them asks what appears to be a routine question.

Is there really such a thing as a routine question, or do even the most innocuous questions mean different things to different persons? Though interviewers are probably accustomed to asking persons their ages, what kind of persons have got used to being asked and to answering such a question? Concretely, what if we were to find that welfare mothers responded differently from the way upper-middle-income mothers did to a series of questions about child care? Could we be confident that the differences in responses told us something reliable and valid about differences either in their true feelings or in their true child-rearing practices? How sure could we be that the difference meant something? This is more than a statistical question about how big the difference has to be before we take it seriously. It is a basic question about what the difference represents. Basically, we have to know whether it is a difference in the true feelings of the two groups or only a difference in the way they approach being interviewed. The welfare mothers may have in common the experience that people who ask them questions are a threat to their well-being. Upper income mothers probably have quite an opposite stock of experiences. Conceivably this could well have a bearing on how they respond to questionnaire items. Further, if the interviewers tend to be middle class (or tend to be drawn from any one class), one group will feel more at home and comfortable with them than the other group. This is not far fetched; it is one of the most consistent findings in sociology.

The point of all this is quite simple, yet it is the most essential point that can be made about the quality of data. *Our data can be only as good as our understanding of the data collection process.* We suffer from a historical tendency to underrate the complexity of data collection, of which one element is to assess the truth or falsehood of responses to questions.

There is good reason to believe that we can validly measure age in a questionnaire because we have the means to verify responses, thereby separating truth out from untruth. What if we were dealing with something more complex, like racial attitudes? Is it still quite so clear what is meant by a lie?

In a famous study years ago LaPiere (1934) presented some very compelling evidence that what people say on matters of race relations cannot necessarily be taken as any sort of predictor of how they will behave. From 1930 to 1932 LaPiere and two Chinese associates traveled twice across the country seeking services, accommodations, or both at hotels, motels, and restaurants. They received service ranging from unexpectedly warm to cordial to reserved in 250 out of 251 cases. In some instances LaPiere accompanied his Chinese friends; in others he did not. After a lapse of six months he sent a questionnaire to each of the establishments asking whether or not they accommodated members of the Chinese race. The answer he received from 92 percent of the same people from whom he had lately received service was a flat "no." Nonetheless, LaPiere's conclusion was not to call these subjects liars. He judged that people typically respond to symbolic situations differently from real ones.

Clearly, LaPiere's and others' studies provide us with empirical evidence that calls into question the simple, common assumption that attitudes are nothing more than predispositions to action waiting to be used by sociologists or social psychologists as handy predictors of future behavior. This discrepancy between people's words and their deeds has been documented in a number of different contexts (Deutscher, 1973).

Even when questionnaire-inspired attitudes do not reflect either the "true feelings" that lie deep in a person's soul or the way that person would act if such an imaginary, hypothetical situation ever did actually present itself, they are often worth studying in their own right. Unfortunately, they are seldom treated as objects of study in themselves or on their own terms: there is almost always the implicit suggestion that they are important as the determinants of future action. When a majority of the American people stated a lack of confidence in Richard Nixon, it was not necessarily important what each of them would actually do as final arbiter in an impeachment trial. The original statement of dissatisfaction becomes a social fact at the moment it is communicated socially. How truly sincere and deeply felt it may be is less important than the way it appears in determining its eventual effect on other persons' attitudes and actions. The sociologist W. I. Thomas put it nicely when he said, "What men define as real is real in its consequences."

Some attitudes are rationalizations, some are stated to test the feelings of another person or group of persons; some are generated momentarily out of the dynamics of group pressure or conversation or other interaction. Other attitudes may be fairly stable predispositions and thus may be useful for prediction. How, then, can we get close enough to what a person is really feeling to sort out stable predispositions? How do we get people to openly discuss their innermost feelings? It is doubtful that this can be accomplished consistently through impersonal interviews by strangers, though there are some cases like the early Kinsey studies of sexual behavior where this technique appears to have been remarkably successful.

Whereas on *a priori* grounds we would expect observational studies to be well adapted to circumvent the problem of lying, few participant-observers have been concerned enough with rigorous measurement and prediction to seriously test the full effectiveness of their method. As always, the method must be matched to the kind of data one is after, and the more deeply personal the data is, the more deeply personal in some sense ought to be the method employed. Where possible, the results should be crosschecked against the findings produced by other methods. As a general rule, the more complex the concepts you are dealing with, the more sophisticated must be your measurement tactics.

Finally, and very briefly, *systematic* errors or biases constitute yet another serious measurement problem.

Systematic Measurement Error

An index could conceivably measure a phenomenon with the same result among a sample of persons each time it is used. There is a certain consistency to the measuring device. Despite this consistency we still cannot be certain that we are accurately measuring the phenomenon of interest to us. Two examples should illustrate how systematic error may produce substantially misleading findings.

Derek Phillips (1971) presents an example from his own research on mental health. In this case, bias on a mental health inventory was so systematically built in that the data produced spurious relationships. Puerto Ricans in New York consistently scored lower on mental health inventories than white, middle class persons. Not willing to accept this relationship at face value, Phillips did some further probing. He found that middle class subjects attached stigma or social undesirability to the very characteristic of psychosomatic disturbances for which they were being tested. His middle class subjects tended to avoid any admission of psychosomatic disturbance. They had reason to avoid telling the truth when that truth appeared damaging to them. In contrast, the Puerto Ricans in the sample felt quite neutral about revealing the information about themselves. Puerto Ricans did not suffer disproportionately from mental health problems as had originally appeared to be the case. Phillips concluded that all his apparently scientific data served only to reflect differences of *attitude* toward psychosomatic symptoms — a far cry from the superficial finding about the relative incidence of mental health problems among different races and social classes. Less industrious investigators might simply have asserted the face validity of their measure, presenting conclusions with potentially racist implications.

Similarly, what if a study were to show that less educated persons in our society tend to have harsher racial prejudices than their more educated counterparts? We might be moved to suggest all sorts of social action policies designed to reeducate the racist lower classes, while simultaneously printing encouraging articles in liberal media sources to reinforce the smug self-righteousness of much of the suburban middle class. Again we could be subject to the same sort of error Phillips frequently found in his and other persons' investigations.

In sum, we have described and given examples of the three major sources of error that beset our measurements. The first source of error is related to the process of measurement itself. We have seen that the measurement of complex, abstract variables is a multistage process, the end result of which is a degree of uncertainty as to whether we have measured what we set out to measure. A second source of error results from respondents who lie for a number of different reasons when confronted by an interviewer with a questionnaire. A third possibility which we have termed systematic measurement error involves those cases where a sample of persons may respond to questionnaire items in a uniform fashion because of commonly held beliefs or ideologies, such as a commonly held sense of stigma about mental illness.

Those who have understood these three sources of measurement error are now in a position to understand the criteria used by social scientists in evaluating the quality of their measures. From our previous discussion it seems plain that there are three major questions social scientists ask about their measures. They are as follows:

1. How much *information* are we being provided by our measures?
2. Is our measuring device *consistent*? Will our measuring instrument produce the same result when applied to the same object twice? This question involves the *reliability* of our measures.
3. Are we really measuring what we think we are measuring? To what extent does an instrument truly represent what it is designed to measure? This last question has come to be known as the *validity* question.

Put most plainly, we evaluate the quality of a measure in terms of its ability to produce valid, reliable information. We can consider in the next section how such evaluations are made.

EVALUATING THE QUALITY OF A MEASURE: INFORMATION, RELIABILITY, AND VALIDITY

We have seen that in the simplest, most concrete sense, measurement is no more than a method of representing facts, objects, or characteristics with numbers assigned by some consistent rule. We will take up the matter of consistency shortly. Right now it is important to note that all sets of numbers are by no means equal in the amount of information they contain.

The Information Criterion and Levels of Measurement

Researchers use the information criterion to distinguish four levels of measurement. The lowest of these (the level providing the least information) is the *nominal* level of measurement. If the categories of a variable are *mutually exclusive* (no person in the sample can fit into more than one category) and *exhaustive* (every person in the sample can be classified into one of the categories), the nominal level of measurement has been achieved. For example, suppose our variable is "state of birth" and that the variable has fifty categories corresponding to the fifty states. As long as our sample includes only persons who were born in the United States, who know the state they were born in, and who accurately report it, the nominal level of measurement is achieved. If we add a fifty-first category designated as "other" our revised variable achieves the nominal level even if some of the respondents were born outside the country. It should be evident that nominal level measures do not provide us with much information beyond categorizing the elements of our sample along such dimensions as state of birth, religion, sex, race, and the like.

Besides distinguishing units as being the same or different from one another, we often wish to make statements regarding whether some elements in the sample being studied possess "more" or "less" of a particular attribute. A second level of measurement is called *ordinal* because it allows us to place persons along a continuum from the greatest amount to the smallest amount of the characteristic we are measuring. We might, for example, be interested in distinguishing the members of some community in terms of their prestige. We could set up a question on a questionnaire asking a group of judges, let's say, to rank persons in the community in terms of their prestige. We would then be able to rank persons in the community from greatest to least prestige. Most variables dealt with by social scientists are of the ordinal type.

We can do more than categorize responses (at the nominal level) or rank order them (at the ordinal level); we can also measure the distance between points along the scale so that we can know not only that one response is lower than another, but also know how much lower. This level of measurement, the *interval* level, is different from the final level, *ratio measurement,* in that ratio scales also have an exact, known zero point. We might be able to measure prejudice with interval level precision, but we would be hard pressed to state when a respondent had no prejudice at all (the zero point on the scale). Measuring income in dollars, on the other hand, can be expressed in terms of a ratio scale because we have a unit of measurement (the dollar) and we know precisely what point on the scale represents zero income.

It is important to reach as high a level of measurement as possible so that we can legitimately perform a variety of mathematical operations on our data. Whereas we cannot go beyond "greater than" or "less than" inequality statements with ordinal measures, we can meaningfully add or subtract interval measures and can multiply or divide ratio scales. The higher the level of measurement reached, the more powerful statistical techniques we can apply, and the more sophisticated our statistical analysis can become. The information criterion leads us to seek the highest level of measurement our data permits. But at the same time we must also strive to maximize the reliability and validity of our measures.

The Criterion of Reliability

One factor that is known to particularly affect reliability is the temporary personal state of the subject when the data is collected. If one were to take college board (S.A.T.) examinations twice and receive somewhat different scores, part of the difference would probably reflect differences in one's mood, alertness, emotional and physical well-being, anxiety, and the like. This would mean that the test had less than perfect reliability because of its sensitivity to extraneous factors, and we could compute a *reliability coefficient* to measure the amount of that imperfection. However, part of the change may sometimes reflect a true change in the subject rather than just wobbliness in the measure. This latter possibility makes it exceedingly difficult to gauge reliability precisely by the so-called *test-retest* method of comparing different scores from successive test administrations. This is a constant dilemma in measuring either change or reliability, and there is no simple solution to the problem. Sometimes the problem logically resolves itself as when the test and re-test are close enough together in time that imputing significant change to the subject makes little or no sense. Sometimes the direction of change in scores points unmistakably to a reliability problem, as when a person's I.Q. appears to drop twenty points in a week.

Variations in the surroundings and in the data-gathering procedures themselves also affect reliability adversely. The weather, time of year, appearance of the surroundings, or interviewer's appearance or manner of approach can all vary from one administration to the next. Although we cannot control these factors in the strict sense of the term, if we know how they influence the data, we can measure them and correct for their influence as we analyze the data.

Finally, data processing is never subject to perfect quality control, and random errors can thus be introduced after the data has been collected. Experienced survey researchers have developed an assortment of techniques to minimize such errors, and, properly applied, these can be quite effective. But at least one critic has suggested that as long as portions of the research effort are carried out by hired hands who have less of a stake in keeping the data as uncontaminated as possible, large errors will be introduced at this stage and they will quite often go undetected (Roth, 1966).

A second method of testing reliability is available when the instrument is fashioned from a number of subparts, all of which are expected to measure essentially the same thing. Such is the case with most test batteries where a number of questions are designed to get at the same phenomenon. Reliability is tested by computing how closely the items tend to resemble one another in the results they produce. This is done in a variety of ways. Each item can be correlated[1] with every other item and an average inter-item correlation can be reported as a *reliability coefficient*. Alternatively, the scores can be added together to form a single scale and then each item can be correlated with the scale. One can then report an average *item-to-scale* correlation. A third popular technique is called *split-half* reliability testing. Here all the items are randomly divided into two equal groups and a smaller scale is computed for each group. The correlation of these two subscale scores is then reported as the split-half reliability coefficient. Most statistics texts present the details of how to compute and interpret these various coefficients.

Although reliability coefficients are all in widespread use, they seem to share a common assumption which can occasionally be a serious flaw. Each of these coefficients is essentially a test of how closely the separate components of an overall measure resemble one another. Yet, is there any compelling logic demanding that parts resemble one another to form a useful whole? Certainly, a crankshaft, carburetor, valves, and pistons do not resemble one another but no one would seriously suggest that they cannot be combined to form an automobile engine. Why, then, should we expect someone who hates one group to necessarily hate another group before we judge as reliable the person's responses to a prejudice scale. We should, therefore, restrict these inter-item consistency tests to measures where homogeneity is theoretically called for by our definition of the concept.

In practice social scientists have concentrated much attention on problems of reliability and too little attention on matters of validity. The reason for this is quite simple. We know how to conceptualize and deal with reliability, but we feel at a loss to pin down validity with testing operations. This is an undeniable problem, but it should not be used as an excuse for misplaced priorities. The fact is that data can be reliable without being valid, while the opposite is decidedly not true. Of the three criteria mentioned, it seems safe to judge that validity is the key characteristic in evaluating the quality of data.

The Criterion of Validity

Part of the problem with judgments about validity stems from a proliferation of terminology. Since validity cannot be directly tested,

---

[1] See Chapter 15 for a discussion of correlation.

there have sprung up a variety of ways to test it indirectly. To add to the confusion, different authors sometimes use different terms to describe essentially the same judgment criterion. Thankfully, the diverse assortment of terms can be reduced to three basic approaches: *content validation, pragmatic validation,* and *construct validation.*

Content validity, sometimes referred to as *face validity,* refers to whether a question or type of measure appears to be valid "on the face of it." In other words, content validity depends on the plausibility of a measuring strategy in the eyes of the researchers or their critics. When an index is created using a set of attitude questions, the content validity approach usually involves trying to judge the extent to which the questions composing the index or scale are a representative sampling of all possible items. However, the more complicated and disputable the concept, the more any such judgment about the content validity of a measure is likely to reflect the predispositions, status, and role of the researcher.

Consider the problem of measuring the quality of student academic performance. If six different professors were to construct comprehensive examinations for introductory psychology students, there would be a great deal of divergence as to what was deemed important and worthy of emphasis on each of the exams. The exams might say more about the individuals who made them up than they did about students' knowledge of psychology *per se.* Each instructor would probably judge his or her own test to be most valid and would doubtless offer solid logic to back up this claim. Hence, content validation is often less a real testing procedure than a method of justification and legitimation.

The essential problem with face validity is that it assumes rather than proves the content of a measure to be obvious. Can we ever be sure of the obvious? A good example of the dangers of such an assumption is afforded by the comprehension tests given to persons at the conclusion of some commercial "speed reading" programs. Such tests are designed to prove that the course has increased reading speed several times without any loss of comprehension. A standard ploy over the years has been to give comprehension tests on reading passages about which subjects can be expected to have some prior knowledge (such as a basic point from American history or a biographical sketch of Abraham Lincoln). Another ploy is that the comprehension questions asked are often framed in a way so that common sense comes close to suggesting the answer. Consequently, it has been shown that persons reading fast and persons reading at a slow, normal pace score about the same on these tests. What we are not told is that persons who have never seen or read the passages also get about the same comprehension scores as the other two groups.

On the face of it, such a test clearly deals with the topic at hand, so it would appear to be a valid measure of comprehension even though it has virtually no discriminatory power. It is only when we concoct and apply a scientific test (using a third group of persons who have not taken the course as a comparison or control group) that the "self-evident" logic behind the instrument falls apart.

Pragmatic validation judges the validity of a measure strictly according to its ability to predict. A good intelligence test, for example, is one which predicts future success in school reasonably well. This is sometimes referred to as *predictive validity*. It has become a rather popular way to simply sidestep the whole issue of validity. Instead of coming to grips with the meaning of a measure, a researcher can rest content with demonstrating that "it predicts, so it must mean something." Sidestepping the validity question can have serious, unanticipated ideological consequences. Some would argue that intelligence testing, for example, proceeds from and tends to reinforce the Social Darwinist theory — that ability varies widely from person to person and from group to group, and success depends on the survival of the most able. But let us consider this: there is evidence to suggest that intelligence scores predict because knowledge of their results constitutes a self-fufilling prophecy.

The evolution of intelligence tests suggests that they may have been somewhat tainted from their beginnings. Early tests like the Stanford-Binet were validated around a pragmatic method called *concurrent validation,* by which a measure is judged valid if it differentiates between groups already considered different. A test of psychosis should thus distinguish between institutionalized, labeled psychotics and "normals." Such a method automatically reinforces the *status quo,* be it wisdom or folly. In the case of intelligence test derivation, one of the validating procedures was to compare test results against teacher ratings of pupils. If a teacher believed a certain pupil to be dumb, a good test was defined as one which also was likely to find the pupil dumb. To the extent that teacher's feelings about students affect the distribution of rewards (the so-called "pygmalion effect"), I.Q. tests based partly on teacher feelings will necessarily correlate with grades, perseverance, and other teacher-influenced measures of performance. Moreover there are simply too many reasons why a measure might predict for us to allow us to confidently consider predictive potency a sufficient indicator, by itself, of valid measurement.

Probably the most popular roundabout approach is the method of *construct validation.* Here measures of concepts are judged valid if they relate as theoretically anticipated to other concepts. A complex analytical construct like authoritarianism may be defined in the first place by its theoretical relationships to other variables. Construct validation inquires empirically into whether or not these expected relations hold. As an example, we might theoretically expect that there will be a relationship between authoritarianism and voting behavior. More explicitly, we might expect that the more authoritarian an individual is, the more likely he is to support political candidates who advocate a vigorous law-and-order position. If we were interested in validating a measure or test of authoritarianism we might go to some community in the midst of a political campaign. We might choose such a community in which the candidates for office clearly vary in their respective positions on law and order, take a random sampling of persons in the community, score them on authoritarianism, and finally ask them their preference with respect to the candidates running for office. If there is a high correspondence in the predicted direction between persons' scores on the authoritarianism scale and their choice of candidates, we might conclude that our technique or test does validly measure authoritarianism.

This is a valuable and increasingly popular way of approaching the validation of indirectly measurable phenomena. Its main weakness is that, if relations do not hold as expected, does one blame the theory or the measures? Construct validation is a good deal more sophisticated than previous approaches but it is still biased in favor of supporting the assumptions of the researcher. A measure's failure to predict does not mean that one necessarily discards the theory. Instead the researcher typically renews the search for a measure that does predict. Should we find such a measure, we are likely to accept it as valid although the chance still exists that our original theorizing was faulty.

Ironically, the most direct and compelling method of validation has been one of the least often used. Much of the information most essential to sociological studies is available from sources other than the subject. For this reason, much interview data can be *crossvalidated* against independent but parallel sources of information. Official records can be consulted to determine a person's age, marital status, ethnic background, political party affiliation, income, academic records, consumption habits, and so forth. Unfortunately, to do so usually involves much more time and energy than is available. The fact that this is so seldom done, even though the results are startlingly relevant and sometimes eye-opening, shows the low priority researchers and funding agencies have attached to studying validity. Some prominent social scientists have recently expressed the opinion that social research cannot progress much farther until it attends more seriously to questions of measurement, especially to the question of validity.

It is often useful to distinguish between the issue of *internal validity* and the issue of *external validity* (Campbell, 1969). Let us return to our earlier example of the researcher who has prepared a questionnaire to measure happiness. If we question the ability of the questionnaire to accurately assess happiness for the sample of respondents the researcher has interviewed, we are calling into question the *internal validity* of the measure. If we question the extent to which the results based on this sample can be generalized to other segments of the population, we are calling into question the *external validity* of the measure. The external validity of our measure is low if due to poor sampling we have no idea how generalizable our results are.

We have tried to pinpoint some of the major problems faced by the researcher in measuring the variables of interest. The problems that we have mentioned will not be easily resolved. However, we ought to be in a position to suggest some ways of improving the quality of our measures. It is to that final task that we now turn.

STRATEGIES FOR IMPROVING THE QUALITY OF MEASUREMENT

The many problems entailed in producing quality measures of our concepts have lately caused quite a stir among social researchers. In particular, long-overdue discussion and debate about the validity of our measures has begun. One of the effects of criticism leveled at social research techniques has been a growing concern with strategies to better cope with some of the problems outlined in this chapter. The most general outgrowth of this concern and intellectual exchange has been a new emphasis on the use of multiple measurement techniques.

The logic behind the use of multiple measurement techniques is elegantly simple. It is referred to as the logic of *triangulation*. Just as in trigonometry one can indirectly but precisely measure the location of a point by appropriate sightings from two other points, so also can one apply this method of triangulation to social measurement. Specifically, all indirect measures have their own peculiar weaknesses. However, by concentrating on the point at which a series of independent, indirect, and perhaps weak indicators converge, we can effectively minimize their separate errors and maximize their overall validity. Simply put, there can be strength in converging weaknesses.

Triangulation is the best test we have of validity. We can never be absolutely sure of what a test measures. That seems to be a fact to which we must reconcile ourselves. But if we make use of several measuring techniques all producing agreeable results, we can have some greater faith that we are, indeed, measuring the concept of interest to us.

An important caveat is necessary in discussing the logic of triangulation or *multioperationalism*. We must continually bear in mind that the function of using a number of measuring techniques is to better affirm the validity of our measures. The logic of triangulation gets short circuited if the techniques used are based on very similar types of data; that is, unless the data used in our various measures are diverse in nature and method, we will be doing nothing more than testing the reliability of these measures. That is a far cry from the assertion we would like to make — that the techniques used are all measuring the dimensions of some variable.

Consider, for example, tests of the proposition that all falling bodies accelerate at an equal rate in a vacuum. If we dropped a one-pound steel ball and a two-pound steel ball and arrived at measures of acceleration very close to what we expect theoretically, there might still be those who would criticize the test by saying that the two objects had too much in common in the first place. If, on the other hand, we drop, in order, a steel ball, a piece of wood, and a feather and find that the rates of acceleration are identical for each, there would be less reason to question the validity of our original proposition.

The key to triangulation, then, is independence among our various estimates. If a series of measurement estimates are all collected by the same method (let us say a series of questionnaires), they may not be sufficiently independent to meet the required logic demanded by triangulation. Each of these separate questionnaires could conceivably suffer from similar flaws, biases, or errors.

Imagine that we are concerned with assessing worker attitudes in a company town. Suppose, further, that we choose to assess workers' satisfaction with living and working conditions by using a questionnaire with 25 separate "satisfaction" questions. If some 75 to 80 percent of the workers responded to each of the 25 questions by saying that they were quite satisfied, might we still have reason to doubt the validity of our data? In terms of the logic of triangulation, would we be twenty-five times as confident of the validity of our satisfaction measure as we would have been if we had used only one satisfaction question? If we add another 25 questions to our questionnaire and the results still remain constant, will we have doubled our faith in the validity of our "satisfaction" findings? The answer is clearly "no." There are several reasons why we may fail to assess accurately the percentage of satisfied workers in the town; one, for example, is the possibility that workers may fear reprisal by their superiors if they show discontent. Given this type of potential respondent bias toward showing satisfaction, we could multiply our questions ad infinitum and still be uncertain about our results.

Suppose we realize that it is possible to increase the validity of our satisfaction measure by collecting diverse types of data, and for this reason we choose to employ a number of independent data-gathering techniques. Along with our use of a questionnaire, we also send a participant observer into the factory and town. Suppose that over a period of time the observer hears little talk of dissatisfaction and sees few instances of conflict. Suppose, further, that we check migration patterns into and out of the town and find that few persons leave the town while many wish to enter. Beyond that we carefully read the town newspaper and find few expressions of discontent. What we are suggesting is that the larger the number of methodologically independent measures we utilize, the fewer doubts we will have about our assertions.

There is an important analogue to our discussion of multiple operationalism. It seems generally to be the case in sociology that researchers come to adopt a particular methodological approach and virtually all of their work is done using that technique. This is in some respects a function of graduate training in sociology. Certain graduate schools stress the importance of their students' developing quantitative, statistical skills.

Those who earn their degrees at such schools generally do research that utilizes these statistical skills (e.g., survey, research). In other graduate schools the emphasis is on qualitative field work procedures. Students in these programs rarely do research that might involve survey research techniques. And so it goes.

There is an unfortunate consequence of people's firm commitment to one or another methodological procedure: it is that researchers typically allow their methodological preferences to dictate the problems that they will work on. Logically the process ought to work in the opposite direction. Problems for investigation should have highest priority. Once we determine what we consider an important issue for investigation, we ought then to consider which methods are most appropriate for acquiring data relative to that issue.

In terms of our immediate concern in this chapter, the kind of methodological provincialism that we have been describing presents a serious obstacle to better measurement. If we are to treat the idea of multiple operationalism seriously, it demands the simultaneous use of a number of methodological precedures — survey research techniques, participant observation, content analysis, historical analysis, experimental procedures, and so on.

CONCLUSION

At the outset of this chapter we stated that precise, valid, and reliable measurement lies at the very heart of any science. For this reason, the measurement questions raised in this chapter are centrally important in any evaluation of the potentialities and limitations of the social sciences.

The authors hope that the reader has come to share their judgment that the measurement of social variables cannot be viewed as an independent, discrete process. We cannot disassociate measurement from the goals of research, the theoretical predilections of researchers, and most significantly from the processes of data collection. Quality measurement is contingent on the investigator's understanding of the strengths and weaknesses of the various methodological techniques available. That being so, we must be alert to how later chapters reflect back on the concerns and problems cited here.

EXERCISES

1. Choose any research article of interest to you from a social science journal. How much attention does the author devote to discussing and evaluating the quality of his or her measures?

2. Choose a variable or concept of particular interest to you and suggest as many concrete measurement strategies as you can. Try to explain how the different strategies affect or compensate for each other's weaknesses.

3. Select two or three articles from a recent issue of the *American Sociological Review*. For each variable used in the study specify the level of measurement that it would be appropriate to assume.

4. How would you measure poverty? Would income and other "objectively measurable resources" be enough, or would you take into account how people *feel* about their material status? After developing your own definition, read Stephen Campbell's discussion of the difficulties and inconsistencies in official definitions of poverty (Campbell, *Flaws and Fallacies in Statistical Thinking*, p. 16ff).

5. Find a research article that uses a popular test or other measuring instrument, or examine any of the standard scales and indices presented by Delbert Miller in his *Handbook of Research Design and Social Measurement*. Try to think of as many situations, types of persons, or groups of subjects as possible for which the measure would be inappropriate and explain why.

6. Christopher Jencks offers a thorough appraisal of the measurement validity and reliability in the Coleman Report's study of equality and educational opportunity. Read Jencks's critique in Mosteller and Moynihan's book *On Equality of Educational Opportunity* and then read Chapters III and V of Jencks's reanalysis of the same data in Jencks, et al., *Inequality*. Is Jencks's reanalysis of the Coleman study consistent with his own criticism of the data's quality?

SUGGESTED READINGS

Campbell, Donald, and J. Stanley Campbell
1966   *Experimental and Quasi-Experimental Designs for Research*. Chicago: Rand McNally.

The authors assess the validity of a number of experimental designs frequently used in the social sciences.

Deutscher, Irwin
1966   "Words and deeds: social science and social policy." *Social Problems* 13 (1966):226–254.

A clear statement by Deutscher of the relationship between attitude and behavior. He also spells out the policy implications of the contradiction between the two.

Douglas, Jack
1967   *The Social Meanings of Suicide.* Princeton: Princeton University Press.

In the course of generating his analysis, Douglas engages in a lively critique of the measurement procedures that have typically been used in evaluating suicide rates.

Landecker, W.
1951   "Types of integration and their measurement" *American Journal of Sociology* 56:332–340.

> The author takes a very difficult concept — integration — and tries to show how researchers must think about it in order to establish clear measurement procedures. This article provides a model for the way social scientists might think of other equally complex variables.

Osgood, C., et al.
1957   *The Measurement of Meaning.* Urbana: University of Illinois Press.

> Osgood's pioneering use of a device called the "semantic differential" for measuring complex individual attitudes is detailed in this book.

REFERENCES

Bonjean, Charles M.; Richard J. Hill; and S. Dale McLemore
1967   *Sociological Measurement: An Inventory of Scales and Indices.* San Francisco: Chandler.

Blumer, Herbert
1956   "Sociological analysis and the variable." *American Sociological Review* 21 (December):683–690.

Campbell, Donald T.
1969   "Reforms as experiments." *American Psychologist* 24 (April):409–429.

Campbell, Stephen K.
1974   *Flaws and Fallacies in Statistical Thinking.* Englewood Cliffs, N.J.: Prentice-Hall.

Jencks, Christopher, et al.
1972   *Inequality.* New York: Harper & Row.

LaPiere, Richard T.
1934   "Attitudes vs. actions." *Social Forces* 13 (March):230–237.

Miller, Delbert C.
1970   *Handbook of Research Design and Social Measurement.* New York: David McKay.

Mosteller, Frederick, and Daniel P. Moynihan, eds.
1972   *On Equality and Educational Opportunity.* New York: Random House.

Phillips, Derek
1971   *Knowledge from What?* Chicago: Rand McNally.

Roth, Julius
1966   "Hired hand research." *American Sociologist* 1 (August):190–196.

Ethical and Political Issues

CHAPTER FOUR

Consider the following hypothetical research situation. A team of politically moderate social scientists has received a research grant from the federal government to investigate political extremism on both the left and the right in America. The researchers will interview members of the Communist Party and the John Birch Society to find out what their attitudes are on a wide variety of political and social issues. Because they know that their respondents may not give completely honest answers, the research team will use an alternative means of data collection as a check on the validity of the interview results. They will also hire and train research assistants to become members of the Communist Party and the John Birch Society, in order to observe the two groups from the inside without the groups knowing that they are being studied. This secretive or disguised observational data will be compared with the interview data.

This hypothetical research example shows that ethical and political considerations enter into the process of conducting social research. Some of these considerations relate directly to the goal of objectivity which guides scientific research. For example, how can social researchers minimize the effect of personal prejudices and biases on what they observe and how they interpret what they observe? How can a group of politically moderate social scientists examine political extremism without having their values color the conclusions of their study? The researchers should also consider the ultimate social use of their research findings. What role should they play in determining this use? Research findings can be used either constructively or destructively. In our hypothetical situation, the research findings could conceivably be used by the government to undermine politically extreme groups. Does the research team have any ethical or political responsibility with regard to this possibility?

Other ethical and political considerations for researchers are less directly related to the question of objectivity. For example, are there ethical limits on the relationship between researchers and those studied? In our hypothetical example, the second means of data collection involves the disguised entrance of research assistants into the political groups to be observed. The groups will not be asked for their permission to be studied. Does such a research tactic violate the accepted rules of the game in social science research? In this chapter we will consider a variety of such ethical and political issues which confront the social researcher. However, before discussing these issues we must first turn again to the issue of objectivity.

OBJECTIVITY

Most social scientists have immediate intellectual and visceral reactions to the word *objectivity*. To some it is a straightforward term that refers to the scientific method and the belief that researchers should remove the effect of their personal biases on their research so that social reality may be uncovered. To others, the term refers to the disguise that social scientists often use in order to escape moral responsibility. A good starting point for unraveling this diversity of opinion is to examine the position taken by Max Weber.

Weber is generally considered to give strong support to the traditional position that social scientists should rule out biases or *value judgments* in doing research. Value judgments are our personal evaluations of the goodness or badness, rightness or wrongness of what we are investigating. In other words, value judgments depend on our personal belief and biases. According to Weber (1968), it is impossible to establish the ultimate validity or invalidity of such judgments on the basis of scientific investigation alone. Related to this point is Weber's argument that the goal of the social sciences is to understand "what is" and not "what ought to be." The latter, or normative type of knowledge, lies within the domain of social philosophy. Consider the sociologist who studies homosexuality. Weber would consider it appropriate for such a sociologist to describe the life styles and socialization of homosexuals, to report on their experience with discrimination at work, and the like, but not to conclude that homosexuality is either superior or inferior to heterosexuality.

Central to the issue of objectivity is Weber's position that the value judgments of researchers should not enter into the collection, analysis, and interpretation of data. This is the strict position on the role of objectivity and, indeed, the strict interpretation of what Weber was saying. One can find in his writing the admission that it is very difficult for social scientists to remove the effect of their own values on the analysis and interpretation of data. Despite these difficulties, Weber seems to be arguing that objectivity is a goal or ideal which should be aimed for in the research process.

We will look at three other ideas of Weber's regarding the role of value judgments. First, although the ultimate validity of value judgments or goals cannot be substantiated by scientific investigation, the means for achieving them can be determined by such investigation. For example, given the goal of racial integration, the social sciences can explore what the best ways are for achieving integration. Second, Weber did not believe that the effect of researchers' values on the problems selected for investigation created any difficulty. An American immigrant might choose to study the assimilation process or a person who is experiencing marital difficulties may want to study the dynamics of the American family system. Weber would point out that the crucial consideration is for such researchers to strive for objectivity in the collection, analysis, and interpretation of data. Third, Weber (1958) encouraged social scientists to distinguish between their role as scientists and their role as private citizens. Such a segregation of roles would, in Weber's view, increase the likelihood of objectivity in social science.

Many objections to the plea for objectivity and a value-free social science have been raised by contemporary social scientists. Gouldner (1962) sees many strict interpreters of Weber's ideas "as narrow technicians who reject the cultural and moral consequences of their work." Behind Gouldner's attack is his belief that Weber's value-free notion once allowed for the growth and independence of the social sciences. Today, however, he believes that the dogma of objectivity is used too often as a rationalization by social scientists; it allows them to sell their goods to the highest bidder while ignoring the possible social consequences of their work. This dogmatic approach also excludes the possibility of any social criticism developing from social science research.

Becker (1967) also critiques the demand for rigorous objectivity. He maintains that we cannot separate our personal values from the research process. For example, Becker argues, researchers' biases influence which societal perspectives are accentuated in research. Becker sees society as based on hierarchical relationships of *superordination* and *subordination*. The superordinates possess authority in a given situation; the subordinates are the "have-nots" in terms of authority. Wardens and prison guards are the superordinates in a penitentiary; the prisoners are the subordinates. Becker argues that research generally does not include both perspectives. In fact, researchers encounter difficulty when they try to avoid this situation.

> A student of medical sociology may decide that he will take neither the perspective of the patient nor the perspective of the physician, but he will necessarily take a perspective that impinges on the many questions

that arise between physicians and patients; no matter what perspective he takes, his work either will take into account the attitudes of subordinates, or it will not. If he fails to consider the questions they raise, he will be working on the side of the officials. If he does raise those questions seriously and does find, as he may, that there is some merit in them, he will then expose himself to the outrage of the officials (Becker, 1967: 244).

According to Becker, the perspective that becomes emphasized is related to the researcher's biases.

There is clearly a great difference of opinion over the role of objectivity. One school of thought maintains that objectivity is achieved by removing the lenses of personal bias to view what really is going on in society. This is the traditional Weberian position. The other position is that objectivity is virtually impossible; it is being used as a shield for escaping moral responsibility. The solution to this seeming contradiction is to develop a balanced position emphasizing both our desire to make scientific observations of society with a minimum of bias and the need for social responsibility. In this chapter we will try to develop such an approach while looking at various ethical and political considerations relating to objectivity in each major step of the research process. The major research junctures to be considered are: (1) formulation of the research question; (2) data collection; (3) analysis, interpretation, and presentation of research results; and (4) application of research results.

FORMULATION OF THE RESEARCH QUESTION

Ethical and political issues relating to objectivity appear at three stages in the formulation of the research question: (1) in choosing the research topic and precisely posing the question to be pursued, (2) in choosing a theoretical model, and (3) in obtaining funds.

Like all beginning steps, choosing the research topic is obviously crucial. Out of all social reality, which slice is to be cut out for examination? Some researchers would suggest that the topic be important in one's field of study and personally interesting. Others would add that it should be relevant to the improvement of society. Such topics are not always easy to come by, but let us assume that the researcher at least picks a topic of personal interest. Suppose that the general topic is crime. We imagine that the researcher has personal opinions and values related to the topic. As we have seen, Max Weber would argue that this situation does not, by any means, automatically rule out objective social research. Such an appraisal becomes more difficult to accept when the precise research question becomes articulated. Will the general topic of crime be pursued from the perspective of the superordinates or the subordinates? What kind of crime will be studied: Lower-class crime or upper-class crime? Theft in the inner city by poor people? Tax evasion by the rich? Illegal political contributions by the large corporations? And, once again, from whose perspective will these more specific questions be pursued? Although the precise questions examined in research cannot always be categorized as being from the perspective of either the super-ordinates or the subordinates, some of them can. Even when they cannot, social researchers should see that their personal biases and values can affect how they conceptualize a research topic. The effect of bias can become apparent when one thinks about which questions and aspects of a topic are ignored and why. Perhaps the researcher should keep a journal during the whole research process, including such thoughts about the conceptualization of the research topic in it, and refer to it when interpreting and presenting the research results.

Closely related to the choice of topic is the choice of a theoretical model that will help us to organize and interpret data. There are many theories in the social sciences, but none has been proved beyond doubt. Many of the theories compete; for example, the functional and conflict theories. In Chapter 2 we saw that functionalists like Talcott Parsons see society as a system made up of different parts. Each part of the system is viewed from the standpoint of what it contributes to the functioning of the system. Some functionalists, for example, believe that social classes in America, which differ widely in terms of economic well-being and political power, are functional. Stratification, they say, operates as a reward system, encouraging people to work hard. In brief, the functionalists tend to view most realities in society as having some positive function. Otherwise, they say, these conditions would not exist in the first place. Researchers who adopt such a perspective are encouraged to predict that social change will be in the direction of maintaining the status quo.

The conflict model, on the other hand, views society from the standpoint of internal strains and conflict rather than consensus. Researchers who choose this theoretical perspective are much more likely to predict revolutionary developments. For example, a conflict theoretician might expect the existence of relatively widespread poverty in our affluent society to lead to upheavals that would transform the very nature of our social system. The choice of theoretical models is not confined to the functional and conflict theories. Recently, social scientists have also tried to develop synthetic theories that achieve balance between these two theories.

The theoretical model chosen to back up a research question is of tremendous importance in determining what will be observed and how it will be interpreted. Do the personal biases of researchers affect which theoretical model will be used? Will conservatives choose the functional theory while radicals opt for a conflict theory? Or, will researchers objectively choose the theory that seems to explain the most? The answer, quite often, may well be the first suggested possibility. The second alternative encourages skepticism. Indeed, how can anyone be sure that personal values have not played a role in the choice of a theoretical model? Oddly enough, Max Weber's position does not appear to be dramatically different from such an appraisal. Weber states that "In the method of investigation, the guiding 'point of view' is of great importance for the *construction* of the conceptual scheme which will be used in the investigation" (Weber, 1968:84). If this is true, how can we still seek objectivity? The solution is similar to the one we suggested for the first problem area. Once again, researchers should try to become sensitized to the role of their own values, perhaps through a journal, and be ready to discuss this during the interpretation and presentation of research results. Furthermore, researchers should aspire to the goal of collecting data that are not contaminated by personal biases. How to accomplish this will be discussed when we deal with data collection.

The third major problem area in formulating a research question is funding. Many social scientists have to depend on allocations from the government, private corporations, and private foundations in order to support their research. Obviously, such sources will support the research in which they are interested. Some social scientists point out that this bias is not always bad; the federal government, for example, supports research that is related to reducing poverty and crime. Other social scientists note that the influence of the funding source explains why research that is likely to support the status quo is more often funded than research that might eventually lead to different societal arrangements. For example, a large corporation is more likely to support researchers who are trying to find out how laborers can work more efficiently than it is to fund research aimed at discovering how workers might better organize themselves politically.

An excellent example of the funding issue can be seen in the case of Project Camelot, a research project sponsored by the Department of Defense which involved a $6 million budget and the services of many social scientists (Horowitz, 1967). The broad goal of the project was to examine social change in underdeveloped countries. However, there was considerable ambiguity about the more specific goals of the project. It has been suggested that the lure of all that government research money may have kept the participating social scientists from caring very deeply about what the exact goals were. However, at least in retrospect, it became apparent that the real interest of the Defense Department was to develop knowledge regarding the possibility of containing political unrest in the Third World countries. The social scientists were not encouraged to deviate from the Defense Department's counterinsurgent perspective. Revolutionary developments as a positive force in the underdeveloped world would have been given little if any attention. This has caused social scientists to describe Project Camelot as an example of "hired hand" research. In retrospect many sociologists are relieved that the project was canceled before it really got off the ground.

What is the solution to the funding dilemma? Are all sources of funding to be suspect and rejected? Clearly, this is a rather extreme and self-defeating position. Caution, however, should be taken in negotiating with any prospective sponsor of research. As Kelman (1968:78) points out, "The crucial issue, it should be noted, is not the sponsorship of the research or the source of the funds, but the nature of the explicit and implicit contract under which the funds are obtained." In brief, no matter who might be supporting a given research project, researchers should know what strings will be attached.

There are broad issues connected to the funding question. Who is going to use the knowledge developed by the research? How will the knowledge be used? Will the knowledge be used constructively or destructively? We will discuss these issues further when we examine the application of research results. As in all research, decisions at each step of the process affect decisions at later steps. One should not begin to worry about the application of research results only after the research is completed; rather, one should begin to worry right from the outset.

DATA COLLECTION

Although it is apparent from the above discussion that the personal values of researchers can color the choice of research topics and theoretical perspectives employed, the quest of objectivity in data collection still remains as an ideal. Social scientists have devised a number of techniques that increase the likelihood that valid and reliable data, minimally contaminated by personal bias, will be obtained. For example, modern sampling techniques enable researchers to include diverse segments of a population in a predictable manner so that their research is really representative of the people being investigated. Advances have been made in questionnaire construction so that "loaded" questions are less likely to appear in surveys conducted today. The point to be emphasized is that our data collection techniques should be used impartially.

> By using our theories and techniques impartially, we ought to be able to study all the things that need to be studied in such a way as to get all the facts we require, even though some of the questions that will be raised and some of the facts that will be produced run counter to our biases. . . . Whatever side we are on, we must use our techniques impartially enough that a belief to which we are especially sympathetic could be proved untrue (Becker, 1967:246).

A crucial issue in collecting objective data is the relationship between researchers and the people who are observed.

> . . . Social research is caught in a highly magnified version of what physicists have termed the "Heisenberg principle": the very process of obser-

vation changes, to a greater or lesser extent in the shorter or longer run, the action it seeks to register (Friedrichs, 1968:9).

Many examples of observation that changes the nature of what is observed can be cited. An interesting case is described by a white social scientist who investigated race relations in South Africa. When he asked black workers about their attitudes toward whites, he received cautiously indifferent replies. When his black research assistant made the same inquiries, however, the responses revealed attitudes bordering on hatred toward the white ruling elite (van den Berghe, 1967).

The effect of observation on what is observed can be diminished. One strategy is to compare what different observers find when they examine the same social phenomena. In the hypothetical study of political extremism mentioned at the beginning of the chapter, it would make sense to have researchers of both radical and conservative political persuasions observe both groups. Another guideline is to make sure that data gatherers are carefully trained to carry out precisely defined observational tasks. They should have no question about what is to be observed and how it is to be observed. A final recommendation is that observations be recorded as soon as possible in order to lessen the possibility that the biases of observers will alter the memory of what has been observed. Mechanical devices such as tape recorders are helpful. Such tactics appear to reduce the negative role which researchers' biases can have on what is observed. However, they do not completely ensure that respondents will willingly display or report their behavior and attitudes to researchers.

The reluctance of respondents is at least partially explained by the fact that some people place a high premium on privacy and do not want their personal lives exposed via the research of social scientists. A very general guideline for overcoming this problem is for social researchers to develop good rapport with potential respondents. One inducement commonly offered is the promise of confidentiality. The question of ethics is relevant here. Obviously, if such a promise is made, it should be kept. Confidentiality can be achieved in large sample surveys by removing the identifying information about individual respondents from the questionnaires. However, when a research project involves a small sample, it may not be possible to ensure confidentiality. In the community study *Small Town in Mass Society* (Vidich and Bensman, 1958), the promise of confidentiality was made to the community members. When the research findings were published, the identities of some respondents became apparent even though code names were used instead of the respondents' real names. Needless to say, this unfortunate result caused an uproar in the community. The lesson to be learned from this example is that it is ethically desirable not to offer confidentiality when it cannot be delivered. Our inability to guarantee confidentiality does not necessarily reduce the possibility of cooperation of potential informants. If researchers can demonstrate the social usefulness and significance of a research project, they may be able to gain cooperation without the guarantee of confidentiality. In fact, the ability to show the social usefulness of a research project to respondents may be just as great an inducement as the promise of confidentiality.

Faced with the possibility of rejection by potential respondents, social researchers have sometimes used deception and manipulation in their work. One example of such deception is disguised observation, in which the people who are being observed are unaware of it. The group might be the army, Alcoholics Anonymous, a street gang, or any group of interest. If you recall, the hypothetical study at the beginning of the chapter included disguised observers of the Communist Party and the John Birch Society. Some social scientists argue that this method of observing is unethical because it invades the privacy of people who have not given their permission to be observed. They maintain that the usage of such research approaches may alienate the larger society and threaten the acceptability of more straightforward research by the broader social science community (Erikson, 1967). Others contend that such tactics should not be rejected automatically, because they may be useful for advancing scientific knowledge in areas where other means of data collection are not feasible (Denzin, 1970).

Disguised observation is not the only research strategy that raises ethical questions concerning the relationship between social researchers and their subjects. Other strategies of deception and manipulation have been used in the experiments of both psychology and sociology. In some cases, the true purpose of such research has been concealed and the human subjects have been treated in less than ethical fashion. A classic example is Stanley Milgram's (1973) experiment which had the apparent purpose of studying the effect of punishment on learning but actually had the concealed purpose of investigating obedience to authority. Subject A enters a laboratory and meets subject B and the experimenter in charge of the research. Subject B is actually a member of the experimental team. The experimenter tells subject A to be the "teacher" in an experiment for studying the effect of punishment on learning. When subject B gives wrong answers, subject A is to give what he thinks are real shocks to subject B. They are not real shocks. The experiment begins. Subject B gives wrong answers and supposedly receives shocks of increasing voltage. Subject B screams and pleads that the experiment stop. When subject A asks the experimenter if he should stop, the experimenter replies in the negative. Subject A continues with the experiment. The real purpose of this experiment is to see whether or not subject A will follow the directions of the experimenter even though he thinks they are causing pain to subject B.

This experiment, and others like it, have been criticized for their unethical treatment of human subjects. Once again, some argue that such research strategies can add to the accumulation of scientific knowledge and, therefore, can be used in certain situations. The question is whether or not the ethical treatment of subjects should be sacrificed for our desire to further scientific knowledge. Some suggest that if more conscientious attention were addressed to this question at the outset of research, fewer studies employing deception and manipulation would be done (Kelman, 1968). The question, however, is a relative one. The practices of deception and manipulation range from the fairly innocent to the outlandish. Some practices should obviously be avoided. When deception is employed, precautions should be taken. For example, if the true purpose of an experiment is concealed, an explanation emphasizing the scientific merit of the research should be given afterward. When researchers decide that disguised observation is ethically tolerable in a particular research situation, special efforts should be made to ensure that the identities of the subjects will be protected. Perhaps the overall ethical guideline is that the people who are being studied should not be hurt by the research process.

It should be underscored that the issues of confidentiality, deception, and manipulation are relevant not only because of ethical considerations but, also, because of their effect on the possibility of objectivity. If respondents fear that their confidences will be broken, that they will be grossly manipulated and deceived by social scientists, how can we expect to gain their trust and find out what is really going on in the segment of society with which we are concerned? In other words, how can we expect to collect objective evidence?

ANALYSIS, INTERPRETATION, AND PRESENTATION OF RESULTS

There are scientific norms which demand that the analysis and interpretation of data proceed in a dispassionate and reasoned fashion, allowing the data to speak for themselves. Constraints, however, do arise which impinge on the ability of researchers to conform to these norms. These constraints range from the biases of researchers, which may direct the analysis and interpretation of data in predictable directions, to outside forces such as one's relationship to the sponsor of the research. For example, a research sociologist employed by a large business corporation makes the following comment on his work:

> But these examples are trivial compared to the distortions and unanalyzed data caused by the pressure for results and restrictions on time. Because our relationship to the organization was both an emergent and continuing one, the results of any study directly affected the possibility of further studies by the involved researcher as well as by the rest of us. This led us to examine the data in order to uncover problems that

management had not been aware of. The more difficult it was to secure permission for a study or to include sensitive questions in a questionnaire, the more we felt we had to justify ourselves by providing results that had a payoff (Goldner, 1967:261).

This assessment reveals a submission to the demands of the sponsor of the research which ideally should be avoided. However, it also shows the difficulties in maintaining a completely dispassionate view.

The processes of determining the facts and assessing the weight of the evidence in order to reach conclusions are crucial to the prospect of attaining objectivity in our research. Regarding the determination of facts, Nagel (1961) discusses the role of value judgments. He makes a subtle distinction between judgments that characterize and those which appraise. Appraising judgments express approval or disapproval of what is under investigation and should be ruled out. Characterizing judgments involve an evaluation of the degree to which some state or condition exists in the phenomena under investigation and is important for analysis to proceed at all. For example, a sociologist who is studying power relationships in the family must make a technical judgment about what kind of behavior is dominant and shows power and what kind of behavior is submissive and shows a lack of power. This would be an appropriate characterizing value judgment. If the sociologist proceeded to argue that either dominant or submissive behavior is good or bad, an improper appraising value judgment would be made. This distinction seems to agree with and clarify Weber's position on the desired role of value judgments in analyzing and interpreting data.

Assessing the weight of the evidence in these steps of research is also important. The process of reaching conclusions from the data can be affected by the values of the researcher in either the natural or the social sciences. To combat this difficulty the researcher should state his or her values clearly. We should remember, however, that we are not always fully aware of our precise values with respect to a particular research topic. In this situation, the worth of any claim we make to objectivity will be measured by the critical evaluation of others in the social science community. This fact, however, should not deter us from striving for an openness in the interpretation of data, and including evidence that contradicts what we might like to find out.

The written presentation of research results should be as thorough as possible. The researcher should discuss his or her methods in enough detail so that other researchers can replicate the work if they so desire. If a complete report of the research is given, the researcher's claim to objectivity can be tested by other researchers with different value stances who may replicate the research and find the same or different conclusions. Another aspect of the complete presentation of research results is discussion of both the positive and negative findings. Sometimes, we are reluctant to discuss findings that do not confirm our hypotheses because we feel that they represent failure. What this attitude overlooks is that, in the long run, such findings may be even more significant from the standpoint of truly understanding social phenomena than the ones we are pleased with. Many of the great breakthroughs in knowledge developed from evidence that contradicted accepted explanations.

A final consideration in the written presentation of research is the statement of the researcher's personal values and biases with respect to the research topic. If, as many suggest, we should state this information, the place for it to appear is here. One rarely sees such a discussion in the professional journals of the social sciences or any other academic discipline encouraging objective scholarship. We hope this situation will eventually change. Earlier we suggested that the social researcher should keep a journal containing reflections on the effect of personal values on the research. A summation of such ideas should be reported in the written presentation of the research results.

APPLICATION OF RESEARCH RESULTS

The findings of social science research quite often have implications for action in public life. A survey on attitudes toward birth control in a particular country can reveal whether or not the implementation of a birth control program is likely to achieve a reduction in population. Studies on black-white relations in America can tell us how to accomplish integration with a minimum of racial conflict. Research on poverty can help us to ascertain the dynamics of poverty, and thus to take steps to reduce the extent of the problem. Michael Harrington's book, *The Other America*, had a profound effect on President Kennedy, who then initiated a war on poverty. Such examples point to the possible relevance of social science research for society.

After a research project is completed, the knowledge gained can sometimes be used in ameliorating social problems. However, as in the case of all new knowledge, it can be used for either constructive or destructive ends. We are all familiar with the example of nuclear energy, which can be used for bombs or as a source of constructive energy. On a somewhat less grandiose scale, the same can be said about social science knowledge. Conceivably, knowledge of black-white relations in America could be used by powerful racists to create backlash conditions that would wipe out what little progress has been made in improving race relations. There is no question that the advertising industry has used social science knowledge to manipulate consumer behavior. The subtle use of opinion poll information by our highest political leaders is often noted. An example concerns our involvement in Vietnam.

> Thus, if 80 percent think it is a "mistake" that we ever "went into" Vietnam, but 51 percent think that we would "lose prestige" if we "pulled

out now," then the "people" have been "consulted" and the war goes on with their "approval" (Roszak, 1969:16).

As mentioned previously, the time to worry about such possibilities is not at the end of the research process, but at the outset, during the stage of problem formulation. Regarding the potential destructive utilization of some research, two social scientists make this observation:

> This is a knotty issue, and one which perhaps can only be resolved by an act of faith. If you believe that in the long run truth makes men freer and more autonomous, then you are willing to run the risk that some people will use the facts you turn up and the interpretations you make to fight a rear guard action. If you don't believe this, if you believe instead that truth may or may not free men depending on the situation, even in the long run, then perhaps it is better to avoid these kinds of research subjects (Rainwater and Pittman, 1967:361).

The message seems clear. If we feel that the knowledge gained from our research will be put to destructive purposes in the long run, we shouldn't do the research in the first place. Many times, however, the situation is not so apparent and we feel drawn to the act of faith noted above.

In the more ambiguous cases, how can we guard against the destructive use of social science knowledge? Two courses of action appear. The first involves trying to form a standard for evaluating a proposed research project; the second relates to the role of the researcher after the research is completed.

In thinking about a standard for evaluating the potential destructiveness of research, we should recall a distinction made by Max Weber. Weber claimed that the ultimate validity or invalidity of value judgments or goals cannot be established by scientific data alone. However, the means for achieving particular goals can be determined by such investigation. Granted this point, perhaps social researchers can commit themselves to doing research aimed at discovering the best means for achieving humane as opposed to inhumane goals. Such research can be described in the following way:

> The research is based on the assumption that social change is desirable. It is designed to contribute to the understanding of ways to facilitate constructive change in the direction of meeting human needs and of expanding the participation of people all over the world in the political, economic, and social processes of their respective societies (Kelman, 1968:65).

It seems less likely that the findings from such research would be used for destructive purposes.

A second safeguard against the destructive use of social science knowledge is for the social researcher to press for the constructive use of research findings after the research is completed. This runs counter to the strict interpretation of Max Weber's plea for role segregation between the researcher as scientist and the researcher as private citizen. The possible social uses of new knowledge should be communicated and commented on by the researcher to the public at large and to those specific groups which are in a position to implement decisions relating to the knowledge. Value judgments are involved in such communication and comment. But, as Gouldner (1962:200) argues:

> If technical competence does provide a warrant for making value judgments then there is nothing to prohibit sociologists from making them within the area of their expertise. If, on the contrary, technical competence provides no warrant for making value judgments then, at least sociologists are as *free* to do so as anyone else; then their value judgments are at least as good as anyone else's, say a twelve-year-old child's. And, by the way, if technical competence provides no warrant for making value judgments, then what does?

CONCLUSION

The focus of this chapter has been on the ethical and political considerations related to objectivity which enter into each phase of the research process. The quest for objectivity is aimed at eliminating the effect of personal bias on observations and their interpretation.

We discussed three processes in the formulation of the research question: (1) choosing a topic, (2) choosing a theoretical model, and (3) obtaining funding. We suggest that personal biases do affect the first two processes, and that the social researcher should become sensitized to this possibility, perhaps by keeping a journal of reflections about the research process. The researcher can then refer to this journal in reporting the findings of the research. In seaching for funds, the researcher should be alert to possible attempts by sponsors to steer research in the direction of their own biases. A recommendation here is for the researcher to be aware of what is being agreed to when a contract with a research sponsor is made.

The ideal of obtaining objectivity in research can be aided by using the techniques of data collection impartially. We should be open to the possibility of collecting data that will prove our hypotheses and biases to be false. The careful training of data gatherers is important with respect to collecting unbiased data.

One should keep promises of confidentiality and minimize deception in research, especially deception that seems to mock the human dignity of informants. We noted that ethical behavior will help social science research to gain the trust of the public at large. If such a trust is lacking, the possibility of collecting objective evidence is diminished.

Again in the analysis and interpretation of data, the biases of the researcher can have a negative effect and nullify the goal of objectivity. A strategy for overcoming this problem is to state one's values in the written presentation of the research. In the long run, the social science community will be able to separate the value-free from the value-laden conclusions. The presentation of the research should also include a thorough description of how the research was done. This allows for replication, which may aid in uncovering nonobjective research.

Both in formulating the problem and after completing the research, the researcher should be concerned about who will use the knowledge he or she has developed and how it will be used — constructively or destructively. We suggested that at the outset of a research project the researcher should ask how well the project is geared toward finding the best means for achieving humane goals. Furthermore, after the research is completed, it is the duty of the researcher to press for the constructive use of the findings in the larger society.

Throughout this chapter, we referred to the position of Max Weber on the role of objectivity in social science research. The position taken in this chapter is similar to Weber's in setting up objectivity as an ideal in the collection, analysis, and interpretation of data. Also, we agreed that personal values do affect the choice of research topic and that social science data cannot prove the ultimate validity or invalidity of particular values. We disagreed, however, with the rigid role segregation suggested by Weber between the researcher as scientist and the researcher as private citizen. We feel strongly that there is an important role for the social scientist to play in pressing for the constructive use of social science findings in the larger society. In this sense, this chapter diverged from a strict interpretation of Weber's position. Indeed, empirical data show that most sociologists today have moved away from such a strict interpretation (Bart, 1970). This looser interpretation does not, however, deny that a premium should be placed on the goal of making scientific observation minimally colored by personal biases. The second major recommendation in this chapter is for researchers to be socially responsible for the research they decide to do, how they do it, and what is done with the new knowledge after the completion of their research.

EXERCISES

1. You wish to interview the residents of a low-income, inner-city area on their attitudes toward governmental social welfare programs. What kind of interviewers would you hire? What advice would you give them regarding the desired goal of eliminating personal bias?

2. Think of research situations where the personal biases of researchers may be problematic. What can be done to increase the likelihood of objectivity in these cases?

3. Think of a research situation where deception may have to be used. Why is this the case? What kind of deception would you use? How would you defend your use of deception on ethical grounds?

4. In what ways could the learning experiment described in this chapter be improved upon from the standpoint of treating human subjects in a humane way?

5. You are approached by a large industrial firm to conduct research on how to increase worker productivity in its factories. What ethical considerations occur to you and how would you deal with them?

6. Think of two research projects whose findings are likely to be used in a constructive manner. Why? Think of two research projects whose findings are likely to be used in a destructive manner. Why?

7. The authors propose that as a general rule the social researcher has an obligation not to harm those studied. Can you think of exceptions to this rule? As an example, you might want to consider the sociologist who has done a study of illegal campaign contributions by officials of large corporations.

8. Do you feel that it is acceptable for a social researcher to seek out funds from the Defense Department for (a) research with clear defense-related applications or (b) research with no direct defense relevance? Is there any ethical problem involved when social researchers lend legitimacy to the Defense Department as a sponsor of social research by accepting research funds from this source?

SUGGESTED READINGS

Becker, Howard S.
1967   "Whose side are we on?" *Social Problems* 14 (winter):239–247.

A concise argument for social scientists to take sides in their research while still seeking to collect valid and reliable data.

Denzin, Norman K.
1970   *The Research Act.* Chicago: Aldine.

A symbolic interactionist perspective on doing research is presented. There is a very thorough treatment of the ethical and political problems in doing social research. Denzin argues for the use of deception as a research strategy in certain situations.

Erikson, Kai T.
1967   "A comment on disguised observation in sociology." *Social Problems* 14 (spring):366–373.

A good statement of the problems in the use of deception in social research.

Gouldner, Alvin W.
1962 "Anti-minotaur: the myth of a value-free sociology." *Social Problems* 9 (winter):199–213.

An excellent statement of some of the problems in maintaining a strict interpretation of the Weberian plea for a value-free social science.

Kelman, Herbert C.
1968 *A Time to Speak: On Human Values and Social Research.* San Francisco: Jossey-Bass.

Kelman discusses the ethical and political considerations at the major research junctures. He is especially good on the ethical implications of foreign research.

Nagel, Ernest
1961 *The Structure of Science.* New York: Harcourt, Brace & World.

One of the best books in the philosophy of science which deals with the difficulties in attaining objectivity in both the social and physical sciences.

Sjoberg, Gideon, ed.
1967 *Ethics, Politics, and Social Research.* Cambridge, Mass.: Schenkman.

An excellent collection of essays by social scientists about the ethical and political considerations that have entered into their own research.

Weber, Max
1968 *The Methodology of the Social Sciences.* Edited and translated by Edward A. Shils and Henry A. Finch. New York: Free Press, 1949.

The classic statement of the traditional position concerning the role of values in social science research.

REFERENCES

Bart, Pauline
1970 "The role of the sociologist on public issues; an exercise in the sociology of knowledge." *American Sociologist* 5 (November):339–344.

Becker, Howard S.
1967 "Whose side are we on?" *Social Problems* 14 (winter):239–247.

Denzin, Norman K.
1970 *The Research Act.* Chicago: Aldine.

Erikson, Kai T.
1967   "A comment on disguised observation in sociology." *Social Problems* 14 (spring):366–373.

Friedrichs, Robert W.
1968   "Choice and commitment in social research." *American Sociologist* 3 (February):8–11.

Goldner, Fred H.
1967   "Role emergence and the ethics of ambiguity," in *Ethics, Politics, and Social Research,* ed. Gideon Sjoberg. Cambridge, Mass.: Schenkman.

Gouldner, Alvin W.
1962   "Anti-minotaur: the myth of a value-free sociology." *Social Problems* 9 (winter):199–213.

Horowitz, Irving L., ed.
1967   *The Rise and Fall of Project Camelot.* Cambridge, Mass.: The MIT Press.

Kelman, Herbert C.
1968   *A Time to Speak: On Human Values and Social Research.* San Francisco: Jossey-Bass.

Milgram, Stanley
1973   *Obedience to Authority.* New York: Harper & Row.

Nagel, Ernest
1961   *The Structure of Science.* New York: Harcourt, Brace & World.

Rainwater, Lee, and David J. Pittman
1967   "Ethical problems in studying a politically sensitive and deviant community." *Social Problems* 14 (spring):357–366.

Roszak, Theodore
1969   *The Making of a Counter Culture.* Garden City: Doubleday.

Van den Berghe, Pierre L.
1967   "Research in South Africa: the story of my experiences with tyranny," in *Ethics, Politics, and Social Research,* ed. Gideon Sjoberg. Cambridge, Mass.: Schenkman.

Vidich, Arthur J., and Joseph Bensman
1958   *Small Town in Mass Society.* Princeton: Princeton University Press.

Weber, Max
1958   From *Max Weber: Essays in Sociology,* ed. and trans. Hans H. Gerth and C. Wright Mills. New York: Oxford University Press.
1968   *The Methodology of the Social Sciences,* ed. and trans. Edward A. Shils and Henry A. Finch. New York: Free Press, 1949.

Sampling

CHAPTER FIVE

Most people are much more expert at sampling methodology than they probably realize. We all engage in various forms of sampling in our everyday lives. When we take a sip of milk from that carton that has been in the refrigerator for the last two weeks to determine whether it is sour, or when we select a few plums at the market for close scrutiny prior to a two-pound purchase, we are carrying out a sampling procedure. When we pick up a book of poems in a bookstore and leaf through it, reading one poem at the beginning, another in the middle, and a third at the end, we are again sampling. In everyday life we adapt our sampling procedure to the situation. We find that for some purposes a sample of one (e.g., the one sip of milk) is more than adequate as evidence for the generalization we are interested in making; for other purposes a more sophisticated sampling procedure is called for, as in the case of the three-poem sample.

In social research as in everyday life, when we sample we gather information about a few cases and seek to make judgments about a much larger number of cases. Sometimes our objective is to sample in such a way as to get an *unbiased* or representative sample, as in our three-poem example; but at other times our objective is to draw a biased sample in an effort to find the best. This procedure can be seen in mate selection for marriage. Young men and women usually go through a phase of their lives where they date many people with the intention of finding the best possible husband or wife. Obviously, we cannot date all possible candidates for the position of marriage partner. Some people would like to try, but the exigencies of time and money rule out this alternative. In other words, in this crucial part of our lives we are forced to sample from among the possibilities. Our final selection is hopefully one of the best of the contenders (most of whom we never meet). The sampling process is in evidence to some extent when we choose a school to attend, look for a job, or pick a place to live. To the extent that we are free to choose in these areas of our lives, we want the best as defined by our personal likes and dislikes. The emphasis in these situations is not upon finding the average or typical mate, school, job, or home; but rather, the best. We want a sample which will be disproportionately weighted in favor of our biased objective of finding the best.

Social scientists use sampling in their research because typically they do not have the time and money to study all the cases in the population of interest to them. The usual aim of the social researcher's sampling is not to find the best case, but rather to find a *representative distribution* of cases which will allow for generalizations about the average or typical. In other words, social researchers often want an unbiased sample so that on the basis of the cases considered they can *generalize accurately* from the sample cases to all the cases in the population.

A well-designed sampling plan contributes to both the *reliability* and the *validity* of our research findings. If we do our sampling carefully and in accordance with one of the standard sampling plans, it should be possible for another researcher to replicate our findings; this is an important aspect of reliability. Careful sampling ensures we have drawn our cases so that our sample accurately reflects the composition of the population of cases to which we wish to generalize; this contributes to the validity of the generalizations we make on the basis of our sample.

It is as important to the consumers of social research as to the producers of the research to know the logic behind sampling, the alternative sampling methods available, and the relative precision that can be expected from each of these alternatives. A major objective of the present chapter is to present a nontechnical introduction to each of these issues. It is a common misconception that sampling is relevant only to quantitative social research. While it is true that sampling procedures for use in quantitative research are more highly developed, it is also true that sampling can play a very important role in qualitative research. We will first consider sampling as it is typically treated in the context of quantitative research, and then turn to a discussion of the use of sampling in qualitative research. We must begin by clarifying some basic terms employed in any discussion of sampling.

BASIC TERMS

As we know, a *sample* is made up of some but not all instances or cases of some general category of people, things, or events. It is the group of cases selected from all the possible cases of interest in a particular research project. The term used to describe all the possible cases of interest is the *population*.[1] The population for a particular study might be all adult women in the United States, all Jews living in Cairo, or all students at Easy College. The population of interest varies, depending on the purpose of the research. A particular subgroup within the population is referred to as a *stratum*. All the male students at Easy College would make up one stratum, and all the female students would make up another stratum. Different strata within a particular population are usually formed on the basis of such characteristics as age, race, and sex. The characteristics of relevance for determining strata depend, of course, on the purpose of the study.

Any individual case in the population is called an *element* of the population. For example, in the study of Easy College, Fred Fraternity and Suzie Sorority are two different elements of the population. Usually the elements are individual people but they can also be poems, newspaper articles, families, plums, or even nations. Another key concept is that of *sampling frame*. Once a population has been defined for a particular study, it is necessary to list all the population elements so that a sample can be drawn from the population. The sampling frame is such a list. For example, the sampling frame at Easy College would probably be all the students registered at the school during the semester when the study was being conducted.

SAMPLING PLANS

There are two basic kinds of samples: *probability* and *nonprobability*. In a probability sample, every element of the population has a known, though not necessarily equal, chance of being selected for the sample. Furthermore, every element has at least some chance (a nonzero chance) of being included in the sample. Neither of these conditions generally holds for nonprobability samples. Probability sampling plans allow us to estimate how closely our sample results approximate what we would have found out had we instead considered the total population. The reason for this is that there are certain statistical regularities associated with probability sampling which are related to our knowing the chance which each element has of being included in a given sample. In contrast, such estimates of precision generally cannot be made with nonprobability samples because we do not know the chances which each element has of being selected for a particular sample. Nonprobability sampling is actually quite similar to the kind of sampling that we do in our daily lives. One type of nonprobability sampling (accidental) could be referred to as unscientific. Accordingly, it makes sense to describe it in detail first.

[1] The term "universe" is also used to refer to the population.

Nonprobability Sampling

Nonprobability sampling is particularly well suited for exploratory research where the focus is on the generation of theory and research ideas. It also proves useful in observational research and qualitative research more generally. In this section we will consider the three most important types of nonprobability sampling: accidental, quota, and purposive. In a later section we will discuss the analytic sampling used in qualitative research, which turns out to be a variation of purposive sampling.

Accidental sampling comes closest to what we are all familiar with as the "man in the street interview." We've heard this on the radio and seen it on television. An important event has occurred in the news, such as the landing of men on the moon. The media coverage of the event switches to various reporters who stand on busy streetcorners and interview people as they pass by. The same kind of sampling is sometimes (but not frequently) done in social research. For example, a survey of student attitudes at Easy College might be carried out by having interviewers stand at the main entrance door to the student union and ask students who enter and leave how they feel about a number of issues. The assumption behind such a strategy is that by simply interviewing whomever happens to stroll by we should get a reasonably representative cross-section of the population of interest. The obvious problem is that there is no assurance this is going to be the case. Indeed, it may well be that the people who congregate in Times Square do not represent a cross-section of the American people. And the group of students who frequent the student union may be overrepresentative of nonacademically oriented students. Academically oriented students have a tendency to cluster near the building on campus called the library. In any event, there is no reliable basis for checking how representative a sample is when it is an accidental sample. In view of this we must be particularly cautious about generalizing from the data acquired through accidental sampling.

A *quota* sample is one in which interviewers are told to screen potential respondents in terms of desired characteristics. A quota is sometimes established in accordance with the percentage of the population which the stratum makes up, and sometimes established in accordance with the theoretical focus of the study. For a survey on attitudes towards the women's movement, the quota sampling plan might call for 50 percent of the interviews with women and 50 percent with men, or the plan might call for 50 percent of the interviews with white women and 50 percent with black women; the first example illustrates quotas based on the proportion of the population that the stratum represents; and the second example illustrates quotas based on a study's theoretical focus — assuming that there were theoretical reasons for expecting the attitudes of black women to differ from those of white women. The main advantage of quota sampling over accidental sampling is the assurance that certain strata of the population will be included in the sample. The fact remains, however, that the sampling done from the different strata in quota sampling is essentially accidental sampling. The "man in the street interview" is still being conducted, but interviewers are told to make sure to stop certain kinds of people. This means that interviewers are afforded a large degree of latitude in the quota sampling procedure which can lead to biased sampling.

The tendency for interviewers to search for respondents in congested areas has already been mentioned. Another bias is that if interviewers are sent out into a neighborhood to interview householders, they are likely to skip houses that aren't as physically appealing (poorer families?) or houses that have a "Beware of Dog" sign in the yard (insecure or sadistic people?). Possibilities such as these reduce the precision of estimates based on quota samples.[2]

Purposive sampling refers to a judgmental form of sampling in which the researcher purposely selects certain groups or individuals for their relevance to the issue being studied. This sampling method is often used in studies of deviance or other social phenomena which are too rare to be dealt with effectively using a representative cross-section of the population. If, for example, we were interested in assessing whether or not there is an impact of pornography on sex crimes, one thing we might decide to study is the pornography consumption habits of those who are or have been in prison for sex crimes. If we were interested in monopolistic practices among large corporations, we might select a specific industry such as the computer industry and attempt to get interviews with top management at several of the major firms. While management at IBM might have very little to say about their own practices, the management of their competitors might have a good deal to say about actions taken by IBM. In such situations the researcher must often make do with whomever will grant an interview. Elaborate sampling procedures are out of the question. A major advantage of purposive sampling is that it is a way to assure that we get at least some information from respondents who are hard to locate and crucial to the study. A major drawback with such samples is that there is little or no control over who is selected within the category. There is no assurance that those selected are in any way representative of some clearly specified population of more general interest.

Probability Sampling

A probability sample is one in which every element of the population has a known, nonzero chance of being selected for the sample.

---

[2] Sometimes quota sampling is combined with probability sampling in such a way as to produce a sample that is a reasonably good approximation to a probability sample. We will have more to say about this in our discussion of probability sampling.

The probability of selection does not have to be equal for each element of the population. Because we know the chance each element has of being included in the sample, we are in a position to estimate how accurately results for the sample estimate the characteristics of the total population. We will consider the four most basic probability sampling plans: simple random sampling, systematic sampling, stratified random sampling, and cluster sampling.

Simple random sampling is the simplest of the probability sampling plans, and the others involve some form of it. A simple random sample is one in which each element of the population has an *equal* chance of being included in the sample. Let us assume, for example, that the library at Easy College has one hundred books on the subject of marine biology. Fred Fraternity has to write a term paper on marine biology and he decides that he needs five sources for the bibliography of the paper. It is late in the semester and Fred does not have time to do a purposive sample of the best books in the library on the subject of marine biology. As a compromise, Fred decides to write down the names of all the books on marine biology on individual slips of paper. He then places the slips of paper in a box and shakes up the box in a thorough manner. After the slips of paper are well mixed, Fred proceeds to pick out five slips of paper from the box and copies the book titles for his bibliography. The bibliography represents a simple random sample of all the library books on marine biology because each book has been given an equal chance of being included in Fred's sample.

The requirement that every element of the population have an equal chance of being selected for a simple random sample has an important implication: a complete listing of all population elements must be available. In other words, an adequate *sampling frame* must be located. (Notice that this requirement was not mentioned with respect to any of the nonprobability sampling plans.) Sometimes this requirement presents no major problem. In studies of college students, for example, a list of registered students often serves the purpose. In other research situations, however, a good sampling frame may be difficult to find.

When complete listings of a given population are not available, some researchers may be tempted to use incomplete listings which are readily at hand. This must be done with caution because an incomplete sampling frame can lead to biased results. For example, some survey research is conducted by telephone and the telephone directory is used as the sampling frame. It should be noted that a substantial number of homes either have no telephone or have an unlisted number. In some areas, fewer than eighty percent of the households have listed telephone numbers. Unlisted telephones are located in upper income households (which can afford them and which try to avoid being besieged with solicitations or checked out by would-be robbers) and in low-income households (which use the device to escape the pressure of creditors). Also, all the families that have moved into new homes in the past year are unlikely to be listed; in our mobile society, that can be a good-sized percentage of the population of a town. Households without telephones are predominantly low-income. The findings of a study that employs the telephone directory as its sampling frame are going to be biased because the sample underrepresents the very high-income, the very low-income, and the newly relocated households.

For a simple random sample the choice of elements from the sampling frame must proceed in a manner that gives every element an equal chance of being chosen. The method used by Fred in his term paper quandary can be described as the "picking a name from the hat" approach. This is a feasible method when small samples are being selected. The process becomes awkward, however, when larger samples are chosen.

Let us assume that Easy College has four thousand students and that we want to select a simple random sample of four hundred students. The list of currently registered students has been obtained and will be used as our sampling frame. A table of random numbers is commonly used for the process of selecting elements from a sample of this size.[3] Tables of random numbers are composed of random numbers that range from one to as high a number as the total size of any sampling frame is likely to be. Such tables are in the appendices of most statistics textbooks. In order to use a table of random numbers for the purpose of selecting elements, one has to first number all the elements in the sampling frame. In our case, each of the four thousand students would be assigned a number from one to four thousand. If the first number picked from the table of random numbers is 379, the student who has been assigned the same number in the sampling frame would be selected for inclusion in our simple random sample. We would continue picking random numbers until we had selected four hundred students for the sample.[4]

We need to introduce two new terms at this point. A *parameter* is a characteristic of the total population. The percentage of all four thousand students at Easy College who feel that students should have a

---

[3] Suppose we were to put the number 1 on 100 gum balls, the number 2 on 100 gum balls, and so on up to the number 1000 which we would also put on 100 gum balls. Then suppose we were to very thoroughly mix all these balls and put them into a large fish bowl. If we now select a very small fraction of these balls one at a time recording the numbers as the balls are selected (e.g., 243, 71, 528, etc.), the resulting list of numbers could be used to construct a table of random numbers. This table would allow us to select numbers between 1 and 1000 at random; with appropriate modifications in the procedures used we could construct a table that would allow us to select numbers between one and a million or one and a billion at random. It is possible that some of the numbers in the specified range will be selected several times and that others will never be selected. In actual practice computers are used to construct such tables.

[4] In practice we might first select the 400 random numbers between 1 and 4000, put them in ascending order, and then count down an alphabetical list of the 4000 students selecting student numbers 7, 29, 36, 53, and so on until the 400 students had been selected.

responsibility in the hiring and firing of faculty members is a population parameter. A *statistic* is a characteristic of a sample. The corresponding percentage of students in our sample of four hundred who hold this opinion is a sample statistic. The issue of precision may now be rephrased. How accurately do sample statistics reflect population parameters?

Probability theory tells us that for a simple random sample such statistics as the sample mean fluctuate around population parameters in a known manner.[5] If many samples are drawn from the same population, the resulting sample estimates cluster around the population parameter. The measure of this variation is called the *standard error*. In general, the larger the sample size, the smaller the standard error of our estimate. That is, the larger our sample, the closer our sample estimate is likely to be to the true population value. If for one of the samples in the preceding example we found that eighty percent of the students agreed with the proposition that students should be given responsibility in the hiring and firing of faculty, we could then estimate (using a formula which is beyond the scope of the present discussion) the standard error to be two percent. The true population parameter (that is the result we would get were we to do a complete count of the attitudes of all the students) will generally be within two standard errors of our sample estimate.[6]

A *systematic sample* is very similar to a simple random sample. Like a simple random sample, a systematic sample initially requires an adequate sampling frame. A random starting point is selected on this list and every *n*th name or unit is selected from that point on.

If we decided to select a systematic sample of four hundred students from the list of currently registered students at Easy College, we would first obtain a *selection interval* by dividing the population size (four thousand) by the desired sample size (four hundred). In this case, the selection interval is ten which means that every tenth student would be selected from the sampling frame for the systematic sample. In order to ensure the possibility that each student has an equal chance of being selected for the sample, the starting point for the selection process must be randomly chosen. In other words, the first student would be selected from somewhere in the first interval of ten on the list and the "somewhere" is determined randomly. Let us assume that the numbers one through ten are thrown into a hat and the number five is selected. The initial student selected for our systematic sample would be the fifth student on the list of currently registered students at Easy College. The selection interval would then be applied by adding ten to five so that the fifteenth student on the list would be selected next. This process would continue until we had chosen four hundred students for the sample.

[5] For a more complete discussion of this issue consult any introductory statistics textbook.

[6] You will note that we have selected a range of plus or minus two standard errors. For an explanation of why we have done this and a discussion of the formula used to compute the standard error, see an introductory statistics book.

The principal advantage of systematic sampling over simple random sampling is the relative ease in executing the selection process. Only one act of randomization is required (selecting a random starting point) with systematic sampling, whereas simple random sampling requires the random selection of *every* element to be included in the sample. We do not have to constantly refer back and forth between the sampling frame and a table of random numbers when systematic sampling is employed. One disadvantage of systematic sampling is that it may be subject to bias if the sampling frame which is used has a regular, recurring pattern or cycle. Consider a research situation where the sampling frame is a list of street addresses for housing units (the population elements are housing units rather than individual people). Imagine that the selection interval is ten and that the randomly chosen starting point for the selection of elements is also ten. If city blocks containing ten housing units apiece are being studied, this might mean that one of the corner housing units on every block would be selected for the systematic sample. It is possible that corner housing units tend to be inhabited by people with higher incomes because corner housing units have larger lots or better views and consequently command higher rentals. The same problem could occur if we did a systematic sample of newspapers with a selection interval of seven. This could result in a sample which contained only Sunday newspapers. It should be clear from the above examples that if systematic sampling is used, the sampling frame should be checked beforehand for the possibility of such cyclical bias.

Stratified random sampling is another form of probability sampling. It involves dividing the population into two or more strata and then taking either a simple random sample or a systematic sample from each stratum. (Notice that quota sampling is very similar to this. The difference is that accidental samples are taken from different strata in quota sampling.)

The hypothetical behavior of Suzie Sorority offers an illustration of stratified random sampling. She has just met Fred Fraternity outside the library and he has related to her how he has handled the problem of researching the literature for his paper on marine biology. We recall that Fred in his inventive way has done a simple random sample of five books from the one hundred which are in the library. Suzie is in the same class and is faced with a similar time pressure; but she knows intuitively that there is something shaky about Fred's procedure. She decides that obviously some of the books on marine biology are more important than others. Suzie has a suspicion that the hardbound books are more scholarly than the paperbacks and, therefore, she wants to make sure that at least some are included in her bibliography. There are sixty hardbound books and forty paperback books on marine biology in the library. Suzie writes down the names of all sixty hardbound books on individual slips of paper and places them in one box. She does the same for all forty paperback books, and she places these slips of paper in a different box.

She shakes up both boxes thoroughly and then proceeds to pick out three slips of paper from the first box and two slips of paper from the second box. Suzie copies the selected book titles for her bibliography, which represents a stratified random sample of all the library books on marine biology.

It is not just the Suzies of the world who use stratified random sampling. Social scientists often use it in their research. It is necessary, of course, to have an adequate sampling frame in order to implement a stratified random sample. The sampling frame must be divided into separate lists for each stratum. The next step is to take a simple random or systematic sample from each of the lists. As with quota sampling, the strata are selected on the basis of variables relevant in the context of a particular research project.

A very important reason for selecting a stratified random sample is that if it is chosen correctly, it should yield more precise results than a simple random sample. The trick is to form strata which are internally homogeneous yet different from one another with respect to what one is studying. For example, in a survey on attitudes toward U.S. foreign policy in the Middle East, it would be appropriate to consider stratified sampling by religion or ethnicity so as to assure that there would be a specified proportion of Jews in the sample. If strata are formed which are internally homogeneous yet different from one another, the amount of sampling error is less than with a simple random sample of the same size. In brief, the sampling error (as estimated using the standard error) is smaller for a stratified random sample than for a simple random sample. This means that the precision of a stratified random sample is greater than that of a simple random sample.

The general procedure in stratified random sampling is to sample from each stratum according to its percentage in the total population. If a particular stratum makes up twenty percent of a given population and the designated sampling size is five hundred, one hundred elements from that stratum should be selected. This is called *proportionate sampling*. There are research situations, however, where it becomes apparent that a proportionate sample will result in very small numbers of elements for particular strata. In cases such as these, it is more appropriate to select a *disproportionate sample* in which the strata are not sampled according to their percentages in the population. The goal in disproportionate sampling is to select enough elements from each stratum so that a fairly detailed statistical analysis of each stratum can be carried out.

In a study of the student body at Easy College, for example, the population might be stratified by subject major. Some majors have very few students (e.g., physics) and for some purposes it would make sense to sample from them in larger numbers than their proportion of the entire student body warrants. When a disproportionate sample is selected, all of the elements of the population no longer have an equal chance of being included in the sample. Remember, however, that the crucial aspect to probability sampling is that we have to know what the chance is of each element being selected. We might decide to give physics majors at Easy College twice the chance they would have of being selected for a simple random sample. When our goal is to estimate a population characteristic (e.g., mean income) based on a disproportionate sample, the results for each stratum must be weighted according to the percentage which the stratum represents of the total population. Since physics majors have been given twice the chance of being included as students from other majors, their responses must be weighted by a *correction factor* of one half when information about the total student body is calculated. If physics majors had been given four times the normal chance of being included in the sample, the correction factor would have been one-fourth.

One potential difficulty with all the probability sampling plans discussed so far is the requirement of ascertaining an adequate sampling frame. In some cases, an actual list of the elements of the population is not readily available. It is not too difficult to find a sampling frame for the student population of Easy College. The list of currently registered students serves the purpose well. It would be difficult, however, to find a good sampling frame for all students who are currently enrolled in all of the colleges and universities throughout the United States.

Cluster sampling can sometimes be used in situations where it would be difficult or impossible to obtain a complete list of all the elements in the population. Cluster sampling involves an initial sampling stage wherein sampling is done from groups of elements which are called clusters. A simple, systematic, or stratified random sample of clusters from a total list of clusters is selected. Once a sample of clusters has been selected, a simple, systematic, or stratified random sample of individual elements is selected from the chosen clusters. In the case at hand, one might first sample from a list of colleges (clusters of students) in the United States which could be derived from a publication such as the *Comparative Guide to American Colleges*. A stratified sample by size of institution might be very appropriate. The final stage of sampling would entail the selection of a simple, systematic, or stratified random sample of individual students from the chosen colleges. For example, we might decide to carry out a stratified random sample of students at each college according to their subject major.

A key advantage of cluster sampling is that a complete listing of all the elements in the population is not necessary. Only a listing of the relevant clusters is required. One disadvantage of cluster sampling is that the precision of estimates based on such samples is less than that for other probability samples of the same size. One way to deal with this problem is to select a larger sample size. In cluster sampling interviewers are sent to a few randomly chosen areas and they interview a substantial number of people in each. In contrast, a simple random sample might result in a situation where interviewers are dispatched to many more locations and they might interview only one person in each. The obvious advantage of cluster sampling is a saving of time and money.

Let us look at another example of cluster sampling which involves more stages of sampling from clusters than the example just cited and also illustrates the advantage of cluster sampling regarding the saving of time and money when interviewers are used. Imagine that we are interested in conducting a survey of the entire adult population in the United States. A list of the entire adult population would be impossible to obtain. Therefore, we decide to use multistage cluster sampling on an area basis.

In our first stage of sampling, we might define counties as our initial sampling clusters. A list of every county in the nation is not difficult to obtain. Suppose we begin by selecting a simple random sample of seventy-five counties. This is the first stage of our cluster sampling procedure and it yields county-sized clusters. (Incidentally, when selecting the seventy-five counties, we should take account of the varying population sizes through a weighting process which makes the probability of selection for any given county proportionate to the relative population size of that county compared with the other counties.[7])

The second stage of sampling would be designed to produce even more manageable cluster sizes. We would select three census tracts (for which listings are readily available) from each of the seventy-five selected counties by using the same probability sampling procedure described above. Even census tracts are quite large and are not easy to work with for the purpose of assigning neighborhoods to interviewers. Therefore, we could proceed to a third stage where we would select city blocks or census enumeration districts. This would depend on the relative urbanization of each area. (In rural areas, it is sometimes necessary to designate physical boundaries such as streams because there is an absence of regular artificial boundaries such as city blocks.) If we select three blocks (or block equivalents) from each census tract by using probability sampling methods, we would have a total of 675 blocks in our sample. We would then proceed to take a probability sample of dwelling units from each block equivalent. If we select two dwelling units from each block and interview one adult in each unit, our total sample size will be 1350. It should be apparent from this example that the cost of interviewing would be considerably less for a national cluster sample than it would be for any other probability sampling plan at the national level (if, indeed, other probability sampling plans could be carried out at the national level). In any event, when a cluster sampling procedure is used, a relatively small number of interviewers is needed to cover the entire sample.

To this point we have discussed probability and nonprobability sampling as if the choice were to use one or the other. In actual practice

---

[7] To actually do this would get us into more sophisticated sampling designs than would be appropriate to consider here.

the two are often combined. When we combine probability and non-probability stages in our sampling design, the final sample is always a nonprobability sample. Despite this it is very common for such well-known public opinion organizations as Harris and Gallup to do so. The sampling design for a national sample typically combines probability cluster sampling at the initial stages (e.g., county, census tract) with quota sampling at the final stage. When probability sampling is combined with quota sampling in such a way that the interviewer has relatively little freedom of choice with respect to where to obtain respondents, the resulting sample can be a very close approximation to a probability sample. The success of such organizations as Gallup and Harris in forecasting national elections is evidence of the accuracy that is possible with a sampling design which combines probability and nonprobability procedures.

PROBLEMS AND ISSUES IN SAMPLING

There are still some key problems and issues relating to sampling which need attention. The following section of the chapter focuses on three areas: (1) selection of sample size, (2) nonsampling error, and (3) sampling in qualitative research.

Sample Size

One of the most frequent questions put to the sampling expert is, "How large must my sample be?" The question is of crucial importance because it has a major impact on the amount of time and money that must go into the data collection phase of the research. Under very special circumstances it is possible to give an explicit answer to this question. But far more common are situations in which the researcher does not have all the information that must be available for there to be a precise estimate of the necessary sample size.

We can precisely specify the sample size that a study calls for if the investigator: (1) can specify a specific population parameter that is the primary focus of the study (e.g., the answer to a question asking how the respondent intends to vote in November); (2) can make a reasonable estimate of the split on the question (e.g., 50/50 or 90/10 on a question with two choices); and (3) can tell us how precise an estimate is desired (e.g., will an error of 1 percent, 2 percent, or 5 percent be tolerable). If these conditions have been met and simple random sampling has been used, then using Table 5.1 we can specify the sample size that will be needed. You will note that a larger sample is needed for 99 percent confidence limits than for 95 percent confidence limits. (If we use the 95 percent confidence limits, then we can be sure that 95 out of 100 samples of the specified size will be within the specified percent error of the population parameter.) These estimates are given for a question with a 50/50 split, but can be used with other splits because the error is greatest for the 50/50 split; that is, the sample sizes specified are conservatively large for items with more extreme splits.

In most studies the investigator is interested in not one but many questions. If each of these questions has a different split among the response categories, then a case can be made for a different sample size for each question. The way this problem is usually handled is to select a sample size appropriate for a 50/50 split; this provides a conservative estimate of the sample size needed for all others. It is also quite possible that different levels of error are acceptable from one question to the next. If the question is how the respondent intends to vote, we would not want to accept more than 2 percent error if the expected split were 52/48. On the other hand, if the split were 90/10 we could predict the election outcome with a much smaller sample and we would be willing to tolerate a much greater error in our estimate. One way to deal with this problem is to select the question that is of greatest importance and use the sample size that corresponds to the acceptable level of error for this question. Another alternative is to select the question for which the acceptable level of error is lowest and choose the sample size that corresponds to this question. However, for most studies neither of these alternatives is possible because the investigator does not have a clear idea of what level of error is acceptable. The acceptable level will in large measure depend on aspects of the statistical analysis which are difficult to anticipate prior to the data collection.

In general, the larger the sample, the less the sampling error, and the more precise will be estimates based on the sample. As can be seen

TABLE 5.1 Simple Random Sample Size for Several Degrees of Precision*

Tolerated Error	Confidence Limits	
	95 Samples in 100	99 Samples in 100
1%	9,604	16,587
2%	2,401	4,147
3%	1,067	1,843
4%	600	1,037
5%	384	663
6%	267	461
7%	196	339

* Source: Charles H. Backstrom and Gerald D. Hursh, Survey Research (Evanston: Northwestern University Press, 1963), p. 33.

in Table 5.1, the increase in precision with increased sample size does reach a point of diminishing returns. We need much more of an increase in sample size to reduce the level of error from 2 to 1 percent than from 7 to 6 percent. With a stratified random sample, lower sample sizes are needed for a specified level of precision. For such samples the estimates presented in Table 5.1 can be used because they are conservative. For cluster sampling a larger sample size is needed for a specified level of error than is the case for a simple random sample. Thus Table 5.1 would not be appropriate for use with a cluster sample. One estimate is that a national cluster sample of 1500 cases is roughly equivalent in terms of precision to a simple random sample of 1000 cases (Davis, 1973:72). Typically Harris and Gallup use cluster samples of between twelve and fifteen hundred respondents to reflect the opinions of the adult population of the United States. It turns out that approximately the same size sample would be needed to estimate the opinions of the adult population of one state (or even one large city) with the same degree of precision.[8]

As we mentioned at the outset, it is usually not possible to meet the conditions necessary for making a precise estimate of the needed sample size. In such situations the researcher is forced to fall back on the experience of others. If the topic of the research or the population being sampled is of great interest and if it has not been studied before, it is quite possible that even a study based on a small sample (and consequently of low precision) will be of general interest. On the other hand, if the topic is one that has been repeatedly studied using large national samples, then it is quite possible that there will be little interest in the proposed study unless it too is based on a large national sample.

Often the funds available set an upper limit on the possible sample size for a study. When this is the case, a judgment must be made as to whether the precision that is possible with a sample of this size is adequate to justify carrying out the study.

Nonsampling Error

There are many sources of error in the research process. We have already discussed the error due to sampling fluctuation which represents the difference between a sample statistic and the corresponding population parameter in the absence of any nonsampling error. We should recall that this *sampling error* is typically estimated by the standard error. However, in most research there are also a variety of sources of *nonsampling error* (this term is used to refer to all sources of error other than sampling error) that tend to reduce the accuracy of estimates based on

---

[8] For smaller populations (e.g., 10,000 and under) it is appropriate to take into consideration the size of the population when deciding on a sample size. For a table of use in doing this, see Slonim (1960:78).

sample results. The term *bias* is also used to refer to the distortion caused by the various sources of nonsampling error.

One source of bias is the failure to choose an adequate sampling frame. A classic illustration of this error was the 1936 presidential poll conducted by *Literary Digest* to see whether Landon or Roosevelt would win. Telephone directories and lists of automobile owners were used as the sampling frame. Questionnaires were sent to ten million adults in the United States who owned a phone or an automobile; more than two million responded. The prediction made on the basis of the poll was that Landon would win by a landslide. Unfortunately, the *Literary Digest* sample was severely biased. Only forty percent of the homes in the United States had telephones at the time. Only a slim majority of families owned a car. This meant that the sample was biased in the direction of higher socioeconomic groupings, which traditionally vote Republican. More sophisticated researchers were well aware of the flaws in the *Literary Digest* poll considerably before history proved it to be wrong. (Gallup, 1948:73–75).

Another potential source of bias which may lead to inaccurate sample findings is nonresponse. In sample surveys of many types (door-to-door, mail, or telephone), there may be a difference between those persons who respond and those who do not. The potential differences are greatest in mail surveys (such as the Literary Digest poll) where the opportunity to refuse cooperation with the survey is almost completely unrestricted. Nonresponse, however, is a problem with all methodologies. When door-to-door interviewing is used, people who are very active are less likely to be at home than nonactive people. Consequently, a good survey will allow for several call-backs of the not-at-homes. The call-backs will be more successful if they are staggered over various times of day and different days of the week. One technique that has been proposed for dealing with the nonresponse problem is to ask those people who *are* at home during the initial call how many nights of the previous week they had been at home. Those who were not usually at home but happened to be there when the interviewer called are weighted more heavily in the data analysis stage of research than the people who were always at home (Politz and Simmons, 1949).

A special biasing factor occurs in panel studies wherein the same respondents are interviewed repeatedly over time on the same subject or different subjects. The original composition of the panel may be representative of the population of interest, but over a period of time, people leave the panel (because of moving, death, or lack of interest). Unless some provision is made to assess the change in makeup of the panel and to compensate for this change, the results will be biased. Another potential problem is that some panel members may become "expert respondents" during the course of their association with the panel. They may thoroughly research the various topics covered in the questionnaires (which are frequently self-administered) and then try to give the "right" answers. The general point is that membership on a panel may encourage some panel members to become less than representative of their counterparts in the population of interest. In order to circumvent this possibility, panel studies are sometimes supplemented by concurrent studies of "fresh" respondents to determine whether there is serious bias caused by membership on a panel.

There are a variety of sources of bias which may be introduced during the interviewing phase of a study. One is the tendency for some interviewers to cut corners on the sampling; this is particularly likely when the interviewer is being paid by the interview rather than by the hour. Another is the tendency for some interviewers to communicate (often nonverbally) the answer they want to hear. Closely related is the desire among many respondents to give the interviewer an answer that the interviewer wants to hear. A less dramatic example of the same phenomenon is the respondent who at least tempers his or her responses to make them more socially acceptable. There is also potential for error if the respondent does not hear the question correctly or the interviewer does not hear the response correctly. Sometimes the question is loaded (written in such a way that the alternative response categories are unlikely to be considered equally acceptable) or includes words that are not clear to the respondent; this is a potential problem when middle class researchers prepare questions to be administered to lower class respondents without adequate pretesting to make sure the questions can be understood.

After the interviewing has been completed, there are still many other possible sources of nonsampling error. The responses to open-ended questions must be coded and coding error is a possible problem. There is even room for error at the stage when the data is being key-punched and prepared for statistical analysis. It should be clear by now that there are numerous sources of bias which can undo the best laid plans of the most conscientious sampling expert. Unfortunately, while chance error due to sampling fluctuation can be estimated, there is no simple formula for estimating the magnitude of the various sources of nonsampling error and bias. The best the researcher can do is to be aware of these sources of error and attempt to keep them to a minimum.

Sampling in Qualitative Research

We have seen that a major reason for sampling in survey research studies is to ensure that the people from whom we gather our data are representative of the larger universe of people about whom we seek to generalize. One might suppose that sampling procedures are unnecessary in the case of qualitative research. Those doing field research typically observe only one case; one organization, one community, one area of the city, one asylum, or one set of events. Since participant observers rarely seek to acquire systematic information from a large number of persons, they do not ordinarily randomly select persons to interview, nor do they typically create quota samples. Nevertheless, sampling procedures are used in qualitative investigations. Participant observers must fashion sampling procedures to be certain that *observations* made in some setting are representative of what generally goes on in the setting. To see how and why field researchers might sample "times," "places," "roles," or "statuses," we will imagine a field researcher who begins an investigation of a large city hospital.

After a few weeks of preliminary observation the researcher recognizes that activities in the hospital vary at different *times* during the day. Perhaps more automobile accident cases show up in the emergency room in the early hours of the morning, or certain types of operations are scheduled at certain times. Perhaps the researcher begins to sense that there are times when doctors are not easily accessible and that this might alter the functioning of the organization. In short, as in virtually all contexts, there is an ebb and flow to activity. If a researcher wants to get a total picture of some setting, she must avoid doing all the observational work at the same time each day. Field researchers will often sample times for doing their observation so as to ensure that their image of the organization is not based solely on the kinds of activities occurring during a particular time interval. It would be possible for the researcher to break the 24-hour day into discrete time units and let the times of observation be dictated by a random sampling of these time units.

Activities and events also vary in different *places* within an organization. Imagine the biased picture of the hospital obtained if a field researcher restricted all observation to the emergency room. The activities of doctors, nurses, patients, and administrators observed in this particular area of the hospital are likely to be quite different from those in other areas. Our researcher correctly decides, therefore, that it is necessary to witness activities in different *places* within the hospital. One strategy might simply be to make a list of various strategic locations within the hospital (e.g., the emergency room, the nurses' station, the admitting office, the cafeteria, the waiting rooms, and the like) and to systematically do observations in each. It might be reasonable in some studies to combine time sampling and place sampling. Researchers must, of course, use good judgment with regard to place sampling. They might discover after a short period of observation in a particular place that they have likely seen all the essential activities that go on there. Our researcher would be foolish to spend hours observing clothes drying in the hospital laundry room simply because a regimented sampling plan demanded it.

Related to time and place sampling is *event* sampling. Schatzman and Strauss (1973) note that in any organization there are typically three types of events: routine, special, and unexpected events. In organizations like hospitals, the vast majority of events are routine — meetings at specific times, meal serving, visiting hours, doctors' rounds, and so on. Alternatively, although special events occur infrequently, they may still be anticipated. If the researcher learns, for example, that an examining board responsible for continuing the hospital's accreditation will be visiting, he or she surely would want to observe how this special event alters the routine operation of the organization. Once researchers have gained the trust of persons in the setting, they may even ask to be called if unexpected events are in the process of occurring. It is possible to make a list of routine events and selectively sample each. Although it is more difficult to plan observations of special and unexpected events, researchers will want to make a determined effort to observe them. Past research experience suggests that a great deal is learned about the functioning of any social system by observing its responses to special events.

Finally, there will be occasions when a participant observer wants to observe the behavior of, or to interview, specific types of persons in an organization. Several persons in unique positions within an organization or setting will have quite different perspectives on the organization. Field researchers rarely try to systematically interview a large number of persons in the setting studied. They might determine, as the research progresses and theoretical ideas begin to take shape, that persons occupying certain statuses in the organization can supply them with important information. They may choose, therefore, to sample *statuses and roles*. In the hospital setting the researcher might want to observe the behavior of, or talk to, persons who serve specific functions. David Sudnow (1967), for example, who studied death and dying in one hospital, made it a special point to observe the activities of the hospital morgue attendant. If the researcher wanted to find out the kinds of changes that have occurred over time in the hospital, it might be reasonable to sample some of the "old timers" there. As an extension of status and role sampling, a field researcher might even be interested in sampling social relationships. The researcher might decide that it is theoretically important to observe a sampling of interactions between, let us say, doctors new to the job and nurses who have long service on the staff.

An important point emerges from several of the examples offered of the sampling procedures frequently employed in qualitative research. It is that the basis for sampling in many qualitative studies is not to make statistical estimates of population parameters based on sample data; rather it is, in the terms of our discussion in Chapter 1, to make analytical generalizations. Certainly the researcher wants to ensure that observations made of persons, events, and places are typical. At the same time, the qualitative researcher would rarely be concerned with having observed every type of event, situation, status, or role. The concern in qualitative research is more usually to sample from among the universe of events, statuses, and the like, only those that are most integrally related to emerging theoretical ideas. It is not a criterion of such sampling that the elements of the sample closely approximate the characteristics of some known universe. In survey research, to draw the contrast, sampling procedures are employed only once at the beginning of the research. In qualitative research employing analytical sampling procedures, sampling is an ongoing procedure throughout the history of the research project.[9] As theoretical ideas develop during the course of the researcher's observations, he may find it necessary to sample features of the situation he had not anticipated at the beginning of the research. In sum, the sampling procedures employed in qualitative research reflect the internal logic of the method itself. As we saw in the first chapter, those using unstructured research techniques seek to let their theoretical ideas emerge out of their observations. The ongoing sampling procedures used by the qualitative researcher aid the realization of this goal.

CONCLUSION

Our objective has been to look at a nontechnical introduction to sampling. We began by discussing ways in which sampling is an aspect of everyday life. One characteristic that distinguishes sampling in social research from sampling in everyday life is the greater concern among social researchers with the precision of sample estimates.

What are the advantages of sampling? (1) It is often much easier and quicker to collect the data we need from a sample than from the total population of interest. (2) It is often much less expensive. (3) In many cases it would be impossible to carry out the study on the entire population of interest owing to the lack of adequate funds or an adequate sampling frame. (4) For many research questions a high degree of precision in our estimates is not needed; the information on the rest of the population adds unnecessary precision (e.g., if our goal is to forecast who will win an election and it turns out that 80 percent of the electorate plan to vote for one of the candidates, we can make a very reliable forecast based on interviews with a small sample of the population).

It is generally assumed that results based on a total count are more reliable than results based on a sample. This is not always the case. One reason is that when a study seeks to obtain information from all elements in the population, the goal is rarely achieved. For example, the U.S. Census misses several million people, particularly those who are very poor, in the underworld, and the like. Thus it is sometimes possible to get a more accurate estimate of the true population parameter from a study based on a sample than from a study which uses the same resources in the effort to obtain information from each element in the population.

[9] What we are referring to as analytical sampling can also be referred to as purposive sampling. The only difference is the emphasis in analytical sampling on the flexibility to change the sample design as the study progresses; however, this is not inconsistent with the goals of purposive sampling.

In the study based on a sample, the researcher will be able to work harder to reach and obtain interviews from those who fall into the sample. The funds will allow the researcher to hire more highly qualified interviewers, or alternatively to put more effort into the training of interviewers. For a smaller well-funded study, it is possible to supervise the data collection more closely and to deal more adequately with the various sources of nonsampling error.

We have considered the criteria for the selection of an appropriate sample size, and it turns out that such criteria tend to be of rather limited use because researchers generally do not have the information needed to make these estimates until after the data has been collected. In general, if the goal is to generalize to a more homogeneous population, a smaller sample is needed than when the goal is to generalize to a more heterogeneous population. In the extreme case in which each element of the population can be assumed to be identical, a sample of one would be quite adequate (as with the single sip of old milk). Sometimes the researcher has in mind a type of statistical analysis that will require a sample of a certain size. If the sample is small, for example, under 100 respondents, the number of alternatives for statistical analysis is quite limited.

Even more troublesome than sampling error are the various sources of nonsampling error or bias. We have reviewed several of the sources of bias that survey research is vulnerable to — including inadequate sampling frames, nonresponse, interviewer effects, coding errors, and errors in the preparation of the data for statistical analysis. We know these sources of nonsampling error can severely bias our findings and, to make matters worse, we have no way to accurately estimate their impact.

We rounded out the chapter with a discussion of sampling in qualitative research. In this situation, the objective is to make analytical generalizations rather than statistical estimates of population parameters. The analytical or theoretical sampling which proves to be so useful in qualitative research turns out to be a special case of the purposive sampling used in survey research.

We are continually exposed to sampling through the mass media in a variety of ways. We hear the results of surveys on a wide range of topics broadcast over television and radio. We are also exposed to the use of sampling in television and radio commercials. There are two extreme reactions to this experience with sampling which, hopefully, have been modified by this chapter. One reaction is to blindly accept sample results — without inquiring as to whether an appropriate sampling plan has been employed. The other extreme reaction to this experience with sampling is to reject all sampling as fallacious. That much skepticism is unnecessary and probably detrimental. We should now realize sampling can be executed in such a way that what we find out from the sample is almost identical to what we would find out from a complete count of the population.

EXERCISES

1. Discuss the sampling in your everyday life with respect to dating and marriage, selecting a school to attend, and buying a car. What kind of sampling do you do? How good a sample do you choose? Is the issue of accuracy relevant in your sampling? Why?

2. Suppose you were sampling the households in a metropolitan area and you wanted a sample of 600 households. The area is covered by 4 telephone directories, one of which contains 300 pages of central city listings. Each of the other 3 telephone directories covers a portion of the suburbs and contains 100 pages. Since the 4 directories have a total of 600 pages and you desire 600 interviews, what problems of bias, if any, might be involved if you randomly selected one name from each of the 600 pages for your sample.

3. Suppose you want to observe the interaction of people who attend rock concerts and you have a limited budget. What sampling method would be best for your purposes. What, if any, limitations must you accept by using this method?

4. Discuss the problems you might run into in an attempt to draw a simple random sample of the U.S., your state, your city, and your school.

5. Qualitative research is sometimes criticized for its lack of attention to sampling design. What sampling related criticisms can be made of most observational studies? How would those who choose to do such studies answer these criticisms?

6. Discuss the strengths and weaknesses of what the authors refer to as "analytical sampling."

7. Think of a research situation in which a probability sample would be most appropriate. Which probability sampling plan would you select? How large a sample would you choose? How would you attempt to minimize bias in the execution of your sample?

8. Think of a research situation in which a nonprobability sample would be most appropriate. Which nonprobability sampling plan would you select? How large a sample would you choose? How would you attempt to minimize bias in the execution of your sample?

SUGGESTED READINGS

Babbie, Earl R.
1973   *Survey Research Methods*. Belmont, Calif.: Wadsworth.

Chapters 5 and 6 give a thorough coverage of sampling logic, concepts, and plans. The latter chapter shows how samples are selected in different research settings.

Backstrom, Charles H., and Gerald D. Hursh
1963   *Survey Research*. Evanston: Northwestern University Press.

> Chapter 2 is a nuts-and-bolts-level treatment of sampling that will be of use to those who plan to actually draw a sample for a survey research study.

Blalock, Hubert M.
1972   *Social Statistics*. 2d ed. New York: McGraw-Hill.

> Chapter 21 on sampling will be of interest to the reader with some background in statistics. It goes into more depth on a number of issues that we have treated in a nontechnical way.

Cochran, William G.
1963   *Sampling Techniques*. New York: John Wiley.

> The treatment is thorough but highly technical.

Denzin, Norman K.
1970   *The Research Act*. Chicago: Aldine.

> Chapters 4 to 6 discuss the relationship between theory and sampling procedure. Denzin raises a number of issues of interest to those who do qualitative research.

Kish, Leslie
1965   *Survey Sampling*. New York: John Wiley.

> This is considered by many to be the most thorough book on sampling available. It requires extensive mathematical background for full comprehension.

Schatzman, Leonard, and Anselm L. Strauss
1973   *Field Research*. Englewood Cliffs, N.J.: Prentice-Hall.

> In Chapter 3 there is a discussion of sampling in qualitative research which is very useful.

Slonim, Morris J.
1960   *Sampling*. New York: Simon and Schuster.

> An excellent nontechnical introduction to sampling. It is written in a humorous vein and contains a number of illustrations.

REFERENCES

Davis, James A.
1973   *General Social Survey: 1973 Codebook*. Chicago: National Opinion Research Center.

Gallup, George
1948   *A Guide to Public Opinion Polls.* Princeton, N.J.: Princeton University Press.

Politz, Alfred, and Willard Simmons
1949   "An attempt to get the 'not-at-homes' into the sample without call-backs." *Journal of the American Statistical Association* 44 (March):9–31.

Schatzman, Leonard, and Anselm L. Strauss
1973   *Field Research.* Englewood Cliffs, N.J.: Prentice-Hall.

Slonim, Morris J.
1960   *Sampling.* New York: Simon and Schuster.

Sudnow, David
1967   *Passing On: The Social Organization of Dying.* Englewood Cliffs, N.J.: Prentice-Hall.

Procedures of Social Research

PART TWO

Survey Research

We are all exposed, fairly regularly, to survey research in one form or another. We are stopped on the street by interviewers who ask our opinions on current local issues or new food products. We get telephone calls from survey research organizations asking how we intend to vote in the upcoming election or why we fly with one airline rather than another. Perhaps we get mail questionnaires from hotels we once patronized requesting comments on the service received. Certainly we see person-in-the-street interviews reported on T.V. and we read newspaper reports of the latest Gallup or Harris poll results. These are all forms of survey research. Surveys attempt to collect information in a systematic manner which allows for the description and explanation of the beliefs, values, and behaviors of people. Virtually every topic of interest to the social researcher has been approached using the survey method. This adaptability is one of the greatest strengths of the method.

One characteristic of surveys is that they generally involve a reasonably representative cross-section of the population, whether the population be the entire United States voting public or all the people who stayed at a certain hotel during the past month. They typically use a predetermined sampling plan which specifies how respondents are to be selected. When appropriate sampling procedures are used, it is possible to estimate how accurately the sample results represent the population from which the sample was drawn. While surveys typically involve interviews with a sample of respondents drawn from a population of interest, some studies using survey research techniques involve interviews with the entire population of interest. An example is the use of survey interviews to conduct a census.

Another characteristic of survey studies is that the sample tends to be larger than is typically the case in observational, intensive interviewing, or experimental studies. For example, Stouffer (1966) conducted a survey study of beliefs about the threat of communism and beliefs about those civil liberties which might have to be sacrificed in order to deal with this threat. The study was based on two national samples carried out by independent polling organizations totalling approximately 5000 persons who represented a cross-section of the population. The study also included interviews with some 1500 community leaders. Stouffer's sample was larger than that of most surveys. The standard sample size for most national samples is in the vicinity of 1500 respondents, but for some purposes much larger samples are used. One example is the Current Population Survey of approximately 50,000 households conducted monthly by the Bureau of the Census for estimating labor force characteristics, such as unemployment rates.

A third feature of survey research concerns the means of data collection used. The most common means of data collection are: face-to-face interviews, self-administered questionnaires (e.g., mail questionnaires and questionnaires such as those often filled out by students in undergraduate courses), and telephone interviews. Typically the questionnaire or interview schedule is set up so that the same questions are asked of each respondent in the same order with exactly the same wording. With other forms of data gathering, such as observation and intensive interviewing, researchers have much more latitude with respect to what they ask (or observe), how they ask it, and how much emphasis they give to each issue.

Another characteristic of most surveys is that the data is collected at one point in time. The sample is most appropriate for describing the population from which it was drawn at the time the interviewing was done. Such *cross-sectional* studies have limited utility for the study of historical trends. However, the survey approach can be used to study trends in opinion and behavior over time by, for example, interviewing a completely new sample of respondents each month or each year. The Roper Public Opinion Center at Williams College is one of several centers around the country which has data from national surveys conducted during the past several decades. Many of these surveys include the same question so that it is possible to trace trends over the years on such issues as anti-Semitism, racism, and sexism. Another method of conducting trend studies is to reinterview the same group of respondents several times. This is called a panel study. *Panel studies* have proven particularly useful in the study of the process by which voters make up their mind as an election approaches (Lazarsfeld et al., 1944). They have also been used to study movement into and out of poverty as well as to study the physical, psychological, and social aspects of the aging process.

The reliance of survey research upon interviews and questionnaires is part of the reason for the popular equation between survey research and the opinion polling done by such organizations as Gallup and Harris. The major distinction is that in academic survey research there is typically much more of an attempt to provide a causal explanation for the attitudes and behaviors reported. In contrast, a Gallup poll usually stops with a simple description of how many people hold a specified opinion or how many people in different demographic categories (i.e., categories of sex, race, age, or some other factor) hold that opinion.

In summary, survey research aims for a systematic and comprehensive collection of information about the attitudes, beliefs, and behavior of people. This collection is accomplished through interviewing and administering questionnaires to relatively large and representative samples of the population of interest. We now turn to the most important steps in the process of carrying out a survey research study. For the purposes of our discussion the steps will be categorized as follows:[1]

1. Research question formulation.
2. Survey design.
3. Sampling plan.
4. Data-gathering technique.
5. Questionnaire construction.
6. Survey execution.
7. Data analysis and reporting.

Any such ordering of research steps is somewhat artificial. Such a listing could be taken to indicate that once a particular step is covered, there is no turning back. To the contrary, it is often necessary to alter decisions made at an earlier point in light of developments during later stages of the research. Problems encountered in the actual execution of a survey, for example, may make it necessary to modify the sampling plan in some way. It is also a mistake to assume that these steps can be followed one at a time, without any regard for subsequent steps. In reality, it is often important to have in mind the intended data analysis procedures when constructing the questionnaire.

RESEARCH QUESTION FORMULATION

By "research question" we mean the major goal, problem, or objective of the study. We are *not* referring to the specific question to be included in the actual questionnaire. The first step in a survey research study is the formulation of the research problem. In fact, formulation of the problem should precede the selection of survey research as the data

---

[1] This list does not include all possible steps in the survey research process, and some of these steps could be broken down into two or more steps. For an alternative formulation of the steps in the survey research process, see pp. 7–8.

collection method. While the method has wide applicability, it may turn out that for the problem we have selected intensive interviewing, observation, or some other approach would be more appropriate.

There are a variety of criteria which can be used in selecting the research question. For some a criterion is that the project have significant social policy implications; that is, the information should be relevant to social improvement, social change, or social action. For others the goal is to produce information which can be used in social criticism. Another criterion is that the project deal with one of the fundamental issues that have concerned social theorists over the years. Often a major factor is the researchers' curiosity about a particular phenomenon. These are just some of the criteria that can be used. Some research questions will meet several of these criteria, but it is rare that the question will meet all of them.

Also of importance in the formulation of the research question is the choice of a theoretical framework or theoretical model. The choice of a theory or model will have implications for the kinds of data that will be needed. If we are to compare the efficacy of alternative theoretical explanations for a phenomenon, we must be sure we have collected the information needed to make the comparison.

Another aspect to question formulation is the process of narrowing down a general area of interest to a level that is specific enough for concrete, empirical research to be carried out. This involves the identification of major variables to be examined. Suppose that the general area of interest is marital difficulty. The focusing process might proceed in the following manner. With what kind of marital difficulty am I concerned? Unhappy marriages? Separations? Divorces? Am I interested in the causes of marital difficulty? If so, which ones? Am I interested in the consequences of marital difficulty? If so, which ones? Thinking through the question area and narrowing down in this manner is of crucial importance for virtually all of the subsequent steps in the survey research process.

A thorough review of the existing literature (books and journal articles) on the topic is generally useful when attempting to narrow down the topic. This literature is helpful because it tells us what has been done and how the project we are considering will add to or extend what is already known. The review of literature will help us find important gaps in existing knowledge which we can attempt to fill with our research.

There are other aids in research question formulation. One is the pilot study. A *pilot study* is a tentative and relatively unstructured investigation of a few respondents who are similar in many respects to those we intend to study as part of the main investigation. If we are planning to investigate alienation among the poor, the pilot study might involve in-depth or intensive interviews with several different categories of poor persons. One goal of such a study is to stimulate our thinking as to the most important sources of alienation in their lives. We would also want to find out how a concept such as alienation can be discussed. Many of our subjects will not understand what we mean by the term "alienation." In short, the pilot study can be useful in deciding what the important issues are and in formulating questionnaire items that are meaningful to those we intend to interview.

One other aspect of question formulation is that it can be very useful to consult with those who are knowledgeable about the topic and who have done related research. Those with practical experience can be particularly useful in helping us anticipate some of the major pitfalls in our planned research. Finally, in the initial phase of the research, as in all other phases, the importance of the researcher's intuition and common sense cannot be underestimated.

SURVEY DESIGN

After we have formulated our research question and have decided that survey research is the most appropriate data collection method for our study, we must decide the type of survey design to employ. Research designs for surveys can be classified as being either cross-sectional or longitudinal. In a *cross-sectional* design, the data is collected at one point in time. This category of designs is most appropriate for making inferences about the characteristics of the population from which the sample is drawn, and inferences about the relationships between variables at that point in time at which the data was collected. The interviewing for such studies is sometimes carried out in less than a week, but more typically requires a few weeks and in some cases a few months. In a *longitudinal* design, data is systematically collected over a period of months or years in such a way that it is possible to observe trends in attitudes or behaviors over the specified period of time.

Consider the following example. A team of researchers is interested in exploring the sex role attitudes of homemakers in New Haven. They select a sample of households in the community and hire interviewers to interview the homemakers in the selected households. After the interviews are completed, the researchers analyze the collected data and draw conclusions that allow for generalizations about sex role attitudes for all homemakers in New Haven.

The research design involved in this example is that of a cross-sectional survey because it calls for the collection of data at one point in time. It represents a snapshot of all homemakers in New Haven at the time during which the survey was conducted. The cross-sectional survey is used much more extensively than are longitudinal designs. This survey of homemakers could be used to obtain a descriptive profile of, say, the age, education level, and religion of male homemakers. Or it could be used in causal analysis, as in a study of the effect of religious background on degree of satisfaction for all persons who are homemakers.

By asking questions about the past it is possible to study certain longitudinal (over time) social phenomena such as social mobility using a cross-sectional survey. An example is the causal modeling with path analysis discussed in Chapter 2; with that model the researcher was able to trace the effect of the father's education and occupation on the respondent's educational achievement, first job, and present occupation. The relationship among these variables was summarized in Figure 2.4. The important point to make here is that this data was collected at one point in time using a cross-sectional survey design.

A *panel study* successively surveys the same respondents at different times. A classic example of this survey design is found in *The People's Choice* by Lazarsfeld, et al., (1944). The researchers interviewed a panel of 600 residents of Erie County, Ohio once a month between May and November of 1940 with respect to how they intended to vote in the presidential election of 1940. Of particular interest to these investigators was the process by which panel members decided to vote in the way that they eventually did. A more recent illustration of such a study is the Survey Research Center's (1972) *A Panel Study of Income Dynamics*. In this survey, approximately 5000 households throughout the United States were personally interviewed during the spring of each year from 1968 to 1972. The survey obtained detailed information about various sources of income. It has been used to study among other topics the characteristics of those moving into and out of poverty during the five-year period.

There are both advantages and limitations to the panel study approach. Most of the advantages relate to being able to interview the same respondents repeatedly over a period of months or years. If we find shifts in attitudes or reported behavior we are in a better position to argue that there has been a real change in the population of interest than a researcher who undertakes a trend analysis based on several independent cross-sectional surveys. When we attempt to compare two different cross-sectional surveys, we know that any difference we find can be attributed either to a real change in attitude or behavior in the population of interest or to a difference due to *sampling error* (i.e., even if two samples are drawn from the same population there will be some differences in observed values due to random fluctuation).[2] This sampling error difference can be ruled out when we use a panel design.

Another advantage of panel studies is that they permit much more information to be collected about each respondent than is feasible with a cross-sectional survey design. Panel studies also avoid a heavy dependence on the memory of respondents for information about the time period covered by the panel; however they may still rely on memory for questions about respondent's past.

Panel studies are not without their limitations. One problem is that over a period of time there is bound to be some sample mortality;

---

[2] For a discussion of sampling error, see Chapters 5 and 15.

that is, there will be a loss of panel members owing to difficulty in reaching them, lack of cooperation, and death. It has been estimated, for example, that approximately one out of every five Americans change residence every year. The record-keeping problems caused by such mobility for a panel study are substantial. In the *Panel Study of Income Dynamics* cited earlier, considerable effort went into minimizing sample loss, but still only 62 percent of those in the original sample remained at the end of five years.

Another limitation of panel designs is that it takes a long time to collect the data. Related to this is the increase in cost per respondent. An indirect consequence of this inflation is the tendency to conduct panel studies on smaller, less representative samples; for example, we might decide to do a panel study of a single community when with the same money we could have obtained a cross-sectional national sample. Some panel studies involve periodic interviews with the respondent for his or her entire adult life. This does not mean that we must wait until all the respondents are dead to analyze the data. It is quite common to analyze the data as the panel progresses. In some studies questions are added to subsequent interviews on the basis of the results of preliminary analysis while the panel is still in progress.

An additional problem with panel studies is that repeated surveys may cause respondents to become overly sensitized to their role as "selected" respondents. They may feel that if they are important enough to be selected for the study, they should express the views which are appropriate for an "important" person. It is not uncommon for panel members, having once been interviewed on particular social issues, to make extensive investigations on these issues before their next interview. As a result, these respondents become inordinately well informed on the topics under consideration. When asked why they have made these investigations, a common reply is that it will "help" the researchers to be dealing with better informed respondents. Others indicate that they would not have continued in the panel unless they had upgraded their levels of knowledge because of the embarrassment caused by not knowing the "right" answers to questions.

SAMPLING PLAN

After a survey design has been selected, a sampling plan must be chosen. A brief review of major points regarding the choice of a sampling plan is provided here. For a more detailed discussion of sampling, the reader is referred to Chapter 5.

Sampling plans are either of the *probability* or *nonprobability* variety. Probability sampling plans all share the characteristics that every element in the population has a known chance of being included in the sample. This allows for estimates of the accuracy of sample findings in approximating what we would find out if we had conducted a census of the total population. With nonprobability sampling plans, we do not know the chance which each element of the population has of being selected for a particular sample. Hence, statistical estimates of precision cannot be made with nonprobability samples. For this reason, probability procedures are preferred when they are feasible.

Of the major probability sampling plans, *simple random* and *stratified random* sampling plans provide the most accurate estimates of true population figures. In order for either of these plans to be implemented, a complete listing of all population elements (a sampling frame) must be available. Good sampling frames can be obtained for some survey research situations (a survey, for instance, of pupils in a given school); but in other situations it is very difficult or impossible to locate a good sampling frame. Furthermore, for a nation, state, or even a large city there is no way to get an accurate list of all possible respondents. Even if the city or state has just done a census, we can be sure that many who are, for example, poor or in the underworld, will have been missed. In addition if we try to use a list that is several months or several years old, many people will have moved. Even if it were possible to actually obtain an accurate list for a state or nation, for most studies the cost of interviewing a truly random sample of any size would be prohibitively high because of the necessary travel from respondent to respondent. Consequently, other types of sampling plans are more common in large-scale survey research studies.

The most widely employed probability sampling plan in survey research is *cluster sampling*. This involves an initial sampling stage (or stages) wherein sampling is done from groups of elements called clusters. A cluster sample of a city, for example, might begin with a probability selection of census tracts.[3] In turn, a probability sample of city blocks might be made within each of the chosen census tracts. Finally, individual households from each of the selected city blocks might be picked by means of probability sampling. When such a sampling plan is used, interviewers spend less time and money than they would have to spend in any sampling plan employing a simple random sample. Interviewers end up working in each of several neighborhoods rather than visiting households randomly scattered throughout the city.

Several types of nonprobability sampling are used in survey research. The *quota sample* is one of the most frequently used. Survey research organizations such as Gallup are able to achieve results using quota samples which closely approximate those which would be obtained using probability samples. This is possible because of the care with which the quotas for various categories of respondents are constructed and the careful control exercised over the way in which interviewers fill their

---

[3] A census tract is an area made up of some thirty to forty city blocks.

quotas. However, more typically, the quota sample of a single researcher cannot be considered a reasonable approximation to a probability sample.

With *quota sampling* the effort is typically to get a cross-section of the population, but with *purposive sampling* this is generally not the goal. Here the researcher purposely selects certain categories of respondents for their theoretical relevance to the issue being studied. It is quite possible that many categories of people will not be included at all in such a sample. Purposive sampling is often used, for example, in studies of elites or of deviance.

Accidental sampling refers to sampling in which there has been little or no systematic control over the respondent selection procedure. If an instructor in a research methods class were to ask each of fifty students to obtain interviews with ten people, and gave no further instructions about how to select them, the result would be an accidental sample of five hundred respondents. Accidental samples occur in social research much more frequently than many would have us believe. Often a study begins with a sampling plan that calls for a sophisticated probability design, but the researcher runs into such difficulty (e.g., in getting agencies to cooperate) that the actual sample at the end of the study can only be described as an accidental sample. Even the major survey research firms have been finding it increasingly difficult to obtain interviews with those selected for interviewing by very careful sampling procedures. This nonresponse problem is a major threat to the representativeness of the resulting sample. If a careful probability sample ends up with only 50 percent of those respondents originally selected for interviewing, the resulting sample might better be classified as an accidental sample than as a probability sample. In short, when nonresponse rates are really high (in some mail surveys, up to 95 percent), it is misleading to think of the resulting sample as a true probability sample.

A final sampling alternative is to combine probability and non-probability sampling, as when we combine a multistage cluster design with quota sampling. For example, we might draw a probability sample of different regions of the country (clusters) and then within each of these regions draw probability samples of smaller geographic regions (clusters), continuing this process for three or four stages until we get down to areas the size of a city block. Then at the block level we may use quota sampling. The decision to use quota sampling at the last stage saves time and money, but it does add some sampling error.

DATA-GATHERING TECHNIQUE

We recall that there are three principal data-gathering techniques used in survey research: self-administered questionnaires, face-to-face interviews, and telephone interviews. Self-administered questionnaires (whether sent by mail, passed out in a classroom, or distributed in some other manner) are distributed to a sample of the population and the respondents fill out their answers to a set of questions by themselves. In both face-to-face interviews and telephone interviews, questions are asked of respondents by an interviewer. Note that answers to the same set of questions can be elicited by each of the three techniques. What varies is the extent to which respondents have contact with an interviewer. Self-administered questionnaires do not involve an interviewer; telephone interviews use the voice of an interviewer; face-to-face interviews employ the total presence of an interviewer. This difference has implications for the quantity and the quality of information derived.

Each of these alternative data collection methods has its advantages and disadvantages. *Self-administered questionnaires* have a clear advantage regarding cost. Since interviewers are not part of the data-gathering process the expense of interviewing is minimized. This reason alone probably accounts for the fact that so much survey research is conducted by self-administered questionnaires. Another advantage of this technique is that respondents have time to consider questions carefully. There is no pressure to react to questions right away as is often the case in an interview. Some respondents feel more comfortable expressing their real reactions to questions on personally sensitive topics (sex, politics, and religion) on a self-administered questionnaire than they do in an interview situation.

There is, of course, a double-edged aspect to these advantages of a self-administered questionnaire. Respondents may not only feel more comfortable — they may also decide to dispose of the questionnaire via the wastebasket. The response rate of self-administered questionnaires is considerably lower than that of either face-to-face interviews or telephone interviews. When the attempt is to reach a cross-section of the population, response rates of 10 percent and less are not uncommon with self-administered mail questionnaires.

A partial explanation for this lower response rate is that some people have a difficult time filling out questionnaires. It has been estimated that, "for purposes of filling out even simple written questionnaires, at least ten percent of the adult population of the United States is illiterate. For complex questionnaires, the percentage would undoubtedly be considerably higher" (Selltiz, et al., 1959). If one adds to those who are unable those who are unwilling, the lower response rate becomes even more comprehensible. The representativeness of those who do respond also becomes a serious question.

The leeway that respondents have in responding to a self-administered questionnaire means that the researcher does not have very much influence over the conditions under which the questionnaire is completed. Some respondents may fill out the questionnaire by themselves; others may seek the aid of friends or family members. Some respondents may complete the questionnaire at a time and place where they feel comfortable and have the leisure to think out their responses thought-fully; others may respond when they are rushed and consequently not give much thought to their answers. In other words, it is difficult to standardize how respondents will respond to a self-administered questionnaire.

Face-to-face interviews are generally the best data-gathering technique for survey research. This approach enables the researcher to obtain information from a much larger percentage of those sampled than do self-administered questionnaires, particularly the mail questionnaires. One reason is that it is more difficult for respondents to refuse cooperation when they are directly confronted and asked to respond to questions than when they receive a questionnaire and are asked to fill it out themselves. The interviewing situation also increases the response rate because many people who are unable to fill out a questionnaire by themselves can and will respond to the same questions when they are asked by an interviewer.

Not only the quantity, but also the quality of responses can be improved by the presence of an interviewer. When questions are not understood by a respondent, the interviewer can clarify their meaning by the use of probing questions. If a respondent does not answer a question in the proper frame of reference, an interviewer can follow up by asking: "Could you explain what you mean by what you just said?" The use of such *probes* can eventually bring the respondent around to providing the information sought by a particular question. Aside from clarifying matters, this additional questioning by an interviewer can add to the depth of the information which the respondent provides for the research. A further advantage of face-to-face interviews is that the presence of the interviewer can sometimes be used as a check on the validity of the answers to questions by respondents. It is less likely that outlandishly false answers will be given by respondents directly to an interviewer.

We should realize that the advantages of face-to-face interviews over self-administered questionnaires are conditional: the effectiveness of the confrontation depends on good interviewers who achieve the respect of and rapport with respondents. One considerable disadvantage of face-to-face interviews is the expense of paying interviewers. The cost can be prohibitive for many survey research situations.

A less expensive interviewing technique for survey research is the *telephone interview,* which can often provide as representative a sample at less than half the cost of face-to-face interviewing. The flat-rate plans provided by the telephone company have made it an increasingly feasible data-gathering technique. However, telephone interviewing does suffer from certain limitations. People without telephones (normally, poor people) and people with unlisted telephone numbers (the well-to-do and those who have recently moved) are usually excluded from telephone surveys. Normally, telephone interviews yield only one-third or one-quarter the amount of information that could be obtained by face-to-face interviews. In the telephone interview, the interviewer cannot use the visual questioning technique (e.g., handing the respondent a lengthy list of alternative response categories) available in self-administered and face-to-face interviews.

QUESTIONNAIRE CONSTRUCTION

All three of the data-gathering techniques we have discussed employ a set of questions to which respondents are asked to reply. This set of questions is referred to as a questionnaire for self-administered questionnaires and as an interview schedule for face-to-face interviews and telephone interviews. In the text that follows we want to consider two general issues: (1) the types of questions asked in survey research and (2) guidelines for designing and organizing the entire questionnaire.

There are two kinds of questions used in questionnaires: structured and unstructured. *Structured questions* (or closed questions) provide the alternative (multiple-choice) answers from which the respondent must choose a reply. The following is an example:

If the presidential election were held today, for whom would you vote?

_____ Calvin Coolidge
_____ William Jennings Bryan
_____ Millard Fillmore
_____ Other (please specify)
_____ Don't Know

The alternative answers for a structured question are printed on the questionnaire form, and either the respondent or the interviewer (depending upon the data-gathering technique employed) checks off the appropriate response. Another example of a structured question is the following:

How do you feel about the federal government giving encouragement to the building of low-income housing in the suburbs?

_____ Strongly Approve
_____ Approve
_____ Ambivalent
_____ Disapprove
_____ Strongly Disapprove
_____ Don't Know

The second question is a better example of a structured question than the first question because the alternative responses cover the full range of relevant (approving and disapproving) answers. The first question obviously fails by this criterion of completeness because it does not include current political figures who are potential presidential candidates. Notice that both questions do include a "Don't Know" category. It is important to have such a category for structured questions because some respondents really may not know how they feel about certain issues. However, the interviewer generally does not volunteer this as a response alternative because many respondents would use it just to avoid making a decision among the other alternatives.

Unstructured questions (or *open-ended questions*) do not predetermine the possible answers from which the respondent must choose. The following is an example:

> What do you feel are the major social problems
> facing our nation today?

Instead of providing the possible answers, the questionnaire form leaves a space for the respondent to answer the question in his or her own terms. In other words, the issue is left open. Such questions have the advantage of allowing for the expression of the depth and complexity of the respondent's feelings and attitudes about a particular topic.

One disadvantage of unstructured questions is that they produce data which is sometimes difficult to analyze quantitatively because the categorization of responses must take place after the data has been collected. In some cases, the answers given by respondents vary so much that it becomes impossible to discern a relatively small number of response patterns. This problem does not occur with structured questions because the categories of response on the questionnaire become the categories used for data analysis. A further important use of structured questions is in the measurement of abstract concepts. We typically operationalize such concepts as morale, anomie, and social class using an index or scale which combines several structured questions.[4]

It should be clear that structured and unstructured questions have their relative advantages and disadvantages and that some topic areas are best covered by one or the other question type. For example, issues for which there is general agreement about the possible alternative replies are best tapped by structured questions. A good illustration is the sex of respondent. Structured questions lend themselves more readily to statistical analysis than do open-ended questions. However, structured questions sometimes inappropriately force respondents to select an answer from irrelevant and predetermined pigeonholes. This is a major, *potential* drawback with structured questions.

Unstructured questions, on the other hand, provide respondents the opportunity to "open up" and answer questions in their own terms. Unfortunately, such responses are sometimes difficult to interpret and analyze. Consequently, in the construction of the questionnaire, it makes

---

[4] Among the most well-known scaling procedures are those referred to as Likert scales, Guttman scales, and Thurstone scales. For a discussion of each, see Miller (1970).

sense to formulate both structured and unstructured questions. The responses to the two kinds of questions can be compared for consistency.

The suggestion to include both structured and unstructured questions is a major guideline for designing and organizing a questionnaire. Other such guidelines are included in the following list.

1. *Introduction.* Every questionnaire should have an introduction which gives a description of what the study is about. The introduction should also provide instructions for responding to the questionnaire and, if the promise of confidentiality is being extended to respondents, this is the appropriate place to make that plain.

2. *Order of Questions.* Most researchers like to begin a questionnaire with one or two questions that will be easy to answer, such as questions about the respondent's household size. However, it is important not to make these questions so personal (e.g., income level) that respondents will be put on the defensive or terminate the interview immediately.

As another rule of thumb, the line of questioning generally is broader at the beginning than later in the questionnaire. For instance, in a politically oriented survey, the opening questions might probe in a general way (including some open-ended questions) for the respondent's opinions on the most important issues of the day. Later in the questionnaire, the interviewer might read a list of specific issues and ask the respondent to appraise the relative importance of each.

The questions should be placed in an order which facilitates an orderly progression of the interchange between interviewer and respondent. One would not, for example, ask a few questions about the most important issues of the day, then skip to questions about political leaders, then skip back to more questions on the issues of the day, then ask some questions about the respondent's characteristics, then skip back to more questions about political leaders.

Finally, the most personal questions are usually saved until late in the questionnaire, so that if the respondent refuses to answer or terminates the interview at that point, most of the information will already have been obtained. A typical cooperation rate on most questions would be well over 90 percent, but on some of the more sensitive questions (e.g., income), this figure can dip as low as 70 percent. It sometimes helps to use display cards to ask the sensitive questions; listing income groups on a card with a letter in front of each group and simply asking the respondent to select a letter is not nearly so threatening as simply asking the respondent's income.

3. *Form of the Questions.* It is important to determine whether structured or unstructured questions are best suited for a given objective. We have stressed the importance of interspersing both types throughout the questionnaire to maintain the interest of the respondent and to com-

plement each other in eliciting both precategorized and free-response information. Even more detailed decisions are necessary. Should a structured question take the form of a numerical scale (for instance rating something from 0 to 9 in terms of favorability) or a verbal scale (e.g., highly favorable, somewhat favorable, somewhat unfavorable, or highly unfavorable)? In making decisions of this type, the reader is advised to refer to some of the texts recommended at the end of this chapter.

4. *Clarity.* It is crucial to make sure respondents will be able to understand the meaning of each question. In other words, the researcher must phrase questions in terms the respondents will understand, but he must be careful not to seem patronizing to respondents. This is often a difficult balance to achieve and is usually best gained through extensive pretesting of alternative questions.

5. *Avoiding Slanted Questions.* Very occasionally, a researcher will deliberately slant a question toward a particular advocacy position. For instance, half the respondents in a survey might be asked, "Do you agree with the people who feel that the quality of life in this country is better than ever before?" The other half might be asked, "Do you agree with the people who feel that the quality of life in this country is at an all-time low?" The intent in this case would be to force respondents to be very sure of their answers, because in effect, the interviewer is daring the respondent to disagree with the hypothesized "form." The key to analysis of these questions would be to compare the percentage of people *disagreeing* with the first question form with the percentage *disagreeing* with the second — in other words, examining how many respondents "held their ground" in the face of encouragement not to do so. This type of questioning ploy, however, is relatively rare and should not be overused. More often than not, if you see a slanted question of this type, it simply represents poor questioning technique on the part of the researcher — sometimes intentional, sometimes unintentional. In the desire to obtain a finding consistent with their hypotheses, some researchers succumb to the temptation to slant questions so they will produce answers favorable to the hypotheses. Needless to say, this should be avoided.

Another subtle way of slanting a question is to exclude certain possible categories in a structured question; the researcher simply includes those categories which he favors and lumps the others into an "all other" category. This is often done unconsciously and can be avoided by a thorough pretest of questions and recording of all responses.

6. *Cross-check Questions.* It is a good policy to include several different questions on one topic area to see if respondents will answer in the same way. Such questions allow for an appraisal of the validity of the questionnaire and of the accuracy of the respondents' self-reports. A special type of a cross-check question is the *random probe*. Each

respondent is asked to explain what was meant by his or her responses to a few randomly selected structured questions. Different respondents are asked to do this for different structured questions. This procedure enables the researcher to eliminate from the analysis phase of the research any structured questions which have been misunderstood by many respondents.

7. *Interviewer Control.* The questionnaire should not only elicit information; it should facilitate control of the quality of the interviewer's work. For instance, the questionnaire should explicitly instruct the interviewer what to do whenever a specific procedure might be in question. The instruction, "Give the respondent two or three minutes to think about this question," may be necessary in certain cases, since some interviewers are more impatient than others. An instruction to "Show respondent card containing income groupings" will alleviate any confusion on exactly how the income information is to be elicited.

It is important to let the interviewer know, through the questionnaire, that his or her work will be thoroughly evaluated after it is completed. Not only should there be a section at the end of the questionnaire for the interviewer's signature and the date of the interview, but this section should be headed with a statement like, "I certify that this is a complete and honest interview, conducted in accordance with the instructions." This phrase implies the sort of commitment which helps motivate interviewers to their best effort.

Another section on validation is sometimes even more persuasive. A portion of each interviewer's work should normally be "validated" by a member of the research staff, who either telephones or writes to a portion of the interviewer's respondents (usually about 15 percent) to make certain the interview was completed, roughly how long it took, whether there were any irritants to the respondents, and whether the respondent confirms the answers to two or three questions. It is important to let the interviewer know that this type of validation will take place; and the questionnaire may end with a section which has space for the validator's comments and recommendations.

8. *Pretest.* All the interviewing experience and wisdom in the world cannot replace the pretest as a means of ensuring that all the above considerations are observed to the fullest possible extent. In a pretest, the proposed questionnaire is actually administered to a very small sample of respondents (anywhere from 10 to 100, depending on the size of the eventual sample). It is a good idea for the research team to conduct some of these interviews and for the people who will actually be administering the eventual interviews to conduct others. The research team can keep an eye on the theoretical implications of the information produced, while the actual interviewers will be more mindful of the practical problems inherent in the questionnaire. Sometimes, several pretests are necessary, with the questionnaire being revised between pretests.

SURVEY EXECUTION

There are a number of problems that may arise in carrying out a survey after all the plans have been formulated. We will concentrate on a few of the problems associated with implementing research that is based on either self-administered questionnaires or interviews.

A major problem connected with self-administered questionnaires is how to get them returned. We already know that respondents face a considerable temptation not to fill out questionnaires that are mailed to them. The suggestion has been made that something in the range of a 50 percent return rate be used as the minimum level of acceptability for survey research based on self-administered questionnaires. This level can be achieved in some situations, but rarely when data collection is based on a mail survey. However, there are things which can be done to maximize the return rate. An introductory letter should accompany the questionnaire in the mail. This letter should explain the purpose of the study and who is sponsoring the research. A good introductory letter can be an incentive for the respondent to fill out the questionnaire. Aside from this letter, the inclusion of a stamped, self-addressed envelope for the respondent to return the questionnaire in is a virtual necessity if a good return rate is to be achieved. In some cases, special incentives such as a pen or a small amount of money are also sent to the potential respondent in order to encourage cooperation. Finally, what is crucial to a good return rate is an intensive followup campaign which attempts to encourage those who have not returned their questionnaires by a certain time to fill them out and send them back.

Even if all these means for increasing the return rate of self-administered questionnaires are employed successfully, it is unlikely that more than 70 percent of the questionnaires will be returned. The question then remains just how the 30 percent who do not respond affect the research findings. Can it be safely concluded that the representativeness of the results is not jeopardized? One way of dealing with this question is to compare information about those who do respond with information derived from some other source about the total sample. For example, assume that a self-administered questionnaire is mailed out to a simple random sample of the students at Easy College and that 60 percent of the sample return their questionnaires. Information from the survey about the respondents' age, sex, and major could be compared with similar information derived from materials available on the total student body. If there were no startling differences between the survey data and the data from these other sources, it could be safely concluded that the 40 percent of the sample which did not return their questionnaires are quite similar to the 60 percent who did return them. In this case, the issue of representativeness would be favorably resolved. This is not a perfect solution, however, as one might question whether there is some other way (aside from age, sex, and major) in which the non-responding group differs from the responding group (e.g., social class background or interpersonal trust).

Even though the response rate is considerably higher for interviews, there are similar problems involved in face-to-face and telephone interviews. Some strategies for improving the response rate in interviews are the following:

1. The refusal of cooperation by potential respondents can be lessened by first training the interviewers in ways to establish rapport with respondents.
2. The temptation of interviewers to avoid certain respondents (for example, homeowners who have a "Beware of the Dog" sign in their front yards) can be diminished by emphasizing the validation procedure and requiring interviewers to account for the reasons for each noncompletion.
3. Respondents are often not home when the attempt is made to contact them via the phone or doorbell. It is therefore important that several call-backs be planned. It is best to make the call-backs at different times of the day and on different days of the week.

If these strategies are used effectively and the response rate is average or better, there is still the question of how representative the respondents are of the total group one has tried to survey. The same advice given above with respect to self-administered questionnaires applies here: compare survey information on the respondents with other information about the total group.

We realize that a crucial problem area for both face-to-face interviews and telephone interviews is the selection and training of the interviewing staff. The nature of this process depends on the organizational setup of the research effort. The researcher may elect to forego the cost and effort involved in hiring and training interviewing staff by subcontracting the interviewing to an independent research firm. If she does, the researcher has two options. One is to employ a nationally known organization such as the National Opinion Research Center. This is a common practice in national studies since these organizations have national staffs of field interviewers. The other alternative, exercised particularly in regional or local studies, is to employ the services of a local interviewing firm. This alternative is more risky because the capabilities of local organizations vary widely. But it is frequently selected as a means of shifting interviewing responsibility elsewhere without incurring the costs associated with national firms. The advisability of this approach depends almost entirely on the reputation of the local firm in question.

When interviewers are hired and trained by the researcher, there are a number of points to keep in mind. We have already mentioned that a positive point of the interviewing approach to data gathering is that the presence of the interviewer can serve as a check on the self-reports of respondents. The other side of the coin is that the presence of an interviewer may bias the answers given by respondents. We must remember that the interview situation is one of social interaction, where the respondents may be affected by the interviewer. Differences in such characteristics as race, sex, religion, and social class position between the interviewer and respondent can have an impact on the answers elicited. In general, respondents give false self-reports when they feel threatened by the interviewer or want to please the interviewer — so they give answers they think the interviewer wants to hear (Phillips, 1971). Some tips for training interviewers so that they will be less likely to elicit biased information from respondents are the following:

1. Train interviewers in how to establish rapport with respondents in order to gain their cooperation. However, be sure they understand that the rapport should not take on a "chummy" quality because this is likely to encourage "pleasing" answers.
2. A desired quality for interviewers to develop is a nonjudgmental attitude toward respondents. This quality should make respondents feel comfortable in expressing their true feelings.
3. It makes good sense to hire and train interviewers who are not radically different from the people whom they will be interviewing. For example, it would not be advisable to hire conventional middle class people to carry out interviews with respondents who are living in communes.

Aside from these guidelines, there are more general points about the training and supervision of interviewers which should be considered. For one thing, extensive training should precede the actual interviewing for the survey. A manual should be prepared for interviewers which deals with general interviewing techniques as well as with the unique requirements of the particular study in question. The questionnaire to be employed in the survey should be used by the interviewers for the purpose of conducting practice interviews with each other and with supervisory personnel. The overall interviewing approach, the probing techniques, and the method of recording information should be carefully critiqued after these trial interviews. Only after interviewers have demonstrated the ability to perform satisfactorily should they be permitted to begin the actual interviewing for the survey.

After the actual interviewing process begins, interviewers should be asked to return their first few completed interviews to the supervisory personnel for critical evaluation. At this point, some validation interviews should be conducted by telephone or in person to ensure that the interviewers are not irritating any respondents and that they are really conducting the interviews according to instructions. Such an assessment also can be helpful for the purpose of evaluating the questionnaire under actual field conditions. Independent validations of the interviews should continue throughout the time period that the interviewing is being conducted. Respondents are unlikely to be irritated by a second, "check" interview if the reason given for it is to make sure that none of the subject matter in the questionnaire proved to be embarrassing or disconcerting in any way.

DATA ANALYSIS AND REPORTING

An important first step in the preparation of data for processing is to *edit* the returned questionnaires to make sure they have been filled out properly. This is painstaking work but it can be very fruitful if erroneous information is corrected and if some spaces left blank on the questionnaire can be filled in on the basis of information from other questions. In sum, a good editing job can add substantially to the quality of the collected data.

   Coding is a crucial phase in the preparation of data for statistical analysis. It refers to the numerical categorization of responses on the questionnaire into groupings that can be keypunched for tabulation and statistical analysis. Coding is fairly straightforward for responses to structured questions. The alternative responses allowed for a structured question are simply assigned numbers ranging from one to the total number of alternative responses. For unstructured questions, the categories of response have to be determined after the data has been collected; categories are decided on the basis of an intensive examination of how the respondents have actually answered the questions. To accomplish this, the following procedure is suggested. A large number of questionnaires are selected at random by the coding supervisor. The responses to the unstructured questions on these questionnaires are reviewed to set up the categories of response. Each category is illustrated by several examples so that coders can get a proper "feel" for what kind of response should be placed within that category. This procedure should be carried out simultaneously by two or more persons who can then compare notes and synthesize their coding schemes. Once the categories have been determined and illustrated in the above manner, coding proceeds by assigning numbers to the now defined categories of response. It should be clear that the coding of unstructured questions can be problematic because the coders must interpret the answers and decide into which of the defined categories of response they fit. To minimize error, after each coder has completed the coding of a certain number of questionnaires (perhaps 50), the coding supervisor should double-check them to to make sure that all coders are using correct and similar interpretations of the responses to the unstructured questions. After that time, the supervisor should continue to spot-check questionnaires periodically throughout the duration of the coding process.

It is difficult to discuss the *data analysis* phase of a survey research project without assuming some knowledge of quantitative data analysis procedures. For this reason we will not go into detail about data analysis at this point (see Chapter 15 for a comprehensive treatment of the subject); however, a few observations on the topic are appropriate. The first step in any quantitative analysis of survey data is to compute a set of marginals describing each variable of interest; the *marginals* for a variable is a listing of each possible response for the variable (question) together with an indication of the number of respondents in each.[5] The information obtained from these marginals should then be taken into consideration in planning other phases of the statistical analysis. The marginals, for example, will indicate which categories of respondents have sufficient numbers to constitute subsamples for independent statistical analyses. Whatever data analysis plan is followed, it is important to include as many cross-checks and quality control measures as feasible. One example is a procedure for cross-checking a table by summing the totals for rows to determine if this sum is equal to the sum of the totals for the columns.

The written presentation of the results of the study should be as clear and complete as possible. The following are some questions that are useful for evaluating the quality of a survey research report of findings.

1. Could the reader replicate the report on the basis of the information provided? Are all phases of the survey research process explained in adequate detail?
2. Are all the potentially relevant data provided or are only highly selected excerpts included? Most studies call for much more in the way of preliminary statistical analysis than it would be appropriate to include in the final report. Thus some selectivity is always necessary. But we can question the nature of the selectivity when data for what seem to be superior indicators of the phenomenon of interest are not presented and no rationale for their exclusion is provided.
3. Are all the data provided supportive of the researcher's hypothesis? When there is no data to contradict the researcher's original hypothesis, we might question the selection procedure used in deciding what results to present. Also related is the tone of the report. Is it one of justifying the hypothesis or of critically evaluating it?
4. Are the study's conclusions warranted on the basis of the data that have been presented? It is not uncommon for investigators

[5] For a more detailed description of what marginals are, see pp. 406, 416–17.

to inflate the substantive significance of their data to the point that the reader of the text is led to the conclusion that the relationship is very strong when the actual statistical analysis yields a weak or at best moderate relationship. It is not wise to skip the tables in a report and rely on the author's conclusions about the content of these tables as presented in the text of the report.

5. Have the authors demonstrated a desire to put their hypotheses in jeopardy and to really dig up any contradictory evidence that may exist? Or, in contrast, do the authors seem to be interested only in presenting results that support their hypotheses?

6. Is there any discussion of the authors' values and the ways in which they may have had an influence on the outcome of the study?

SECONDARY ANALYSIS OF DATA

As more and more research is conducted, an ever-increasing amount of data becomes available to social scientists. It is often possible to obtain the data desired simply by re-analyzing data produced by someone else. This is called "secondary" analysis of data. For instance, a researcher might be interested in isolating factors which predispose people toward racial prejudice. A study might already exist in which a scale of racial prejudice was developed as one of many indicators of voting behavior. The new researcher might use the scale of racial prejudice as a dependent variable, employing numerous demographic, social, and economic factors from the same study as independent variables. In other words, simply by conducting a new analysis of the data, the researcher has obviated the need for a completely new and expensive data collection process.

Secondary analysis of data may involve survey data, as in the hypothetical case presented above. However, it may also involve information not collected by a formal survey process. For example, the famous suicide study conducted by Emile Durkheim involved a secondary analysis of approximately 26,000 suicide records, collected long before survey research was a recognized methodology.

In most cases, however, survey data are the most likely candidates for secondary analysis, largely because of their ready availability in well-organized form. Imagine having to pore through 26,000 suicide records in gathering data; the cost alone might well be more than that of a survey, although of course there would be no practitioners of suicide available for a survey.

Secondary analysis is useful in several ways. It may be the only way of obtaining data from the past, especially in view of the problems in relying on people's memories to obtain data. To ask an elderly person to recall the "mood of the thirties" might not be nearly as fruitful as to analyze people's responses to a questionnaire at that time, although the anecdotes provided by the interview of the elderly person could well provide much illuminating and complementary information.

Another utility of secondary analysis involves trend studies. If we wished to conduct a ten-year study of trends in racist or sexist attitudes, we could initiate a study and continue it for ten years; or we might utilize secondary analysis for the entire study; or we might utilize several years of secondary data and extend the same study format a few years into the future. In other words, the availability of secondary data means that trend studies need not always use the present as the initial time period.

Sometimes, before embarking on costly research, investigators may do some secondary analysis to assess the potential fruitfulness of their objectives or of specific questioning techniques. Even though the data from an earlier study may be out of date, the investigator can appraise the potential usefulness of comparable contemporary information. Thus, secondary analysis can provide a nice lead-in to "primary" research.

As with all research techniques, there are potential problems inherent in secondary analysis. As already indicated, the results may be out of date. Views on sexual mores collected in the early 1960s, for example, would not be at all representative of attitudes prevailing in the mid-1970s.

Secondly, depending on how well documented the earlier research is, contemporary investigators may not know enough about how the study was conducted to assure themselves that the data are sufficiently reliable and valid for their purposes. For example, there may be inadequate documentation of the sampling procedures used.

Another problem is that the contemporary researcher is at the mercy of the earlier researcher in terms of what questioning devices were employed to collect the data. Were the indicators of social class adequate, in view of the current methods of evaluating social class? Were the earlier questions worded so that they do not quite reflect the contemporary researchers' hypotheses? If not, will researchers be tempted to compromise the hypotheses slightly to obtain the advantage of data availability?

There are many ways in which secondary data may be utilized. A single survey may be reanalyzed. Several different surveys may be pooled and treated as one survey. (Problems of different time periods may occur here.) Several different surveys may be compared with one another and treated as replications of one another. Several different indicators (e.g., several different questions on racial prejudice) may be compared from within a single survey. Other research designs for secondary analysis are described in Hyman (1972).

As indicated previously, there are numerous sources of data collected by surveys and available for secondary analysis. These sources are often called "data banks." Hyman's publication contains an extensive listing of many such sources, a few of which are:

> Louis Harris Political Data Center, University of North Carolina, Chapel Hill, North Carolina (sample surveys conducted by the well-known Harris agency)
>
> National Opinion Research Center, University of Chicago, Chicago, Illinois (a general collection of N.O.R.C. studies)
>
> Roper Public Opinion Research Center, Williams College, Williamstown, Mass. (a large collection of sample surveys from all over the world)

Usually, the data are available on punched cards or magnetic computer tape. The *bugs* (errors) are supposed to have been *cleaned* (removed) from this data, but we often find that this is not the case. Sometimes there are punches for a variable that do not correspond to any known category given in the code book.

In general, secondary analysis of data can represent a viable alternative to primary survey research as long as the researcher is assured that the earlier data are still relevant and that the earlier methodology was sufficient to produce highly reliable and valid data.

CONCLUSION

Survey research is a procedure for systematically and comprehensively collecting information about the attitudes, beliefs, and behavior of people. It does so through interviewing and administering questionnaires to relatively large and representative samples of the population of interest. In the present chapter we have reviewed seven critical aspects of the survey research process: (1) research question formulation, (2) survey design, (3) sampling plans, (4) data-gathering technique, (5) questionnaire construction, (6) survey execution, and (7) data analysis and reporting.

Survey research is the most frequently used data collection method in sociological research. Most topics of relevance to social researchers have been approached using the survey method. This flexibility is one of the major strengths of the method. Another major strength is its ability to generalize from a relatively small sample to a much larger population of interest.

Survey research also has its limitations, as does every research method. It is not the panacea for every research question or issue. Perhaps the greatest weakness of the method is its dependence on the memory and honesty of respondents. All the data-gathering techniques for survey research require the self-reports of people regarding their attitudes, beliefs, and behavior. Deliberate deception on the part of respondents is only one potential threat to the validity of survey research results.

In addition to deliberate deception, there are a variety of other threats to the validity of survey research data. Many respondents will seek to give socially desirable answers or will at least temper their views in light of their beliefs about what the interviewer wants to hear. There will be some respondents who get into *response sets;* that is, they will answer a whole series of questions using the same category quite independent of the actual content of the question. There will also be respondents who give irrelevant answers because they do not understand certain words used in asking the question or they understand the word in a way quite different from that intended by the researcher. Finally there is the problem of dishonest interviewers. Some will attempt to cut short the interview by asking only a few questions and then filling in the others themselves. Others will fabricate the entire interview. While any well-designed study will build in measures to catch such sources of error, it is not possible to entirely eliminate the possibility that such corner-cutting will occur.

In this chapter we have reviewed a number of the limitations of the survey research approach. In our chapters on other data collection approaches, particularly intensive interviewing (Chapter 7) and participant observation (Chapter 8), further consideration is given to the limitations of survey research with which each of these methods attempts to deal. Since survey research is presently the most widely used data collection method (at least among sociologists), other competing methods are often presented as dealing with certain of the limitations of the survey research approach. While it is true that these competing methodologies can deal with some of the limitations, it is often at the cost of giving up other positive characteristics of the method, such as the generalizability of results.

EXERCISES

1. Design a brief questionnaire that might be used in a study of the type conducted by G. F. White (see "Suggested Readings Showing Use of the Method.") What sources of bias do you think are inherent in this kind of study? If the occupations of the criminals and victims are reversed in half the cases and the sample is thus split into two halves for analysis, how do you know that the two halves are similar in terms of socioeconomic characteristics? How can you ensure this similarity in conducting the study?

2. Design a very brief questionnaire asking what people consider the main problems facing the leaders of the United States. Have another student design a similar questionnaire. One questionnaire should ask the question without suggesting any answers; the other should contain a list of possible answers

which will be shown to the respondents. Administer the two questionnaires to ten classmates apiece. Compare the answers received. What implications are there for questionnaire design? Which question format is preferable and why? In what situations might the other format be better?

3. One concern of *The People's Choice* by Lazarsfeld, Berelson, and Gaudet was to determine why people vote the way they do. Consider an upcoming election or one that has recently taken place. Conduct a modest survey to attempt to find out the reasons that people intend to vote for (or actually voted for) the candidate of their choice.

4. Two students should work on this question together. Work up a brief list of questions on a topic area of interest to both of you. Each of you should select five people to interview by means of these questions. One will conduct face-to-face interviews while the other will carry out telephone interviews. Which will use which data collection technique should be determined by the flip of a coin. After the interviews are completed, compare notes on your interviewing experiences.

5. Think of a topic area about which you want to find out information through a questionnaire. Construct three structured and three unstructured questions for the topic area. Ask another student in the class to respond to these questions. Also, ask the student to offer constructive criticism on how adequate the questions are.

6. Think of survey research situations where it would be most appropriate to use each of the following data collection techniques: a self-administered questionnaire, a face-to-face interview, and a telephone interview. Compare your answers with others in class.

7. Conceptualize a research question that asks whether or not there is a relationship between two or more variables. Show how you would approach the question by both a static and a dynamic survey design. Compare the merits of both approaches.

8. Choose a topic of special interest to you. Compare how you would carry out research on the topic by a survey and another method. What ethical problems might occur in each instance? Does the survey method appear to have more or fewer ethical problems than the other method?

9. Suppose you wish to obtain data on the ethnic backgrounds of wealthy persons. You must represent the entire United States with your research. How will you go about the study if:

a. you have an extremely limited budget?

b. you have an unlimited budget?

Discuss the problems that may be caused by budgetary limitations, as pertaining to the data collected.

10. Considering the substantial costs attached to survey research, why is it the most widely used social science methodology? In your answer, consider factors such as acceptability of results, availability of preexisting data, convenience to the researcher, reliability and validity, and statistical measurement.

SUGGESTED READINGS

Readings about the Method

Babbie, Earl
1973   *Survey Research Methods.* Belmont, California: Wadsworth.

> This book gives an excellent treatment of all aspects of survey research design and analysis. It begins with a short history of survey research and then delves into a coverage of different survey designs. The topics of sampling, questionnaire construction, interviewing, and data processing are then handled in a very satisfactory manner. The analysis section of the book covers measurement, table construction, the use of statistics, and complex forms of data analysis such as path analysis and factor analysis. The book is highly readable and yet quite sophisticated. Good examples are provided throughout the text.

Backstrom, Charles, and Gerald Hursh
1963   *Survey Research.* Evanston: Northwestern University Press.

> A good description of various phases of survey research. The heaviest concentration is on questionnaire construction and sampling. In addition to a detailed discussion of survey research, a series of useful checklists for the actual execution of survey research is presented. These checklists are very practical and helpful for the student. An example is the checklist for the process of drawing a sample. This includes nineteen separate things for the researcher to consider when sampling is done. There are fourteen similar checklists for other phases of survey research.

Hyman, Herbert
1972   *Secondary Analysis of Sample Surveys: Principles, Procedures and Potentialities.* New York: John Wiley.

> Advantages and pitfalls of secondary analysis are discussed in depth. Various approaches to this technique are examined in relation to the underlying theoretical perspectives. Numerous case studies and examples of empirical work are employed to illustrate various categories of secondary analysis. The author identifies problems in the analysis of secondary data and suggests means of alleviating them. Also included are references to many collections of secondary data (sometimes referred to as archives or data banks). An original survey among users of secondary analysis provides many insights into practical application of the method.

Phillips, Derek
1971   *Knowledge from What?* Chicago: Rand McNally.

> This is a critical appraisal of the empirical methods used in sociological research. By means of analysis of numerous studies (involving other

methodologies as well as survey research), Phillips discusses potential sources of invalidity and bias. An extensive section on interviewing cites studies indicating that characteristics such as the interviewer's race, sex, religion, and social status may affect respondents' answers. Phillips suggests means by which interviewers may be included as one factor in the research design in order to facilitate better control of the "interviewer effect" on respondents' replies.

Selltiz, Claire, et al.
1959   *Research Methods in Social Relations.* New York: Holt, Rinehart & Winston.

The conceptual and methodological aspects of social research are discussed, with emphasis on survey research. The book contains extensive sections on causal analysis, problems in measurement, questionnaire design, scaling techniques, analysis and interpretation, and the research report. The appendix contains suggestions for estimating time and personnel requirements for a study, as well as an introduction to sampling and an illustrated guide to questionnaire construction. For the most part, the text deals with generalized concepts rather than practical examples.

Readings Illustrating the Method

Blau, Peter M., and Otis Dudley Duncan
1967   *The American Occupational Structure.* New York: John Wiley.

This study of the American occupational structure involves analysis of secondary data. Rather than conducting original interviews, the researchers utilize preexisting data from the U.S. Census. Data on more than 20,000 American males aged 20–64 are examined to isolate trends and phenomena in American occupations. The volume contains an excellent discussion of quality of the data, notably bias due to "no answers." The authors discuss the questionable usefulness of statistical significance tests in surveys utilizing very large samples, in which virtually every minute difference appears to be significant.

Campbell, Angus
1975   "The American way of mating: marriage si, children only maybe." *Psychology Today* 8 (May):37–43.

This article is based on the findings of a survey of over two thousand U.S. adults. A number of interesting questions are explored. Are married couples happier than single people? Does the presence of children lessen the happiness of married couples? What happens to the level of happiness for a married couple when their children grow up and leave home? Do men need relationships with women more than women need relationships with men?

Coleman, James S., et al.
1966   *Equality of Educational Opportunity.* Washington, D.C.: U.S. Department of Health, Education and Welfare, Office of Education.

This is an epic study dealing with segregation in public schools and its implications. Massive numbers of teachers and students provided information about themselves. The fact that the questionnaires were controlled or administered by the teachers themselves rather than by trained professional interviewers may represent a methodological problem. Supplementary studies investigated black college students and school enrollments based on 1960 U.S. Census figures. Several case studies were also employed. This study is an excellent example of what happens when several methodologies and sources of data are included in one study.

Lazarsfeld, Paul; Bernard Berelson; and Hazel Gaudet
1944   *The People's Choice.* New York: Columbia University Press.

This is a classic example of the survey design referred to as the panel study. A panel consisting of six hundred residents from Erie County, Ohio was interviewed several times between May and November of 1940. Of central interest was how the panel members intended to vote in the presidential election of 1940. Special attention is devoted to how panel members who experienced "cross-pressures" (conflicting voting tendencies) eventually decided to vote.

Pettigrew, Thomas; Robert Riley; and Reeve Vanneman
1972   "George Wallace's constituents." *Psychology Today* 5 (February):47–92.

Through survey research the attempt is made to explain the source of George Wallace's political support. One of the major contributing factors to such support is discovered to be relative economic deprivation. In particular, bluecollar respondents who feel deprived because their economic gains are less than those of whitecollar workers have a marked tendency to back Wallace. Status inconsistency is also considered a possible motivating force for those of this political persuasion.

Reed, John S.
1972   *The Enduring South.* Lexington, Mass.: Lexington Books.

Reed employs secondary analysis in a study of the Southern United States. His objective is to determine whether, as the South and other parts of the country become more similar demographically and economically, they are also becoming less distinguishable culturally. He utilizes survey data, but it is data from public opinion polls conducted by someone else. Surveys covering three decades are involved in the study. Reed discusses the advantages and limitations of secondary analysis and the related effects on the study.

Stouffer, Samuel
1966   *Communism, Conformity, and Civil Liberties.* New York: John Wiley.

This work constitutes another classic example of research conducted via the survey method. It is based on a 1954 survey that examines the opinions of Americans concerning internal and external threats of communism. The attitudes of people are also explored concerning what civil liberties might have to be sacrificed in order to develop controls over communism. The survey consists of interviews conducted with a national cross-section of the population and a selected sample of community leaders throughout the country.

White, Garland F.
1975   "Public responses to hypothetical crimes: effect of offender and victim status and seriousness of the offense on punitive reactions." *Social Forces* 53 (March):411–419.

A door-to-door personal interview survey in a large Midwestern city is the source of data for this study. The objective of the research is to determine how occupational status of criminals and seriousness of their crimes affect people's conceptions of "fair punishment." The rigidly structured sample of 523 persons was exposed to each of several hypothetical crime episodes, which mentioned the criminals' and victims' occupations as well as the nature of the crime. In roughly half the cases, the occupations of the criminal and victim were reversed. Respondents were asked how severe the punishment should be. The seriousness of the crimes described in the episodes varied substantially. Thus the researcher was able to compare the suggested punishments for various degrees of crime severity and for differing occupations of the criminal for the same crime.

Williamson, John B.
1974   "The stigma of public dependency: a comparison of alternative forms of public aid to the poor." *Social Problems* 22 (December):213–228.

Williamson's study of 230 women in the Boston Metropolitan Area appraises the stigma attached by the public to thirteen possible programs or proposals for aiding the poor. Door-to-door personal interviews were conducted in which each of the thirteen alternatives was described briefly; a scaling technique was employed to elicit a measure of stigma. The scaling device is of particular interest, as is the translation of results into policy implications.

Wingrove, C. R., and Jon P. Alston
1974   "Cohort analysis of church attendance, 1939–69." *Social Forces* 53 (December):324–331.

Secondary analysis of preexisting survey data obtained by the American Institute of Public Opinion (the Gallup Poll) six times from 1939 to

1969 forms the basis of this study. Various "age cohorts" (or groupings) were analyzed to determine whether church attendance varies significantly by age. The study illustrates the use of cohort analysis and secondary analysis.

REFERENCES

Hyman, Herbert
1972   *Secondary Analysis of Sample Surveys: Principles, Procedures and Potentialities.* New York: John Wiley.

Lazarsfeld, Paul; Bernard Berelson; and Hazel Gaudet
1944   *The People's Choice.* New York: Columbia University Press.

Miller, Delbert
1970   *Handbook of Research Design and Social Measurement.* New York: David McKay.

Phillips, Derek
1971   *Knowledge from What?* Chicago: Rand McNally.

Selltiz, Claire, et al.
1959   *Research Methods in Social Relations.* New York: Holt, Rinehart & Winston.

Stouffer, Samuel
1966   *Communism, Conformity, and Civil Liberties.* New York: John Wiley.

Survey Research Center
1972   *A Panel Study of Income Dynamics.* Ann Arbor, Mich.: Institute for Social Research.

Intensive Interviewing

CHAPTER SEVEN

Let us suppose we are studying the processes by which individuals seek acceptance into so-called "deviant" groups. Let's say we have decided to investigate occupations generally regarded as deviant and wish to begin by studying male go-go dancers. What method of data collection shall we employ?

We know relatively little about male go-go dancers, except that they are widely considered a deviant occupational segment. Will they agree to be interviewed? If so, will they be evasive or deliberately misleading in their responses? In what setting should they be interviewed? What types of questions should we ask?

We quickly dismiss the possibility of sending a task force armed with questionnaires to interview a random sample of male go-go dancers. The logistical problems alone could prove overwhelming; imagine arranging for a number of interviewers to obtain access to this group of people. Of even greater consequence could be the difficulty of anticipating what the most productive lines of questioning will be. The very fact of engaging in an unusual occupation may mean that the respondents will prove unpredictable and will vary greatly in their reactions to specific questions; so how do we devise a standard set of questions that will be productive in each interview and will be easy for "hired-hand" interviewers to administer?

Is there a data-gathering method other than traditional survey research which might better meet our needs? We know that participant observation has been useful in studying some deviant groups (see Chapters 1 and 8). However, no one on our research team has the inclination to become a participant in the male go-go dancer occupation. Observation alone would seem of minimal value. We suspect that, when not on stage, male go-go dancers do not congregate in places where they can be observed unobtrusively. We feel so poorly informed about this occupation and its practitioners that we might misinterpret at least some of the actions we would observe. It becomes apparent that information will have to be obtained directly from the go-go dancers themselves.

Some sort of direct interview seems a necessity, but the traditional form of survey research interviewing will not suffice. Faced with a similar dilemma in their study of stripteasers, Skipper and McCaghy (1972) settled on a method of data collection that is called *intensive interviewing,* or *depth interviewing.* They personally interviewed a number of strippers individually, but the interviews were conducted differently from the way most survey research interviews are done.

The researchers prepared a list of questions which they thought might be useful. However, the use of each specific question was guided by the progress of the interview. If a respondent proved especially responsive to a particular question, the topic was *probed extensively* via supplementary questions (some prepared in advance, others devised on the spot). Questions evoking minimal response were sometimes *restated* in different words, and, if they still bore little fruit, were usually discarded until the next interview. In short, these interviews were *customized* to each individual respondent and interviewing situation, as the researchers took their cues from interviewees in determining what interviewing directions to pursue at any given juncture.

The interviews were *lengthy,* involving more than one meeting in some cases. In fact the researchers interviewed some strippers in more than one setting, as they found certain environments (notably backstage) to be distracting and disruptive to the interviews.

These interviews were even more dependent than most face-to-face interviews on the rapport, mutuality of trust, and sense of reciprocity which developed between researchers and respondents during their transition from strangers to confidants of sorts. The quality of the *incipient relationship* (or emerging relationship) between interviewer and interviewee is the cornerstone of the intensive interviewing method.

The preparation of the interviewers was also intensive. They attempted to gird themselves for any contingency by compiling a list of alternative reactions to possible developments during the interviews. The objective was to encourage spontaneity in stripteasers' comments while minimizing the possibility that the interviewers would be so surprised by a remark or turn of events that they would retard the interview's momentum.

The intensive interviewing technique offers an opportunity to probe extensively for "sensitive" information from potentially evasive persons, tailoring each interview so the interviewee feels as comfortable as possible in the interviewing situation and will be encouraged to provide candid self-reports. The format is usually flexible, with the types and order of questions, the setting, and even the manner of the interviewer being governed not only by the study objectives and the cumulative information flow, but also by a continuing assessment of what it will take to make the interviewee maximally responsive. While some standardized questions may be asked of every respondent, the interviewer takes account of each respondent's individuality in deciding what to ask, as well as when and how to ask it.

Most intensive interviews are apt to last a long while, with three hours not uncommon. This length of time provides an opportunity for the good intensive interviewer to nurture the incipient relationship with the respondent, enhancing the development of a conversational, give-and-take relationship and, hopefully, the likelihood of frank revelations. Obviously, this form of interviewing places a premium on the interviewer's ability to make quick judgments concerning what to say or do next at any given point in the interview. This factor, more than anything else, is probably what makes the greatest difference in the ultimate productivity of the interview.

APPLICATIONS OF INTENSIVE INTERVIEWING

The use of intensive interviewing to obtain information from strip-teasers is just one example of how this method may be employed in studies of deviance. Becker (1955) conducted intensive interviews with marihuana users, eliciting information on their experience with and attitudes toward the drug. Lindesmith (1947) interviewed opiate addicts intensively, seeking to identify the processes involved in becoming addicted, remaining addicted, and breaking the "habit."

Denzin (1970:103) and Spitzer conducted a study among mental patients, examining changes in patient attitudes as they moved in and out of hospitals. Although they employed a highly structured questionnaire in the interviews, the researchers allowed sufficient flexibility in questioning techniques to result in the following phenomenon when one question was simply asked twice (Denzin, 1970:129): "One respondent, when asked if she 'would be against a daughter of hers marrying a man who had been to see a psychiatrist about a mental problem,' answered, 'I know I shouldn't say this but I don't want any daughter of mine marrying a man who has been through what I have been.' Notwithstanding this, when the question was repeated, the woman replied, 'No, I guess I wouldn't be against this!'" The persistence of the interviewing technique revealed what appeared to be the difference between a hasty judgment and a more considered opinion.

There is ample evidence that the field of deviance represents only one of many possible applications for intensive interviewing. When Zuckerman (1972) was faced with the requirement of obtaining information on a highly prestigious elite — Nobel laureates in science — she chose intensive interviewing as her data-gathering method and wound up interviewing 41 of the 55 laureates who lived in the United States at that time. Lipset, et al. (1956) utilized four methods — participant observation, intensive interviewing, examination of records and documents, and survey research — in studying the organization and internal politics of a trade union. Holmstrom (1972) engaged respondents in "flexible" or "free-style" interviews in her study of the two-career family; later she collaborated with Burgess (Burgess and Holmstrom, 1974) in applying the same type of interviews to the study of rape victims. In the latter study, which was aimed at the clinical objective of developing a strategy for counseling rape victims, the interviews were designed to be both therapeutic to the victim and informative for the interviewer. Kubler-Ross (1969) produced a veritable wealth of data from perhaps the most difficult group to interview — dying people — via intensive interviews in her study on death and dying.

The study by Lipset, et al. (1956) concerning the politics of a labor union is an excellent example of how intensive interviewing can make an important contribution when several other data-gathering methods are also employed in the same study. One of the researchers in that study, Martin Trow, indicates that the review of documents and voting records, survey research, and participant observation were all useful in dealing with various objectives in the research. However, he points up the importance of intensive interviewing in evaluating the amount of legitimacy imputed to the party system by various groups and social categories within the union (Trow, 1957:34):

> The workings of the party system inhibited direct expressions of hostility to the system. In the ordinary give and take of conversation in the shop, party meeting, club meeting, informal gatherings after hours, such expressions were not likely to be expressed; they violated strongly held norms, and called down various kinds of punishments. It was only when we interviewed leaders individually and intensively that we could get some sense of the reservations that they held about the party system, how widely and strongly those reservations were held, and thus could make some assessment of those sentiments as a potentially disruptive force in the party system.

In short, intensive interviewing has applicability to a wide variety of social research investigations. Whether it is employed as the sole data-gathering technique or in combination with other methods depends on a number of considerations to be discussed later. For the moment, let us turn from the applied aspects to the more theoretical implications of this methodological tool.

THEORETICAL UNDERPINNINGS

Interviews involve direct interaction between two parties — the interviewer (or enumerator) seeking information from the interviewee (or respondent). As in any interaction, the ultimate value of the interview depends on a number of considerations, among which are:

1. *Commitment:* the intensity of interest among both parties in making the interaction mutually beneficial.
2. *Meaning:* the ability of each party to understand the true intent of the other's actions and statements.
3. *Fluidity:* the extent to which the course or content of the interaction may be adapted to meet the needs of either party.
4. *Assimilation:* the ways in which the two parties digest and interpret the content of the interaction.

Intensive interviews may be contrasted with highly structured interviews using these four criteria. By "highly structured," we refer to interviews utilizing a questionnaire with precisely worded questions appearing in a certain sequence and administered by an interviewer who has no authority to change or amend either the wording or the order of these questions. Most survey research studies employ structured questionnaires.

Commitment

Throughout any interaction, each party consciously or subconsciously makes a series of decisions concerning the presentation of self to the other. Each is constantly determining how much to reveal and what impression to make. The benefits each party feels as the interaction progresses will govern the extent and nature of continual personal *commitment* to the interaction. Theoretically, as the interaction continues, the relationship supplies sufficient rewards for each party so that it can continue; if it fails to provide these rewards, it will be terminated either mutually or unilaterally. The burgeoning rapport between the two parties may be one source of satisfaction. Receipt of valued information may be another. Gratification at being the object of another's interest may be yet another perceived reward, and undoubtedly there are many additional possibilities.

Most interviews, no matter what type, are forced interactions on the part of at least one participant. The initial contact between interviewer and interviewee is usually an arbitrary meeting of two strangers. A key difference between structured interviews and intensive interviews is that, in the former, the relationship is not likely to progress far beyond its initial abruptness, arbitrariness, and remoteness. Intensive interviews, on the other hand, are normally conducted in ways that encourage and nurture the development of the *incipient relationship* mentioned earlier. In other words, the interviewer is relatively free to guide the emerging relationship into directions which offer the best chance for mutual reward.

If a respondent is not conversant with or is irritated by the first few questions in a structured interview, the interviewer is not allowed to revise or skip the remaining questions in that section; consequently, the respondent may terminate the interview early or may give superficial answers. An intensive interviewer, sensing a lack of respondent effort, has the freedom to try another approach to obtaining the same information or to switch to a different topic. In other words, the format of the intensive interview is sufficiently flexible to offer a variety of avenues for sparking and maintaining respondent commitment.

We are not referring simply to obtaining participation. This is not usually a severe problem, and cash payments are useful incentives in difficult cases. It is the *quality* of participation that is crucial — the motivation and ability of respondents to provide introspective and candid responses to the best of their ability.

An intensive interviewer may frequently *praise* the effort of the respondent, contributing to the latter's self-esteem. Interviewers may reveal facts about themselves, facts that will not influence the respondent's opinions but will position the interaction as one of information exchange rather than a one-way flow. Reinforcement of self-worth and a sense of reciprocity are but two of several techniques for gaining maximum respondent commitment to the interview.

Meaning

Even if interviewees are highly motivated to provide extensive and accurate responses, their ability to do so is at least partly dependent on their interpretation of the questions. Will a given question mean to the respondent exactly what it meant to the person who prepared the question? This problem increases as the level of abstraction in the question becomes greater. For example, if a question refers to "success in life," will a given respondent interpret "success" as being measured by level of affluence, or esteem from one's peers, or occupational status, or some other indicator? To provide a detailed definition of "success" for respondents' edification might be helpful, but a questionnaire filled with definitions usually proves boring and fatiguing to interviewees.

A related consideration is whether respondents' answers mean to researchers what the respondents intended. Most structured interviews include a few "open-ended" questions which ask respondents to answer in their own words (e.g., "What do you think are the most important problems facing the president of the United States?"). The people who analyze the answers to these questions are generally not the ones who conducted the interviews. Considering the various possible meanings or nuances of each comment, how likely are these analysts to interpret correctly the intended meanings of people they have never met?

Becker and Geer (1957:29) recount a situation in their study of medical students when a student used the word "crock" to describe a patient. The student explained that the term referred to any patient with psychosomatic complaints. Only after observing medical students for some time and hearing the word used frequently did Becker and Geer realize that "crock" meant a patient in whom the students had invested substantial diagnostic time without finding a real malady. It was the perception of "wasted" time, rather than simply the patients' fantasies, which precipitated use of the derogatory term. If the researchers had accepted the initial definition reported by the medical student, they would have overlooked a factor that eventually proved important in the direction of the study. This example, although drawn from an observational study, illustrates the pitfalls of interpreting interviewees' comments on face value alone.

Structured questionnaires are usually pretested on several respondents to determine what kinds of response they produce, which questions are unclear, and how long they take to administer. Unfortunately, since many of the questions have multiple-choice answer categories, which allow even the most confused interviewee to take a guess, it is sometimes difficult to ascertain confidently that the intended meanings of questions are clearly understood by respondents. Regardless of the steps taken to safeguard against it, the possibility of misinterpreted meaning is greater when there is no direct interchange between respondents and the persons who will analyze their responses. There is no opportunity on either side to ask, "Could you explain that a little more?" or to indulge in any of the little clarification mechanisms that pervade most conversations.

Intensive interviewing emphasizes the direct interchange between a respondent and an interviewer (often the director of the study) who is actually conducting an analysis during the course of the interview and is sensitive to when and how to ask for clarification. Either respondent or interviewer may ask the other to restate something or to expand on it. The following hypothetical exchange would not be unusual:

INTERVIEWER: Do you consider this community a good place in which
              to live?

RESPONDENT: Do you mean generally or for me in particular?

INTERVIEWER: Well why don't you discuss it generally at first and then
              for you in particular.

RESPONDENT: Generally speaking, it's a dump. It used to be nice but
              then it started going downhill.

INTERVIEWER: What do you mean by "downhill?"

RESPONDENT: Well, it started with parlors. And then we have lots of drug pushers in town. They hooked our kids on dope.

INTERVIEWER: Parlors?

RESPONDENT: Betting parlors. Bookie joints. Aren't you from around here?

INTERVIEWER: No, but I'm enjoying getting the inside story from you.

RESPONDENT: Well these are places where you can go make a bet, like on the horses. They're illegal, and they operate in the backs of stores. Everyone has been in there at one time or another. I've been in there. The police know about them, but they look the other way. I think it's the money from the parlors that financed the dope peddlers in the first place.

This brief example illustrates how both interviewee and interviewer obtained clarifications — the former asking for a more precise definition of the initial question, and the latter eliciting amplification for "downhill" and "parlors." In a structured interview, much of the information yielded by the respondent might never have surfaced. In fact, a simple "yes" or "no" answer would have sufficed for the first question.

While each respondent in an intensive interview study is likely to be asked a variety of questions tailored to his or her own unique knowledge or experience, there may be some questions that must be asked of all respondents. In these instances, the emphasis is on *equivalence of meaning*. The objective is for a question to have the same *meaning* to each interviewee, even though it may have to be phrased differently from interview to interview to achieve this goal.

Suppose we were interested in the following question:

> If some people in your community suggested that a book written by a socialist and advocating socialist policies be taken out of your public library, would you favor removing the book, or not?

For some respondents we might be able to ask the question in its present form, but for others it would not be safe to assume that they understood what we meant by such terms as "socialist" and "socialist policies." In view of this impediment, the intensive interviewer posing the question would not hesitate to reword the question as follows:

> Suppose a person who favored government ownership of all the railroads and all major industries such as the steel industry, the auto industry, and so on had written a book which was in your public library advocating government ownership of the railroads and major industries. If some people in your community suggested that the library get rid of the book, would you agree that it would be a good idea to make the library get rid of the book, or wouldn't you agree?

This revision might seem overly simplified, redundant, and even patron-izing to some respondents; but it would be used only in those cases where it promised to communicate an equivalent meaning to the original question, and to do it more easily than the original question itself.

In any conversational interaction, the meaning of what participants say to one another is not always readily apparent. We have seen that intensive interviews afford participants the same opportunity to obtain immediate clarification and definitions as would be available to people in normal discourse. A key reason for this characteristic of intensive inter-views is their relatively flexible or fluid format.

Fluidity

In any conversation, the participants are not usually aware of exactly what direction the interchange will take until they are in the midst of the interchange. They have certain objectives to pursue, but the way they do it hinges on the flow of the conversation. Depending on what they discover during the exchange, they may revise their objectives and strike out in new directions. In a sense, conversation is like a chess game, where a given move depends on what the other player has just done.

Intensive interviewing attempts to incorporate the same sort of flexibility. We have already described how the researchers who studied stripteasers prepared a list of questions but also were equipped with a number of alternative questions for use in various contingencies. They could not foresee all possible eventualities, but they did the best possible preparation job. Most important, they were not restricted by either the wording or the sequence of the initial list of questions.

The flexible format of intensive interviews is important for a num-ber of reasons. First, the interviewer has the opportunity to *probe imme-diately* for additional information whenever the interviewee mentions anything of particular interest. For example, in our hypothetical example involving comments about betting parlors, the intensive interviewer would probably want to probe extensively the respondent's personal experience with these parlors, which the respondent inadvertently mentioned in de-scribing what they were. Since the interviewee herself made this revela-tion, the interviewer almost has an implicit license to pursue the subject. The respondent might consider such a line of questioning to be an invasion of privacy if she hadn't brought it up herself. She has now taken the interviewer into her confidence, and it is a perfectly natural thing for the interviewer to want to know more.

Thus, the flexibility of intensive interviewing facilitates the devel-opment of the incipient relationship between interviewer and inter-viewee, by allowing the former to follow up immediately on spontaneous comments by the latter. This display of interest helps to solidify the relationship as well as to gain valuable information.

In some intensive interviews, the respondent will spontaneously bring up a topic which the interviewer intended to discuss later. The good interviewer will immediately *switch topics,* to capitalize on the momentum provided by the interviewee. Once again, this tactic reaffirms the interviewer's interest in the respondent's concerns.

Intensive interviews may be useful in probing *sensitive subject matter.* If an initial question does not prove productive, the topic can be approached in a different way later in the interview. For example, suppose family relationships are being studied, and the intensive interviewer asks about problems existing in the interpersonal relations within the respondent's family. The respondent says, "I don't want to talk about that." The interviewer, sensing there may be some very real problem, waits until later in the interview, when the rapport between herself and the respondent has become stronger. Then she asks about problems that are prevalent in contemporary families in general. In such instances, it is not uncommon for the interviewee to answer in detail which no second-hand knowledge could generate; the implication is that the respondent is really talking about her own family.

It should be noted that intensive interviews are not a flawless way for delving into sensitive subject matter. Only the most highly trained and perceptive interviewers can successfully examine highly personal topics with a respondent. In addition, on some sensitive issues a form of research that allows the respondent a considerable degree of anonymity (e.g., a mail questionnaire) will elicit more revelations than an intensive interview with even a highly skilled interviewer.

We have seen that the intensive interview offers researchers many options, in terms of what to say as well as when and how to say it. Most important, these options make it possible for the interview to reflect the sort of continuity and momentum characteristic of a productive conversation — a fluidity of exchange seldom possible in structured interviews.

The notions of commitment, meaning, and fluidity have been suggested as representing important similarities between the data collection method known as intensive interviewing and normal discourse — similarities that may make this the preferred methodology in many research situations. However, one of the most distinctive attributes of the method involves the ways in which it may be organized and used in the researcher's analysis.

Assimilation

Since the intensive interviewer is usually either the director of the research project or a highly trained, well-informed coworker, he or she has the opportunity to assimilate or digest the results of one interview before undertaking another. This is a twofold benefit. First, the interviewer does not have to formulate arbitrary answer categories prior to the interviewing and adhere dogmatically to them throughout the process. Each succeeding interview may help *refine the answer categories* until they represent the best possible way of describing the data produced by respondents.

The question, "Should possession of marihuana be legalized?" might evoke an affirmative response from interviewee number one and a negative answer from number two. However, number three might offer a qualifying comment, such as "Only for people under age 30." The intensive interviewer would then recognize the question as not simply a dichotomous one and would incorporate a "qualified" category into the analysis. A corresponding structured interview (pretests notwithstanding) might have forced responses into either the "yes" or "no" directions. By establishing answer categories as the interviewing progresses, the researcher better describes the full range of respondent opinion.

The sequential nature of intensive interviewing has another key advantage. Data from structured questionnaires are not usually analyzed until all questionnaires have been collected and tabulated. Consequently, methods such as intensive interviewing and participant observation, which involve sequential assimilation of data by a researcher over time, have the advantage of facilitating the process of inference known as *analytic induction*. The following steps briefly summarize what is referred to as the process of analytic induction:

1. We formulate a rough definition of the phenomenon we want to explain.
2. We formulate a preliminary explanation of that phenomenon.
3. At this point we examine only *one* case in light of our proposed explanation. We try to determine whether the facts of that one case can be accounted for by our preliminary explanation.
4. If the explanation fits the facts of that one case, we turn to other cases to see if the explanation still fits. If the explanation does not fit the one case, we have two options. Either we can reformulate the original theoretical explanation or we can redefine the phenomenon which we wish to explain.
5. We keep examining a number of cases in sequence, reformulating our theory each time that a new case cannot be explained by the existing theory.
6. This process of examining cases, redefining phenomena, and reformulating hypotheses and explanations continues until we are satisfied that we have formulated an explanation that will not be abrogated by additional data.

The strategy of the researcher using analytic induction is to systematically look for negative cases, to seek out cases that cannot be explained by the present theoretical model. This search for negative cases is thoroughly consistent with the argument made in Chapter 1 that science proceeds by attempting to disprove theories. Intensive interviewing lends itself nicely to this analytical technique. With each new interview, the researcher is able to challenge previous hypotheses and to try new ones. The more challenges a hypothesis successfully meets, the more credibility it has.

Suppose we were doing a study of attitudes toward gay rights among the students at Easy College. Suppose the question, "Do you think there should be laws against marriages between members of the same sex?" elicited negative responses from the first six students interviewed. We suspect that some people are giving what they think is the most socially acceptable reply. Consequently, we revise the question to make the less acceptable answer more palatable: "Many people suggest that there are good reasons for maintaining laws against marriage between members of the same sex. Would you agree with these people?" If responses continue to be negative, we may impute more credibility to the hypothesis that students at Easy College are relatively free of prejudice against homosexuals on this issue; or we may wish to continue making it easier and easier to give the socially unpopular answer so that we can determine at what point (if ever) respondents do embrace that sentiment.

Intensive interviewing has important contributions to make to the analytical process, both in terms of how the data are organized to be maximally representative of responses and how they are analyzed. This is not unlike the process we all use in living our daily lives. We tend to categorize facts and perceptions in ways our experience tells us will be most functional to our needs. We utilize our most recent observations to reevaluate and perhaps redefine our preconceptions. An obvious example would be the case of a white person who has always harbored the belief that blacks are inferior; but when a black family moves next door and friendship ties develop, the long-standing perception of inferiority undergoes an abrupt reevaluation. The sequential execution of intensive interviews makes it possible for researchers to assimilate information in the same manner by which we absorb our life experiences.

PROCEDURAL ISSUES

We now turn to a more concrete discussion of the procedural aspects of intensive interviewing. We want to present an overview of how to do intensive interviewing and of the various issues — such as control of the interview, nonverbal communication, and rapport — which are central to an understanding of the method. Up to this point we have emphasized differences between intensive interviews and structured interviews. To make this contrast we have used somewhat oversimplified conceptions of each and we have explicitly avoided any discussion of the alternatives that fall along the continuum between these two. In view of this we turn first to the issue of degree of structure.

Degree of Structure

Interviews are usually characterized as being one of three types:

1. *Structured* or standardized: All questions are asked exactly the same way and in the same order for all respondents.
2. *Nonschedule standardized:* All questions are asked of each respondent, but they may be asked in different ways and in different sequences.
3. *Unstructured* or nonstandardized: No standardized schedule of questions is used.

There are variations involving some combination of these three types. For example, *semistructured* interviews are inquiries in which certain questions are asked of all respondents (either in structured or nonscheduled form) but also other unstructured questions may be asked as well. Semistructured interviewing was used in the stripteaser study cited earlier. This is a relatively popular form of interviewing, since it provides some data (such as age, marital status, and level of affluence) that are comparable for all respondents, as well as other data derived from questions tailored to take advantage of the unique experiences and perspectives of each individual.

We include nonscheduled standardized, unstructured, and semistructured interviews under the heading of *intensive interviews,* since they feature the kind of probing, individualized pursuit of information we regard as intensive. Structured interviews are excluded; although they may be lengthy and may sometimes seem intensive to interviewees, they do not incorporate the sort of format flexibility that intensively seeks out the ways in which each individual respondent may be most informative. This is why we have contrasted structured interviews with intensive interviews at several junctures.

In discussing the procedural aspects of intensive interviewing, we shall employ a hypothetical case; we shall assume we are about to embark on a study of upper-middle class suburbanites and their participation in community-oriented voluntary organizations. This segment of the population has been selected deliberately for the example because it tends to be among the most suspicious and evasive groups to interview and should exemplify most of the problems to be encountered in intensive interviewing.

Access

Our first problem is to entice upper-middle class suburbanites to submit to intensive interviews. Let's say we cannot afford to pay them for their trouble. We wish to interview them at length in their homes —

adult female household heads in half the cases and adult male household heads in the remainder. Why should they have the slightest inclination to participate in the study? Ordinarily we might seek the endorsement of a respected and well-known local organization, as a means toward establishing our credibility. However, because the study involves the topic of organizations, we cannot risk any respondent's thinking we represent a specific organization, so we abandon the endorsement idea.

However, we write a letter to the Chief of Police, with details of the manner in which we intend to go about our study. We state that our objective is to determine what kinds of organizations people belong to and reasons for membership. We guarantee that no participant will be identified with his or her specific comments in our report. The ultimate beneficiaries, we state, will be the organizations that are sponsoring our endeavor. We formally request permission to conduct the study as outlined in the letter, and we follow up the letter with a personal visit to the police station.

Armed with police approval, we now send letters to a sample of homes (selected randomly if the study is a large one or perhaps selected to reflect widely disparate neighborhood conditions if we will be conducting only a few interviews). Again, we explain the broad purpose of our research, with no reference whatsoever to sponsorship of the study.

Now comes the tricky part — actually obtaining respondent cooperation. We visit a few homes which have received our letter and ask for an appointment to conduct an interview, stating that the interview may last as long as two or three hours. Most of the people we approach perceive themselves as being quite busy. Despite our preparations, some will be suspicious of us and our motives.

We emphasize that their participation is extremely important to us, because we have selected only a few households to represent the entire community. We also stress that the information we obtain will not be linked to them personally and will enable community organizations to direct their goals and activities so as to make them most consistent with the needs of the community. We may offer to make a synopsis of the results available. We assure them that our intent is not to inconvenience or exploit them but simply to collect information at their convenience, which will be of benefit to a great many people. When they express concern over the length of the interview, we explain that it can be divided into more than one session and suggest that they start the interview to see if they find it as interesting as most people do.

In other words, we use a *combination of inducements* designed to take advantage of two basic premises. The first premise is that an intensive interview *approaches* the sort of *sociable conversation* enjoyed by most people. It is not, strictly speaking, a sociable occasion, but it tends in that direction and can be a positive interlude for people who are gratified at being asked their opinion.

A second premise is that in presenting ourselves as interviewers we may be viewed by the people we approach as what Goffman (1963: 129) calls *opening persons* — individuals such as newspaper reporters who, because of their roles, are implicitly granted the license to approach strangers without causing the suspicion and rejection often accompanying such confrontations. Although the intensive interviewer is not a long-standing acquaintance of the respondent, she may be accorded the deference such an acquaintance would receive (at least for the duration of the interview) because of her uniquely perceived role as a person whose "job" is to talk to strangers.

Preparation

In preparing for the actual interviews, our chief concern should be to accumulate existing information on community organizations. This includes published material (e.g., newspaper articles, brochures printed by the organizations themselves, and books on the history of the community) as well as other sources. Perhaps we will want to talk to a few community leaders. We will almost certainly converse with leaders of specific organizations, assuming they are aware of what we are doing.

As we perform this initial investigation, we should begin preparing an outline for the interview. Our initial hypotheses or informational needs should be formed. For example, as our familiarity with community organizations increases, we may hypothesize that people join these organizations primarily as a means of accumulating power over others in the community. An alternative hypothesis might be that voluntary organizations are used by members primarily as a means of socializing with others or escaping family routine. Or, we might hypothesize that the community social patterns tend to subjugate individual identities, with the result that people join voluntary organizations mainly to gain access to a social milieu small enough to permit the emergence of well-defined personal identities.

These hypotheses may be strengthened, refuted, or modified as the interviewing progresses. Other hypotheses may supplement or replace them. The important thing is that before and during the interviewing process we are continually working from and reevaluating a specific theoretical perspective.

Our initial preparation is valuable in another way. By learning as much as possible about community organizations before we commence interviewing, we are less likely to be at a loss if a respondent mentions a term or concept which is unique to an organization. For example, mention of a "hit" might require you to ask for a definition unless you know in advance that this term is used by one organization as slang for "dues." While there is nothing wrong with asking respondents for clarification, a repeated need to do so may reflect negatively on the credibility or even the intelligence of an interviewer.

Finally, intensive preparation gives us a better "feel" for the community in general and for its voluntary organizations in particular. Our investigation emerges from abstraction to reality. Our sense of personal involvement and commitment is heightened, and we gain confidence in our ability to cope with any exigencies which arise during the interviews.

Execution

We arrive at the home of the first appointment and reintroduce ourselves to the respondent. We restate the purpose of the study and mention any pertinent ethical considerations. We might say something like:

> Hello, I'm _____. We spoke the other day about the study I'm conducting on community organizations. Thank you for the opportunity to ask you some questions. I'm particularly interested in people's views on what these organizations are like, how they function, what purposes they serve, why people join them, and anything else you can tell me about your impressions of voluntary community organizations. As I said the other day, I can promise that your name will never be linked with anything you say; you will remain completely anonymous. I'd like to tape-record our conversation, although I don't want your name to appear on the tape. Taping our discussion means that I don't have to take a lot of notes, which speeds up the process and ensures that I have an accurate record of what we say.

This introduction has suggested the range of topics to be discussed. The term "impressions" is important, as interviewees may incorrectly assume that, since they do not belong to one of these organizations, their views have little or no validity. The interviewer can assure them that people's *impressions* are important whether or not they belong to an organization. Tape-recording the interview, in addition to providing a substantive record, will enable us to evaluate our interviewing technique after the interview is completed.

Note that, nowhere in that introduction did we refer to the interaction as an "interview." It is important at the outset to position the exchange as a conversation or discussion between two *participants,* rather than as an inquisition.

Once the interview begins, we follow a predetermined topical outline, until it seems natural to deviate from it. Let's say we have decided to conduct semistructured interviews, in which we will ask every respondent a few standard questions about the organizations to which he or she belongs. These questions are relatively easy to answer, so we ask them at the beginning. The respondent is thus immediately assured that participation in the discussion will not be a difficult task, and we now have knowledge about the respondent (membership in organizations) which may be used as a frame of reference throughout the interview.

From this point, the course of the interview and the questions that are asked will depend largely on the inputs of the interviewee. As in every conversation, many devices may be used by either the interviewer or the respondent in manipulating the interchange to achieve a given purpose. A task of the interviewer is to guide the discussion in a way that the purposes of both parties are as harmonious as possible.

As an example of the various intents which may motivate interviewer or interviewee inputs, a hypothetical interview excerpt appears below. Beside each comment of the interviewer or interviewee is an explanation of the intent underlying the comment. The abbreviations IR and IE are used to indicate the interviewer and interviewee respectively:

Conversation	Intent
IR: Let's talk for a moment about the reasons why someone might join a voluntary community organization.	Definition of purpose.
IE: (Silence)	Encouragement to proceed.
IR: What are some of the reasons why someone might join a voluntary community organization?	Restatement of purpose into question.
IE: Well, you want to be of service to the community.	Indication of opinion in response to direct question.
IR: Uh-huh!	Encouragement to proceed.
IE: I mean you join that kind of organization to help other people.	Restatement of earlier response.
IR: I understand.	Indication that no further restatement is needed; encouragement to proceed in another direction.
IE: And of course you enjoy belonging to a club or you wouldn't be a member.	Additional opinion response to earlier question.
IR: Club?	Echo statement to elicit more information.
IE: Well, most of the organizations I can think of are clubs — at least the ones I'd want to join.	Expanded definition in response to echo request.
IR: So there are some types of organizations you would want to join and some you wouldn't want to join.	Restatement of IE's comment to elicit more information.

Conversation	Intent
IE: Sure. The Committee on Recycling may have a useful function, but you never think of them as having much fun together. The Garden Club does a lot of things to make the town more beautiful, and we also have a lot of fun at our meetings and outings.	Clarification of former statement in response to IR's restatement.
IR: What are some of the things that the Garden Club does to have fun?	Probe for additional related information.
IE: Well, there are many ways to have fun. My daughter was telling me the other day that their class is planning to put on a dance where the music will be provided by members of the class.	Evasion of question, perhaps because earlier response is difficult to substantiate, or because the topic is too sensitive, or because IE is tired of discussing topic.
IR: That's interesting. How does the Garden Club decide what to do for fun?	Initial support, so as not to alienate IE. Refocus on previous topic, approaching question from different perspective.

In addition to the diversity of manipulative conversational devices which may be employed by either party, this example shows how the interviewer may seize on just one word ("club") to propel the interview in a related and useful but slightly different direction. The factor of enjoyment, which might or might not be covered later in the interview, emerged at this point and provided important insights into the respondent's real outlook on organizational membership.

Control

While the interviewer was not abrasive or authoritative in the example presented above, she did maintain control of the interview by guiding the respondent into productive conversational directions. She did not allow the interviewee to evade questions and was not satisfied with superficial or cursory answers. Moreover, the interviewer appeared to maintain a steady *pace* in the interview. The conversational exchange did not bog down with redundancies and did not skip too lightly over important points. The matter of pace is important, because it is highly detrimental for the interview to gain momentum and then deteriorate because the pace suddenly becomes too slow or too fast. The momentum we want to maintain is one that produces a steady and productive conversational flow. If either one of the participants speaks for a long time without some input from the other, the interview is suffering from a lack of control. On the other hand, if the interview consists of a series of rapid-fire inputs between interviewer and interviewee, this is a sign that the interviewer is failing to elicit responses in sufficient length to obtain relevant information. Banaka (1971:107) states that a 60-minute depth interview (a synonym for intensive interview) should average between two and four inputs per minute (combining inputs of both parties). This is just a rule of thumb, but a pretty good one.

Nonverbal Indications

At one point in the hypothetical interview, the interviewee remained silent at a time when it might have been appropriate to say something. This was a nonverbal means of indicating to the interviewer — in this case, encouragement to proceed because the respondent had nothing to say. Nonverbal communication is an important part of any conversation and therefore of any intensive interview. Many signals may be given by either party, involving tone of voice, eye contact, body position, gestures, facial expressions, and pauses. Even the point at which one person interrupts the other can be meaningful.

As an example, Burgess and Holmstrom (1974:144–145) illustrate in their book *Rape* how one rape victim used nonverbal means to indicate her feelings of distress during an intensive interview:

> Laura, age 13, wouldn't say anything. She sat holding a little pink coin purse. Then she bent over and picked up a short screw from the floor that her mother had dropped. She took the screw and kept hitting, with some force, the purse with the screw. First she drew lines across the purse; then she really stabbed it, making holes in the purse.

Nonverbal indications obviously play an important part in intensive interviews. They offer interviewers a diversity of ways in which to manipulate the conversation while not appearing to do so. Since the same devices are available to interviewees, it behooves interviewers to be aware constantly of any nonverbal communication in which the other party indulges.

Rapport

We have stated more than once that the quality of the incipient or emerging relationship between interviewer and interviewee is the key to how productive the intensive interview will be. We do not mean that the two will become close friends, and in fact there is a danger of "over-rapport" which could compromise the researcher's detached perspective.

However, it is important for the intensive interviewer to nurture rapport with the other party, within the framework of an appropriate degree of objectivity.

The best avenue for gaining and perpetuating rapport with respondents is to ensure that they receive sufficient and continuing rewards from the relationship without feeling that these gratifications are artificially contrived. For example, it is beneficial to praise the interviewee's contributions occasionally, but not to the point where it is overdone. In the hypothetical conversation presented earlier, the interviewer gave some praise ("That's interesting.") concurrently with attacking the apparent evasiveness of the respondent. There was the chance that the interviewee would be irritated at the refocus on a topic just evaded, and the interviewer sought to soften any possible irritation by offering praise. This suggests that it is the *timing* rather than the amount of praise which is most important.

One of the attractions intensive interviewing has for respondents is that it gives them an opportunity to reveal in a nonjudgmental environment the multiple identities they perceive themselves as having. A woman who may know she is criticized by neighbors for "going off and leaving her child" with a babysitter while pursuing a career need fear no recriminations in this respect from the skilled intensive interviewer. In this sense, the interaction of an intensive interview may offer benefits not available in most day-to-day encounters. The intensive interviewer who accepts without judgment the various self-identities indicated by the interviewee is facilitating development of strong rapport with the other party.

One of the easiest ways to undermine rapport between interviewer and interviewee is for the former to look or act outside the bounds of acceptability. In most suburban communities, for example, a stranger entering one's home is implicitly expected to present a neat appearance and not to be dressed too informally. Although someone interviewing on a Saturday might expect to find the respondent clothed in faded, torn jeans while doing household chores, the interviewer should not attempt to duplicate this appearance, as it may be interpreted as a lack of respect for the home being entered. Neither should the interviewer be so splendidly dressed that the respondent will feel uncomfortable by comparison. In other words, interviewers should not attempt to look the same as respondents. They should maintain their own identities without overemphasizing differences between themselves and interviewees.

Similarly, in action and word, the interviewer should be prepared to perform within the respondent-defined bounds of propriety, while not compromising her own identity in doing so. It is not wise to alter one's manner of speaking to try to conform to a respondent mode. With rare exceptions, an intensive interviewer would look silly if she tried to adopt the jargon of a specialized group, such as physicians or hippies.

The mood of the intensive interviewer goes a long way toward encouraging rapport with the respondent. The interviewer must appear enthusiastic about the interview and about the prospect of being allowed to converse with the interviewee. Patience is an important interviewer attribute, and there may be times when the interviewer will, or at least should, recognize the respondent's need to take a "vacation" from the topic, in the form of either irrelevant conversation or an actual hiatus in the interview.

We have alluded to the importance of intensive preparations for intensive interviewing. There will be certain fundamental facts that respondents may expect interviewers to know in order to establish their credibility — the size of a community, the typical climate of the area, key industries in the vicinity, and so on. Failure of the interviewer to "do his or her homework" can result in a loss of credibility and can make rapport that much more difficult to establish and maintain.

The respondent's commitment to the interview and rapport with the interviewer are likely to be heightened if the interview is perceived as an information exchange rather than a one-way flow of data. This is why we previously suggested that the interviewer slip in comments about herself — comments which are not apt to change respondents' views. For example:

> IE: It's important to get out of the house once in awhile. I love my kids, but they really get on your nerves. The din is sometimes incredible!
>
> IR: I can understand. I have kids of my own.

The concept of information exchange is greatly aided if the researcher offers to present a summary of the study results to the interviewee. Respondents are often curious about how they compare with others, and the reciprocity of information represented by this gesture can be highly beneficial to rapport.

Setting

In our hypothetical study, we initially decided to hold the interviews in people's homes. However, there was no assurance that this would be the best setting. In fact, there is every likelihood that the respondents might have been distracted by events around them (e.g., telephone calls or the needs of other family members) or by the very presence of onlookers in the form of other residents of the home.

The intensive interviewer should be prepared to change the setting of the interviews. The researchers in the striptease study mentioned at the beginning of this chapter took their subjects out to dinner rather than continuing to interview them backstage. If our suburbanites prove to be distracted by the home environment, we should be prepared to request that interviews be held elsewhere (e.g., in an anteroom at the Town Hall or library or at some other public place).

In a sense, the interviewer becomes part of the setting of an intensive interview. It is a fact that respondents generally (although not always) relate better to interviewers of the same sex. Thus it may be necessary to change the "setting" by changing interviewers, if this seems to be a problem in a particular study.

COMPARATIVE STRENGTHS AND WEAKNESSES OF THE METHOD

In this section we review a number of issues that should be taken into consideration when deciding whether or not intensive interviewing is the most appropriate method for the study under consideration. It will become evident that many of the method's greatest strengths are also the sources of its most significant limitations. Much of what we say here is based on comparison with other approaches, particularly survey research and observational methods. We will first review the major strengths of the method.

There is less chance of the interviewer and the interviewee misunderstanding one another with intensive interviewing than with the structured interviewing used in survey research. The interviewer has the opportunity to cast questions in terms that are clear to a specific respondent and to ask the same question in a variety of different ways if there is any doubt as to the respondent's comprehension. If respondents seem to be inconsistent, there is the opportunity for the interviewer to confront them with the apparent inconsistency. In so doing it is often possible to resolve the apparent contradiction.

Intensive interviewing has the potential for providing more accurate responses than survey research on certain sensitive issues. There is a greater opportunity to develop rapport with the respondent. It is also possible to approach a sensitive issue from a variety of directions. If the interviewer senses that the respondent is shading the truth, it is possible to ask another question to test the previous answer. For example, interviewees who claim to have a high degree of racial tolerance may be asked how they would feel about their children getting married to a person of a different race or how they feel about a busing policy which would bring about a substantial shift in the racial composition of the local schools.

We cannot always count on intensive interviewing to provide more accurate responses on sensitive issues. With some respondents the more formal survey research interviewer (or the still more anonymous mail questionnaire) may get a more honest answer. For some topics the intensive interview may yield the most honest responses, but for other topics this may not be the case. Unfortunately, there are no clear guidelines available to tell us when the intensive interview will yield the most honest answers on sensitive issues.

In intensive interviewing questions and response categories can be tailored to fit the respondent's way of looking at the world. There is less danger than with survey research of imposing a set of irrelevant categories on the interviewee or casting the question in a form that does not make sense given the respondent's view of how the world works. Typically the intensive interviewer is the researcher who is carrying out the study, but with many survey research studies the researcher in charge of the project does not do any of the actual interviewing. Thus the intensive interviewer is directly confronted with the difficulty respondents are having understanding the questions and the tendency of respondents to interpret the questions in ways other than those originally intended; in contrast, the survey researcher may be quite insulated from such problems.

Intensive interviewing provides a more complete and more in-depth picture of the individual respondent than is the case with survey research. In this respect the method is similar to participant observation. In survey research we get a flat view of the respondent. The respondent is reduced to an atomized set of background characteristics and specific attitudes. In intensive interviewing there is an attempt to round out our image of the respondent by exploring underlying motives and personal experience which can be linked to specific attitudes and beliefs.

In intensive interviewing there is a continual assimilation and evaluation of information by the researcher. When appropriate such information can be used to shift the line of questioning to a more fruitful direction. Depending on where the interview is conducted, observation of the environment may provide an important perspective on what the interviewee is saying. For example, if a respondent describes himself as being extremely thrifty, but the interviewer notices lavish furnishings in the other's home, the credibility of the respondent's remarks may be called into question. The interviewer might interject a comment to challenge the respondent such as:

> You are very fortunate to have such a beautifully furnished home while being able to save a lot of money at the same time (or while operating on a limited budget).

The respondent might reply that the furnishings were inherited, that he dislikes them, and that he intends to change homes in the near future; or he might say something like:

> What I meant before was that I think it is important to save systematically, but I don't believe in living like a monk.

In survey research, interviewing efficiency is often a major consideration and cost per interview is often an important measure of an interviewer's performance. In some studies interviewers are paid a fixed amount of money per interview, an unfortunate practice which implicitly encourages them to conduct the interview as quickly as possible so as to maximize their income per hour. When such interviewers find a person who meets their sampling criteria, they will often attempt to complete the interview on the spot at all costs. If the respondent is about to go shopping, the interviewer may try to administer the interview in half the usual time with obvious implications concerning the quality of the data which is produced. Such interviewers will usually make every attempt to complete even a very long interview in one sitting.

In contrast, the intensive interviewer is more conscious of the need to develop the best possible rapport with each respondent. An attempt is made to be sensitive to the needs and convenience of the interviewee. If the timing of a contact proves to be inconvenient, another meeting is arranged. Since most intensive interviews are arranged by appointment, this is rarely a necessity. If the interview becomes drawn out and the interviewee shows signs of fatigue, the interview is continued at a later time.

There are certain categories of the population which can be reached by the unstructured interview format but not by either the observational approach or the standard survey research approach. One of the clearest examples is the study of elites such as U.S. senators or the presidents of major corporations. It is generally all but impossible to use the participant observation approach when studying such issues as elite decision making. It is also very difficult to get the persons primarily involved in these issues to take the time to respond to a survey research questionnaire. But in some cases such persons will grant an interview that follows the conversational form used in intensive interviewing. However, even here the interviews will typically be short and lack much of the depth that is usually identified with the intensive interviewing approach. It is very difficult to use the observational approach to study a highly dispersed group, such as U.S. senators when Congress is not in session. One strength of intensive interviewing is that it can be used when the group of interest is widely dispersed.

As a general rule, a study based on intensive interviewing can be carried out more quickly than an observational study, but less quickly than a survey research study. One reason that survey research studies tend to be quicker is that the interviews are typically shorter. Another is that the interviewing is generally divided among several interviewers. Observational studies typically take from several months to a few years, which is more time than is needed for most intensive interviewing studies. Perhaps the greatest advantage of intensive interviewing relative to participant observation is the speed with which in-depth data may be collected. Since some survey research projects call for data collection over a period of years and since some observational studies are based on data collected in one afternoon, any generalization about the speed of the alternative approaches must be interpreted with caution.

A study based on intensive interviewing will generally cost less than a survey research study. If we do not figure in a salary for the investigators, the costs of both intensive interviewing and of observational studies can be quite modest. If we do figure in a salary for the researcher, then the cost per interview is greater than for survey research. However, the total cost of the study may still be lower than for a survey research study because the typical intensive interview study is based on fewer than fifty respondents and the typical survey research study is based on several hundred respondents.

We now turn to a review of the most significant limitations of intensive interviewing as a research method. It is possible to take measures to minimize some of these problems, but many are unavoidable consequences of characteristics that represent the greatest strengths of the method. The advantages of intensive interviewing do not come without their costs, that is, their methodologically undesirable consequences.

It is very difficult to say anything about the generalizability of studies based on intensive interviewing. Such studies share a variety of the problems typically associated with observational studies. The issue of generalizability is much less problematic with survey research studies. This is not to say that generalizations are not made on the basis of intensive interview studies. They are. The problem is that we typically have no way to assess the accuracy of these generalizations.

One source of the problem is the sampling procedure. Intensive interviewing studies are generally based on small nonprobability samples. Typically no effort is made to obtain a random sample of some clearly definable population. A sample of as many as fifty respondents is rare. Even if probability sampling procedures are used, with such small samples the error involved in attempting to make any statistical generalization from the sample to the relevant population would be too large to be useful. That is, it would not tell us much to know that 50% ± 30% (i.e., between 20% and 80%) of those in the population of interest oppose gun control legislation. One reason for the small sample is that the interviewing is typically done by one or two people on a limited budget. Another reason is that the data produced does not lend itself to quantitative statistical analysis. Thus if the number of respondents starts to even approach the several hundred that is common in survey research studies, it becomes very difficult to analyze the data using procedures appropriate to qualitative analysis.

Another threat to generalizability is the lack of standardization in the interviewing procedure. The way in which a question is asked differs from one interview to the next. The goal is to ask the question in such a way as to get the most complete and accurate information possible on the issues of interest from each respondent, but we have no way of knowing that the alternative ways in which the question was asked really are comparable in meaning. Many argue quite sensibly that the comparability is less than in the case of the standardized survey research question which is asked in exactly the same way each time (even taking into consideration the possibility that the question will be interpreted in slightly different ways from one respondent to the next).

Another aspect of the lack of standardization in the interviewing is the variation in the degree of emphasis given to a question from one respondent to the next. Typically there will be a whole series of questions that are unique to a specific respondent and not asked of any other respondent. For those questions asked of all or most respondents there is considerable variation in the length of the responses. This lack of standardization in the length of responses is in part due to differences between respondents with respect to how much they would volunteer in response to the same question asked in exactly the same way. It is also in part due to variation in the extent to which the interviewer probes the issue or in other ways communicates an interest in the topic to the interviewee. As a result, to the same general question there will be three-word responses from some respondents and three-thousand word responses from others.

The lack of standardization in the data collection procedure makes it difficult to replicate an intensive interview study. Suppose we try to replicate a study based on intensive interviews and come up with different conclusions. It will be difficult to say whether the discrepancy is due to differences in interviewing procedure, differences in the sampling procedure, or something else. This difficulty in replicating the sampling and interviewing procedures of the original study means that the reliability of the method is low relative to that of survey research. There is generally no way to make statistical estimates of the reliability of results.

Intensive interviewing is highly vulnerable to interviewer bias. There are a variety of potential sources of interviewer bias in any form of data gathering based on interviewing, but some sources pose a much greater threat to the validity of intensive interviewing than to the structured interviewing used in survey research.

While interviewers are always instructed to avoid communicating their own personal views on the issues covered in the interview, an interviewer always gives off some cues that can be used by the respondent as a basis for at least guessing where the interviewer stands on a variety of the issues being considered. This is particularly true in intensive interviewing which is much more informal and approaches a conversation. Even if the interviewer is successful in avoiding verbal cues, there are a variety of forms of nonverbal communication which the interviewer is not fully aware of and does not have full control over. In a long intensive interview it is more than likely that interviewers unintentionally communicate a great deal about themselves, their values, and their attitudes on the issues being considered. This unquestionably has an impact on the opinions expressed by interviewees. The desire to give socially desirable answers and the desire to please the interviewer are problems in any kind of interviewing, but they are particularly problematic in intensive interviewing.

The flexibility the interviewer has in how a question is cast and how much the question is probed is another potential source of bias. In the simplest case the interviewer can ask leading questions or loaded questions, that is, questions that make it easier for the respondent to answer in one category than in another. If the interview is taped, it is possible to check for evidence of loaded questions, but usually it is only the researcher (who was also the interviewer) who goes over these tapes. This arrangement makes it less likely that any bias present will be picked up. By the time the results are prepared for publication, any such bias will be all but impossible to detect. In addition to what the interviewer actually says in the course of the interview, there are a number of nonverbal cues that will not be picked up on the tape, but can have a substantial impact on how much the respondent elaborates on a specific issue. These unrecorded cues can lead to an increase in the amount said when the respondent is supporting the investigator's thesis, theoretical perspective, or ideological outlook.

The quality of the data collected using the intensive interviewing approach depends very heavily on the skills of the interviewer. In this sense it is similar to participant observation research which depends heavily on the skills of the observer. In survey research it is also important to have skilled interviewers, but the skills required are much more narrow and are much easier to teach. It is rare for any hired-hand interviewers to be able to do what most investigators would consider an adequate job in an intensive interviewing study. This is one of the reasons that such studies are typically based on small samples.

With intensive interviewing studies there is also a lack of standardization in the data analysis procedures. In this sense the method is similar to observational research and in this sense it differs from the typical survey research study. Given a single body of data generated from an intensive interviewing study, it is quite possible for two data analysts to come up with quite different interpretations. Owing to the lack of any systematic procedures for analyzing such data, it is very difficult in such a situation to decide which interpretation is most valid; however, the situation does not come up very often because it is typically the same person who did the interviewing who also does the analysis of the data. This heavy dependence on the judgments of one or two investigators when it comes to interpreting the data leaves the door wide open for the researcher's theoretical perspective and personal ideology to substantially influence the reported findings of the study.

Throughout the chapter we have discussed a variety of potential strengths as well as the major limitations of the intensive interviewing approach. It is important to bear in mind that the strengths mentioned are only potential strengths. If the interviewer is not highly skilled, the actual research results may reflect all the potential pitfalls of the method and virtually none of the strengths of the method.

CONCLUSION

Intensive interviews differ from other interviews in that they are less structured or standardized. They allow the interviewer flexibility in questioning the respondent — flexibility which enables the interviewer to ask for or give immediate clarification in cases of misunderstandings, probe for additional detail on interesting comments volunteered by the interviewee, defer or rephrase questions producing sensitive reactions from respondents, and achieve many other benefits.

Most importantly, the intensive interview's effectiveness is predicated on the interviewer's ability to know what to ask, when to ask it, how to ask it, and how to conduct a continuing and cumulative analysis of the entire process. One advantage of the sequentiality of intensive interviews is that the investigator is usually equipped to conduct analysis while asking questions; and this ability enables the researcher to challenge and adjust or refute hypotheses as the study progresses and more interviews are conducted.

Unlike a survey research study utilizing structured questionnaires that are typically administered by hired-hand interviewers and analyzed in their totality by a researcher who has never met a respondent, intensive interviewing emphasizes the incipient relationship between interviewer and interviewee. The quality of this relationship is what determines how productive the interview will be. If both parties obtain sufficient rewards from the relationship as time passes, the interview will proceed; otherwise it will terminate. Thus, the intensive interview should be more of an information exchange than a one-way flow of data and of rewards or benefits.

In a sense, the intensive interviewer is the data-gathering tool (as is the field worker in an observational study), in contrast to the questionnaire, which is the data-gathering instrument in a structured interview. In fact, intensive interviews usually employ no questionnaires, although they may use topic guides and may even include a few structured questions to be asked of every respondent (a semi-structured interview).

Intensive interviewing is sometimes employed in exploratory studies, in which the researcher desires to obtain a "feel" for what to ask and how to ask it in a large survey research study. In other cases, it may be the only method of data collection. Some investigations involve the use of several data-gathering devices, including intensive interviewing. Intensive interviews are particularly useful when there is virtually no other means of reaching respondents, such as in the study of U.S. senators, presidents of major corporations, and male go-go dancers.

Like all research methods, intensive interviewing has its limitations and potential pitfalls. The data generated does not lend itself to quantitative analysis and does not permit statistical inference about the population from which the respondents were drawn. The method is greatly dependent on the capabilities of the interviewer. The lack of standardization in sampling, interviewing, and data analysis make it difficult to determine how generalizable the results are. This lack of standardization also increases the chance that the researcher's theoretical perspective and personal ideology will have a substantial impact on the outcome of the study.

Intensive interviewing emerges as a technique that is highly useful in obtaining information in a relatively short space of time from potentially elusive or inaccessible respondents. The method permits a direct solicitation of information from a respondent rather than the development of inferences through observation. Those studied may be located in a relatively confined area or spread throughout the world.

EXERCISES

1. Organize the class into pairs, and have one member of each pair interview the other intensively about the most outlandish thing the interviewee has ever done. When the interview is completed, the interviewer should interpret the findings for the respondent, and the respondent should comment on these interpretations. The Banaka book (see the Suggested Readings section of this chapter) will be helpful in determining how to conduct and interpret the interview.

2. Using the same pairs of students, have the interviewer and interviewee switch roles, with the *new* interviewer asking the *new* respondent's opinions of people who do outlandish things like those described in the first interview.

3. Discuss the differences which might arise between the intensive interviews you have just conducted and similar intensive interviews among factory workers you have not met, conducted during their lunch breaks. What problems might arise in the factory worker interviews which were not present during your classroom interviews? What problems in the classroom interviews might be alleviated during the factory worker interviews? Why?

4. Discuss the ethical considerations and potential methodological pitfalls of conducting intensive interviews among dying patients in a hospital. Reference to *On Death and Dying*, by Kubler-Ross (1969), will be helpful. Consider the possibility that intensive interviewers might alienate the "affections" of patients from the hospital staff. Think about the likelihood that respondents will be so grateful at receiving attention that they will simply try to find the "right" answers to "please" the interviewer.

5. In Kubler-Ross's book, *On Death and Dying* (1969:22), the author says:

> We had no other preconceived ideas (other than who would be the interviewer and who would observe) nor did we read any papers or publications on this topic so that we might have an open mind and record only what we ourselves were able to notice, both in the patient and in ourselves. We also purposely did not study the patient's chart since this too might dilute or alter our own observations. We did not want to have any preconceived notion as to how the patients might react. We were quite prepared, however, to study all available data after we had recorded our own impressions. This, we thought, would enhance our perceptiveness and, we hoped, desensitize the rather frightened students through an increasing number of confrontations with terminally ill patients of different ages and backgrounds.

Discuss this viewpoint on preparation in light of the fact that most intensive interviewers obtain as much information as possible before starting the interviews, so as not to be shocked by a respondent's comment any more than is necessary and so as to be able to interpret *immediately* what each interviewee says within the context of known data on the interviewee's frame of reference, background, and so on. The Stebbins article (see the Suggested Readings section) may be helpful in deliberating about the proper balance of subjectivity and objectivity in conducting intensive interviews.

6. Some researchers who use the intensive interview approach say their studies are meant to complement more quantitative data. Some methodologists, notably survey researchers, have suggested that this kind of statement is merely a disclaimer designed to cover up the inadequacies of the small sample and that readers of the report will forget the disclaimer and will inappropriately assume a high degree of reliability in the findings, even if subconsciously. What do you think?

7. The article on female blacks in professional life by Fuchs states that the study was initiated to examine a hypothesis she had developed earlier. The study eventually supported this hypothesis. Discuss the likelihood that the flexibility offered by intensive interviewing could allow a researcher to force the results to support an hypothesis. How might the researcher bring about this kind of manipulation? What might the author have included in the article which would have removed any suspicion along this line?

8. Devise a list of topics you might consider including in an intensive interview of two-career families, with the objective of determining what compromises the members of such families are forced to make. Conduct an intensive interview with one such family. What additional topics surfaced during the interview? Compare your findings with Holmstrom's and discuss the differences.

SUGGESTED READINGS

Readings About the Method

Banaka, William H.
1971   *Training in Depth Interviewing.* New York: Harper & Row.

> This book contains detailed procedures for training oneself or others to become "depth" (or intensive) interviewers. There is an extensive listing and discussion of pitfalls of intensive interviewing and procedural details involved in conducting interviews. The author stresses the interactive process between interviewer and interviewee, including means of manipulating the conversation to the interviewer's best advantage. A lengthy section on methods of evaluating intensive interviews emphasizes the competency of the interviewer. Numerous rules of thumb are given for conducting this analysis.

Kahn, Robert L., and Charles F. Cannell
1957   *The Dynamics of Interviewing.* New York: John Wiley.

> This is not a detailed methodological primer. It is a largely theoretical discussion of various interviewing forms. An important aspect of the volume is the comparison of the advantages and disadvantages of intensive interviewing versus other interviewing forms. Of chief value to the intensive interviewer is a section on learning how to interview, including examples of interviews, and emphasizing probing techniques.

Richardson, Stephen A., et al.
1965   *Interviewing, Its Forms and Functions.* New York: Basic Books.

> The value of this book is largely theoretical. The interview as a data gathering device is compared with other methods of data collection. The authors discuss the interviewer's role, characteristics of interviewers, and relationships between interviewer and interviewee. Although valuable in providing an excellent philosophical overview, the volume is not oriented toward applications for the most part.

Stebbins, Robert A.
1972   "The unstructured research interview as incipient interpersonal relationship." *Sociology and Social Research* 56 (January):164–179.

> Stebbins discusses in depth the interviewer-interviewee relationship in an intensive interview. His focus is on the incipient (or emerging) relationship between the two. Drawing from various theoretical perspectives in sociology and social psychology, the author suggests many ways in which the nature of this incipient relationship enhances the likelihood of acquiring valid data. This is a strictly theoretical exposition, but an important one for the practitioner of intensive interviewing.

Readings Illustrating the Method

Becker, Howard S.
1963   *Outsiders.* New York: Free Press.

> In a classical study, Becker utilizes both participant observation and intensive interviews in studying the sociology of deviance through the media of two subcultures — users of marihuana and dance hall musicians. This is one of the best examples of the way in which data not collected from a large, random sample with a structured questionnaire may be utilized in developing generalizations about society.

Epstein, Cynthia Fuchs
1973   "Black and female: the double whammy." *Psychology Today* 7 (August): 57–61, 89.

> Epstein conducted intensive interviews among 31 female blacks engaged in professional careers. The article contains limited information on the methodology, but is a good example of the way in which inferences can be developed from intensive interviews and the potential problems involved in making such inferences.

Holmstrom, Lynda Lytle
1972   *The Two-Career Family.* Cambridge, Mass.: Schenkman.

> The author uses intensive interviews to study the two-career family. Investigating a number of factors, including life cycle of the family, division of labor, and compromises, she develops conclusions about the nature of such families — their problems, their viability, and so on. An interesting feature of the book is an extensive section on methodological considerations, notably the advantages of intensive interviewing versus other data-gathering techniques.

Kubler-Ross, Elisabeth
1969   *On Death and Dying.* New York: Macmillan.

> This study of dying patients in a hospital setting used intensive interviewing as the sole data-gathering technique. On the basis of these interviews, Kubler-Ross developed a theory that people who face a gradual dying process go through five stages: denial and isolation (refusal to accept), anger, bargaining (attempts to postpone the inevitable, often by prayer), depression, and acceptance. She found nonverbal communication between the interviewer and interviewee to be very useful. The incipient relationship and its importance in eliciting information is well illustrated in this study.

Skipper, James K., Jr., and Charles H. McCaghy
1972   "Respondents' intrusion upon the situation: the problems of interviewing subjects with special qualities." *The Sociological Quarterly* 13 (spring): 237–243.

The researchers engaged in the difficult task of obtaining information about stripteasers from the strippers themselves. They encountered numerous problems, particularly in terms of the disconcerting nature of the interview surroundings. This is an interesting example of the kinds of difficulties which can arise in the study of deviant groups, the creativity involved in meeting these crises, and the applicability of intensive interviewing to such studies.

Tavris, Carol
1974   "The speak bitterness revolution." *Psychology Today* 9 (May):43ff.

This was not set up to be a social research study as such but rather a field trip to China to study "their brand of psychology." Thus it is more a report on that trip than an attempt to develop social research implications. However, the description of Chinese society contains, by implication, comparisons for other societies. A key data-gathering method involved intensive interviews conducted through an interpreter. The main interest to the intensive interviewer is in the presentation of results and the interweaving of interview vignettes with conclusions.

Zuckerman, Harriet
1972   "Interviewing an ultra-elite." *Public Opinion Quarterly* 36 (summer):159–175.

A study of Nobel laureates is the focus of this piece. The intensive interview is the sole data-gathering device. Zuckerman demonstrates the problems of eliciting cooperation, the importance of preparing intensively for the interviews, and pitfalls in the actual interviewing transaction. This is a methodologically oriented article, with several excerpts from interviews. The author compares the interviewing of elites with other types of interviewing. This is a good example of a situation in which intensive interviewing represented virtually the only viable option to the researcher.

REFERENCES

Banaka, William H.
1971   *Training in Depth Interviewing.* New York: Harper & Row.

Becker, Howard S.
1955   "Marihuana use and social control." *Social Problems* 3 (July):35–44.

Becker, Howard S., and Blanche Geer
1957   "Participant observation and interviewing: a comparison." *Human Organization* 16 (fall):28–32.

Burgess, Ann Wolbert, and Lynda Lytle Holmstrom
1974   *Rape: Victims of Crisis.* Bowie, Md.: Brady.

Denzin, Norman K.
1970   The Research Act. Chicago: Aldine.

Goffman, Erving
1963   Behavior in Public Places. New York: Free Press.

Holmstrom, Lynda Lytle
1972   The Two-Career Family. Cambridge, Mass.: Schenkman.

Kubler-Ross, Elisabeth
1969   On Death and Dying. New York: Macmillan.

Lindesmith, Alfred R.
1947   Opiate Addiction. Bloomington, Ind.: Principia Press.

Lipset, S. M.; Martin A. Trow; and James C. Coleman
1956   Union Democracy. Glencoe: Free Press.

Skipper, James K., Jr., and Charles H. McCaghy
1972   "Respondents' intrusion upon the situation: the problem of interviewing subjects with special qualities." The Sociological Quarterly 13 (spring): 237–243.

Trow, Martin
1957   "Comment on 'participant observation and interviewing: a comparison.'" Human Organization 16 (fall):33–35.

Zuckerman, Harriet
1972   "Interviewing an ultra-elite." Public Opinion Quarterly 36 (summer):159–175.

Observational Field Research

CHAPTER EIGHT

The famous sociologist Robert Park is quoted as having once issued the following methodological directive to his students:

> You have been told to go grubbing in the library, thereby accumulating a mass of notes and a liberal coating of grime. You have been told to choose problems wherever you can find musty stacks of routine records based on trivial schedules prepared by tired bureaucrats and filled out by reluctant applicants for aid or fussy do-gooders or indifferent clerks. This is called "getting your hands dirty in real research." Those who counsel you are wise and honorable; the reasons they offer are of great value. But one more thing is needful; first-hand observation. Go and sit in the lounges of the luxury hotels and on the doorsteps of the flophouses; sit on the Gold Coast settees and on the slum shakedowns; sit in Orchestra Hall and in the Star and Garter Burlesk. In short, gentlemen, go get the seats of your pants dirty in real research. (McKinney, 1966:71)

Park's statement implicitly contains the central point of this chapter on participant observation. It is that one important way to gain an understanding of human action and social process is for researchers to enter, as far as possible, the worlds of those whose behaviors they are trying to fathom. Researchers use participant observation so that they might better see the world as their subjects see it, so that they might capture those whom they study "in their own terms" and thereby learn how they achieve a coherent, ordered existence. The method of participant observation is, therefore, based on the presumption that by studying persons in the "natural, ongoing environments where they live and work,"

(Schatzman and Strauss, 1973:9) social scientists will maximize their ability to grasp the motives, values, beliefs, concerns, troubles, and interests that underlie the actions of their subjects.

Participant observation has a long history of use in anthropological research[1]; thus there is justification if the term conjures up the image of a social scientist living with some preliterate tribe, perhaps for several years. The sociologist who becomes a member of a relatively unfamiliar American subculture is, in a real sense, doing anthropology. There are many studies in which sociologists have become part of cultures otherwise unfamiliar to them. In his now-classic work, William F. Whyte (1943) spent more than two years living in Boston's North End. Herbert Gans (1969) moved into Levittown, a new suburban community, in order to understand the quality of life in such a context. Eliot Liebow (1967), in his book *Tally's Corner,* describes his observations of the Negro street-corner men with whom he spent more than a year.

The community studies mentioned constitute only one area in which observational field work[2] has been done. Beyond that, the range of contexts dealt with by the "naturalistic" field worker has been considerable. Schools (Jackson, 1968), hospitals (Sudnow, 1967), industrial organizations (Gouldner, 1954), and asylums (Goffman, 1961) have all come under serious consideration at one time or another. Nor have marginal institutions such as the taxi-dance hall (Cressey, 1932) or the pornographic bookstore (Karp, 1973) escaped qualitative researchers' attention. Deviant groups or subcultures have made up another major area of inquiry for observational work: prostitutes (Greenwald, 1958), alcoholics (Lofland, 1970), professional thieves (Sutherland, 1949), and more recently, hippies (Davis, 1970), draft resistors (Thorne, 1971), drug users (Pope, 1971), homosexuals (Sagarin, 1969), have all come under investigation.

There are also those researchers who have gathered observational data from a number of diverse settings in order to better understand processes of social interaction. Edward Hall (1969) and Robert Sommer (1969) have, for example, studied proxemic or spatial patternings among human beings in a number of different contexts. Hall, particularly, has put his observational powers to use in conducting cross-cultural studies. Finally, we would be remiss here if we did not single out the naturalistic inquiries of Erving Goffman (1959, 1963, 1971) who, more than any other

---

[1] For a more complete description of the uses of anthropological field research in sociology, see pages 355–359 of Chapter 13 (Comparative Research Methods).

[2] The terms *field research* and *field work* are sometimes used in a comprehensive, generic fashion to include any methodology requiring that researchers collect data from persons in nonlaboratory settings. Given this definition, survey research and field experimentation could, for example, be labeled field research techniques. To avoid confusion, the authors wish to indicate that the terms *field research* and *field work* are being used in a more limited way here. They will use these terms interchangeably with observational research throughout this chapter.

sociologist, has combined observational data with personal insight to provide substantial understanding of face-to-face behavior.

As indicated by our examples, field work, concentrating as it does on the subjective side of experience, is inherently person oriented. It is not well suited to the study of large, complex organizations, large social institutions, comparative international events, or generally to issues of a macrosociological scope. Typically, observation-centered field work is done to study relatively small groups or well-defined social settings so that the researcher can establish and maintain close, first-hand contact with subjects and their actions.

It is difficult not to sympathize with the goal of providing rich, ethnographic analyses of one or another culture. Unfortunately, however, advocates of participant observation have been much more diligent in making claims for the benefits of that methodology than they have in explicating just how field research gets done. Although it is certainly useful to read accounts of those who have done observational studies, we are nevertheless left with an uncomfortable feeling. If we want to do this type of research ourselves, we are going to have to resolve a number of questions: How exactly ought I to proceed? What exactly should I observe? How should I behave in the field? Just how much should I participate with those whom I am studying? How will I know which data is important and which unimportant? What kind of identity should I adopt in the field? How long must I spend in the field? What must I do to gain access to those whom I want to study? And so forth.

The standard response to such questions is that they cannot be definitely answered. We are told only that although observation is the primary and indispensable tactic distinguishing the method, field researchers must proceed by way of a kind of methodological eclecticism, choosing the method that suits their purpose and present circumstances at any given point in time. Hence, unobtrusive measurement, life history studies, documentary and historical analysis, statistical enumeration, indepth interviewing, imaginative role-taking, and personal introspection are all important complements of direct observation in the field worker's repertoire. We are typically told that whatever method of inquiry can enrich researchers' insight into the social processes they are observing, and in which they may be participating, is ipso facto appropriate.

Perhaps the most comprehensive statement we frequently hear is that observational field work aims at a thorough and systematic collection, classification, and reporting of events as well as the specification of the relations between those events. Thus, while field workers set out to narrate and describe a "slice of social life," they must make their description more than a journalistic account of these events. By employing (or fashioning) sociological concepts and propositions to order collected data, researchers try to illuminate the less visible, latent structure of social organization. If successful, researchers do a good deal more than simply use abstract categories to describe the events observed: they add a new dimension to our understanding of a social setting or set of events. If successful, they break through the facade of faulty knowledge formulas that earlier observers have constructed to account for social labels, stereotypes, cultural taboos, fear, ignorance, indifference, or avoidance. And in so doing, observational researchers give us, as well, a fresh perspective on our own social positions. All these related aims of observational field research provide us the criteria according to which such research ought to be evaluated.

Impressionistic statements like those above are helpful. They give one a feeling for the nature of fieldwork. However, it is one thing to be told that the aim of participant observation is discovery of substantive theory, and quite another to know when this has been adequately accomplished. The rhetoric demanding that field researchers "take the role" of those whom they are studying and thereby "see the world from their standpoint" is sensible in the abstract, but it certainly fails as a clear guideline for researchers in the field. It is, further, undoubtedly disconcerting for the novice field researcher to be given the following kind of advice: "Don't worry about clearly delineating your problem too early. The focus of your research should emerge as you become involved in the context of your observation. Try to be sensitive to the underlying dimensions of the behaviors you are studying. Be flexible and responsive to changes in the setting investigated. Try to be complete in noting your observations and descriptions of persons, places, and events."

Our discussion to this point makes it quite apparent that one of the most striking aspects of observational field research is the absence of standardized operating procedures.[3] Since all cultures have their own distinctive characteristics, different demands are placed on researchers. A set of rules for doing good field research would be rather like a sex manual: though we are surely better off with a discussion of techniques that have worked for other people than with nothing at all, we can never carry out the actual practice with manual in hand. Both sex and field research are instances of intimate and sensitive human interaction, and neither can be reduced to a simple set of techniques. The object sought by the field worker, a deep understanding of the meaning of social action, cannot be realized by mechanically and unfeelingly using a simple set of instructions.

We acknowledge that the field research process cannot be rationalized or mechanized, but we are resolved to study the benchmarks along the path that observational field work "typically" follows. As we proceed through the remainder of this chapter, we will also offer some practical suggestions based on the accumulated successes and failures of many

---

[3] The general description of the research process offered here does not extend to those cases in which researchers do quite *structured* observation. In some instances researchers decide in an *a priori* fashion the data necessary to test their ideas and then construct standard coding categories for its collection. See pages 296–298 of Chapter 11 (Content Analysis) for a discussion of structured observation.

field research projects. It is, then, to a more explicit description of field research as a method that we now turn.

THE METHOD

Beginning with some general notions and perhaps some tentative hypotheses, field researchers observe a set of behaviors in detail. They then begin to formulate a series of questions, guesses, and hunches relative to the meaning of those observations. As more data accumulates, some hunches are supported, others eliminated; and hopefully some general analytical structure begins to suggest itself. Hunches become more formal hypotheses; inquiry begins to center around these hypotheses; and tentative conclusions begin to solidify. Truly craftsmanlike field workers, however, begin to refine their propositions through a vigorous search for negative cases — phenomena that do not seem to fit into their developing structure of explanation. In other words, theoretical propositions are not only generated in the field, but, insofar as possible, *tested* in the field.

In sum, field workers do not begin with all their propositions. They follow a long, arduous path which begins with a *sense of something problematic to be investigated,* and gradually they try to formulate a more sharply defined theoretical model for explaining the events at hand. Within this general process there are a number of stages through which the research can be seen to pass. By definition, the first of these stages involves choosing a research site.

Beginning the Research: A Question and a Research Site

Field research begins with these rudimentary elements: a general area of inquiry, a sense of something problematic that calls for explanation, and a potential site where a phenomenon of interest may be observed. When we speak here of an area of interest, we mean that in the broadest sense. A researcher might initially be interested, for example, in the culture of college students, in the way that power is exercised in a community, or in the possible alienation of workers in large organizations. Whatever area of interest is chosen, researchers do well to begin by asking themselves what they know and don't know about the area. If, for example, you have a general interest in social movements ask yourself where this interest comes from. Have you had first-hand experiences that led to this interest in social movements? Have particular social movements been a prominent part of the recent social scenery? Have you read books or heard lectures or discussions that deal either directly or peripherally with social movements? What unanswered questions have been raised for you through these intellectual experiences? Is yours a generalized interest, or are you more intrigued by specific social movements?

These preliminary ruminations are important for three reasons. First, they should help to pinpoint a manageable area for further inquiry. Second, they may help us specify what we know already about the area of inquiry, and, therefore, suggest the issues needing further inquiry to round out our personal knowledge of the subject matter. Finally, some serious reflection on what motivates the choice of one sociological topic instead of another will prove an invaluable base from which we may continually assess and reassess potential sources of bias as we collect and analyze data. This introspective questioning will also help in making explicit to an audience our personal sentiments — and so better allow them to assess for themselves the probable validity of our findings.

Most methodologists would argue that the choice of a research site should follow this general problem formation process. There is a rub, however. Although some formulation must necessarily precede the choice of a setting, the very logic of naturalistic inquiry demands that such a *priori* conceptualizations must not become so elaborate and compelling that they take on the character of self-fulfilling prophecies. There is the danger of leaping from the choice of a generic problem area to the assumption that the research setting is indeed a species of that genus. (This is the logical fallacy of "begging the question.") Suppose that a researcher has an interest in studying expressions of Black Power in the United States. The researcher should not set out with the absolutely rigid idea that Black Power is *in fact* a social movement with all the characteristics that have come to be associated with such phenomena. This is a matter to be investigated.

It is a sound principle of qualitative research (though perhaps not a widely practiced one) that one's initial interest should be with situations and settings more than with concepts and theories. If one starts with the idea that Black Power is a social movement, then it is likely that he or she will uncover a good amount of evidence that it is one. If, alternatively, one sticks to the more open-ended guiding question, "How can Black Power best be understood sociologically?" the self-fulfilling prophecy risk is reduced. Put simply, researchers must consciously avoid switching from inquiry to rhetorical demonstration.

We can see that the choice of a context for investigation is rarely made without some kind of rationale; somehow, we expect the context chosen to inform us about some feature of social life. Whether we make them explicit or not, we must have some set of questions that leads us to a particular setting for observation. Even researchers who claim to be merely curious about behavior in one or another place, must have some prior idea about that place. They know enough about it to be curious. Rather than pretending, therefore, that we have absolutely no a *priori* assumptions in such cases, we ought to make our assumptions explicit and put them to work. If we make our assumptions clear we can submit them to testing. If we allow our assumptions to remain hidden to us, they are potential obstacles to a full understanding of the situation under investigation.

We begin to perceive a dialectical relationship between our initial questions about a phenomenon, the choice of a research setting to answer these questions, and the data collected in the setting. Later, collected data may cause us to ask some questions more insistently, reject other questions as unimportant, and create the need for answers to previously unformed questions. As a research strategy, then, field work ideally allows us to create a beneficial balance between theory and data. We must not develop such an investment in one set of questions or theoretical ideas that we become blind to events in a setting unrelated to these questions or ideas. We must be prepared to accept the possibility that our original questions or ideas about a setting are irrelevant to an understanding of it.

Gaining Access and Taking a Role

Once we choose a site for study we must face the guardians of that social arena to obtain entry. Some settings provide virtually free access while others are nearly impenetrable. In some settings the field workers may be freely admitted with the full understanding of their hosts that they are researchers. Access to other settings may require the researcher to conceal both motives and profession. In still other instances, observation may be done so unobtrusively that the issue of motives never arises.

The degree of difficulty faced by researchers in gaining access to settings and to persons in those settings seems to be a function of two basic elements. First, just how public is the setting? Is involvement and membership in the setting clearly restricted, or is the setting open to anyone who might choose to be there? Fully public settings — such as bars, museums, department stores, and the like — pose no problems of access in the most immediate concrete sense. In other cases, membership and participation is clearly restricted or, at least, monitored, as in private country clubs or labor union organizations. We could, of course, envision any setting as lying somewhere along this public/private continuum.

There is a second dimension that is perhaps of even greater importance. Do the participants in the setting perceive the need to keep part or all of their activity (perhaps even their very membership) secret? To choose an example at the extreme end of the continuum, it would be virtually impossible for an outsider to study, first hand, certain features of organized crime.

Given these two dimensions, we could conceive of situations in which access to the setting itself would pose no problem, but it would be difficult to talk to participants directly. This might, for example, be the case for the researcher trying to study behavior in pornographic movie theaters. As a general rule, however, we can expect to have the fewest problems of access in those settings that are most public and in which people do not engage in secretive activities.

One researcher, Laud Humphreys (1970), was forced to disguise his identity in order to study homosexuality. The sites for his observations were public restrooms (called "tearooms" by the participants) where homosexuals met for impersonal sexual encounters. Humphreys legitimated his presence in these settings by adopting the role of the "watchguard." By watching for approaching police and outsiders, Humphreys became privy to the intricacies of a little-known but widespread activity. In addition, he secretly recorded the license plate numbers of "tearoom" participants and then later interviewed them at their homes. In order to conduct these interviews, Humphreys presented himself as a researcher merely interested in certain aspects of family relations. These novel strategies, developed by a researcher who would otherwise not be able to study this "unusual" public sexual behavior, set off a torrid debate in both the professional and popular press about the ethicality of disguised observation.

Few research settings of interest to the observational sociologist pose such difficult problems. There have been many community studies done, for example, without raising the suspicions of the "locals" so much that they felt the need to extensively question the researcher's motives. Others have conducted observational studies where it was not even necessary for researchers to identify themselves. Studies of bars, waiting rooms, subways, and the like pose few problems of the dramatic sort faced by Humphreys. Still others have taken advantage of a role they normally occupy or have taken on a specialized role for the sake of research. Howard Becker (1963) put his musical talents to work in order to study the professional musician. Joan Emerson (1970), a nurse, studied problems of maintaining reality definitions in gynecological examinations. Others have taken on roles as tame as pedestrian in a large city (Wolff, 1973) or as racy as member of a nudist camp (Weinberg, 1968) when the exigencies of research have so dictated.

Raymond Gold (1969) has summarized this array of possibilities into four basic roles which the field worker can assume: *complete observer, observer-as-participant, participant-as-observer,* and *complete participant.* The specification of these four conceptual roles results from Gold's response to two basic questions: How involved should researchers become in the ongoing activity? To what extent, if any, should researchers conceal their intentions?

The complete participant and the complete observer both remain totally disguised. The complete observer remains relatively or completely detached from the situation studied. He may operate from behind a one-way mirror, at the listening end of a tape recorder, or from some concealed observational vantage point. The complete participant, as in

Humphreys's case, becomes almost fully involved both behaviorally and emotionally. The two remaining roles differ according to the amount of emphasis placed on detached observation as opposed to involved participation. The participant-as-observer tends to get quite involved affectively and to downplay or conceal his role as researcher. The observer-as-participant, on the other hand, is completely open about his research objectives and he approaches people on that basis. The choice of any one of these roles depends on both the situation and the nature of the information sought.

Roles tending toward the covert, participatory end of the spectrum are generally preferred when actors consider the sharing of their knowledge potentially dangerous to themselves, or when the information is highly ego involved (lying buried under a protective layer of rationalization such that direct methods of information seeking could well elicit faulty data). Moreover, the choice of a covert role always raises serious ethical dilemmas. Is the information sought in any sense public? If it is strictly private, then what justification can the researcher give for "stealing" it? Whose interests must researchers protect? Do they owe anything to the subjects who have made the research possible? In general, are there any limits to the sociologist's right of inquiry?

These are, if not unanswerable, at least moot questions that continue to spark lively professional debate. Humphreys justified his work by articulating the high sense of ethical duty he maintained toward his subjects throughout the study. But others have argued that laudable personal morality is no substitute for codified professional ethics that can be employed to evaluate systematically and uniformly any research effort in the social sciences. After all, good intentions are no assurance that the researchers can anticipate all the effects of their research. If subjects are harmed unwittingly, the researcher can in no way reverse these negative effects.

In a discussion of disguised observation, Kai Erikson (1970) lays down two ethical principles to guide the choice of a role. First, researchers must never deliberately misrepresent their identities to enter a private domain where they would otherwise have no legitimate access. Second, investigators must never misrepresent their research intentions. Interestingly, Humphreys accepts these two principles and argues forcefully that he did not violate them.

The more that naturalistic observation involves interaction between researcher and subjects, the more the role taken by the researcher has to be individually tempered to the personalities involved and the situations in which they mutually find themselves. Hence, the only general rule that can be laid down is that each researcher must find his or her own best role and then adapt it according to the problem at hand. Some will find that the persons studied allow them to raise questions aggressively and vigorously. But others may see the need, at least at the outset, to remain unobtrusive. Finally, it should be noted once more that a researcher's role does not necessarily remain static. At different points during the research project, and in the company of different respondents, different roles may be demanded.

One thing is clear. Whenever research involves interaction between subjects and investigators, there is no such thing as total, bland unobtrusiveness. In effect, the ideal of "naturalistic" inquiry can never be fully realized. Subjects always "locate" researchers in some meaningful frame or context and relate to them accordingly. Researchers who maintain a mechanically objective detachment may create an uncomfortable ambiguity that forces subjects to interpret their actions as best they can, possibly resulting in behavior toward the researcher that is atypical and detrimental to the research goals.

Participant observers should try to understand and take into account the identity which their subjects attribute to them. How does a researcher's race, sex, ethnicity, physical appearance, known affiliations, and the like affect subjects' behavior? Does the researcher pose any kind of threat to the group or to any particular individuals or factions? Is he or she being manipulated to serve the overt or latent interests of anyone? How do subjects interpret the researcher's intentions? What kinds of rewards might especially cooperative subjects be anticipating? A serious consideration of these and related questions can help researchers to see their already collected data in proper perspective and may, as well, suggest useful strategies for future data collection.

Finally, since so much research takes place in organizational settings, we should say something about problems of access in those cases. Virtually all organizations are characterized by an elaborate stratification system such that certain persons or groups of persons have clearly more power and authority than others. Researchers who become too closely identified with one or another of these strata (subgroups) are likely to lose access to other groups in the setting. Robert Kahn and Floyd Mann (1969) have explicitly focused their attention on this problem of access to organizations where there may be intraorganizational disputes or competing hierarchies of authority. Their solution is for researchers to seek "dual or multiple entry." They advocate that researchers seek the acceptance of representative leaders from each faction before beginning to solicit any information. Hopefully, field researchers can thus sidestep the sometimes fatal problem of partisan identification with one or another faction.

The sociologist Myron Glazer (1972) has documented how harmful partisan identification can be. While studying student life in Chile amidst a highly politicized and suspicious atmosphere, he and his wife sought the approval of student leaders from each major campus faction. Unfortunately, members of the Christian Democrats noticed him being introduced to and having coffee with the Socialists just hours before the two researchers sought the good will of the Christian Democrats. Consequently, they were greeted only with coldness and a lack of cooperation by this latter group.

Generally speaking, groups being pursued, persecuted, or stigmatized by public authorities or private moralizers are least likely to accept an inquisitive outsider seeking their friendship and admission to their worlds of private knowledge. Researchers like the Glazers, who encounter difficulties in foreign countries holding a poor image of the "Yanqui," are likely to find similar sentiments among many in the United States as well. Many New Left and minority groups have become increasingly suspicious, if not openly hostile, to sociological "snoopers." We can no longer assume that social research will be unquestioningly accepted as a legitimate enterprise.

What all these tales of failures and mistrust signify is that researchers' conduct during the first few days and weeks in the field may be an enormously significant factor in eventually determining the success or failure of their study. If observers are initially viewed with distrust and suspicion by those whom they seek to study and do not handle the situation well, it may spell the end of their work before it really begins. Perhaps the most appropriate way, therefore, to summarize the issues we have been considering is in the form of some guiding suggestions. Needless to say, if any suggestion offered below seems inappropriate for the situation being studied, it should be utterly discarded. But here, in the abstract, both common sense and previous research experience lead the authors to make the following suggestions:

1. Whenever possible, level with people about what you are up to. This does not mean that you must engage in a detailed exposition of any developing theoretical ideas you might have. It might be useful for you, though, to develop some standard explanation that you can give of your work if asked. Generally, we agree with the maxim that "honesty is the best policy." If you feel that it is impossible to tell the truth or, even further, that you must actually disguise your research identity, you should take a particularly careful look at the ethical implications of your research.

2. For the first few weeks in the field it is probably best to adopt, if possible, a fairly passive research role. After all, your first task as a field researcher is to get a feeling for the context you are studying. Before you know the "rules" of a particular setting or culture, you run the risk of unwittingly engaging in behaviors that persons may find objectionable.

3. As a corollary to our second suggestion, it is probably unwise to conduct any in-depth interviews with informants at the beginning of your work. You simply do not know as yet what to ask. This does not, of course, mean that you should discourage persons from talking to you if they seem eager to do so.

4. Do not get into the position of offering advice to persons. Many have the conception of sociologists as therapeutic agents who can solve personal or organizational problems. Make clear that you are an investigator rather than a therapist. If persons still want to tell you their problems, listen sympathetically, for what you are being told may constitute valuable data.

5. Don't be afraid to ask questions if the situation calls for it, but do not assume the role of expert on anything. Make it plain to people that they are the experts and that you are there to learn from them.

6. Don't let persons force you into one or another particular role. Don't let your subjects decide for you what you should or should not be interested in observing. If you do not make plain that your job as a researcher is to investigate all features of the situation, you may find yourself observing only a limited number of events.

7. Don't become closely aligned with one or another group in the context you are studying. If you become viewed as a partisan during internal political battles, it will likely become impossible for you to observe certain segments of the organization.

At this point we will make the happy assumption that a researcher has successfully gained access to his or her setting. Of course, he or she has already been collecting data — in that preliminary thoughts about the broad area of concern, considerations of the best context in which to do observations, and experiences in making initial contacts with persons in the chosen setting all constitute relevant data. But once the researcher has gained access to the setting designated for study, the collection and continual interpretation of data becomes the most preoccupying research task. After all, we should state once more, the essential strength of participant observation is that it allows the researcher to continuously integrate the processes of data collection and analysis. While it is inappropriate to speak of the notation of data as merely one step in the process of "discovery" demanded by field research, we should look at some practical suggestions at this point concerning the nature of data that ought to be collected, and therefore, the content of the notes that should be kept by field researchers.

Note Taking

The substance of systematic, objective, and analytical participant observation lies in keeping accurate and detailed field notes. The first and perhaps only unequivocal rule that we will state about the content of field notes is that they must be *complete*. This is particularly crucial at the outset of a field work project. We say that because researchers do not go into the field with a well-formulated problem or an explicit set of hypotheses to be tested. They simply cannot know which data may ultimately be important and which not. For that reason, researchers who fail to be complete in their note taking at the outset may very well miss a good deal of data that later on turns out to be important. For purposes of continuing our descriptive account of field notes, let us assume that we have begun to observe behavior in some reasonably well-defined organizational setting. Especially during the first few weeks of field work, the following kinds of categories of data ought to find their way into our field notes.

First, we ought to strive to produce a complete *description of the setting* under investigation. The description of the setting offered in the field notes should provide enough information so that anyone reading the notes will have a clear picture and a "feeling" for what that setting is like. In order to accomplish this end, we must develop an eye for detail. Let us suppose we have begun to investigate one or another small religious group, such as the devotees of Krishna. We would likely begin the research by visiting their temple. In the description of that setting we will want to note a number of details — the colors of the walls, the general condition of the place, the kinds of objects to be found there. If we see that there is, for example, a bulletin board in the setting, we do not simply note its existence. We make some assessment of the kinds of things that are important enough to find their way onto the bulletin board. If there are magazines lying around on a table, note the titles. After all, the kinds of things that persons read is often a good unobtrusive indicator of their interests, beliefs, or ideological outlook. In short, the researcher's description of the setting should include anything that informs a reader about the nature of the setting or the persons who use it. One useful strategy in this regard is to draw maps of the setting itself. What might the spatial arrangement of furniture, for instance, say about the quality of interactions occurring in that setting?

As with descriptions of places, *descriptions of persons* should accurately portray to any reader what our subjects are like. Again, such a task necessitates our developing an eye for detail. Note the distribution of males and females, persons' racial groups, their ages, and so forth. Try to be aware, as well, of less visible but important indicators of status. How are persons dressed? What proportion of persons wear wedding rings? Do persons have noticeable accents? Do persons have tattoos or other body markings such as scars? It might be useful in some settings to get an indication of persons' physical health: Are persons' teeth in good condition? Is their skin condition good? Are they as a group disproportionately underweight or overweight?

The task of complete description may sound a bit overwhelming. It would, of course, be impossible to note down every possible piece of description about the setting and persons in it. We have to be selective to some degree. Full descriptions of persons and places need not be accomplished during the first visit or two to the setting. We can keep adding to our description on subsequent visits. Beyond that, it should become clear after a time that some persons are more "important" than others in the group studied. After it becomes clear who are the influential members of the group, we may want to give a more detailed description of them. In this sense, our descriptions will be cumulative.

Along with descriptions of persons and places, our notes should ideally be filled with quotation marks. It is very important that we include in our notes both conversations we directly have with persons and conversations we might overhear. Once more, the task is not to record every conversation that occurs, but rather to convey to the reader of our notes a good sense of the general content and tone of conversation typical in the context studied. It is not particularly imperative that we remember the exact words of a conversation. It *is* imperative, however, that we maintain the integrity of the substance of the conversation. We should also work to recreate phonetically the dialects that persons may use. If persons have a distinctive way of speaking, try to capture it. If persons say, for example, "Duya wanna gow-owt?" record it that way instead of "Do you want to go out?" If a group has its own distinctive argot, it is our job to understand it and ultimately present it to our readers. We should also keep in mind that a good deal of communication between persons is nonverbal. Part of our descriptive task, therefore, will be to include nonverbal gestures, postures, facial expressions, and the like.

We should also give serious attention to the suggestion (perhaps it ought to be elevated to the status of a rule) that we go out of our way to *record anything we find inexplicable or unusual.* Any data that we simply cannot understand often turns out to be among the most significant that we collect. The fact that we cannot make sense out of a conversation or an event is itself indication of an important aspect of the meaning fabric of the setting which is eluding us. Our essential task as field researchers is to arrive at some understanding of the meaning structures of those being studied. We should, therefore, hold these inexplicable conversations and events in mind as we continue to collect data. We must try to orient our data collection in such a way that these inscrutable phenomena are ultimately understandable.

To this point we have stressed the elements of description that ought to be found in our notes. Along with this task of providing description, it is our continual task as field researchers to be formulating tentative explanations of the things we are seeing. An absolutely crucial element of the data collection note-taking process, therefore, are *statements of personal feelings, hunches, ideas, or hypotheses.* We should include in our notes any guesses we might have about why persons are acting as they are. Try to continuously weave observations into some kind of theoretical or explanatory structure. If at any point during our observations we feel that we are seeing a theme that might possibly emerge as the focus of our work, we must get it down in our notes. Don't worry about the quality of the explanation offered. We shouldn't refrain from putting an explanation in our notes because we feel it may be incorrect.

We must force ourselves to be speculative. Remember that our notes do not constitute a finished product.

It would be sensible to include even brief theoretical ideas such as the following:

> There may be some kind of link in this organization between the status of persons and the kind of conflict and hostility that I am seeing.

In other cases we may want to expand our theoretical ideas into a larger memo. In these theoretical memos we will want to use some of the data already collected to show how it supports our theoretical ideas. We may also want to engage in some discussion of already published research that bears on the theoretical ideas we are raising.

Aside from the actual collection of data, our continual attempt at theorizing is the most important activity we can engage in. As we go along we will continue to refine these preliminary theoretical ideas. As these ideas develop they will be instrumental in helping us narrow the range of the data we collect. Indeed, as we write, amend, expand, assess, and reassess these theoretical ideas in our notes, we are actually writing substantial portions of our final research report.

Finally, in terms of the content of our field notes, we should say a word about *methodological notes*. Methodological notes consist of a recording of, and commentary on, the success or failure of our data-gathering approach(es). Our own feelings and the reactions of our subjects as we attempt to explore various features of their lives can be used as an index of the quality of the data obtained. Resistance can be a valuable clue that more is going on than meets the eye. When subjects suddenly become recalcitrant, is it because we have touched on a particularly sensitive area which they would sooner bury than uncover? Or, does it have something to do with the way we approached them? Might we have broken an informal norm by asking someone in a group to comment on the activities or character of another group member? If so, what might this imply about the maintenance of group solidarity? Much can be learned about a group by analyzing how and why they expose or conceal knowledge about themselves.

There is one last word about recording field notes. It is often impossible to record notes as action is taking place before us. In these cases, it is important that we look for opportunities to jot down key phrases so that we can later recapture the proceedings in full. In addition, it is important to sit down to record our notes as soon as possible after the actual observations are made. Memory tends to flag in short order unless stimulated by the active attempt to reconstruct events.

Our recent discussion of field notes should have been sufficiently clear to indicate that in the case of field work research a number of activities are carried out simultaneously. Methodological problems are dealt with while data is being collected and data analysis accompanies both of these operations. If, however, for purposes of creating benchmark guidelines, we were to divide the field work process in terms of time and energy expended by the researcher, we would name three phases. We have already dealt with two of them. The first phase would consist of gaining access to the setting and beginning one's observations. The second phase would involve reconstructing past events and seriously collecting data. The last phase of field research would consist of analysis per se.

At this point we will assume that we have left the field altogether and are now trying to come to grips with our collected data. Analysis has already begun in that we should at this point have accumulated a good number of theoretical notes and memos. That being so, we should by now have a pretty good idea of the alternative theoretical directions that the final research report might take. The time has come, however, to decide on the theoretical framework that will best allow us to order the bulk of the collected data. Given this problem, we must now occupy ourselves with the question: What procedures might be most helpful in producing a comprehensive analysis of the collected data?

Formulating an Analysis

We hesitate to offer an absolutely clear set of criteria for evaluating the quality of an analysis. It is perfectly plausible that two researchers independently entering the same social situation might emerge with two quite different analyses of data collected. We would add to this idea that each of these analyses might be equally cogent. It may simply be that the two researchers have seen quite different features of social life illuminated in the context studied. We should recall from our discussion in Chapter 1 that qualitative research seeks to discover generic "forms" of social life and that any one context may potentially display a number of these forms. The heart of an analysis, therefore, involves the researcher's application of a small number of well-selected concepts to show his or her reader the dimensions of social life reflected in the data. If successful, an analysis will cause us to see relations between pieces of data that might at first seem wholly discrete. In addition, the discovered elements of social life uncovered through an analysis of the collected data may challenge, specify, or confirm some already existing theoretical view of social life.

The beginnings of an analysis must be generated through a search for descriptive categories that serve to order good portions of the collected data. Standard sociological concepts or categories such as social class, ideology, identity, status, role, deviance, stigma, socialization, informal organization, and the like may provide a core for initial data classification. Sometimes these categories alone are sufficient to an analysis because they are flexible enough to be molded around the events at hand. Additionally, the unique linking of these categories can

itself be a creative and theoretically informative expression of the sociological imagination.

In other instances, the nature of the empirical setting and the
data collected necessitates the development of new conceptual categories. David Sudnow (1967), for example, needed to develop the concept
of "social loss" to explain observed variations in the attitudes of medical
personnel towards dying patients with different social statuses. His data
allows us to see how the death of some persons constitutes, in the minds
of the hospital personnel, a greater social loss than the death of others.

John Lofland (1971) suggests six classes of the initial ordering of
observational data: *acts, activities, meanings, participation, relationships,*
and *settings.* Each class further suggests a series of questions to be asked
of the data. For example, what are the basic types of acts and activities
that go on? What is the typical frequency of each activity and what is its
duration? How do actors meaningfully define the situation? What does
their action mean to them, and what kinds of collective norms dictate
their choice of action? How deeply does each participant get involved?
Are some participating more than others? Who relates to whom and
how? Who avoids whom and why? Is there a chain of communication
or command? Which persons appear to be central? Finally, what are the
distinctive characteristics of the setting and to what extent do they affect
or limit what takes place, how it takes place, and who gets involved?
How might the participants and their actions be different in another
setting?

The organizing categories suggested by Lofland are helpful, but
they will not fully solve the problems of the researcher who has collected
a large volume of field notes. Beyond raising the questions suggested by
Lofland's categories, researchers must somehow take into account the
specific type of data they have gathered. A usual procedure engaged in
by field workers in order to get a closer picture of the content of their
data is to somehow *code* that data. While there are many ways to code
qualitative data, they all represent variations of an essentially similar
process. We will look briefly at one coding procedure which may serve
as a basis for any specific variation demanded by a researcher's own data.

The first step in coding qualitative data is to generate as many
descriptive categories as possible. To accomplish this, researchers should
carefully read through their data and, each time a new category is suggested, write it down on a separate sheet of paper. Let us return to our
investigation of the Krishna religious group. We could well imagine the
collected data yielding the following kinds of categories: description of
setting, description of persons, eating habits, treatment of outsiders, internal conflict, proselytizing activities, value expressions, economic considerations, street behavior, the conversion process, and patterns of
leadership. It would not be unusual for one to produce a hundred or
more categories through this first close inspection of the data.

After such initial categories have been produced, we will begin to work with them more carefully. We may decide that some of the categories need to be broken down into even more categories and that a number of others really reflect one broader category. We arrange and rearrange the categories until we are satisfied that they are reasonably discrete and comprehensive of the collected data. At this point we can simply assign each of the developed categories a number. Having done this, the next task is to once again examine the data in the field notes indicating by number the category(ies) into which each piece of data appropriately fits. We will find, of course, that one verbal statement, one story or one event might properly be coded into a number of different categories.

In order to make the data more manageable we might at this point turn to a pair of scissors and a pile of index cards. If possible, we should duplicate several copies of the field notes. We keep one copy intact and use the other copies to cut out specific pieces of data, placing each on a separate index card. If a specific piece of data fits in more than one category, make as many copies of that data specimen as there are categories to which it applies. As we go through this process, we will want to record on the back of the card the category number to which the data refers. We may now put together the cards of each category. After reading all the data referring to each category, we may choose to refine the categories even further. At the very least, the kind of coding procedure described will give us a clear idea of the areas where we have the most data. It would certainly say something if we were able to uncover fifty pieces of data on, let us say, the conversion process, and only a couple on eating habits, or what-have-you. The sheer quantitative volume of data on one or another feature of the situation studied will almost necessarily influence the organization and content of the final report.

We have described the process of formulating an analysis largely in technical, procedural terms. Everything suggested to this point is preliminary to the actual writing of one's analysis. It is, most frequently, the work of writing the data analysis in a coherent fashion that causes a reevaluation of old ideas and leads to the formulation of new ideas. The process of writing allows the researcher to see more clearly the possible solutions to theoretical problems. New ideas reflect back upon the organization and statement of initial ideas and so on. Ideas that may at first have been terribly jumbled and inarticulately framed assume new vigor and demand expansion. Analysis, we mean to suggest, is not produced in a predictable, serial, linear fashion. There is a reciprocal relationship between ideas, such that one idea suggests others which in turn reflect upon and change the original idea, and so on.

Our final comment, therefore, would be that categorization alone will not produce a striking, convincing, compelling analysis. An analysis will be successful if the researcher can, through the use of the procedures described, complemented by personal insight, uncover in the data what Schatzman and Strauss (1973) refer to as a "key linkage" — an overriding pattern or story line which provides new insight into the situation investigated.

Such key linkages are at the heart of a developing theoretical perspective. We know that different observers can look at the same set of events and come up with very different key linkages. A psychiatrist and a city planner could analyze the same problem and produce quite different interpretations and suggestions. This is inherent in the nature of analysis because the description of a phenomenon is dependent on the choice of conceptual categories and any system of categories is some-what arbitrary and artificial. Just as wave theory and particle theory produce different interpretations of the nature of light, a functionalist and a Marxist analysis of any phenomenon will differ. It is not, therefore, important to produce a final, definitive interpretation of one or another phenomenon. It is important, however, to add something to the ongoing practical and intellectual discussion surrounding a phenomenon.

For most of this chapter, we have worked to understand the theoretical basis for field work, the areas in which field work has tradi-tionally been done, and the nature of the field work process. We have also considered, where appropriate, some practical guidelines for those who may eventually do field research. We shall end our discussion of observation and field research by looking more closely at some of the limitations of the method.

LIMITATIONS OF OBSERVATIONAL FIELD RESEARCH

It is already apparent that qualitative field methods cannot be used as a substitute for good quantitative research. Rather, as we have so often emphasized, structured and unstructured techniques ought to be used in conjunction with one another. The type of in-depth understanding of one or another social situation provided via field research methods con-stitutes an important contribution to our knowledge. At the same time, we must recognize that qualitative research does not easily allow a re-searcher to produce reliable measurements of phenomena, and conse-quently is of limited utility in definitively testing quantitative propositions. In addition to this general limitation we might list the following fre-quently mentioned and related weaknesses of qualitative field research:

1. The method is not applicable to the investigation of large social settings. The context studied must be small enough to be dealt with exhaustively by one or a few investigators.

2. There are few safeguards against the particular biases, attitudes, and assumptions of the researcher who does field research.

3. In the case of the field work the likelihood of the researcher's

selective perception and selective memory possibly biasing the results of the study is very great.

4. There is the related problem of selectivity in data collection. In any social situation there are literally thousands of possible pieces of data. No one researcher, in other words, can account for every aspect of a situation. The field researcher inevitably pulls out only a segment of the data that exists and the question inevitably arises as to whether the selected data is really representative of the situation.

5. The mere presence of the researcher in one or another group may change that social system to something different from what it would be were he not present. It is often argued that it is impossible to observe human beings without both influencing their behavior and being, in turn, influenced by them.

6. Because there is no set procedure defining the field research process, it is difficult for a researcher to explain to another exactly how the work was done. It is, therefore, virtually impossible to replicate the findings of a particular field work study.

Taken together, these various problems add up to a major, severe criticism of field research. Aside from our own private feelings and experiences, there is no way to easily assess the reliability and validity of the interpretations made by the researcher. We are forced to presume that researchers have been careful in their data collection and interpretation. However, as long as data is collected and presented by one or a few researchers with their own distinctive talents, faults, and foibles, there will remain suspicion concerning the validity of their rendering of the phenomena studied. Qualitative field researchers often respond to these criticisms by suggesting that the cost of imprecision is more than compensated for by the in-depth quality of the data produced.

Herbert Blumer (1954) has, for example, argued that we have not reached the point in our understanding of social processes (if, indeed, we ever can or will) where we can formulate our explanations using "definitive concepts" whose terms are unambiguous and whose empirical referents are precise. Blumer has argued for the necessity of using "sensitizing concepts" whose exact meaning can flexibly be adapted to our further unfolding of the mysteries underlying the "stubborn empirical world."

Such a position has a certain plausibility, but it can easily become an umbrella protecting shoddy research practices. In reviewing the substantive contributions of field workers one is immediately struck by the failure of most to conscientiously review the validity and reliability of their data and the inferences made from that data. There have been many theoretical discussions (Becker, 1969; Becker and Geer, 1969; Schwartz and Schwartz, 1969) of the relative merits of field work as well as consideration of the special problems in evaluating qualitative data. However, one finds few cases in which authors self-consciously consider these kinds of questions in the body of their research reports. We could, of course, raise the same questions about the effectiveness of quantitative researchers' checks against invalidity and bias. Those using structured techniques might not fully and satisfactorily resolve the questions raised here, but any review of quantitative research work does reveal a concerted effort to assess the reliability and validity of findings.

We would ask field researchers to work harder at explicating the procedural and analytical processes through which they produce their data and interpretations. In order to better evaluate the quality of data presented us, we need to know more than we normally do about the researcher's sampling procedures.[4] We need to know more about the basis for data selectivity. We need to have a fuller sense of the researcher's biases and assumptions. We need to know more about the procedures used in developing the analysis produced. Field researchers must, in short, be more fully responsible for specifying the methods used in seeing what they have seen. We do not read these requests as an unnecessary imposition on field researchers because our methodological judgments lie at the root of the analyses we produce. The requests made, then, are not antithetical to the goals of field research. To the contrary, closer attention to the quality of data produced via field work techniques seems a necessary step in evaluating how well we have "respected the nature of the empirical world" (Blumer, 1969:60).

CONCLUSION

For a period of time in American sociology, especially throughout the 1940s and 1950s, there was a considerable decline in the use of observational field research techniques. This decline was related to the simultaneous and rapid growth of quantitative methods. Survey research particularly grew in popularity as it allowed researchers to reach large numbers of people, increase the certainty of generalizations made from collected data, replicate the findings of earlier studies, and test theoretical ideas with increased precision.

Quantitative techniques such as survey research correctly remain central methodological tools today. There has been, however, a reemergence, a rebirth of the use of qualitative techniques. We make this judgment based on the large number of studies within the last fifteen years relying on qualitative methods, as well as on the growing volume of books describing the underlying logic of observational field work and the strategies found useful in its execution. This change has been brought about in part by the recognition that other techniques alone cannot

---

[4] For a discussion of sampling procedures in qualitative research, see pages 123–126 of Chapter 5 (Sampling).

provide the rich insight and human understanding that comes when scientists directly involve themselves in the worlds of those they study.

EXERCISES

1. Choose some relatively familiar context such as your dormitory room or a classroom and spend a couple of hours doing careful observation. Try to consider some of the elements of good observation mentioned in the chapter. Write a brief essay indicating the things, events, or processes observed that you had previously taken for granted during your normal involvement in the setting chosen.

2. Along with two or three other persons in your class, visit and observe some public context such as a bar, a public park, a bus station, or an event such as a rock concert, or a sporting event. Imagine that your collective goal is to understand how strangers either interact or fail to interact with each other in public places. Each of the persons with whom you are working should independently make her own observations and record her own field notes. At the end of the observation period you can meet as a group and compare your respective observations. What similarities exist? What differences are there in your observations? After discussing your separate observations write a brief report analyzing some feature of the situation studied (You might, for example, focus on how persons avoid one another, spatial rules governing interaction, how persons begin conversations, etc.). As an aid in producing your own analysis you may want to look at research on the conduct of persons in public places. As examples of such research we would mention Lyn Lofland's articles on "Self management in public settings" or Erving Goffman's book, *Behavior in Public Places* (see references for full citation).

3. Assume that you are about to embark on an observational study of a weight watchers group. Briefly indicate some of the methodological problems you might anticipate having. Do you speculate that there might be problems of access? Will there be difficulties in talking to persons? Might your own values intrude into your findings?

4. We mentioned in the chapter that Kai Erikson (1970) has established two rules concerning the ethicality of observational work. First, researchers must never deliberately misrepresent their identities to enter a private domain where they would otherwise have no legitimate access. Second, investigators must never misrepresent their research intentions. Write an essay indicating whether you think these rules are too restrictive. Will it be possible to follow these two rules and still study most social groups?

5. Read any article of your choice presenting data acquired through participant observation. As a source for a number of interesting articles you might want to look at the journal called *Urban Life*. After reading the article answer the following questions:

a. How fully did the author describe his or her methodology?
b. What additional discussion could have been included to give the reader a clearer idea of the procedures used?
c. Did the analysis conform well to the data presented?
d. What questions would you have about the reliability and validity of the findings?
e. Could the subject studied be investigated using methods other than participant observation? If so, indicate the methods that could have been used.

SUGGESTED READINGS

Readings about the Method

Bogdan, Robert
1972   *Participant Observation in Organizational Settings.* Syracuse, N.Y.: Syracuse University Press.

> Bogdan's short book is useful on two counts. First, he includes a sensible discussion of some of the central problems researchers are likely to encounter as they do observational field research. His discussion of the stages in participant observation should complement our own discussion in this chapter. Second, the book explicitly focuses on observational research in organizational settings. It is one of the few books to have this focus. The reader should also appreciate the appendix of the book in which the author includes some examples of field notes.

Filstead, William J.
1970   *Qualitative Methodology: Firsthand Involvement with the Social World.* Chicago: Markham.

> In this edited book the author has compiled a number of important essays on nearly all features of observational field research. Among the general topics discussed the reader will find articles on field work roles, processes of data collection, data analysis and ethical problems in field studies. Several of the articles to which we made reference in this chapter are included among Filstead's selections.

Glaser, Barney, and Anselm Strauss
1967   *The Discovery of Grounded Theory.* Chicago: Aldine.

> This book is among the most important published within the last few years on qualitative methodology. In it, the authors provide a theoretical rationale for observational work and describe the logic of inductive inquiry. Concerned primarily with the question of how researchers

generate theory from collected data, this book presents one of the most articulate descriptions available on the development of analysis from qualitative data.

Lofland, John
1971   *Analyzing Social Settings.* Belmont, Calif.: Wadsworth.

Lofland's book attempts to cover in a simple, straightforward fashion some of the major elements of observational field research. In the first part of the book the author offers a broad description of the purposes and goals of qualitative analysis. In the second part of the book he establishes guidelines for collecting and then analyzing observational data. Although Lofland's discussion tends to be somewhat "cookbookish," it should serve as a useful introduction to observational techniques for the student entering the field for the first time.

Webb, Eugene J., et al.
1966   *Unobtrusive Measures: Nonreactive Research in the Social Sciences.* Chicago: Rand McNally.

As indicated by the title, the authors of this book describe a number of different types of measures that may be acquired without the direct intervention of a researcher. This book is included here because some of the measures suggested can profitably be used by researchers doing qualitative field work research. The reader should especially note Chapter 5 of the book, "Simple Observation."

Whyte, William Foote
1943   *Street Corner Society.* Chicago: University of Chicago Press.

Whyte's *Street Corner Society* stands as a classic example of observational field research. It is also one of the few qualitative studies in which the researcher describes in an in-depth fashion how the study proceeded. To get a feeling for some of the typical problems any researcher doing participant observation is likely to experience, read the appendix of this book titled "On the Evolution of Street Corner Society." It is an honest, sensitive statement on the practical, intellectual, and ethical issues Whyte had to face as he did his research. It is fascinating and informative reading.

Readings Illustrating the Method

Becker, Howard S.
1963   *Outsiders: Studies in the Sociology of Deviance.* New York: Free Press.

Through his research on two separate subcultures — marihuana smokers and jazz musicians — Becker develops the theoretical idea of labeling to explain how and why certain persons embark on a "deviant career."

The studies reported in this volume demonstrate the use of analytic induction as the major method of inference in participant observation. The theoretical ideas raised in this work have had considerable impact on later studies of deviance as labeling theory gained considerable prominence during the mid-1960s. The book is also instructive for students wishing to see how qualitative data is presented in a study.

Cavan, Sherri
1966   *Liquor License: An Ethnography of Bar Behavior.* Chicago: Aldine.

In this study, Cavan develops a typology of bars that usefully organizes an enormous volume of qualitative data on various features of bar behavior. Along with detailing the different normative structures in each of the four bar types, she distinguishes the functions performed by each. Readers will want to consider, possibly on the basis of their own experiences, whether Cavan's typology does, in fact, allow for an insightful analysis of variations in bar behavior. They might want to consider whether bars familiar to them fit neatly into one or another of her categories.

Hall, Edward
1969   *The Hidden Dimension.* Garden City, N.Y.: Doubleday.

In this highly interesting and readable book, Edward Hall investigates some of the spatial norms that govern everyday behaviors in different cultures. In the first few chapters, the author reports on research concerning spatial regulation among lower animals and the effects of crowding on pathological behavior. The remainder of the book is devoted to a description of spatial regulations among human beings. Aside from its contribution to the study of proxemic or spatial behaviors, Hall's work demonstrates the value of cross-cultural observational research. While one might take issue with some of the inferences Hall draws from his data, he or she ought not miss the obvious policy implications of the research.

Humphreys, Laud
1970   *Tearoom Trade.* Chicago: Aldine.

In this book Humphreys reports the results of more than two years of field research on the behavior of homosexuals meeting in public bathrooms (called "tearooms") for impersonal anonymous sexual encounters. Because of the topic investigated and the methods employed, *Tearoom Trade* has been an extremely controversial book. Some have applauded it for its ingenious field research techniques and others have damned it as yet another example of illegitimate, immoral sociological voyeurism. As you read Humphreys's account of the field roles he adopted, try to consider your own position on the ethicality of his research. Ethical issues aside, notice how Humphreys continuously integrates descriptions of the setting, observations of particular events, over-heard conversations, and direct statements from respondents.

Liebow, Eliot
1967   *Tally's Corner.* Boston: Little, Brown.

In this lively, enormously popular and well-written ethnography, Eliot Liebow analyzes various features of the lives of black street-corner men in Washington, D.C. He analyzes the relationship of these men with each other, with women, and with their children. His data is used to construct a convincing argument that the behaviors of these men are explicable in terms of the obstacles they face in trying to realize the "middle class" values of achievement and success. From a methodological point of view, the reader will want to consider the threats to validity in a study in which a white researcher studies black persons. This is one of the several methodological issues Liebow raises in the appendix to his study.

Sudnow, David
1967   *Passing On: The Social Organization of Dying.* Englewood Cliffs, N.J.: Prentice-Hall.

Sudnow explores how death and dying are dealt with by staff members in two large municipal hospitals — one public and one private. Among other issues Sudnow analyzes differences between the two hospitals in the care of the dying, the effects of persons' social class on their treatment, the techniques of breaking "bad news," and the rituals associated with bereavement. Throughout, the author uses collected data to sustain the theme that death is as much a social as it is a biological fact.

REFERENCES

Becker, Howard S.
1963   *Outsiders: Studies in the Sociology of Deviance.* New York: Free Press.
1969   "Problems of inference and proof in participant observation." In *Issues in Participant Observation,* ed. George J. McCall and J. L. Simmons. Reading, Mass.: Addison-Wesley.

Becker, Howard S., and Blanche Geer
1969   "Participant observation and interviewing: a comparison." In *Issues in Participant Observation,* ed. George J. McCall and J. L. Simmons. Reading, Mass.: Addison-Wesley.

Berger, Peter, and Thomas Luckman
1967   *The Social Construction of Reality.* New York: Doubleday.

Blumer, Herbert
1954   "What is wrong with social theory." *American Sociological Review* 19 (February):3–10.

1969   *Symbolic Interaction.* Englewood Cliffs, N.J.: Prentice-Hall.

Cressey, Paul
1932   *The Taxi-Dance Hall.* Chicago: University of Chicago Press.

Davis, Fred
1970   "Focus on the flower children: why all of us may be hippies someday." In *Observations of Deviance,* ed. Jack Douglas. New York: Random House.

Emerson, Joan
1970   "Behavior in private places: sustaining definitions of reality in gynecological examinations." In *Recent Sociology* no. 2, ed. Hans Peter Dreitzel. New York: Macmillan.

Erikson, Kai
1970   "A comment on disguised observation in sociology." In *Qualitative Methodology,* ed. William J. Filstead. Chicago: Markham.

Gans, Herbert
1969   *The Levittowners.* New York: Random House.

Glazer, Myron
1972   *The Research Adventure.* New York: Random House.

Goffman, Erving
1959   *The Presentation of Self in Everyday Life.* New York: Doubleday.
1961   *Asylums.* New York: Doubleday.
1963   *Behavior in Public Places.* New York: Free Press.
1971   *Relations in Public.* New York: Basic Books.

Gold, Raymond
1969   "Roles in sociological field observations." In *Issues in Participant Observation,* ed. George J. McCall and J. L. Simmons. Reading, Mass.: Addison-Wesley.

Gouldner, Alvin
1954   *Patterns of Industrial Bureaucracy.* New York: Free Press.

Greenwald, Harold
1958   *The Call Girl.* New York: Ballantine Books.

Hall, Edward
1969   *The Hidden Dimension.* New York: Doubleday.

Humphreys, Laud
1970   *Tearoom Trade.* Chicago, Aldine.

Jackson, P.
1968   *Life in the Classroom.* New York: Holt, Rinehart & Winston.

Kahn, Robert, and Floyd Mann
1969   "Developing research partnerships." In *Issues in Participant Observation,* ed. George J. McCall and J. L. Simmons. Reading, Mass.: Addison-Wesley.

Karp, David A.
1973   "Hiding in pornographic bookstores: a reevaluation of the nature of urban anonymity." *Urban Life and Culture* 1 (January):427–451.

Liebow, Eliot
1967   *Tally's Corner.* Boston: Little, Brown.

Lofland, John
1971   *Analyzing Social Settings.* Belmont, Cal.: Wadsworth.

Lofland, John, and Robert A. Lejeune
1970   "Initial interaction of newcomers in Alcoholics Anonymous." In *Qualitative Methodology,* ed. William J. Filstead. Chicago: Markham.

Lofland, Lyn
1971a   "Self management in public settings, part I." *Urban Life and Culture* 1 (April):93–117.
1971b   "Self management in public settings, part II." *Urban Life and Culture* 2 (July):217–231.

McKinney, John C.
1966   *Constructive Typology and Social Theory.* New York: Appleton-Century-Crofts.

Pope, Harrison
1971   *Voices from the Drug Culture.* Boston: Beacon Press.

Sagarin, Edward
1969   *Odd Man In.* Chicago: Quadrangle Books.

Schatzman, Leonard, and Anselm Strauss
1973   *Field Research: Strategies for a Natural Sociology.* Englewood Cliffs, N.J.: Prentice-Hall.

Schwartz, Morris S., and Charlotte G. Schwartz
1969   "Problems in participant observation." In *Issues in Participant Observation,* ed. George J. McCall and J. L. Simmons. Reading, Mass.: Addison-Wesley.

Sommer, Robert
1969   *Personal Space.* Englewood Cliffs, N.J.: Prentice-Hall.

Sudnow, David
1967   *Passing On: The Social Organization of Dying.* Englewood Cliffs, N.J.: Prentice-Hall.

Sutherland, Edwin
1949   *White Collar Crime.* New York: Holt, Rinehart & Winston.

Thorne, Barrie
1971   *Resisting the Draft: An Ethnography of the Draft Resistance Movement.*
        Unpublished Ph.D. dissertation: Brandeis University.

Weinberg, Martin
1968   "Sexual modesty, social meanings and the nudist camp." In *Sociology
        and Everyday Life,* ed. Marcello Truzzi. Englewood Cliffs, N.J.: Prentice-
        Hall.

Whyte, William Foote
1943   *Street Corner Society.* Chicago: University of Chicago Press.

Wolff, Michael
1973   "Notes on the behavior of pedestrians." In *People in Places: The Sociol-
        ogy of the Familiar,* ed. Arnold Birenbaum and Edward Sagarin. New
        York: Praeger.

Experimental Research

CHAPTER NINE

The idea of experimentation should not be foreign to most of us. We all use loose or incomplete forms of experimentation in our daily lives. A husband or wife "experiments" with different ways of preparing food, noting their spouse's reaction to each modification of the prepared dish. A salesperson intent on finding the most persuasive "line" to use in selling a product may systematically test out a number of approaches until he finds the one that works best. Teachers experiment with a variety of teaching formats, hoping to find the one that allows students to learn the most. Vacationers in Las Vegas try out a number of different systems at roulette or blackjack, hoping to find the one that will make them winners.

Any time that we somehow systematically "manipulate" our surroundings and try to assess the effects of these manipulations, we are engaging in an experiment. In all the cases mentioned, actors looked for changes in one or another phenomenon (expressions of pleasure in eating, number of sales made, and so on) after systematically manipulating some feature of the environment. The presumed purpose of our everyday experimentation is to safely assert the existence of a *causal connection* between two or more variables.

What, then, distinguishes our everyday experimentation from scientific experimentation? The most basic answer is that most of us do not typically go to the trouble of creating rigorous safeguards to ensure the correctness of the causal relationship suggested by our experimentation. Consider the teacher who has been experimenting with a number of teaching methods. Suppose he finds in one of his classes that small-group discussion seems to produce the greatest amount of learning, as measured by a test on the material. Would we be satisfied that he has uncovered the best teaching technique and that he should now use small-group discussions in all his classes? Are there, in short, any kinds of procedural considerations that might cause us to question the validity of his "findings"?

Among other questions, we might ask: "Isn't it possible that the class responding well to the small-group discussions had better students in the first place and would have learned more regardless of the method used? Might the size of the class have had an effect on the amount learned — independent of the method employed? Might it have made a difference that the teacher's classes met at different times during the day and that, again, independent of the method used, students are more or less attentive during certain school hours? What about the distribution of males and females in the class? Is there any possibility that the sex composition of the class alters the willingness of students to participate in small-group discussions?

It seems plain that in order to make "safe" causal inferences we must somehow ensure that factors wholly unrelated to what we presume to be the cause of some phenomenon can be excluded or discounted. In the ideal experimental situation the only thing that will vary from group to group or situation to situation is the experimental treatment. Unless the situations studied are similar in all respects other than the presence or absence of an experimental treatment, we cannot be certain that it is the experimental treatment rather than some other difference existing between the groups that causes certain changes in the groups. If we hope to isolate the effects of one or another experimental treatment we must somehow *control for,* or rule out, all those factors other than the experimental treatment which could affect the behaviors of those studied. In the case at hand, if we want to demonstrate that *small-group discussion* makes a difference in student learning, we must be careful to rule out class size, gender composition, the time of day the class is taught, and other such factors.

Both everyday actors and scientists are concerned with demonstrating causal connections between various features of the social world. The essence of the scientific experiment, however, is that scientists make every effort to set up their experimental procedures in such a way as to clearly demonstrate that any changes in behavior following an experimental treatment are not "contaminated" by factors extraneous to that treatment. Experimental research, therefore, may be defined as research in which one or more variables are manipulated by the experimenter under carefully controlled conditions. The task of scientists is to assess clearly the effects of their experimental manipulation by measuring changes in a specified variable. The key phrase in this definition is that experimental research is conducted under *carefully controlled conditions.* For most of the remainder of this chapter we shall consider some of the difficulties involved in achieving such control. We shall see that some research problems do not easily submit to pure experimental procedures and others do. The degree of control possible must be taken as the major criterion in assessing how surely we can claim the existence of a causal connection between two or more variables.

THE ELEMENTS OF TRUE EXPERIMENTATION

Perhaps we can achieve a better picture of how control is exercised and how causality between variables is established by looking at a hypothetical example — an experiment that might be conducted in some social psychologist's laboratory. We can follow the researcher through the process of experimentally testing her idea. We shall want to offer a rationale for each step in that process. With this goal in mind, we choose to begin our discussion by assuming that a researcher has a theoretical reason for believing there is a relationship between the degree of anxiety in a group and the cohesiveness of that group. Further, she states the hypothesis she will want to test experimentally as follows:

> The greater the anxiety among the members of a group, the greater will be the cohesion of that group.

In order to determine the experimental procedures needed to test this hypothesis, the researcher must look carefully at the elements of the hypothesis. Clearly, the two variables being related in the hypothesis are anxiety and cohesion. The convention in scientific research is to label the proposed causal variable in a relationship the *independent variable* and the proposed effect of the independent variable, the *dependent variable*. In her hypothesis, the researcher has proposed that anxiety causes cohesion. Hence, given our definitions, anxiety is the independent variable and cohesion is the dependent variable.

Logic demands that in order to test this hypothesis the researcher must necessarily compare at least two groups. The simplest test of her hypothesis would be to compare a low-anxiety and a high-anxiety group with the expectation that cohesion would be greater in the latter group. At this point, we may mention one of the great strengths of experimental procedure: the experimenter is in a position to create just the groups that she needs in order to test her hypothesis. More explicitly, the experimental researcher is in a position to manipulate her independent variable: that is, she can cause it to vary. In this case, the experimenter must think of some way to introduce or produce anxiety in one of the two groups she will assemble and compare. In this simplest form of experimentation, where the researcher works with only two groups, the group in which the experimental, independent, or test variable (in this case anxiety) is introduced is called the *experimental group;* and the group in which it is not introduced is called the *control group.*

We may now consider how the experimenter works to create her two groups and how exactly she manipulates the test variable. It is not uncommon for university-associated researchers to put an advertisement in their school newspaper asking for student volunteers to participate in an experiment. Usually those students who volunteer are paid a nominal sum of money for their participation.

While we will want to discuss more fully at a later point the possible weaknesses of experimental procedures on human subjects, we may note two possible difficulties raised by the recruitment procedure we are outlining here. First, students represent only one sector of the whole society. They are likely younger, better read, possibly more intelligent, and so on than the average person in the society. If we use only students because of the convenience of their accessibility, we must recognize that there will be limits to any generalizations made from our experimental findings. It may very well be that groups more heterogeneous in terms of age, ethnicity, intelligence, and the like would behave quite differently from the relatively homogeneous groups of students. Second, our subjects would consist of those persons who *choose* to participate in an experiment. This raises another problem of selectivity. Might there be some systematic difference between the types of persons willing to participate and those not willing? Researchers must be cognizant of these factors as they ultimately attempt to make generalizations about group process from their data.

Bearing these problems in mind, let us assume that volunteers have been instructed to sign up some time in advance of the date when the experiment will actually be carried out. For purposes of convenience we shall say that thirty students have indicated their willingness to participate in the experiment. Since group size might very well affect people's behavior, the researcher makes the reasonable decision to have fifteen students in both the experimental and control groups. The next decision must be to determine which fifteen will be in each group. This decision is an absolutely crucial one, and if improperly made could void the results of the experiment. Let's consider the logic of the assignment of the students to the two groups.

We could ask, "What would be wrong with simply assigning the first fifteen names on the list to the experimental group and the last fifteen to the control group?" Recall the purpose of the experiment: it is to assess the effects of anxiety on group cohesion. All other variables must be ruled out. This being so, we may begin to see why simply splitting the list in half to create the two comparison groups would be an unwise decision. It might be that women, or poor students, or psychology majors have a tendency to sign up for participation in experiments before others. The first fifteen students who sign up might, in other words, differ in important respects from the last fifteen. Since the researcher wants to rule out or control for any such systematic differences she must adopt a different procedure for assigning subjects to experimental and control groups.

The researcher correctly chooses to assign students to her groups *randomly*. The laws of statistical probability dictate that neither of the two groups would be over- or underrepresented by persons with one or another distinctive characteristic. Random selection is, therefore, a key feature of experimental procedure, allowing the researcher to effectively control for all possible factors extraneous to the specific relationship under investigation.

Now the day has arrived when the volunteers will show up to participate in the experiment. Having solved the problem of group assignment, the researcher must be prepared to manipulate the independent variable in the experimental group (somehow create anxiety in that group) and to measure any changes that occur in group cohesion. At this point there are a number of variations that might be pursued. The following type of procedure would not be unusual:

1. After assignment of persons to the two groups, the researcher asks the members of each group to work together on some reasonably simple problem. The researcher is not, in this case, interested in their ability to do the assigned problem. She merely wants to get persons interacting as a group so that she might measure certain features of that group interaction.

2. Prior to the arrival of the subjects she has determined how to *measure* cohesion, the dependent variable. While the difficulties of measurement are great and the researcher must be concerned with the reliability and validity of her measures, let us say for simplicity's sake, that she measures cohesion in terms of the number of times group members refer to the group as a whole by using the collective "we." She might do this by observing the groups through a one-way mirror.

3. After observing each group for a time, she will have arrived at a quantitative measure of cohesion for each group prior to the introduction of the test variable. Measurement of the dependent variable prior to the manipulation of the independent variable is often referred to as a *pretest*.

4. At this point the experimenter is prepared to manipulate the experimental group by somehow introducing or raising the level of anxiety in that group. Perhaps she might, as one example, communicate to the members of the experimental group that they are not performing as well as they should be on their assigned task and that unless their performances get better they can expect a reasonably unpleasant punishment. Through such a communication the researcher has presumably increased the level of anxiety in the experimental group and is now in a position to observe any changes in group cohesion.

5. The researcher returns to her place behind the one-way mirror and again assesses the degree of cohesion in each group as measured by the frequency of collective group references by group members. The measure of the dependent variable following the experimental treatment is often referred to as the *posttest*. Any change in subjects' behaviors or attitudes is established by comparing pretest and posttest measures.

If, when the researcher compares the pretest and posttest measures of cohesion for both the experimental and control groups, she is able to show a substantial increase in cohesion after manipulation of the independent variable in only the experimental group, this may be taken as evidence that the initial hypothesis relating anxiety and cohesion is correct. More than that, however, the experimental procedure she used allows the researcher to make the even more powerful statement that anxiety is a *cause* of cohesion. Properly executed experimental research allows for collection of the evidence necessary for making causal statements. A review of the hypothetical research we have described will reveal that the researcher has met the following three criteria for establishing causality between variables:

1. First, the researcher must be able to show that the independent and dependent *variables are associated*. She must be able to show, in other words, that any measured change in the independent variable will be accompanied by a measured change in the dependent variable and vice versa.

2. The idea of causality implies more than simple association, however. The idea of causality involves, in addition, the *direction of the relationship* between two variables. It is one thing to say that variables X and Y are related and quite another to say that X caused Y. In order to establish the more precise direction of causality between two variables, the researcher must show that there is a time sequencing to any measured change in both independent and dependent variables. That is, showing the direction of causality is contingent on the demonstration that a change in Y clearly *follows* a change in X, and not the other way around. The experimental procedure involving the manipulation of an independent variable clearly allows the researcher to illustrate the time sequencing of events. One of the strengths of the experiment resides in the fact that the researcher frequently controls the timing of events. She is able to demonstrate that any measured change in the dependent variable occurs *only after* the independent variable has been introduced.

3. Finally, in order to establish a causal relationship between two variables, the researcher must be able to give evidence that it is indeed the proposed independent variable and not some other unknown factor that is responsible for any measured change in the dependent variable. The experiment which allows for *random assignment* of subjects to both experimental and control groups ensures that the two groups are not substantially different in important respects. The control over extraneous

variables exerted through random assignment allows the researcher to make a very important assertion; namely, that the only difference between the groups studied is that one has not been exposed to the experimental treatment and the other has.

We have set the stage for further discussion by presenting in some detail, through example, the logic and structure of experimental research. We cannot assume, however, that once the conditions for a true experiment are met, researchers can unequivocally establish just how the variables examined in their studies are causally related. As in all the methodologies employed by social scientists there are sources of distortion, bias, or error that may render invalid the findings produced in a study. We turn, then, to a discussion of some of the threats to validity where the classic experimental design is employed.

THREATS TO VALIDITY IN EXPERIMENTAL RESEARCH

Methodologists typically distinguish between threats to *internal validity* and threats to *external validity* as they consider sources of distortion in experimental research.[1] When we speak of internal validity, we are referring to the ways in which the conduct or process of experimentation itself may affect the results obtained. Is there anything about the procedures used in conducting an experiment that may distort the "truth value" of the data collected? It is important to remember that the researcher wants to isolate the effects of specific independent variables. Threats to internal validity exist when our ability to see the effect of some independent variable is blurred because the experimental procedure used has itself affected subjects' behaviors.

When researchers speak of external validity, they refer to difficulties in *generalizing* the findings of experimental research. A frequent criticism of laboratory experiments is that they are artificially constructed situations and that people do not act in the real world as they do in constructed experimental situations. For this reason there are limits to the generalizations we can make from experimental research. The external validity question asks whether groups created for purposes of experimentation are sufficiently different from naturally occurring groups that generalization beyond the experimental situation is unwarranted. We will want to address ourselves to this so-called "reality" problem. First, however, we need to consider some of the specific obstacles to internal validity in studies using the classic experimental design.

---

[1] In our discussion of internal and external validity we draw heavily upon the work of Campbell and Stanley (1963).

Internal Validity

Internal validity is the *sine qua non* of experimental research. We must be able to ascertain whether the experimental treatment is, in fact, responsible for any measured changes in a dependent variable. We saw earlier that random assignment of subjects to experimental and control groups ensures, according to the laws of probability, that the groups compared do not significantly differ from one another in their composition. Through random assignment we achieve a degree of control over the range of variables, other than the chosen independent variable, that could be causally related to the dependent variable in our study. We must now examine those factors associated with the experimental procedure itself that cannot be controlled through random assignment.

In all cases, the concern of the researcher is to measure *change* in some dependent variable after the introduction of a test variable. In order to assess precisely the change in a dependent variable, she must measure it at least twice — once before the introduction of the test variable and once after. There are, however, some complications that enter into the researcher's assessment of change.

Immediately we may see that the subjects of an experiment may become *sensitized to the measurement procedures used*. Any initial measurement (pretest) of subjects may sensitize them to the interests of the experimenter and affect their responses to the second measurement (the posttest). Suppose, for example, researchers want to determine whether a movie showing natural childbirth makes persons more or less favorably disposed toward natural childbirth. If the experimenters decide to use the control group/experimental group design and to show the movie (the independent variable) in the experimental group, they would undoubtedly want some initial measure of subjects' attitudes about natural childbirth. But if they ask persons to fill out an attitude questionnaire on childbirth, the very activity of filling out the questionnaire might affect their attitudes. If this occurred, the experimenters would not easily be able to assess the effects of the movie itself (their independent variable) in changing subjects' attitudes.

Along with the danger of pretest sensitization there may be *maturational processes* through which members of either or both groups go. That is, the subjects of an experiment may experience an event or input from the general experimental environment which is unrelated to the experimental treatment per se but which may nevertheless influence their behaviors and attitudes. We could, for example, envision influential leaders becoming established in a group that has been meeting for even a short time. These leaders could modify the behaviors of other subjects in the study. Or, as another example of maturational effects creating changes in behavior apart from the experimental manipulation, there is the simple possibility of subjects becoming bored or fatigued or growing hungrier during the course of an experiment. There are, in other words, a number of factors associated simply with the passage of time that might cause persons to change their behavior.

Closely related to the effects of maturation are the potentially confounding effects of *history*. It could happen, especially in experiments where there is a reasonable span of time between pretest and posttest measures of the dependent variable, that subjects will learn about an event that has occurred in the society which will influence their attitudes. Campbell and Stanley (1963) cite the example of a study done in 1940 in which the researcher wanted to assess the effects on students of Nazi propaganda. During the days in which the students were reading the propaganda materials, France fell to the Nazis. It is very likely that any changes in student attitudes were more directly a result of this historical event than of the materials they were reading.

In addition to the factors already named, researchers concerned with the internal validity of experimental procedures have mentioned that there are occasions when the dependent variable is not measured exactly the same way in the posttest as in the pretest. There are many experimental studies where observers, scorers, or raters evaluate changes in the dependent variable after some experimental treatment. It could happen that these persons themselves go through a maturational process — become fatigued or bored — and do not, therefore, use exactly the same measurement criteria for the posttest as they did for the pretest. This problem of *measurement decay* is further exacerbated if pretest and posttest measurements are done by altogether different sets of persons. It could happen, in other words, that any measured change in the dependent variable is due to inconsistencies in measurement rather than to the experimental treatment.

Finally, we must mention the possibility that subjects will drop out of the experiment before it is completed. *Experimental* or *subject mortality* will, of course, influence the comparability of the control and experimental groups and will cause researchers to question whether any measured changes in a dependent variable following the experimental treatment might be a function of the changed composition.

In order to combat some of the threats to internal validity we have been considering, experimental researchers have invented elaborations on the classic experimental design. To illustrate the ingenuity of researchers who are intent on maximizing the internal validity of their experiments, we shall examine a frequently used variation of the control group/experimental group design. In the case we have chosen, researchers employ four comparison groups. This design has come to be called the Solomon Four-Group Design and takes the form illustrated in Table 9.1. The reader should note that the form of the design up to experimental group 2 is identical to the classic experimental design already discussed. Two additional groups have been added to the design. In these two additional groups no pretest measure of the independent variable is made.

TABLE 9.1 The Soloman Four-Group Design

	Experimental group 1	Control group 1	Experimental group 2	Control group 2
Pretest conducted	yes	yes	no	no
Exposure to test variable	yes	no	yes	no
Posttest conducted	yes	yes	yes	yes

Consider along with us the logic of adding experimental group 2 and control group 2.

We begin with the assumption that because persons have been randomly assigned to all four groups they do not systematically vary from each other in any important respect. Although no pretest measures are taken in experimental group 2 and control group 2, we can assume, because persons have been randomly assigned to all four groups, that if a pretest *had* been given in these groups, the results would not differ substantially from the pretest measures of experimental group 1 and control group 1. We can also assume that the effects of any maturational processes would be the same in all four groups.

Now, let us suppose that the researchers were concerned with the possible sensitizing effects of a pretest measure. We draw your attention to the comparison they could make between experimental group 1 and experimental group 2. The only thing differentiating these two groups is that a pretest measure has been conducted in one and not the other. Therefore, if the pretest has had no effect in changing the attitudes or behaviors of persons, we would expect that there will be no substantial difference in the posttest measures for these two groups. If there is a substantial posttest measure difference between experimental groups 1 and 2, the researchers can estimate how much influence the pretest has had in producing that change, since the only thing distinguishing those two groups is the absence of the pretest in one of them. Moreover, by comparing these experimental groups with control group 1 (pretest done, no experimental treatment), they can assess the effects of their experimental treatment.

What about maturation and history as confounding factors? How can the effects of those two related factors be evaluated? These possible biasing factors can be evaluated by means of control group 2. Subjects in control group 2 have experienced neither a pretest nor the experimental treatment. Only a posttest has been done. Any change in control group 2 (the difference between the posttest measure and the pretest measure inferred to be the same in experimental group 1 and control group 1) must, then, be due entirely to maturational processes and not the effect of the experimental treatment. The pure effect of the experimental treatment can be determined by subtracting the posttest score of control group 2 (effects of maturation) from the posttest score of experimental group 2 (effects of maturation and experimental treatment).

In conclusion, we can see that the elaboration of the classic experimental design to include a larger number of comparison groups better allows researchers to determine exactly the effects of their stated independent variables. There are several design variations possible. By using a number of groups, researchers can administer several pretests; they can control in a number of ways the timing of events (that is, the timing of the introduction of the test variable); they can sometimes vary the *intensity* of the test variable in different groups (a researcher interested in the effects of anxiety could, for example, control the degree of anxiety created in groups studied); and they can administer a number of different posttests. While it goes beyond the scope of our discussion to study all these design variations, we must at the least understand their purpose. All elaborations on the classical experimental design allow researchers to evaluate more precisely the causal effects of their chosen independent variables.

External Validity

Even when researchers conduct experiments in which they minimize the threats to internal validity, they must still worry about whether they can generalize from their experimental findings. After all, persons may not behave in their "natural life situations" as they do when they know that their behaviors are being watched, measured, and evaluated by a scientist. Can we be certain that persons conform, react to anxiety, learn how to perform tasks, respond to group leaders, develop group norms, and the like just as they would in situations in which they are not being studied? When we inquire into the correspondence between persons' behaviors in experimental situations and their "natural world" behaviors we are raising the question of external validity. If there is no correspondence between the two, it becomes logically dangerous to generalize beyond the experimental situation itself.

The fact that persons' behaviors may be altered because they know they are being studied was clearly demonstrated in a 1939 study of workers in the Hawthorne plant. The biasing effect of subjects' knowledge that they are part of a study has, therefore, come to be called the *Hawthorne effect*. In the Hawthorne study a number of researchers set out to investigate factors affecting worker productivity. They manipulated patterns of lighting, monetary incentives for production, patterns of managerial leadership, and so on. The major finding of the study was that regardless of the experimental manipulations employed, the production of workers seemed to improve. One reasonable conclusion from this research is that the workers were pleased to be part of an experiment — they were pleased to receive attention from re-searchers who expressed an interest in them — and this was the most influential factor affecting productivity. We can, however, be somewhat more specific regarding how persons' knowledge of their participation in an experiment might cause them to modify their "normal" behaviors.

One danger is that subjects in an experiment may try to behave in accordance with the way they believe the experimenter expects them to behave. When this occurs we can speak of an *expectancy* or *modeling effect* operating. All of us have a need to order and to make intelligible the situations in which we are acting, and the experimental situation is no exception. We ought to expect that subjects in an experiment will try to figure out what the experiment is about, what the researchers wish to know. Subjects no doubt have some conception of how persons participating in an experiment ought to act; they realize their behaviors are being evaluated and, in most instances, will want to "look good." Given their definitions of the experimental situation, subjects will often model their behavior on what they believe the experimenter is looking for. The problem is compounded by the demonstrated possibility that experimental researchers do sometimes unwittingly convey their attitudes and expectations to their subjects with the result that the subjects conform to those expectations.

The operation of expectancy effects was pointedly shown by Rosenthal and Fode (1963) in an experiment of their own. One group of researchers were given a number of laboratory rats and told that these rats had been specially bred genetically and could be expected to be fast learners. Another group of researchers were told that their rats were dull and consequently would not easily learn to run a maze. Despite the fact that there was in reality absolutely no difference between the two groups of rats, the "superior" rats performed much better than their "dull" counterparts. Rosenthal and Fode offer the following tentative account for these surprising findings:

> Rats are sensitive to visual, auditory, olfactory, and tactual cues. These last, the tactual, were perhaps the major cues mediating the experimenter's expectancy to the animal. . . . Experimenters expecting and obtaining better performances handled their rats more and also more gently than did the experimenters expecting and obtaining poorer performances. (Rosenthal and Fode, 1963:165)

Rosenthal and Fode's experiment is particularly striking in that these unwitting "communications" occurred between experimenters and non-symbol-using animals. When we think of the utterly enormous capacity of the human animal to symbolize, to pick up subtle cues, and to engage in elaborate processes of interpretation, we must recognize the heightened likelihood that expectancy effects are operative in determining the outcomes of experimentation with persons.

We mentioned earlier that there are frequently special *sampling* problems in the conduct of experiments that may also flaw the representativeness of findings. More specifically, the subjects of laboratory experiments are often drawn from readily accessible populations. Very often, the subjects are students and then only those students who express a willingness to participate. The generalizability of our findings might therefore be compromised by selection processes that favor the inclusion of certain types of subjects and the exclusion of others. Consider, as an example, the implication of the fact that experimental subjects are often volunteers. Substantial evidence has been accumulated to show that volunteers differ from nonvolunteers in the following ways (Jung, 1971:28):

> Volunteers are higher in the need for social approval.
> Volunteers tend to have more unconventional personalities.
> Volunteers more often tend to be first born.
> Volunteers for certain experiments are less well adjusted.
> Volunteers tend to have higher need for achievement.

It is important to know that the problem of generalizability does not belong to the experimental researcher alone. Systematic sample selectivity and expectancy biases must certainly be considered as obstacles to generalization in participant observation and survey research studies as well. In the case of experiments, the problems of internal validity, we have seen, can be dealt with through the use of ingenious experimental designs. There is no such similar logical response to the question of external validity. As we saw in earlier chapters, satisfaction that the results of our research allow for generalization always demands a leap of faith to some degree. While we should refrain from claiming a one-to-one relationship between the laboratory situation and the "real world," we should not dismiss the power of the experiment in sensitizing us to important processes of social life. A social psychologist named Leon Festinger says it well and his words are worth quoting at some length:

> It should be stressed . . . that the problem of application of the results of laboratory experiments to the real-life situation is not solved by a simple extension of the result. Such application requires additional experimentation and study. It is undoubtedly important that the results of laboratory experiments be tested out in real-life situations. Unless this is done the danger of "running dry" or "hitting a dead end" is always present. A continuous interplay between laboratory experiments and studies of real life situations should provide proper perspective, for the results obtained should continually supply new hypotheses for building the

theoretical structure and should represent progress in the solution of the problems of application and generalization. (Festinger, 1971:326)

Festinger's request that there be a continuous interplay between experimental procedures and studies of real life situations provides a useful transition to the next section of this chapter. We have strongly implied so far that laboratory experiments have the great virtue of letting researchers exercise control over variables extraneous to their research interests in a particular study. As a general rule we may suggest that as research is done in the real world — that is, as we try to study persons in their natural environments — it becomes increasingly more difficult to isolate a few variables for investigation. At the same time, we wish to emphasize that it *is* possible to conduct experiments outside the laboratory situation; it is sometimes possible to have, as the saying goes, the best of both worlds. Researchers who are legitimately concerned with the artificiality of the laboratory situation often have the opportunity to conduct their experimental inquiries in natural settings. In the next section we want to look at some examples of sociological field experiments.

SOCIOLOGICAL FIELD EXPERIMENTATION

Very often the social phenomena or processes of interest to sociologists are not easily investigated within the context of a laboratory. It is difficult to study such issues as the development of group culture, consumer behavior, and the effects of mass communication, in experimental laboratories. At the same time, sociologists, aware of the multitude of factors that may inhibit their attempts at establishing causal relationships between variables, want to utilize experimental models whenever possible. In this section of the chapter we shall study some selected examples of sociological field experiments.

True Field Experiments

We mentioned in earlier chapters that one goal of sociological research is to use the knowledge acquired through investigation to formulate sound social policy. American society is beset by many social problems that demand solutions. What is the best way to deal with poverty, racial segregation, delinquency, and the like? Very often we read about alternative programs suggested by citizens, social scientists, and legislators to ameliorate social ills. We must have some intelligent basis for choosing between alternative policy proposals. There are situations where social scientists may employ experimental procedures for gathering evidence about the likely success or failure of alternative policy proposals. As one example of the type of field experimentation that might be done, we shall consider the New Jersey negative income tax experiment.

The idea of a negative income tax was first suggested in 1962 by the economist Milton Friedman. The basic idea of a negative income tax is to have the federal government pay out cash to families on the low end of the income scale so as to ensure a minimum income to all in the country. The amount of money paid by the federal government to a family would decrease as the income level of that family went up. The amount paid to a family without any income might hypothetically be $3000. The idea behind the negative income tax would be to subsidize a family while still providing some incentive to work. It has been suggested, therefore, that there might be a tax rate of 50 percent which would be applied to persons who are working but whose income still makes them eligible for government support. It would work this way: Suppose a family of four had an income level of $1000. The 50 percent tax rate would demand that half of the $1000 ($500) be subtracted from the guaranteed $3000 baseline, reducing the government payment to $2500. The total family income would then be $3500. An understanding of this hypothetical formula should allow us to compute that the total family income for a family earning $2000 would be $4000. Such a system would continue until the family's earnings reached $6000, at which point they would be paid no further subsidy.

There are a number of questions raised by both opponents and proponents of the negative income tax. On a technical level persons disagree on what ought to be the baseline guaranteed income for a family of four. There is also disagreement concerning what ought to be the tax on earned income for the same family of four. Disagreement exists around these technical features of the negative income tax plan because it is argued that these figures are crucial in determining whether the tax plan would kill any incentive for persons to work. It is feared that if the subsidy were too high persons would be disinclined to seek work. It is also felt that the different versions of the plan would have differential effects on family patterns of consumption, family attitudes toward education, and the like. All these questions remain unresolved.

Here, then, we are confronted by a social policy plan with potentially great implications for the welfare and labor force participation of the poorest segment of our society. We are also confused about which version of the plan would have what kinds of effects. Without any empirical data we would find ourselves accepting or rejecting a proposal without much sense of the potential effects of the plan. It is in the context of this ignorance that researchers have endeavored to set up an experiment to find out the likely effects of the various plans. It seemed reasonable that one way to resolve some of the arguments centering around different versions of the plan was to let the different plans themselves constitute experimental treatments. The researchers proceeded to set up their experiment as follows. We ask the reader to attend to the fact that the experimental procedure devised meets the criteria of a true experiment.

> . . . Twelve hundred low income families (were selected) from four metropolitan areas in the state. These families have a number of characteristics in common in addition to the obvious characteristic that they are urban: each has a non-aged male head, an employable (although not necessarily employed) member, and a total family income below 150 percent of the poverty line. . . . Following a process of random selection, families are assigned to one of eight negative income tax plans in addition to a control group which does not receive payments. . . . Each of these families receives a regular cash payment for three years, the amount being based on the size of the family, the plan to which the family is assigned, and the current income of the family. In addition to these payments, each family will be interviewed quarterly for the three-year period. (Kershaw, 1969:17)

The purpose of the sequence of planned interviews was, of course, to measure various dependent variables of interest to the researchers: family life style, the effort expended by persons in looking for a job, patterns of economic consumption, and the like. While there are a total of nine groups involved in this experiment, it should be clear that it is a true experimental design. Families were randomly assigned to each of the nine groups, the different plans constituted variations of the experimental treatment, there was a clear control group which did not receive any experimental treatment, and there were a succession of measures designed to evaluate the effects of each experimental treatment.

We should be quick to note that the experimental procedure outlined has its difficulties. There are several potential sources of bias. First, the families involved knew that they were participating in an experiment and this knowledge might affect their behaviors. Second, the experiment was designed to run for only three years and the subjects' knowledge of this fact may also have affected their behaviors. After all, no one could be complacent about a guaranteed income for the rest of his life because the experiment's termination date was known in advance. The employable members of these families were probably more motivated to seek jobs than they would have been if they had thought they would never again have to make any greater efforts at income production than they had been making when selected for the experiment. Related to these two points, the subjects were to be measured on various dependent variables a number of times during the course of the three years and this frequent series of posttest measures might have some biasing effect. Even with these limitations, it seems clear that the experiment described should provide the most valid data possible on this complex problem — short of fully instituting a negative income tax plan.

The possibility of conducting naturalistic field experiments of the sort just described should be important to both social scientists and government officials concerned with social policy. Armed with powerful experimental procedures, we should not have to embark on social programs in ignorance of their possible effects or outcomes. If the government is about to institute one or another social program that would entail the expenditure of billions of dollars, it does not seem unreasonable to invest a much smaller sum to determine the effects and viability of the proposed policy.

Not all true field experiments involve the large expenditure of money necessitated by the negative income tax experiment. Nancy Jo Filipe and Robert Sommer (1966) have, for example, conducted a number of simple field experiments on persons' use of space. In one of these studies, conducted at a state mental hospital, Filipe and Sommer wanted to document persons' behaviors when their personal space had been violated. The violation of personal space was the experimental treatment. The experimenter would sit within six inches of randomly selected male patients who were sitting alone on benches scattered throughout the hospital grounds. A comparable control group consisted of persons sitting by themselves who were left alone by the researchers. In both instances researchers quantified the rates at which subjects vacated their seats. Rates of vacancy in both experimental and control groups could be easily compared. The results of their elegantly simple experiment are graphically expressed in Figure 9.1.

FIGURE 9.1 Cumulative Percentage of Patients Having Departed at Each One-Minute Interval

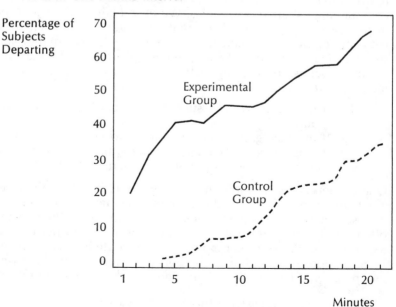

If you have understood the techniques used in the two quite different field experiments just described, you should be able to guess without much difficulty the kinds of experimental procedures that have been devised in natural settings to study such diverse social phenomena as the effects of leafleting on political behavior (Hartmann, 1972), the effect of teacher expectations on student learning behavior (Rosenthal, 1963) and the effects of physician demands on the behavior of nurses (Hofling, et al., 1972). We have particularly meant to demonstrate through our examples that we need not think of the true experiment as possible only in the laboratory situation. There are instances in which we can create a kind of natural laboratory. There are situations in the natural world in which it is possible to randomize subjects and to make clear group comparisons. The social scientist whose goal is to establish causal relations between variables ought to seek out these situations for natural experimentation whenever possible.

While the two field experiments we have described to this point meet the criteria of the true experiment, the problems that sociologists wish to investigate frequently do not lend themselves to true experimentation. We would like, then, to make a distinction at this point between true experiments and what have come to be called *quasi experiments*.

Quasi-Field Experiments

Quasi experiments stand in contrast to the true experiment in terms of the degree of control exercised by the researcher over possibly confounding extraneous variables. We have defined the true experiment in terms of three structural elements or conditions. When these three elements operate simultaneously in a research design they afford researchers maximum control and give them justification for maximum faith in any causal assertions they make. In order to qualify as a true experiment, the project must meet the following criteria:

1. It must achieve its results through comparison of at least two groups.
2. It must assign persons or subjects to groups randomly.
3. It must be constructed so researcher has control over, or is able to evaluate, the timing of the experimental treatment.

Quasi experiments are those in which all the elements of the true experiment are present *except for* the random assignment of persons to groups. As researchers try to conduct their inquiries in natural field settings they often find it either unfeasible or impossible to assign persons randomly to the groups. We can offer examples to illustrate how and why this is so.

Suppose a group of researchers are interested in the formation of *group culture*.[2] Further, let us imagine that they have theoretical reason

---

[2] We are indebted to Gary Alan Fine for this example.

for believing that the development of group culture is enhanced or retarded by the relative success experienced by a group in realizing its collective goals. Stated more explicitly, they believe that the more successful the group in realizing collective goals, the more rapid and complete will be the development of a distinctive group culture. Conversely, the failure of a group to realize collective group goals will retard the development of group culture.

It would be possible for the researchers to set up their own groups through random assignment of individuals and to then somehow create a situation where these groups would be more or less successful in realizing artificially established goals. It would be possible, in other words, to create the conditions for a true experiment. In this case, however, the researchers have reason to believe that this kind of manipulation might have some distinctive drawbacks. They recognize that the theoretical problem they have posed does not easily submit to solution through pure experimental techniques. That is, the researchers recognize the difficulty of detailing the development of group culture in the short time they would be able to observe artificially created laboratory groups. Elaborated cultures simply do not develop in an hour or two, a day or two, or even a week or two.

At the same time, the researchers realize the strength of experimental procedures in establishing causal relationships. They wish at least to approximate a true experimental procedure in testing their hypothesis. They decide, therefore, to look for some naturally occurring situation where they might be able to test their ideas. The researchers are willing to give up some of the rigorous control afforded by true experimental procedure in order to study the phenomenon of interest in a more natural situation. They engage, in other words, in a kind of trade-off. They know that it is virtually impossible to assess fully all the contemporaneous inputs from a natural environment which could affect behavior. Very importantly, they know that by choosing to investigate already existent groups in some natural setting they will be unable to randomly assign persons to groups; they will have no control over the composition of the groups studied. (As noted earlier, much control is lost by the inability of the researchers to randomly assign subjects to groups, and where that inability exists, the research, by definition, fails to qualify as true experimental research.)

In this search for a context best allowing them to approximate the conditions of true experimentation, the researchers first consider the type of situation demanded by their theoretical concerns. In the case at hand, they consider if there are any naturally occurring situations where the following conditions obtain:

1. A situation where one will be able to observe a number of groups from their inception over a long enough time period to see and somehow measure the development of group culture.

2. A situation where, although persons have not been strictly assigned to groups randomly, one might expect that the members
   of the various groups will not vary in any substantial respect.
3. A situation where some groups are successful and others un-
   successful in realizing their collective group goals.

After giving some considerable thought to whether there are
natural situations where these three theoretically dictated conditions
might hold, one of the researchers hits on an idea. Why not study the
formation and operation of Little League baseball teams! Here, after all,
one can observe a number of groups (teams) over time from the point of
their very formation. The groups will all be of the same size. The age
composition of the groups will be the same. Although the researchers
will want to check out the procedure through which individuals are
assigned to teams, they have no reason immediately to assume that there
will be any gross or systematic variation in the background characteristics
of the players from team to team. Finally, the researchers will not have
to artificially manipulate the test variable — the relative success the
groups experience in realizing their goals — since they can presume the
dominant goal for each group will be to win ball games, and it will
naturally occur that some teams will be winners and others losers. As a
matter of fact, they will be able to observe teams at a number of points
along the continuum of goal realization because the better win/loss record of one team ensures that another team has a worse win/loss record.

As a second example in this section, we will consider the kind of
field experiment that can be conducted in large-scale organizations.

The famous sociologist Max Weber (1947) noted that the trend of
Western history is toward the ever-increasing bureaucratization of social
life. Virtually all of us find that a large portion of our daily lives is conducted within large-scale bureaucratic organizations. As students, our
lives are bounded in important ways by the educational institution. Later
on many of us take jobs and have careers that are carried out within
the context of a large-scale organization. And as we move through our
life cycle we unavoidably come into contact with a variety of large-scale
organizations: churches, hospitals, various government agencies, and the
like. To the extent that large-scale organizations so thoroughly dominate
modern life, much sociological effort has been expended in analyzing
how they operate, how they shape our lives, and how persons respond
and adapt to them. In their studies of "life" in contemporary organizations, sociologists have most commonly employed such methodological
tools as participant observation of a single case, in-depth interviewing,
the analysis of documentary materials, and sample surveys. Ever more
frequently, however, sociologists (e.g., Evan, 1971) are seeing the value
of adding the *field experiment* to their repertoire of methodological tools
for analyzing organizations.

In institutional settings researchers must normally conduct their
experiments on *already existing groups* within the organization. It would

cause too much disruption for researchers to randomly assign students to classes, employees to work groups, and so forth. In such cases researchers often use strategies alternative to random sampling in choosing the groups they study. One such strategy designed to increase researchers' faith in the initial comparability of the groups is to be certain that the groups chosen are alike or *match* each other in obviously important respects. For example, if researchers want to study the effects of a new teaching technique in grade schools, they will, at the very least, want to make sure that the classes chosen do not differ widely in such important characteristics as the racial, sex, age, and social class attributes of the students. As an illustration of the type of organizational experimentation where a matching procedure was used, we will briefly describe a classic study on workers' resistance to organizational change.

A pressing problem in the study of organizational life has been to understand why workers are so resistant to any form of organizational change. In their early and influential study, Lester Coch and John French (1948) wanted to answer two related questions: (1) Why do people resist change so strongly? and, (2) What can be done to overcome this resistance? The study was carried out in a manufacturing plant employing approximately 500 women and 100 men. The workers, who were producing pajamas, were paid on an individual incentive system; that is, they were paid in terms of the number of "pieces" or units they produced. Because their pay reflected the efficiency of their individual production, the workers were very hesitant to change from one type of work to another since the number of units they produced would decline while they were learning the new job. The policy of the company had been to give workers a "transfer bonus" when they were asked to change from one type of work to another. Presumably with this "transfer bonus" the factory operators would not suffer any loss of earnings while learning their new job. Nevertheless, workers were quite resistant to job changes and many preferred to quit rather than change. Believing that resistance to change stemmed from a combination of individual motivation and strong workgroup norms, Coch and French designed an experimental procedure to test whether greater worker participation (the test variable) in change decisions would lessen resistance to change.

The researchers decided to compare four already existing work groups — three experimental groups and a control group. In experimental group 1, a small number of employee representatives participated with management in designing their group's work changes. In experimental groups 2 and 3 the treatment was identical — all the workers in these groups participated in designing work changes. Changes in the work routines of the control group were made according to the traditional company policy. The researchers could not use random procedures in assigning workers to the four comparison groups and were, therefore, careful to choose four work groups matched with respect to:

1. The efficiency rating of the groups before job transfer.
2. The degree of change involved in the job transfer.

3. The amount of we-feeling (cohesiveness) observed in the groups.

The results of this experiment demonstrated very clearly that the more participation the workers had in determining the nature of work changes, the less resistant they were to the change itself. In this study the dependent variable was a measure of how quickly the separate groups learned their new jobs and were able to produce pieces at an efficiency rate comparable to their rate prior to the transfer. Experimental group 1 (representative participation) showed a good relearning rate. During the period following their job change they cooperated well with their supervisors. Also, none of the workers in this group quit their job during the first forty days following the work change. Experimental groups 2 and 3 (full democratic participation) learned their new jobs more quickly than those in experimental group 1 and eventually produced at a level 14 percent higher than the prechange level. The control group, however, fell in its efficiency ratings and never improved during the forty days after their job change. Seventeen percent of the workers in this group quit within forty days of the job change. Moreover, "Resistance (in the control group) developed almost immediately after the change occurred. Marked expressions of aggression against management occurred, such as conflict with the methods engineer, expressions of hostility against the supervisor, deliberate restriction of production, and lack of cooperation with the supervisor." (Coch and French, 1948:522).

For the last few pages we have been looking at how experimental procedures can be employed in real world situations. As part of our discussion of field experimentation we distinguished between true experiments and quasi experiments. In quasi experiments researchers are unable to use random assignment procedures in creating experimental and control groups. True and quasi experiments do not, however, exhaust all the types of research that have been termed experimental. We should like to add to our discussion one other variation of experimental research. In what we shall term *demonstrations* two of the criteria for a true experiment are not met. Demonstrations involve neither group comparison nor random assignment of subjects. Demonstrations, which may be conducted both in the laboratory and in the field, involve only the introduction of an experimental treatment in some group.

The Demonstration Experiment

Despite the relative lack of control exercised by the researcher in conducting a demonstration, this variation of the experiment has produced some of the most compelling findings in the social sciences. Stanley Milgram's (1963) study of obedience and authority represents an outstanding example of the power of the demonstration to produce dramatic findings.

Let us recall that Milgram was interested in finding out the effects of authority on the willingness of persons to administer punishments to others (see page 97). Subjects who participated in Milgram's demonstration were told that the object of the research was to better understand how persons learned. At the outset, each of the subjects was introduced to another individual who, they were told, was simply another volunteer like themselves. In fact, this second person was a confederate of Milgram.

The real subject was assigned the role of teacher and Milgram's confederate took the role of student. They were to occupy separate rooms, communicating by use of microphones. The subject taught his student, then tested him. For each wrong answer the student was to be punished by his teacher. The teacher punished by administering electric shocks, each of which was stronger than the preceding one. The teacher could only press the shock button, not control the voltage. Milgram stayed in the control room with the teacher.

The procedure was a deception. Milgram's assistant, the student, did not receive any shocks. As the voltage levels began to increase, however, he did turn on a taped recording of a man indicating various degrees of pain — from slight involuntary pained sounds at the beginning to rather lengthy moans as the voltage increased with a succession of "planned" incorrect answers. As the moans became louder and more frequent, and the voltage indicator showed the shocks to be increasingly close to the "extremely dangerous" point, the naive subject would turn to Milgram and show concern, often indicating that he no longer wished to go on with the experiment. Each time, Milgram, dressed in a scientifically authoritative white lab coat, would simply express his wish for the subject to continue. In each replication of the procedure well over fifty percent of the subjects carried the experiment through to the end, administering what they believed to be "extremely dangerous" shocks to the learner.

One of the things suggested by Milgram's "demonstration experiment" is that in some situations persons are capable of rather extraordinary behavior. While most of us, if questioned, would say that *we* would never inflict that kind of pain on another human being, Milgram shows the power of authority in dictating our acts. Despite the nature and possible importance of findings such as those provided by Milgram for understanding, say, the behavior of soldiers in war, many have expressed concern about the ethical implications of the kind of demonstration described. Even though Milgram carefully and at some length debriefed each of his subjects, many question the researcher's right to manipulate and deceive "naive" subjects.

On the methodological side, the Milgram example can be contrasted with true and quasi experiments. In true and quasi experiments we find at least two clear comparison groups that differentially experience the experimental treatment. Such group comparisons are important because they help the researcher to pinpoint more precisely the extent of the subjects' change in some behavior or attitude following an experimental treatment. In the case of Milgram's demonstration, persons certainly experience an experimental treatment. It is clear, however, that there are no discernible group comparisons to be made in terms of the intensity of treatment given. Here, if there are any differences in the intensity of treatment received, they are controlled by the subject rather than the researcher. In the example offered, the treatment continues, in effect, as long as the subject is willing to continue in the experiment. The demonstration, and therefore the experimental treatment, ends when the subject decides that he or she will no longer administer shocks to another. The type of experimental research done by Milgram clearly "demonstrates," highlights, or illustrates certain features or aspects of human behavior (the willingness of persons to obey authority) and is highly informative on that level. The demonstration is, however, to be particularly distinguished from the true experiment in the following ways:

1. There are not clear comparison groups which experience different amounts or intensities of the same experimental treatment.
2. By definition, therefore, there is no random assignment of persons to comparison groups. There is no control group.
3. There is no clear timing to the experimental treatment since it continues as long as the experiment itself continues.

These procedural or structural characteristics of the demonstration tell us something very important. It cannot be the goal of the demonstration to show causal relations between variables. Causality between variables may be strongly implied by the outcome of demonstrations like Milgram's, but given the structural conditions just outlined, causality cannot be as firmly established as is possible in a true experiment.

CONCLUSION

The sociologist Norman Denzin (1970:147) has written: "In a fundamental sense the experiment is the point of departure for all other methods." It is fair to make this claim to the extent that a basic criterion used by social scientists in evaluating their methodologies must be an assessment of how surely they can assert causal relations between variables. The certainty of social scientists' claims to causality rests in turn on how successfully they have been able to *control* those features of the world that could render their stated causal relations specious. We have meant to show that the experiment is the most powerful procedure available to us in achieving this control. This being so, we may use the true experiment as a baseline against which our other methods may be evaluated. It is not inconceivable that we could rank-order our various methods in terms of the amount of control given up in their use.

The matter will not be resolved with such a simple ranking of methods, however. Social scientists will inevitably have to attach to any of their findings, produced through whatever method, the silent caveat that these findings are true "all other things being equal." In short, social scientists must learn to adopt a certain modesty about their research since they must live with the fact that in their investigation of the social world all other things will never be equal.

Indeed, this chapter on experimentation, apart from acquainting us with the techniques involved in the use of the method itself, should stand as testimony to the enormous complexity of the social world. We have seen that the power of the experiment lies in the fact that it goes furthest in making all other things equal. At the same time we are forced to see that even in the most carefully controlled laboratory experiment, we cannot keep potentially contaminating factors out of our findings. We stress again the fact that no matter how elegantly we achieve an internal consistency in our methods, any methodology is, *by its very existence,* potentially reactive or biasing.

In the case of experimental research we have already spoken of the "Hawthorne effect"; the difficulties of dealing with maturational effects; the potentially sensitizing effects of our attempt to measure our dependent variables in an experiment; the frequent artificiality of the experimental situation; the possibility that even with our efforts at randomization, members of control groups and experimental groups could vary in some unknown respect; and the inability of the researcher to fully control for contemporaneous events arising from the general environment. All these factors potentially bias the findings of the experimental researcher.

We should also note again the delicate tension existing between control over extraneous factors in our work and naturalism. As we achieve greater levels of control, as we reduce the possibility of variables unknown to us intruding into our findings, we simultaneously thereby create situations that resemble less and less the kinds of social situations in which persons normally act. As we strive for naturalism, on the other hand, "all other things" become more and more unequal. We are caught in a kind of double bind. We want on the one hand to strengthen our faith in any causal assertions we make. At the same time we must be concerned that the variables operating causally in contrived experimental situations may not operate causally as actors carry out their normal daily lives.

Finally, we cannot leave a chapter on human experimentation without some comment on the ethical issues involved. The examples of experimental research offered in this chapter directly raise questions about the legitimacy of "manipulating" human subjects. What is more, our examples seem to suggest that the successful experiment often depends on subjects' ignorance of the experimenter's manipulations. The successful experiment often necessitates deception, keeping the subjects in the dark, not alerting them to the nature of the experimental treatment they are receiving. Deception is, indeed, part of the language of the experimental researcher who consistently refers to those studied as "subjects," "naive subjects," and even on occasion as "victims." Can we, for example, justify making subjects believe that they are inflicting pain on others as did Milgram in his obedience experiments? Should we even infringe on the privacy of others by purposively transgressing culturally understood spatial norms as Sommer did? In a recent paper the sociologist Everett Hughes (1974) asks the question, "Who can study whom?" We might elaborate that question to ask, "Who can study whom in which ways?"

Questions of ethicality do not submit to simple answers. If there is any resolution it rests in our sensitivity as researchers. We must consider just how important will be the information produced through our research. We must consider the alternative means through which this information can be acquired. We must consider the kinds of threats we pose to those we study. We must consider the personal and social risks we create for persons. We must weigh whether deception is really necessary in order to accomplish our work. As scientists we are appropriately dedicated to using procedures that best help us unravel the complexity of causal relations, that best allow for replication of findings, and that best allow us to reduce bias and error. We have tried in this chapter to illustrate the power of the experiment in meeting these goals. We must not, however, become so committed to these goals that we fail to remember that precisely because ours is a human science it must also be a humane science.

EXERCISES

1. On page 243 of this chapter we briefly described the simple, elegant study conducted by Nancy Jo Filipe and Robert Sommer on persons' reactions to violations of their personal space. Using some convenient context such as a public park or waiting room, try to replicate their study. You may find it helpful to read their study in full (see references for full citation) before you try to set up your own experiment. Indicate in your findings just how well your own study supports the earlier findings of Filipe and Sommer. If your own findings differ significantly from theirs, try to explain the discrepancies.

2. Several years ago a woman named Kitty Genovese was murdered on a New York street while some 38 persons looked on without doing anything to help. No one even telephoned the police. This led many journalists to conclude that city living made persons callous, indifferent, and uncaring. Social scientists, however, were unwilling to accept this simple answer and began to do studies

of helping behavior in city places. They wanted to know the conditions under which persons would either help or not help others. One interesting hypothesis tested was that the *more* persons there are to witness someone in need of help, the less likely, or at least less quickly, was anyone to help. The simple explanation offered was that each onlooker believes that someone else will help and the result is that no one helps. There develops, in other words, a kind of "diffusion of responsibility."

Suppose you wanted to test the diffusion of responsibility hypothesis. Along with a small group of persons in your class, construct a field demonstration to test the hypothesis, carry out the experiment, and report your findings.

3. A longstanding theoretical idea in social psychology is that *frustration* leads to *aggression*. Describe the elements of a true laboratory experiment that could be employed to test this relationship. What would be the experimental treatment in your study? How would you measure the independent and dependent variables? How many groups would you study and why?

4. We commented in this chapter that in many studies experimenters deceive their subjects. In the case of Milgram's experiment on obedience, for example, subjects were led to believe that they were administering painful shocks to others. With regard to this and similar studies, persons have raised strong ethical objections. What is your position on the ethicality of experiments like Milgram's? Do social scientists have the right to mislead "naive" subjects? What do you think are the limits of experimentation on human subjects?

5. An argument in this chapter has been that in the use of any social science methodology there is a continual tension between control on the one hand and naturalism on the other. Briefly answer the following questions in terms of this tension:

   a. Describe how maximum control is achieved through the use of experimental procedures.
   b. Make plain the relationship between control and establishing causality between variables.
   c. Indicate why experimental control is achieved at the expense of external validity.
   d. Discuss briefly the value of the field experiment in terms of your answers to a, b, and c.

6. Outline some of the major threats to internal validity in experiments and then explain how elaborations on the "classic" control group/experimental group research design help researchers to evaluate the effects of these factors.

SUGGESTED READINGS

Readings about the Method

Campbell, Donald T., and Julian C. Stanley
1971   *Experimental and Quasi-experimental Designs for Research.* Chicago: Rand McNally.

In their much cited book, Campbell and Stanley exhaustively describe the various designs typically used in experimental research. They concisely describe the strengths and limitations of each research design. While some of the discussion is at a high level of sophistication, the beginning student should easily be able to follow their description of threats to internal and external validity in experimentation.

Jung, John, ed.
1971   *The Experimenter's Dilemma.* New York: Harper & Row.

In the first half of this book, the author describes some of the central threats to experimental validity. Separate chapters discuss such issues as the way persons' behaviors are affected because they know they are participating in an experiment, the problem of sample selectivity in experiments, and the operation of modeling and expectancy effects. In the second half of the book the reader will find a series of essays written by prominent experimental researchers. Each of these essays focuses on specific problems associated with experimental procedures. The reader may especially want to read those essays on the ethicality of deception in experiments.

Plutchik, Robert
1968   *Foundations of Experimental Research.* New York: Harper & Row.

This clearly written text covers all phases of experimental research. Drawing examples from many areas of social science inquiry where experimental procedures have been used, the author tries to illustrate the typical kinds of decisions faced by experimental researchers and then suggests rational procedures for solving them. In Chapter 2 the author outlines seven major decisions that must be made in any experimental study. In the following chapters each of these decisions is dealt with in greater detail.

Selltiz, Claire; Marie Jahoda; Morton Deutsch; and Stuart W. Cook
1959   *Research Methods in Social Relations.* Rev. ed., New York: Holt, Rinehart & Winston.

In this book we specifically recommend that the reader look at pages 95–127 in which the authors discuss causal inference from experimentation. Along with the usual discussion of types of experimental design, the authors include some discussion of "matching" procedures as a complement to random assignment of subjects to comparison groups. The reader will find several examples illustrating the value of matching procedures to ensure that comparison groups do not systematically vary in their composition.

Wenglinsky, Martin
1975   "Feature essay: Milgram's 'obedience to authority: an experimental view.'" *Contemporary Sociology: A Journal of Reviews* 4 (November): 613–617.

As we have mentioned several times, Stanley Milgram's research on obedience has been highly controversial because of its ethical implications and its findings. In this review of Milgram's latest book, the author strongly takes issue with the idea that the willingness of the subjects in Milgram's experiment to follow his instructions to "shock" others can be taken as evidence of persons' "evilness." The author of the review suggests that experimental subjects simply play by what they see as the rules of the experimental game. This lively essay is important because its implications go beyond an immediate critique of Milgram's research. The ideas contained in this essay cast some doubt on the external validity of any experiment.

Readings Illustrating the Method

Bickman, Leonard, and Thomas Henchy, eds.
1972   *Beyond the Laboratory: Field Research in Social Psychology.* New York: McGraw-Hill.

> In this book the authors have compiled a number of interesting experiments conducted in the field. Apart from their intrinsic interest, the studies included demonstrate the ingenuity of researchers who wish to combine experimental procedures with naturalistic observation. Many of the studies described could be easily replicated by students because they do not necessitate elaborate arrangements or expensive props.

Deutsch, Morton, and Mary Evans Collins
1951   *Interracial Housing: A Psychological Evaluation of a Social Experiment.* Minneapolis: University of Minnesota Press.

> In this well-known, "classic" study, the value of using experimental procedures for planning and social policy purposes is shown. The researchers examined how segregated and integrated housing patterns affected the attitudes of whites toward blacks. The study was conducted in two large-scale housing projects, one in New York and one in New Jersey.

Evan, William M., ed.
1971   *Organizational Experiments: Laboratory and Field Research.* New York: Harper & Row.

> We have indicated that social scientists are increasingly interested in conducting experiments to understand various aspects of organizational behavior. Some of these experiments are conducted within actual institutions and others in the laboratory setting. In this book, Evan has provided outstanding examples of both laboratory and field experiments. The reader ought to consider why most of the studies conducted in actual institutional settings fail to qualify as true experiments.

REFERENCES

Campbell, Donald T., and Julian C. Stanley
1963 *Experimental and Quasi-experimental Designs for Research.* Chicago: Rand McNally.

Coch, Lester, and John R. P. French, Jr.
1948 "Overcoming resistance to change." *Human Relations* 1:512–532.

Denzin, Norman K.
1970 *The Research Act.* Chicago: Aldine.

Evan, William M., ed.
1971 *Organizational Experiments: Laboratory and Field Research.* New York: Harper & Row.

Festinger, Leon
1971 "Laboratory experiments." In *Research Methods: Issues and Insights,* ed. Billy J. Franklin and Harold W. Osborne. Belmont, Cal.: Wadsworth.

Filipe, Nancy J., and Robert Sommer
1966 "Invasions of personal space." *Social Problems* 14:206–214.

Hartmann, George W.
1972 "A field experiment on the comparative effectiveness of 'emotional' and 'rational' political leaflets in determining election results." In *Beyond the Laboratory: Field Research in Social Psychology,* ed. Leonard Bickman and Thomas Henchy. New York: McGraw-Hill.

Hofling, Charles K., et al.
1972 "An experimental study in nurse-physician relationships." In *Beyond the Laboratory: Field Research in Social Psychology,* ed. Leonard Bickman and Thomas Henchy. New York: McGraw-Hill.

Hughes, Everett C.
1974 "Who studies whom." *Human Organization* 33 (4):327–334.

Jung, John
1971 *The Experimenter's Dilemma.* New York: Harper & Row.

Kershaw, David N.
1969 *The Negative Income Tax Experiment in New Jersey.* Princeton, N.J.: Mathematica.

Milgram, Stanley
1963 "Behavioral study of obedience." *Journal of Abnormal and Social Psychology* 67:371–378.

Rosenthal, Robert
1963   "The effects of physician demands on the behavior of nurses." In *Beyond the Laboratory: Field Research in Social Psychology,* ed. Leonard Beckman and Thomas Henchy. New York: McGraw-Hill.

Rosenthal, Robert, and K. Fode
1963   "Psychology of the scientist: three experiments in experimenter bias." *Psychological Reports* 12:491–511.

Weber, Max
1947   *The Theory of Social and Economic Organization,* trans. by A. M. Henderson and Talcott Parsons. New York: Oxford University Press.

Historical Analysis

CHAPTER TEN

It is a fair assessment of American academic life that the practitioners of the several social science disciplines have relatively little contact with one another. Sociologists, psychologists, historians, anthropologists, and economists normally define the boundaries of their respective disciplines fairly rigorously. In each field there is a certain orthodoxy about the relevant questions for investigation, the methodological techniques central to the particular area of inquiry, and the modes of analysis distinctive of the discipline.

In the largest sense, of course, the disciplines named share a concern with understanding "persons in society." They differ from one another in terms of the features of that relationship which they emphasize. We might think of social life as something like a giant jigsaw puzzle and envision various social scientists working on selected parts of it. There is, in other words, a rather extensive division of labor among the social sciences. It is a division of labor brought about by the impossibility of any one discipline being able to attend to the extraordinary number of parts making up the human mosaic.

Each of the social sciences seeks to establish a paradigm, or model, that represents all aspects of that specific science. By indicating the special problems, issues, and modes of analysis that are distinctly their own, members of an academic field better succeed in affirming their expertise in the minds of others. Naturally that is useful to one's career; more importantly, it is also de facto to establish the importance of the discipline itself. A firm indication of the dimensions of a discipline's subject matter facilitates communication between professionals. Clear delineation of boundaries ensures that there is some homogeneity of knowledge shared among the members of a discipline and that therefore there is some consistency to the socialization of new members.

The division of academic labor exists not only between disciplines but within disciplines as well. As knowledge continually grows, specialization within fields becomes nearly inevitable. Just as has been historically the case in fields like medicine, social scientists become increasingly specialized within their own fields. It is common in sociology, for example, for one to develop an expertise in a particular substantive area of investigation — deviance, stratification, large-scale organization, medical sociology, or small-group study. The specialization is not just in subject matter; there are also theoretical and methodological specializations. It is now proper to speak of clear boundaries within the discipline as well as between disciplines.

We can view the development of this sort of separatism between and within social sciences in two ways. From one perspective we may see it as a natural and inevitable consequence of the explosion of knowledge in various fields. On the other hand, we may view it as, in fact, a weakening of our understanding of the human condition. The artificial distinctions maintained prevent us from developing a comprehensive, whole image of social life.

The authors of this textbook submit, despite some social scientists' claims, that there ought to be fewer distinctions between various fields — that in fact psychology, sociology, history, and economics "pour into" one another. At the very least, the authors maintain that the members of one discipline ought not avoid using the concepts, methods, and modes of analysis of another discipline when these could contribute to an understanding of a particular problem under investigation. This chapter contains a strong argument for the necessity of sociologists' engaging in *historical analysis*. The inclusion of historical perspectives and methodologies as part of successful sociological work is not merely a matter of arbitrary choice; it is, beyond that, demanded by the rational acknowledgment that contemporary social forms all have, by definition, a history.

HISTORY AND SOCIOLOGY

Sociologists are largely accustomed to studying social phenomena at one point in time — the present. We typically ask how a particular social institution is operating today, or what constitutes deviant behaviors in a society today. What *are* the elements of a social phenomenon? These are certainly not unreasonable questions, but to answer them only in the form asked may limit our comprehension of contemporary events, situations, behaviors, or institutions.

"Social forms" do not appear spontaneously and autonomously.

Every element of a society — from the individual to the social institution — has a biography, a life history. In some measure we cannot escape the judgment that these elements are a product of their pasts. Moreover, social life is constantly in a state of transformation. If we are to fill out and expand our understanding of contemporary social arrangements we must look to the transformations through which they have already passed. An example should make our point clear. Let us look at the values held by the members of a society.

Whenever persons behave according to their standards of what *ought* to be done — whenever they act according to what they believe is right, proper, decent or moral — they are expressing their values. The fact that social scientists have shown considerable variation between cultures in the central values of their members, signals the need for historical analysis. We must think of value orientations as representing a society's long-term response to its total historical situation. Sparta's emphasis on militarism and courage, the high premium placed on youth and strength by Eskimos, or the place of the work ethic in American society, cannot be understood apart from the historical and environmental factors that shaped those values. Max Weber (1958), for example, in his well-known and brilliant historical analysis of capitalism traces the origin of that economic form to the Protestant work ethic of Calvinist theology.

We may borrow from the writings of the sociologist C. Wright Mills (1968) to further our claim for the inadvisability of segregating sociological and historical analysis. An outspoken critic of contemporary social science, Mills expressed discontent with the nonhistorical nature of most sociological work. As he saw it, the failure of sociologists to view social phenomena in historical perspective was simultaneously a failure to exercise the "sociological imagination." He defines the sociological imagination as reflected in a concern with "problems of biography, of history, and of their intersections within social structures." He states his case (1968:158) this way:

> ... The biographies of men and women, the kinds of individuals they variously become, cannot be understood without reference to the historical structures in which the milieux of their everyday life are organized. Historical transformations carry meanings not only for individual ways of life, but for the very character — the limits and possibilities of the human being. ... Whatever else he may be, man is a social and an historical actor who must be understood, if at all, in a close and intricate interplay with social and historical structures.

For Mills the question of whether sociologists should engage in historical analysis is one that ought not even be asked. Sociology *is* a historical discipline. "Unless one assumes some trans-historical theory of the nature of history, or that man in society is a non-historical entity, no social science can be assumed to transcend history." (Mills, 1968:146)

In calling for a more extended use of historical data as a way of better understanding contemporary societies, we are not asking sociologists to engage in analyses foreign to the tradition of their discipline. Those writers whose research is considered to have provided us with some of the central theoretical ideas in the field nearly uniformly engaged in historical analysis. Indeed, historical analysis was unavoidable for nineteenth-century European sociologists because the emergence of sociology as a discipline followed a major historical transformation in the organization of European society. It was the transformation from a peasant agrarian society to a citified industrial society, a structural change brought about by the French and Industrial Revolutions.

Sociology as an independent, autonomous discipline arose as certain social themes "called out" for analysis after these two revolutions. The social themes of power, wealth, status, alienation, the division of labor, and the nature of community life emerged then and still exist as abiding sociological concerns. Speaking of the importance of the French Revolution as a catalyst for sociological thought, Robert Nisbet (1966:31) comments:

> The French Revolution was possessed of a suddenness and dramatic intensity. The stirring Declaration of the Rights of Man, the unprecedented nature of the laws that were passed between 1789 and 1795, *laws touching literally every aspect of the social structure of France* — were sufficient to guarantee to the revolution a kind of millennial character that was to leave it for a whole century the most preoccupying event in French political history (our emphasis).

Following particularly the Industrial Revolution, the disappearance of the peasant community and the rise of industrial cities caused thinkers to consider the changing basis for social organization in society. For example, the Industrial Revolution thoroughly altered the condition of labor in society. Karl Marx, whom many consider the father of modern sociology, analyzed the developing factory system. His resulting contributions to our understanding of capitalist class structure is, of course, well known. With the development of technology in large industrial cities, there had to develop an extensive and complex system of occupational specialization. This became a theme for the theoretical writings of the French sociologist Emile Durkheim (1947), who, in a book titled *The Division of Labor in Society*, examined the changes we have described. Similarly, Sir Henry Maine's (1870) distinction between societies based on status relations and those based on contract relations, Ferdinand Tönnies's (1940) distinction between community and society, Robert Redfield's (1947) distinction between folk and urban societies, and Max Weber's (1947) discussion of the increasing bureaucratization and rationalization of the modern world are all rooted in their analyses of major social, historical trends. In significant respects, these researches reflect the images of history held by their authors. The concepts generated from their work remain among the major tools for contemporary sociological analysis. Their work stands, therefore, as convincing evidence that the broad contours of modern society are best seen as part of a moving historical scenario.

It would be appropriate to summarize the points made thus far by saying that to study certain features of society in contemporary isolation severely handicaps our ability to answer two questions: (1) How and why have social forms come to assume their present shape? and, (2) What shapes are they likely to assume in the future? However, before we overstate our case for history, its data, and methods, let it be plain that we are not arguing for a naive historical determinism. We would not suppose that *every* present-day aspect of social life stands in a linear relationship to the past. If we try to see every feature of our social lives as a function of historically determined events, we are misusing history.

Neither, we might add, are we asserting that any research without a historical component to it is somehow illegitimate. Immediately, for example, we may see that certain types of evaluation research do not require historical analysis. If the goal of some research were to compare the relative effectiveness of alternative drug, alcohol, or mental health rehabilitation programs, a historical analysis would probably not be called for; to engage in historical analysis might draw the researcher away from the problem at hand.

It is fully legitimate to study persons' present attitudes, values, beliefs, and behaviors. Experimental social psychologists frequently inquire into processes of human behavior — conformity, aggression, patterns of leadership, and the like — many aspects of which can be well understood without historical research. It is certainly proper and useful for social scientists to explain the operation of contemporary large-scale bureaucratic organizations. We need to know how our school systems are functioning; how persons adapt to the imperatives of such institutions as prisons, hospitals, and homes for the aged; how the present legal system distributes justice, and so forth. It is also within the professional domain of sociologists to describe the inner workings of a subculture, to assess the points of conflict between racial and ethnic groups, to learn how persons adapt to the heterogeneity and diversity of mass culture, and so on. We are merely suggesting that sociologists not shy away from historical analysis when they believe it could expand their theoretical understanding of whatever they are investigating. Most importantly, they should not refrain from historical investigation because the methodologies they feel comfortable with do not easily equip them to do historical work. We must see the worth of adding historical methods to our already established bag of methodological tools.

The methodologies most currently in use among sociologists do not easily allow for historical analysis. The questionnaire, for example, while it does allow researchers to query respondents about their pasts, has its greatest utility in uncovering persons' present attitudes. Sociologists using survey techniques sometimes engage in *longitudinal studies,* but even these investigations are relatively short-term affairs and are not examples of historical research. Participant observation does allow the researcher to acquire a sense of process over time in some setting, but again the time frame is normally very limited. Experimental research is nearly always limited to the investigation of behavior at one point in time. Sociologists do, however, make use of such techniques as content analysis of literature, the analysis of institutional records, and the analysis of personal documents. In these instances they are making use of the same types of data sources typical of historical research. In the rest of this chapter we will consider the difficulties faced by the researchers who choose to base their analysis on such data sources as confidential records, personal documents, commercial business records, official government records, and personal life histories. In order to evaluate the methodological problems that the sociologist can expect to encounter in the use of such data we must more fully consider the problems of reliability and validity they engender.

THE NATURE OF HISTORICAL DATA SOURCES

There is a game played by children that works as follows: A number of persons sit in a circle and one person is chosen to begin the game by writing out a two- or three-sentence message on a piece of paper. The individual then puts the paper aside and whispers the message to the person immediately to the right. That person, in turn, whispers the message to the next person, and so on, until the original message is presumably heard by the final person in the circle. This last person writes down the message exactly as he or she hears it. The point of the game is to compare the originally written message with the final rendering of it. That comparison is often the source of considerable humor because the final message usually bears little relation to the original one. The more persons involved in the game, of course, the more garbled the message is likely to become.

Let us consider the possibility that the distortion of messages in this simple game is directly analogous to the distortion of historical messages as they successively change hands. The central methodological question a researcher ponders when he or she works with historical data is: "How much faith can I place in the evidence? To what extent can I believe the data?" Obviously, the closer we are to the events we describe, the more certain we are of the validity of our data. There is a kind of "hierarchy of credibility" when it comes to believing that we have a correct picture of some social event. If we have seen it ourselves — if we have been an eyewitness to the event — we are most certain that we know what went on. If we did not ourselves witness the event, but hear a recounting from an eyewitness, our faith in the picture given is somewhat diminished; but we are still likely to find this first-hand information more credible than second- or third-hand information. As the number of accounts between the actual event and our hearing of it increases, our faith in the accuracy of the accounting diminishes. Since historical researchers can rarely be eyewitnesses to events extending any long distance into the past, the adequacy of their data becomes a preoccupying methodological concern.

The evaluation of historical data, then, poses special problems of reliability and validity that do not normally confront the sociologist who studies contemporary phenomena. A good deal of critical scholarship done by professional historians involves consideration of the validity of data recorded by unseen others. In attending to the distance that data sources stand from the actual events they describe, historians distinguish between primary and secondary data sources. We shall see that one of the quarrels historians frequently have with sociologists engaging in historical investigation is their overuse of secondary data sources when primary sources are available.

Gottschalk (1950) defines a primary data source as "the testimony of an eyewitness, or of a witness by any other of the senses, or of a mechanical device like the dictaphone — that is, of one who . . . was present at the events of which he tells. A primary source must thus have been produced by a contemporary of the events it narrates." Primary sources, then, are tangible materials that provide a description of an historical event and were produced shortly after the event took place. Primary sources may take many forms: newspaper accounts, letters, public documents, eyewitness verbal accounts, court decisions, and personal diaries. Secondary sources, in contrast, borrow the knowledge they contain from other sources, the evidence contained in them being therefore hearsay or indirect evidence.

Let it be clear that even when social scientists have access to primary data sources they cannot be certain of their validity. We must recognize that those who produce accounts of events, in any of the possible forms we have named, may do so with their own peculiar perceptions of the situation or with particular ideological or personal-interest perspectives. Newsmen, for example, may report events in such a way as to sell a maximum number of newspapers. Even a seemingly dispassionate observer to an event may unwittingly have adopted a position on the event. In dealing with any historical record, researchers must be aware that every statement or account is written from a definite perspective and for a specific purpose. There are some records, however, which, by their very nature, we can logically assume to be most accurate. We would, for example, expect there to be no intentional deceit or error in stenographic or taped records of courts, political bodies, or committees. Notebooks and other memoranda are also high in credibility because they are intimate and confidential records. When journals and diaries are written spontaneously and intimately, they are valuable historical documents. In other words, those documents that we can presume were written spontaneously by eyewitness observers with no reason to believe that their accounts would be publicly shared are generally thought as the least biased historical data sources.

Professional historians whose major job it is "to keep the human record straight," frequently have a professional investment in establishing the truth of facts that the sociologist, more intent on *using* historical data, does not. Professional historians are often, for example, concerned with determining the genuineness of a document. The goal of critical historical scholarship may begin and end with a determination of a record's authenticity. Sociologists, intent on placing the data in a larger framework, would rarely be found engaging in this sort of scholarship.

The purpose of much professional historical analysis is to uncover any potentially significant information about a document — its origin, the competence of its author, and whether the document is still in its original form and wording. Extraordinary effort may be expended in determining the date, place, source, or author of a document. In this pursuit, historians may have to become knowledgeable about such fields as paleography (the science of ancient writing), epigraphy (the science of inscriptions and epigraphs), and philology (the science of ancient languages).

More recently, historians have made use of statistical tools more customarily employed in such fields as economics and sociology. Perhaps they were influenced by the ingenuity of statisticians like Frederick Mosteller (1964), who studied the disputed authorship of several of the Federalist papers. Hamilton, Madison, and Jay were the known authors of the Federalist papers, but some of these essays were left unsigned. Who wrote them: Hamilton, Madison, or Jay? Mosteller moved toward a solution this way: he looked at the grammatical structure and word usages in the known writings of each of these three persons. He discovered through this procedure a number of distinctive differences in their literary styles. He then took the disputed papers and subjected them to a statistical analysis designed to establish the frequency of certain stylistic conventions. By so doing he could provide reasonably convincing evidence that it was one and not the others who wrote a particular essay.

Any discussion of the utility of historical data immediately raises the question of generalizability. Sociology, because it seeks after generalization, is a resolutely comparative discipline. Sociologists typically center their investigations on recurrent, repeating, or institutionalized social phenomena that can be directly compared. Sociological analysis is, in other words, normally concerned with "open classes of events" —which are events that repeat themselves in a similar form and thereby allow for comparative analysis. For example, deviance occurs in every society. And every modern society is dominated by complex bureaucratic structures. In every society, by definition, persons are engaged in social interaction. In every society persons can be compared in terms of their religious, ethnic, race, class, and age statuses.

The argument has been made that historical events are spatially and temporally specific, that they are unique, nonrecurrent social events. Those who argue for historical specificity see historical events as "closed classes of events." There was, after all, only one French Revolution; there was only one American Revolution. Strictly speaking, one might suggest that it is logically unfair to compare World War I with the War of the Roses, with the Arab-Israeli War, or with the Vietnam War. To do so is, as the saying goes, a bit like mixing apples and oranges. The supposition underlying this view of the uniqueness of historical events is that the social antecedents of each of these events were very dissimilar.

It is perfectly true that events are best understood in terms of their immediate, specific historical contexts. We certainly would not suggest that one outcome of historical analysis ought to be the production of invariant social laws. Quite to the contrary, we realize that one of the values of historical study is to relieve us of our contemporary provincialism. We sometimes tend to see all of social life as understood by looking at contemporary society. Sociologists sometimes write as if they have uncovered unalterable regularities in patterns of human communication, or the structure of institutions, or the causes of deviance by investigating their own societies at one point in time. Cross-cultural and historical analysis functions to shake us from this unwarranted faith in the universal truth value of much contemporary scientific research:

> Early social theorists tried to formulate invariant laws of society — laws that would hold true of all societies, just as the abstracted procedures of physical science had led to laws that cut beneath the qualitative richness of nature. There is . . . no "law" stated by any social scientist that is trans-historical, that must not be understood as having to do with the specific structure of some period. . . . We do not know of any universal principles of historical change; the mechanisms of change we do know vary with the social structure we are examining. . . . Just as there is a variety of social structures, there is a variety of principles of social change. (Mills, 1968:150)

One of the characteristics frequently distinguishing sociological from historical research involves the sociologist's professional concern with either *testing* hypotheses developed prior to data collection or *developing* theory from collected data. When sociologists turn to historical materials it is usually with the intention of revealing conceptual themes that have an applicability beyond the specific case(s) studied.

Historians seem to be much more cautious in their use of historical materials. Rarely do we find historians attempting to test theory explicitly. They may offer reinterpretations of historical events, as did Charles Beard (1935) in his description of the economic motives of those who drafted the United States Constitution; but in few instances are historians willing to claim a conceptual significance to their findings extending further than the boundaries of the studied events. As we turn in the next section to a consideration of the types of historical research done by sociologists, we shall want to think about the conceptual distance that social scientists should be able to move from collected historical data.

SOCIOLOGICAL USES OF HISTORY: SOME SELECTED EXAMPLES

In order to indicate the problems and prospects of sociologists' use of historical data we shall, at this point, center our discussion on historical research done by sociologists. We can show, through example, the kinds of sociological problems that warrant, perhaps demand, an historical approach. For purposes of convenience and clarity of organization, we shall examine historically based sociological research in the following categories:

1. Sociological attempts to establish long-term cultural trends.
2. The use of historical case studies to test theoretical ideas.
3. The use of personal documents and life histories as part of ethnographic reports.
4. The use of available records to study institutional change.

We have two goals in mind as we proceed with our selective review of literature utilizing an historical approach. First, we hope to get a better sense of the place and importance of historical evidence for understanding contemporary social life. Second, our look at the literature will highlight the methodological problems awaiting the researcher who chooses to consider society in historical perspective. We now turn to those sociologists who have endeavored to document long-term processes and regularities in the growth and development of social structures.

Analyzing Social and Cultural Trends

Classical sociologists were never particularly reticent about postulating global theories of social change; such theories are in important respects also theories of history. August Comte (1896), who coined the term sociology, is probably most well known for his evolutionary theory of the human mind, which he believed had passed through three historical stages: the theological, the metaphysical, and the scientific. Each of these stages, Comte thought, grew out of the previous stage and would be reflected in the social organization of human life. Another evolutionary theorist, Herbert Spencer (1891), conceived of society as analogous to any other organism, reasoning that societal growth and change could be understood in the same terms as organic growth and change.

The failing of early evolutionary thinkers lay in their inability to explain *why* social change took place. Mere explanation by analogy, as in Spencer's case, did not constitute good sociological explanation. For this reason, Karl Marx is often considered the first *sociological* theorist of social change because his primary concern was to discover the *source of change*. For Marx, the answer was to be found in an examination of history, an examination that led him to write in *The Communist Manifesto* (1848) that "the history of all hitherto existing societies is the history of class conflict." Unlike Comte, Marx saw the evolution of society as rooted not so much in ideas as in the material conditions of society. Men made history, Marx insisted, as they transformed these material conditions to their own benefit.

> History does nothing, it possesses no immense wealth, it wages no battles. It is man, real living man, that does all that, that possesses and fights; "history" is not a person apart, using man as a means for its own particular aims, history is nothing but the activity of man pursuing his aims. (Anderson, 1974:7)

As is well known, Marx postulated that the course of man's history making would be toward the development of a classless society.

An equally comprehensive view of history is to be found in the writings of Max Weber (1947). Weber's life-long concern with the increasing rationality of the modern world is a theme that runs through his discussions of religion, authority relations between people, and especially his analysis of bureaucratic structure. Marx saw revolution leading to a one-class society as the future course of history. Ever-increasing bureaucratization was Weber's image of history.

The works of thinkers like Weber and Marx are voluminous and far too complex to analyze within the context of this book. It might be more helpful to turn instead to the recent research of Lyn Lofland. Her research is representative of the type that many modern sociologists are likely to conduct.

In her 1973 book, *A World of Strangers,* Lofland tries to answer these questions: What is the basis for public social order in cities? How is the potentially chaotic world of biographical strangers transformed into a system of predictable social relationships? The central thesis of her research is that public urban order is achieved quite differently in modern cities from the way it was achieved in preindustrial and early industrial cities. The transition has been from a primarily *appearential* order to the *spatial* order of present-day cities. "In the pre-industrial city, space was chaotic, appearances were ordered. In the pre-industrial city a man was what he wore. In the modern city a man is where he stands." (Lofland, 1973:82) We need not concern ourselves with her argument *per se,* but rather with the kind of data she must present to convince us of its correctness.

Clearly hers is a historical argument. She wants to show us through descriptions of both modern and preindustrial cities that there has, in fact, been a transformation in the ordering of city places. To make the comparison necessitated by her thesis, Lofland must reconstruct a situation that she obviously never experienced. She must create for her reader a picture of life in preindustrial and early industrial cities. Her object in one chapter is, as she puts it, to journey backward in time to visit a preindustrial city. (Lofland, 1973:30) Before we think about the threats to the validity of her presentation, we might ask why she chose to frame her analysis of modern cities in historical terms at all. Why didn't she simply present data on modern cities and leave it at that?

Lofland does not directly answer that question in her book, but were this question put to her she would likely respond by saying that the historical comparison helps us to better see how our own lives are unique. We tend to take for granted the way our lives are organized and we need the "shock" provided by history to see our complacency. Moreover, we should realize that Lofland's book is not just about cities: it is about persons' need for order and intelligibility in their lives. It is only through the kind of historical comparison given us by Lofland that we may see how people have continually adapted to and transformed their environment to produce this order. In a real sense all knowledge is comparative; here, it is the historical comparison that gives Lofland's analysis its sociological power.

Now, however, we must ask the question always posed when historical data is presented. Can we be sure of its accuracy? As Lofland describes modern cities we are in a position to judge for ourselves the adequacy of the description given. We can always ask whether the description closely relates to our own experience. We cannot employ this validity criterion when presented with historical data. We must rely on Lofland's good judgment in piecing together, from largely secondary sources, an image of life in these earlier cities. As a sociologist primarily intent on using the preindustrial city as a point of comparison she cannot invest her energies in the arduous, time-consuming search for primary sources. Her work is, in a manner of speaking, a translation of translations. She selectively produces her picture of preindustrial city life from previously written histories. It is in terms of that selectivity that other questions suggest themselves.

We said earlier that one of the distinguishing characteristics of sociological in contrast to historical work is the sociologist's interest in demonstrating the utility of a set of conceptual ideas. Lofland was not merely intent on setting the factual record straight. Her sole objective was not to dispassionately create a picture of the preindustrial city. It was equally to use that picture for a purpose — to show that the most salient basis for order in that type of city was appearential. The problem of validity is complicated as soon as the researcher seeks to do more than transmit the historical message as faithfully as possible. (We do not mean that selectivity is only a problem with historical data. Those who study contemporary events, through whatever method, will also be selective in their data reporting.) For the sociologist who uses secondary historical sources, the problem of selectivity is exacerbated somewhat for two reasons: (1) it is a selectivity drawn from the selective reports of others and, as earlier mentioned, (2) it is a selectivity that cannot be challenged by our own life experience.

It has not been our goal to question Lofland's rendering of history. We have used her study as data to illustrate an interesting case of sociological work having the purpose of specifying long-term historical transformations. We have also meant to raise some of the problems associated with secondary data analysis.

We urge the reader to examine other works, such as David Riesman's (1961) study of changes in American national character, Pitirim Sorokin's (1928) examination of cyclical cultural patterns over a 2500-year period, Karl Polanyi's (1957) description of the rise and fall of market economies, Carr-Saunders's (1933) detailed treatment of the growth of professions in modern societies, or Seymour Martin Lipset's (1963) analysis of the development of democratic institutions in the United States. Although these sociological treatments of historical change and transformation vary considerably in content, you will, in evaluating them, want to raise some of the same questions as have been asked of Lofland's research.

The issues confronted to this point should be helpful in thinking about sociologists' use of historical case study materials. The emphasis of this form of sociological research is not so much to document trends over time as to examine in detail one reasonably limited set of historical events. It is worth repeating an observation of Everett Hughes, reported in an earlier chapter: "Every social situation is a laboratory where some aspect of social life can best be studied because there it is best illuminated." We propose that the past provides us some of our best social laboratories.

The Historical Case Study

A superlative example of an historical case study informed by a sociological theoretical perspective is Kai Erikson's (1966) analysis of American Puritanism. Ever since the classical sociological theorist Emile Durkheim postulated the notion that deviance could serve certain social functions in a society, sociologists have looked for evidence to support that theoretical contention. Durkheim had in mind the idea that a society needed its deviants in order to continually reaffirm the boundaries of propriety in a society. Functional arguments for the importance of deviance are intriguing. They provide a novel way of showing how certain institutions in a society, if not the society itself, continue to operate. Durkheim argues, for example, that without the existence of sinners a church could not exist. The very existence of sin provides the opportunity for believers to reaffirm the faith that has been offended by the sinner. So, the worst thing that can happen to a church is to completely eliminate sin from the world and completely propagate the faith to society!

By choosing a specific, dramatic case, Erikson hoped to show how, to the extent that a common morality exists in a society, the society comes to depend on its deviants for the maintenance of its social boundaries. In *Wayward Puritans* Erikson shows how these theoretical ideas can be applied to understand the witch hunts in Colonial America. Relying most heavily on secondary sources, he describes how the "moral entrepreneurs" of early Massachusetts colonial society, in their zeal to maintain religious purity, launched full-scale attacks on alleged Salem witches. This particular attack on "deviants" is only one of several that Erikson documents and analyzes. Anyone who did not fully identify with Puritanism suffered in these self-conscious attempts to delineate acceptable behavior in the society. A close analysis of the historical case provides compelling evidence for Erikson's theoretical notion:

> . . . Boundaries remain a meaningful point of reference only so long as they are repeatedly tested by persons on the fringes of the group and repeatedly defended by persons chosen to represent the group's inner morality. Each time the community moves to censor some act of deviation, then, and convenes a formal ceremony to deal with the responsible offender, it sharpens the authority of the violated norm and restates where the boundaries of the group are located. . . . (Erikson, 1966:13)

Although Erikson does not draw these parallels himself, we could, on the basis of casual historical knowledge, say that a number of historical cases might be used as additional historical illustrations of the functional view of deviance: the McCarthyism of the 1950s; the events leading up to the laws of discrimination against Jews in Nazi Germany; the internment of Japanese-Americans during World War II; and more recently, the antipathy expressed toward the hippies of the mid-1960s.

We should be motivated by more than just curiosity about the possible parallels in the historically discrete cases named above; there is an important methodological point to make. We know that no matter how interesting the sociologist's rendering of one historical case, we are obligated to question the representativeness of that case. If, however, sociologists can show that their theoretical ideas help to explain a number of cases, two things are accomplished: (1) we are allowed to see underlying dimensions to historical events separated in time, and (2) we have greater faith in the generalizations made from any one case. This positive outcome suggests a strategy for social scientists who see value in historically testing their theoretical ideas. They should be willing to conduct a number of historical case studies as a way of both understanding history and continuing to amplify their theories.

There is another point that our example gives us the opportunity to make. Thus far we have spoken only of the ways in which sociologists can be informed by an historical perspective. Lipset has said that the "way in which one looks at data depends in large measure on the questions asked, the theory employed, and the classifications used." (1968:50) Historians, thus, would expand their own visions by looking at their data from a sociological point of view. The difficulty of establishing such a reciprocal relationship between sociology and history is, however, considerable. Consider the criticisms leveled at Erikson's research by two historians.

Anne and Hart Nelson (1969) find fault with Erikson's work on two related levels. First, they claim that because Erikson began his inquiry with a specific set of theoretical ideas he wished to test, he was caused to "misquote and misrepresent in his efforts to make the data conform to his theory." (Nelson and Nelson, 1969:149) Second, they find fault with Erikson's too frequent use of secondary sources when primary sources were available. They argue that he should have made much more extensive use of sermons, available diaries, and the like. Had Erikson, they claim, done better history rather than stopping "when he finds a secondary source that tells him what he wants to hear," (1969:150) his analysis and interpretation of the historical case studied would have been far more adequate. We are considering these criticisms not because we should either agree or disagree with them, but because they indicate the kinds of issues for which the sociologist utilizing historical data will likely be held accountable.

Erikson's (1969) reply to these methodological criticisms is equally interesting because it helps us to better understand how sociologists are likely to view the use of historical cases differently from professional historians. Erikson tries to make clear at the outset that his response to the Nelsons' critique ought not be read as a quarrel between history and sociology. He admits quite readily that he has no training in historiography and that mistakes might have been avoided had he had that kind of training. He also admits to relying heavily on secondary sources but defends himself by saying that sociologists cannot spend their whole lives becoming intimately acquainted with a particular historical period since their goal is to produce comprehensive generalizations. He ends his response this way:

> I share the Nelsons' hope that sociology and history can manage to create a closer partnership by examining the same data responsibly, and I agree that sociologists would be better prepared for that partnership if they knew more about history. At the same time . . . a fact that serves the

job of historical explanation still has enough vitality and ambiguity left over to serve other purposes as well, and critics from one field cannot do a responsible job of evaluating the way in which a student from another uses his material unless they give at least a glancing thought to the theoretical contours of his argument. (Erikson, 1969:154)

Personal Documents and Life History Reports

Not all historical research must extend back a long distance in time. Rather, the period of interest may be quite recent, and the historical data very far removed from government reports and religious edicts. Personal documents such as diaries, letters, and biographical statements have long been used in sociological research. Perhaps the most well-known example of this form of primary data in sociological work is W. I. Thomas and Florian Znaniecki's (1918) study, *The Polish Peasant in Europe and America.* In this research, the authors consider a long-standing theoretical problem in sociology; namely, how persons adapt to new forms of social organization. The Polish peasant in America afforded an excellent opportunity for understanding the modes of adaptation of persons transplanted from a largely agrarian culture to a modern industrial culture.

The research was based on the letters that these immigrants sent to their families in the "old country." Speaking of that data source, Thomas and Znaniecki (1918:1832) wrote, "We are safe in saying that personal life-records, as complete as possible, constitute the perfect type of sociological material. . . ." Acquiring the letters through an advertisement in the newspaper, Thomas and Znaniecki were able to document the nature of the interaction between these persons and their distant families. The data, in effect, provided a continuous history of their New World experience. These letters, constituting actual interaction between persons, allowed the researchers to assess dynamics of attitude change, changing relations within primary groups, and the development of community life.

Much of the presentation in the two-volume work is thoroughly descriptive: Thomas and Znaniecki appear to have included, in an unedited form, every letter they were able to acquire. This is important because it allows their readers to obtain an overall feeling for the data, better allowing them to judge the adequacy of the researchers' interpretations. At the same time, we must cast something of a wary methodological eye on this type of data. There are two weaknesses that immediately come to mind. First, the letters obtained were necessarily selective. The researchers were able to use only the letters of those who saw fit to reply to their advertisement, and they were provided with only the letters these respondents saw fit to show them. Second, we must recognize that the authors of these documents may have had some reason for presenting the quality of their experiences in a particular light.

As part of their effort to see the New World experience from the subjective perspective of the peasants themselves, Thomas and Znaniecki commissioned selected persons to record detailed life histories of themselves. In these documents, which read much like novels, the critical life events responsible for shaping subjects' perspectives were brought into focus. When contemporaries of Thomas and Znaniecki saw how persuasively the life history documents filled out the general ethnographic descriptions of the immigrant experience, they were led to adopt it in their own later work. This was especially true of sociologists at the University of Chicago who, as a group, were committed to discovering persons' adaptations to city life. Clifford Shaw's (1930, 1931) recording of delinquents' life histories and Edwin Sutherland's (1937) analysis of the professional thief are two frequently cited examples.

Despite the applause that these works still receive, the life history method has, with a few notable exceptions (Hughes, 1961; Williamson, 1965; Bogdan, 1973), been little used in recent years. Even the detailed methodological discussions by Gordon Allport (1942) and Louis Gottschalk et al. (1947) of their importance did not motivate sociologists to continue life history studies. Perhaps we can account for this waning interest in terms of sociology's historical development. As sociological research relied more heavily on quantitative procedures after 1940, social scientists may have come to feel that life history reports were too journalistic in tone; too impressionistic, not scientific enough. Howard Becker (1970) in a recent article on life history data implies that such a view misunderstands the method.

Becker is careful to point out that the life history is to be clearly distinguished from the more literary autobiography. When we read autobiographies we do so with the recognition that authors select their material to present a particular image of themselves. We recognize as well that what an author considers as trivial or unimportant, and therefore chooses not to report, may be quite significant for the sociologist. While we believe that sociologists would do well to make use of such works as *The Autobiography of Malcolm X* (1966) or Claude Brown's (1965) *Manchild in the Promised Land,* these sources do pose special selectivity problems that somewhat diminish their sociological value.

How then does the life history differ? As sociologists gather life history reports, they do not simply rely on subjects to fully determine what will be said. Rather, social scientists, with their particular theoretical interests in mind, maintain a continuous dialogue with their subjects. Through this dialogue subjects are oriented toward specific kinds of events in their lives; clarification is demanded where ambiguities exist; and, where necessary, the scientist will ask for more extensive descriptions of past events. Becker (1970:420) puts it this way:

The sociologist who gathers a life history takes steps to ensure that it covers everything that we want to know, that no important fact or event is slighted, that what purports to be factual squares with other available evidence and that the subject's interpretations are honestly given. The sociologist keeps the subject oriented to the questions sociology is interested in, asks him about events that require amplification, tries to make the story told jibe with matters of official record and with material furnished by others familiar with the person, event or place being described. He keeps the game honest for us.

Becker's statement also alerts us to the fact that the life history must be used in conjunction with other data sources. If we were to rely solely on a few individual case histories to make our generalizations, criticism of our findings would be justified. Just as we must recognize the extent to which historical events are unique, so also must we suppose an individual's life history to be idiosyncratic in some respects. When used in conjunction with other techniques and data sources, the life history will provide a penetrating, in-depth view of events. The life history is, in this respect, an extension of the traditional use of "informants" in participant observation research. Used with proper caution, personal documents and life history reports will further our effort to comprehend the intersection of history, individual biography, and social structure.

The Use of Available Records

As suggested, personal documents and life histories have their limitations as data sources.[1] Although we are able to get an in-depth view of persons and events, we are studying normally only a small number of cases and the data we acquire is relatively unsystematic. Sociologists who wish to comment on the historical experiences of large groups or population aggregates must, therefore, turn to other data sources. Available records have been frequently used by sociologists to provide systematic historical data on large numbers of individuals. Although social scientists must live with the fact that records are not kept with the expectation that they will someday be used for historical investigation, a variety of official records do exist that make possible the statistical analysis of sociohistorical trends. To get an idea of the types of records available for this form of historical analysis in sociology, we may briefly look at the research concerns of those who do demographic analysis.

Demography has traditionally been an important area of sociological inquiry. Simply, demography is the study of population phenomena. Among other issues, demographers seek to document rates of fertility,

---

[1] For a more detailed discussion of a number of the issues taken up in this section see Chapter 12 (Aggregate Data Analysis).

patterns of immigration and migration, changing food resources in a society, birth rates, and death rates. Demographers may examine trends or changes in these population parameters on any of a number of levels: for a selected part of society, for a whole society, for several societies — indeed, even for the world. Obviously, demographers must, in order to produce their aggregate population analyses, rely exclusively on existing records.

Although the data is sometimes spotty or incomplete, demographers have been able to document population trends using such materials as census reports; international migration records; population registers; and records of such "vital" statistics as disease, birth, and death rates. By looking at population trends historically, demographers have shown consistent relationships between various of these population characteristics and a society's level of economic development. It is by now, for example, a well-established "fact" that there is an inverse relationship between a society's level of industrialization and its fertility rate. Generally, as a society becomes more industrialized, persons begin to have fewer children. The importance of such a finding for social policy formation needs no elaboration.

Since all their research depends upon existing records, demographers have been particularly sensitive to methodological problems. Although census records, for example, are considered fairly reliable, we know that they will contain certain types of errors. Many persons lie about their age or income. In the compilation of any record, it could happen that persons will be counted twice or omitted altogether. Those responsible for compiling statistics will incorrectly classify some of the cases. It could happen that for political or ideological reasons, "official" statistics may be altered. It is certainly possible that there will be errors unwittingly committed in *recording* data for official statistics. There can be a temporal problem in certain records: that is, the statuses of a good number of persons will change over time (e.g., marital status, citizenship) and the changes will not be reflected in the records we use. Demographers have taken steps to estimate the degree and direction of these various errors in their data. It is impossible to make aggregate data records error free, but it is possible to be cognizant of likely errors in the data and to consider them in assessing the significance of findings.

We have named only a small number of the official record sources employed by the social scientist who wishes to establish statistical trends over time. To those mentioned we would add the following sources: voting records; lists of school enrollment; city directories; telephone directories; tax payment records; unemployment figures; sports attendance figures; local, state, and national government expenditures; records of police arrests; congressional proceedings; and, of course, codified law in its various forms. Imagine the kinds of historical trends of potential theoretical significance that could be established using records of this sort. Using telephone directories it would be conceivable to assess changes in the ethnic composition of an area; records of police arrests may be used to establish how the nature and type of criminal activity have changed over time; the use of voting records to reflect ideological change in the country has been a traditional preoccupation of social scientists.

Now that we have some idea of the types of records available for historical analysis, we can illustrate their use in two recent studies. Each of the investigations deals with a different aspect of poverty in America. Both rely on available historical records. Both lend validity to the central point of this chapter — that an understanding of contemporary social forms will be increased by seeing how they stand in a broader historical context.

Much of the literature documenting the degree, nature, and amount of poverty in the United States asserts that the plight of the poor today is of a quite different nature from the poverty of early immigrants to the country. The argument goes that immigrants to this country really were, and perceived themselves to be, in an opportunity-filled society. Consequently, they viewed their poverty status as a temporary one and lived out their lives with the reasonably certain feeling that if things did not get much better for themselves, certainly their children would be better off economically. Today's poor, alternatively, are thought to view their economic situation as a permanent one. Although it has achieved some considerable currency among American academics, the truth of this historical comparison has never been put to the test. Stephan Thernstrom (1968), in his attempt to look at poverty in a historical perspective, uses several data sources to test the validity of this longstanding image. Of course, it could be tested only by accurately assessing the poverty experience of immigrants to America of the late nineteenth and early twentieth centuries. We shall not study Thernstrom's entire argument, but we shall take a brief look at some of the ways he used historical records. First, however, let us consider Thernstrom's (1968:161) statement of the aim of his research (beyond proving or disproving the supposed self-image):

> A related, but broader, aim is to demonstrate the necessity of examining in proper historical perspective some of the complex issues involved in current controversies over the poverty problem. Much of the literature dealing with present-day poverty bristles with large unsubstantiated assumptions about the past. . . . (There has been a) failure to take into account relevant portions of the historical record.

He begins his analysis by choosing to look at the "historical record" in Newburyport, Massachusetts, a typical turn-of-the-century manufacturing city that drew to itself large numbers of immigrants. He "combs through" census schedules, tax lists, and savings bank records in order to get some general clues about the welfare status of the immigrants living there at the time. In order to identify this part of a working class culture, he creates a social class index based on existing records of family property holdings. He is able to uncover records that indicate, for a statewide sample of unskilled laborers in Massachusetts in 1874, the mean annual wage of a family head. Seeing at one point the necessity to determine the numbers of unskilled workers who saw fit to leave Newburyport, Thernstrom compares the appropriate sections of the census reports over time — in 1850, 1860, and 1870. Part of his task was to look at rates of occupational mobility. In order to obtain a representative sampling of persons whose patterns of mobility would be examined, the researcher drew names (presumably in a random fashion) from 1910 marriage license records. He drew another sample randomly from birth certificates. We have given only a sampling of the sources from which Thernstrom generates the evidence allowing him to reject the viability of the "new poverty" thesis. In order to discover exactly how he uses collected data to make sense of the historical period, the reader will have to return to the original research.

In *Regulating the Poor* (1971), Frances Fox Piven and Richard Cloward also create an historical analysis of the poor. The purpose of their research is, however, quite different from Thernstrom's. Through a combination of history, political interpretation, and sociological analysis, they endeavor to explain the recent, rather dramatic increases in the number of persons receiving public welfare. They make it plain at the outset, however, that their concern is not simply with describing the welfare system. Rather, they wish to see how the welfare institution in the United States has been linked to other major social institutions; how it functions today and has functioned in the past to serve the larger political and economic order. Their historical analysis traces the welfare system in the United States from the Great Depression to the present, revealing a distinctive pattern of relief policy — at certain times relief policy has been quite liberal and at other times highly restrictive.

Their major thesis which is convincingly documented through their historical investigation is that the welfare system has been used to control and regulate the poor. "Historical evidence suggests that relief arrangements are initiated or expanded during occasional outbreaks of civil disorder produced by mass unemployment, and are then abolished or contracted when political stability is returned." (Piven and Cloward, 1971:xiii) It is by examining the operation of the welfare system in total historical perspective that we can comprehend the explosion of welfare programs following the civil disturbances of the early 1960s.

Starting out with a comprehensive historical analysis based on the writings of professional historians, Piven and Cloward (1971:8) find that the initiation of welfare systems was a response to the "mass disturbances that erupted during the long transition from feudalism to capitalism beginning in the sixteenth century." In considering the beginnings of the relief system in the United States, the researchers examine a variety of historical data sources: newspaper accounts of the tenor of the society in the 1930s, official unemployment statistics, average wage figures, congressional records, accounts of senate debates, voting records, and, of course, records of expenditures for various forms of public relief. As they piece together the relationship between stability in society over time and the expansion or retraction of relief programs, the argument that relief programs have had the function of "diminishing proclivities toward disruptive behavior" (1971:348) becomes indeed compelling.

CONCLUSION

Our intention in this chapter has been to provide an overview of the types of historically based research possible in sociology. We have emphasized the distinction between the particularizing aims of history and the generalizing aims of sociology. The few examples given should have been sufficient to indicate: (1) the wide range of sociological problems that may be investigated historically; (2) the nature and methodological limitations of data sources available for historical analysis; and (3) the inappropriateness of delineating a constant, rationalized set of procedures for conducting historical research. We find that many of the research methods considered elsewhere in the text can be used in historical analysis, but some (such as content analysis) lend themselves to historical analysis more readily than others (such as experimentation).

Historical research shares much in common with such unstructured procedures as participant observation. In both cases the researcher proceeds by way of a kind of methodological eclecticism, making use of any available materials that will enrich insight into the events or processes studied. As the situations studied change, the available data sources change, and so also, then, do the methodological problems. Despite these variations, two questions remain constant in our evaluation of any sociologist's historical investigation: How much faith can we have in the accuracy of the historical picture given? And, are the generalizations made from the historical cases legitimate?

We must acknowledge that problems may exist in the analysis of historical records. But, with a sense of proportion, we should leave this chapter convinced that a comparative historical perspective helps us see with greater clarity both ourselves and the social structures within which we carry out our lives. In recent years considerable progress has been made in the collection and preservation of historical materials. As sociologists begin to acquaint themselves more fully with these data sources, they will benefit from discussions with historians about the historiographic methods that will ensure the proper use of the data. Historians, in turn, can profit by considering how sociological questions and theories might inform their interpretations of the past. Such a happy rapprochement depends on the willingness of social scientists to risk looking beyond the "conventional wisdoms" produced through the histories of their respective disciplines.

EXERCISES

1. Go to the library and read five different newspapers. Choose papers that differ in size and circulation. You might want to include such papers as the *Christian Science Monitor, The New York Times,* a local town newspaper, and your campus newspaper. Describe how these papers differ. Are there differences in how national events are reported? Does each paper have a distinctive ideological perspective?

Speculate on how a historical research report might be affected if the investigator relied on only *one* of these papers as the data source for a study.

2. Imagine that administrators in your college have an interest in producing a short history of the college (how, why, and when it started; what its growth has been like, and so on) and have commissioned a group of students in your class to begin collecting preliminary data. Along with two or three other students, work out some division of labor for collecting whatever institutional records might be applicable to this particular problem. Without doing any in-depth analysis, write a brief report indicating the kinds of materials available for such a study. Also indicate the kinds of information you would like to have about the history of the institution which do not appear in available materials.

3. As an exercise in realizing the variability in eyewitness accounts, ask several persons to give you an account of what went on in a particular meeting or class you did not attend. Write down the accounts of a few persons immediately after the class or meeting and interview a few others a day or two later.

In what way(s) do the reports of your informants differ? What are the points of similarity? Did those with whom you spoke immediately after the event give more detailed accounts? What does the "data" lead you to say about the difficulties of relying on only one or a few eyewitness accounts in historical research? What methodological recommendations would you make to increase the validity of information acquired via eyewitness reports?

4. Read one or two research reports written by historians and one or two written by sociologists. (You might find it convenient to find these reports in Cahnman and Boskoff's book *Sociology and History*; the full reference for this book is noted in the suggested readings for this chapter.) Then answer the following questions:

a. Make a list of the types of historical sources used in the studies. Are they primary or secondary sources?

b. Do the reports differ in terms of the type of generalizations the authors attempt to make from their collected data?

c. What conclusions might be reached about differences in orientation of sociologists and historians?

5. Suppose that one of your roommates was writing a term paper on the segregation of minority groups in large cities and was planning on relying solely on the most recent census data to write the paper. What arguments would you use to persuade your roommate that the term paper could be strengthened were the recent census data complemented by a broader historical approach?

6. On page 260 of this chapter C. Wright Mills is quoted as follows: "Unless one assumes some trans-historical theory of the nature of history, or that man in society is a non-historical entity, no social science can be assumed to transcend history." State in your own words what you believe is the significance of Mills's statement. Do you agree or disagree with the statement? Why? Why not?

SUGGESTED READINGS

Readings about the Method

Cahnman, Werner J., and Alvin Boskoff
1964   "Sociology and history: reunion and rapprochement." In *Sociology and History*, ed. Werner Cahnman and Alvin Boskoff. New York: Free Press.

This is the first article in Cahnman and Boskoff's book and sets the tone for a very worthwhile set of readings on the use of history in sociology. The first article is a strong, cogent statement of the necessity of historical sociology. The remainder of the book provides interesting examples of the application of sociological theory and methodology to historical materials.

Gottschalk, Louis; Clyde Kluckhohn; and Robert Angell
1947   *The Use of Personal Documents in History, Anthropology, and Sociology.* New York: Social Science Research Council.

In recent years sociologists have not paid very much attention to personal documents such as diaries as a data source for research. This book deserves to be rediscovered for it systematically presents a discussion of the use and importance of personal documents. The section on the use of personal documents in sociology is exhaustive and has the special merit of outlining the precautions necessary when using this data source. However, the reader would do well to also read carefully the sections of the book on history and anthropology.

Lipset, Seymour M., and Richard Hofstadter, eds.
1968   *Sociology and History.* New York: Basic Books.

In this book the authors present some outstanding examples of interdisciplinary research. These essays present further verification of the advantages of combining historical and sociological approaches. We particularly recommend Lipset and Hofstadter's introductory essay, which is concerned with the advantages and problems of such interdisciplinary research.

Mills, C. Wright
1968   *The Sociological Imagination.* New York: Oxford University Press.

Of particular interest here is the chapter entitled "The uses of history," which is well worth reading in full. It is a very literate, compelling essay in which Mills demonstrates the central place of a historical perspective in the creation of the "sociological imagination."

Social Science Research Council
1954   *The Social Sciences and Historical Study.* New York: The Council.

Recognizing the need for more historical research in the social sciences, the Social Science Research Council created a special panel in the early 1950s to discuss and report on points of conjunction between sociological and historical research. Most of the ideas and suggestions still apply today.

Winks, Robin, ed.
1969   *The Historian as Detective: Essays on Evidence.* New York: Harper & Row.

The series of articles in this book deal with the actual mechanics of historical research. Special emphasis is given to the problems involved in the collection and verification of historical materials. The book is nicely organized; each article discusses a particular aspect of the historical research process. Among the topics discussed are: difficulties in obtaining necessary materials, detecting inconsistencies in historical records, and verification of historical evidence. The reader will also find descriptions and discussion of famous historical frauds.

Readings Illustrating the Method

Erikson, K.
1966   *Wayward Puritans: A Study in the Sociology of Deviance.* New York: John Wiley.

Erikson's book is a case study of Colonial America done with the intention of providing historical evidence for a certain contemporary theory of deviance. It is a widely read and important book. The reader will particularly want to consider the data sources used by Erikson and the validity of the generalizations made from the one case.

Fogel, Richard, and Stanley Engerman
1974   *Time on the Cross: Evidence and Methods.* Boston: Little, Brown.

Time on the Cross has become one of the most controversial studies done in the last few years, both because of the methods used by the authors and the conclusions they reach. They utilize computer technology to analyze a variety of historical documents; and their quantitative, statistical results lead them to the conclusion that slavery was a much more benign institution than it is generally seen to have been by most historians. Presently, both historians and sociologists are engaged in considerable debate about the significance of the work.

Genovese, Eugene D.
1974   *Roll, Jordan, Roll: The World the Slaves Made.* New York: Pantheon Books.

Writing from a neo-Marxist theoretical perspective, the author combines historical data with sociological theory to analyze how slaves constructed a livable world for themselves under very harsh conditions. This book shows the utility of historical analysis for letting us better understand such contemporary aspects of black culture as its stratification system, its family structure, and its relation to the larger society.

Handlin, Oscar
1968   *Boston's Immigrants.* New York: Atheneum Press.

In this study Handlin attempts to explore the factors influencing the economic, physical, and social adjustments made by immigrants to Boston between 1790 and 1880. Among the data sources used for the study were: newspapers of the period (especially the immigrant press); city, state, and federal census materials; records of town meetings; and immigrant registration records.

Lodhi, Abdul Aqiyum, and Charles Tilly
1973   "Urbanization, crime and collective violence in 19th century France." *American Journal of Sociology* 79 (September):296–318.

Lodhi and Tilly explore alternative arguments which link violence to cities and urbanization. Utilizing historical documents (censuses, newspapers, annual crime reports, archive data) from nineteenth-century France, they carefully document the incidence of crimes and collective violence. Tilly and Lodi's findings cast doubt on theories that interpret crime and violence as a response to the chaos of living in cities.

Piven, Frances Fox, and Richard Cloward
1971   *Regulating the Poor: The Functions of Public Welfare.* New York: Vintage Books.

In this book the authors trace the relationship between welfare expenditures and the maintenance of social order. The underlying thesis of the book is that relief arrangements are expanded during periods of civil disorder and then retracted during periods of social stability. The reader should note the variety of data sources used in the study and consider the validity of the generalizations made for understanding the present welfare system.

Sennett, Richard
1970   *Families Against the City.* Cambridge, Mass.: Harvard University Press.

In this historical study of nineteenth-century city life, Sennett examines such diverse topics as urban class and mobility patterns, urban power structures, and their relation to urban family life. Sennett tries to show how studying the situation of the family in the nineteenth century gives us a better understanding of contemporary city experiences.

Shaw, Clifford
1931   *The Jack-Roller.* Chicago: University of Chicago Press.

In this early study Shaw utilized the life history method to understand some of the factors involved in adolescent delinquency. The study focuses on the life of one such adolescent and contains fascinating, in-depth descriptive material on Stanley's life. Aside from the intrinsic interest of the materials presented in the book, *The Jack-Roller* exemplifies the fruitfulness of the life history method and provides a model for those who would employ this method.

REFERENCES

Allport, Gordon
1942   *The Use of Personal Documents in Psychological Science.* New York: Social Science Research Council.

Anderson, Charles
1974   *The Political Economy of Social Class.* Englewood Cliffs, N.J.: Prentice-Hall.

Beard, Charles
1935   *An Economic Interpretation of the Constitution of the United States.* New York: Macmillan.

Becker, Howard S.
1970   "The relevance of life histories." In *Sociological Methods: A Casebook,* ed. Norman K. Denzin. Chicago: Aldine.

Bogdan, Robert
1973   *Being Different: The Autobiography of Jane Fry.* New York: John Wiley.

Brown, Claude
1965   *Manchild in the Promised Land.* New York: New American Library.

Carr-Saunders, A. M., and P. A. Wilson
1933   *The Professions.* Oxford: Clarendon Press.

Comte, Auguste
1896   *The Positive Philosophy of Auguste Comte.* London: Bell.

Durkheim, Emile
1947   *The Division of Labor in Society.* Glencoe, Ill.: Free Press.

Erikson, Kai
1966   *Wayward Puritans: A Study in the Sociology of Deviance.* New York: John Wiley.
1969   "Response to the Nelsons' 'case example'." *American Sociologist* (May): 151–154.

Gottschalk, Louis
1950   *Understanding History: A Primer of Historical Method.* New York: Knopf.

Gottschalk, Louis; Clyde Kluckhohn; and R. Angell
1945   *The Use of Personal Documents in History, Anthropology, and Sociology.* New York: Social Science Research Council.

Hughes, H.
1961   *The Fantastic Lodge.* Boston: Houghton Mifflin.

Kuhn, Thomas
1971   *The Structure of Scientific Revolutions.* Chicago: University of Chicago Press.

Lipset, Seymour M.
1963   *The First New Nation.* New York: Basic Books.
1968   "History and sociology: some methodological considerations." In *Sociology and History,* ed. Seymour M. Lipset and Richard Hofstadter. New York: Basic Books.

Lofland, Lyn
1973   *A World of Strangers.* New York: Basic Books.

Maine, Sir Henry
1870   *Ancient Law.* London: John Murray.

Malcolm X
1966   *The Autobiography of Malcolm X.* New York: Grove Press.

Mills, C. Wright
1968   *The Sociological Imagination.* New York: Oxford University Press.

Mosteller, Frederick, and David L. Wallace
1964   *Inference and Disputed Authorship: The Federalist.* Reading, Mass.: Addison-Wesley.

Nelson, Ann, and Hart Nelson
1969 "Problems in the application of sociological method to historical data: a case example." *American Sociologist* (May):149–151.

Nisbet, Robert
1966 *The Sociological Tradition.* New York: Basic Books.

Piven, Frances, and Richard Cloward
1971 *Regulating the Poor: The Functions of Public Welfare.* New York: Random House (Vintage).

Polanyi, Karl
1957 *The Great Transformation.* Boston: Beacon Press.

Redfield, Robert
1947 "The folk society." *American Journal of Sociology* (January):293–308.

Riesman, David; Nathan Glazer; and Reuel Denney
1961 *The Lonely Crowd.* New York: Anchor Books.

Shaw, Clifford
1930 *The Jack-Roller.* Chicago: University of Chicago Press.
1931 *The Natural History of a Delinquent Career.* Chicago: University of Chicago Press.

Sorokin, Pitirim
1928 *Contemporary Sociological Theory.* New York: Harper & Row.

Spencer, Herbert
1891 *The Study of Society.* New York: Appleton.

Sutherland, Edwin
1937 *The Professional Thief.* Chicago: University of Chicago Press.

Thernstrom, Stephan
1968 "Poverty in historical perspective." In *On Understanding Poverty*, ed. Daniel P. Moynihan. New York: Basic Books.

Thomas, W. I., and Florian Znaniecki
1918 *The Polish Peasant in Europe and America.* Chicago: University of Chicago Press.

Tönnies, Ferdinand
1940 *Fundamental Concepts of Sociology.* New York: American Book Co.

Weber, Max
1947 *The Theory of Social and Economic Organization.* New York: Oxford University Press.
1958 *The Protestant Ethic and the Spirit of Capitalism.* New York: Charles Scribner & Sons.

Williamson, Henry
1965 *Hustler.* New York: Doubleday.

Content Analysis

Despite recent evidence that chimpanzees may, after much instruction, learn the meaning of a few signs, we may still agree with anthropologists' traditional claim that it is the extraordinary capacity of humans for symbolic communication which sets us apart from the lower animals. Indeed, the argument is made that without language human culture would be impossible. Because language allows us to express and arouse emotion; as well as convey values, attitudes, and knowledge; it is the key factor in the creation of human societies. It is only through language that abstract insights can be formulated as knowledge and then transmitted and shared with others. It is, in other words, through language that knowledge becomes a collective, social possession rather than an individual possession. The continuance of culture depends on each generation communicating its abstract knowledge to the next.

Nearly from the beginning, moreover, persons sought to codify their thoughts and accumulated knowledge. Writing must, in this context, be seen as one of the most profoundly important of human inventions. It is in written communications, from the first stone scratches on cave walls to today's enormous variety of mass-produced printed media, that we find preserved our beliefs, values, understandings of the world, and images of ourselves. Further, the written word is not merely a record of behavior — it is itself a form of behavior. We may seek through our writing to convince others of a point of view, to change attitudes, to manipulate others, to motivate action, and so on.

Writing is, of course, only one medium of communication in contemporary society. Our lives are importantly shaped by movies, radio, and most especially television. The power of television to communicate both orally and visually an extraordinary assortment of factual information, ideas, beliefs, and values to forty million or more persons simultaneously has created revolutionary change in modern society. Television now plays a significant role in the socialization of children. It shapes our knowledge and interpretation of social events. To the extent that it affects our buying habits, it affects the whole economic structure. Some have claimed that television has transformed Americans into a nation of spectators and has, thereby, altered our leisure time activities and the structure of our family lives.

It should come as no surprise that the study of communication content has a long tradition in social scientific work. The analysis of written, verbal, and pictorial communications has been undertaken to reveal significant information about the values of both communicators and their audiences. *Content analysis* is the label that has come to be attached to the methodological procedures for extracting thematic data from a wide range of communications. In this chapter we shall consider the major elements of content analysis, offer some examples of its use in the social sciences, and discuss some of the methodological issues raised for investigators who seek to analyze the content of communication in its various forms. We begin our discussion by outlining the general contours of the method. Let us consider the elements of Bernard Berelson's (1952:18) definition of content analysis as a research technique for "objective, systematic and quantitative description of the manifest content of communication."

THE METHOD: AN OVERVIEW

Researchers who use content analysis, Berelson tells us, are *objective* in their evaluation of the content of communications. We have, of course, seen in other chapters that objectivity is a central feature of scientific investigation. How, then, does the idea of objectivity apply to the analysis of human communications? We can best illustrate the need for objectivity through an example.

Were we to hear persons comment about the liberal stance of the editorials in a particular newspaper, we might be led to ask them a number of questions to determine the validity of their assertion. What exactly is their definition of liberalism? Have they read all the editorials in the particular paper or has their reading been selective? Over how long a period of time have they been reading the newspaper? To what other newspapers is this one being implicitly compared? We ask these questions because we know that persons may interpret the content of any communication in terms of their own particular needs, interests, biases, or ideologies. In short, our questions might be directed at uncovering the *rules* that have been used in categorizing and making evaluations of the contents of a particular written document. The essence of objective, scientific content analysis is that researchers make absolutely explicit the rules they have used in classifying the content of any communication.

We need not agree with the categories that researchers develop for analyzing the content of materials. Nor need we agree with procedures for placing a unit of communication in one or another category. What is important is that, as long as the rules of the game have been spelled out, we can evaluate how conclusions were reached; and we can expect that any researchers who follow those rules, regardless of their own personal values, beliefs or interests, will document the content of materials in exactly the same way. Content analysis done with rule-guided objectivity allows researchers using the same procedures to easily *replicate* the findings of earlier research.

Berelson tells us, secondly, that content analysis is a *systematic* procedure. Actually, systematic procedure is part of the more general criterion of objectivity and refers again to the rule-guided nature of the method. The idea of systematic procedure does, however, add something to our characterization of objectivity. Suppose that we wanted to compare the editorials in several newspapers. In order for our comparison to be a valid one, we must systematically use the same procedures in documenting the content of each of the separate papers. For example, suppose we were to compare the editorial content of *The New York Times, The Washington Post, The Phoenix Sun,* a small local newspaper, and the Easy College newspaper. It would be contrary to systematic procedure to say that because these newspapers differ in size and nature of the audience served, different criteria ought to be employed in analyzing each. Once we commit ourselves to a systematic procedure for evaluating our data we minimize considerably any personal biases that might intrude into that evaluation. It is by applying systematic procedures to all cases studied that we avoid collecting only data congenial to our theoretical ideas.

Third, content analysis most usually provides us a *quantitative* description of communications. Perhaps the most common use of content analysis is to detail the *frequency* with which certain items, symbols, or themes appear in a written document. As we shall see, those who engage in content analysis will also be interested in assessing the *intensity* of particular variables. If we were interested in comparing the attitudes of two candidates for office with regard to their position on welfare, we could do a content analysis of their speeches. We might choose at the outset to count the number of times each candidate makes positive or negative comments about the welfare system. This simple enumeration might be misleading, however. Beyond simply counting the number of references made we could devise some set of rules for measuring just *how positive or negative* each of these assertions is. We can imagine that once the researcher chooses to go beyond measuring simple frequencies, the task of setting up adequate categories becomes more difficult. This is an issue to which we shall return.

There are both positive and negative consequences of the quantification of materials demanded by content analysis. On the positive side, the use of rigorous categories yielding quantitative results allows the researcher to characterize efficiently a large volume of materials. Since the meaning of the numbers produced will be clear to any reader, there is no danger of a reader making impressionistic judgments about the content under investigation. We should also say that a clear quantitative presentation of the content of materials has another advantage: it can often alert us to themes in those materials that we would otherwise miss.

As we study content analysis, let us keep in mind that we risk missing the overall sense of a body of communications if we do no more than offer statistical summaries of their content. Any communication evokes a feeling, an overall impression, or a sense that cannot be captured simply by counting the frequency with which certain items appear. We might say that, in important respects, any communication is going to be more than the sum of its parts. It is for these reasons that we would claim, as we have done in the past, that qualitative and quantitative techniques must be used in conjunction with one another.

Berelson is careful to point out, lastly, that the technique of content analysis deals with the *manifest content* of communication. Content analysis is, by definition, limited to what explicitly appears in a text. Very frequently — we all know this from our own reading — there are levels of meaning implied by the written materials that do not actually appear in the text itself. We "read between the lines" of a text, continually interpreting the meanings lying behind the manifest symbols. As an objective, systematic, quantitative procedure, content analysis must be limited to documenting the elements, symbols, or themes that manifestly appear in a communication. This is not, however, to say that the researcher who chooses to employ content analysis will refrain from engaging in any interpretation of the materials studied. But the timing of the researcher's interpretive inferences is all-important. Reading between the lines must wait for "the interpretation stage, at which time the investigator is free to use all of his powers of imagination and intuition to draw meaningful conclusions from the data." (Holsti, 1969:12)

The preceding paragraphs on the definitional features of content analysis were meant to provide an initial or preliminary sketch of the method's boundaries. We may begin to bring the picture into sharper focus by examining a sampling of investigations accomplished using content analysis. We particularly want to discover, through reading about the types of studies done and the data sources used, the different questions and research goals that frequently motivate the analysis of communications.

APPLICATIONS OF CONTENT ANALYSIS

Social scientists have content-analyzed an enormous variety of materials and have done so with a number of different purposes in mind. Newspapers, periodicals, government records, personal documents such as letters and diaries, novels, recorded speeches, and children's books are among the written communications that have been used. In addition, researchers have analyzed the content of such diverse communications media as inscriptions and images on art work, and television and radio programming. In sociology, another frequent use of content analysis is as part of structured observation. Robert Bales (1950), for example, has used structured observational categories for analyzing the nature of ongoing verbal interaction in small groups.

Whether the data sources are written, visual, or verbal (or some combination), nearly all communications research has been guided by some aspect of the question, "Who says what to whom and with what effect?" In some instances the concern of the researcher may be to analyze the content of a message in order to understand the motives, goals, intentions, or values of its author or source. Here the concern is with the "who says what" part of the question. In other cases researchers concentrate on the communication itself (the what) to determine how larger social phenomena are illuminated in the content. In still other cases the task of the research is to assess the effects of communication on particular audiences (to whom with what effect). In sum, researchers typically investigate the thematic content of communication with at least one of the following goals in mind:

1. To make inferences about the values, sentiments, intentions or ideologies of the sources or authors of the communications.
2. To infer group or societal values through the content of communications.
3. To evaluate the effects of communications on the audiences they reach.

We can order our discussion of some representative content analysis studies in terms of these major research goals.

Inferences to the Source: Who Produces the Communication?

Frequently the concern of content analysis investigation is to infer from themes uncovered in a communication the characteristics of the persons or institutions responsible for creating them. These studies are based on the apparently reasonable assumption that attitudes, values, beliefs, and the like, are revealed in symbolic communications. On this assumption researchers have analyzed a variety of documents ranging from diaries to public speeches in order to understand characteristics of communicators.

In one well-known study (Paige, 1966), the personal letters of a woman, Jenny Cosgrove, were analyzed to better understand certain features of personality structure. The study particularly indicates the value of content analysis to uncover themes that might elude even a clinician trained in the evaluation of such personal materials through careful reading. While clinicians were able to insightfully analyze specific features of the series of letters written by Jenny, a widow, to her son, the statistical analysis produced through content analysis revealed themes that even a careful reading missed. In this particular study the content analysis, done with the aid of a computer, helped to uncover important themes centering on Jenny's conception of herself, her son, her job, and her attitudes toward death.

In similar studies researchers have made use of a variety of documents. Suicide notes (Osgood and Walker, 1959) have been studied in order to understand the quality of consciousness of persons willing to take their own lives. In another study on the same topic (Ogilvie et al., 1966) the researchers were able to develop a set of categories for analysis sophisticated enough that they could distinguish actual from simulated suicide notes.

More recently, Seider (1974) studied available speeches in order to assess the ideology of business elites. This study suggests yet another strength of content analysis. It provides the opportunity to study persons or groups of persons generally inaccessible to social scientists. Elites are one such group. Studies of elites have suffered because it is nearly impossible to observe the daily activities of "powerful" individuals or to personally interview them. Content analysis partially remedies this problem. We say partially because we can analyze only those communications persons consider to be fit for public consumption.

There is something else to take into account in inferring the intentions or values of communications sources. A number of studies have been directed at understanding how the *accuracy* of communications may be affected by the interests of the originating person, or more generally the interests of originating institutions. The concern of this research is frequently to understand how political, economic, or social interests may affect the content of communications. A study of the kinds of images presented on television constitutes a good example. In 1964, Melvin DeFleur sampled 250 television shows during one week which children might watch. He did so to determine how realistically occupational roles were characterized or presented to children in that medium. His major conclusion was that stereotyped images presented in these programs represented romanticized distortions of the actual occupational world. One might infer that such distortion is done to make the shows more appealing to children. Such a finding, we would add, assumes considerable importance when we consider that the images presented on television exert a major influence on childhood socialization.

A number of written communications have been analyzed to illustrate how the coverage of events, phenomena, or social processes might be seen as a function of personal or institutionally based ideological interests. In one cross-cultural study (Wayne, 1956), for example, the content of Russian and American family magazines was compared. Consistent with socialist ideology, Russians were most often pictured as engaged in happy and constructive work and leisure activities. The magazines rarely showed persons displaying aggression of any sort or engaging in any form of even minor deviance. Magazines in the United States, alternatively, much more frequently pictured Americans engaged in "unflattering" activities. In a related fashion, several studies of newspaper reporting (e.g., Allen, 1922; Lewis, 1960; Blumberg, 1971) suggest that the way events are covered may reflect ideological or sales considerations. These are interesting studies because they begin to show how institutional, economic, or political factors potentially affect the production and distribution of information in a society.

We distinguish the types of studies we have been describing from those where the purpose is to infer from themes uncovered in communications the values of the populations or audiences reached by the communications. These studies are concerned with how the content of communication reflects, or is representative of, general social values.

Inferences to Populations: Communication Content and Social Values

In a number of studies researchers have sought to test hypotheses concerning changes in the value structure of societies. One of the more well-known of these studies is David McClelland's (1961) research on the relationship between a society's rate of economic development and the stress it places on achievement values. By correlating achievement themes in some thirteen hundred children's stories from nearly every country in the world with such indicators of economic growth as increases in coal and electricity consumption, he was able to show a greater concern with achievement values in those societies with higher rates of economic growth. In other sections of his book, *The Achieving Society*, McClelland shows how a number of additional communications sources may be used to study value changes historically. He makes use of such literary forms as poems, epigrams, legends, tales, and the writings of major authors to measure achievement motivation in societies extending as far back as ancient Greece. *The Achieving Society* is well worth reading in detail as it illustrates some ingenious uses of content analysis in historical research.

In similar fashion, David Riesman's (1950) well-known thesis that there has been a gradual shift in American national character from an "inner directed" stress on personal achievement to an "other directed" concern with group acceptance, has been tested through content analysis. Partial evidence for Riesman's hypothesis was provided through an analysis of advertisements in the *Ladies' Home Journal* over a 66-year period (Dornbusch and Hickman, 1959). The researchers were able to show a significant increase in other-directed advertising at the historical juncture when Riesman suggests the shift began.

Somewhat "unusual" data sources have been used to assess dominant values in a society. Barcus (1961), for example, studied the themes, type of stories, and type of characters pictured in Sunday comic strips from 1900 to 1959. He found that during that period there was a steady decline in themes stressing domestic or home concerns and an increase in content around crime and romance themes. In other studies researchers make use of multiple sources. One such study (Otto, 1963) centered on themes of sex and violence in a 1961 sample of newspapers, books, and magazines. In that year the investigator sampled all the issues of fifty-five magazines and recorded for each the number of violence and sex incidents mentioned. He also measured the column space devoted to stories and pictures with these themes. The information obtained was supplemented with a similar analysis of all the issues of ten newspapers across the country, and finally with an analysis of the covers of 295 paperback novels published in the same year. Still other researchers have made inferences about cultural values and social change through the analysis of school songbooks (Sebald, 1962), films (Wolfenstein and Leites, 1950), and folk tales (Bradburn and Berlew, 1961).

The concern of "representative value" content analysis need not be to document society-wide values. Sociologists have long argued that specific groups or subcultures of persons generate and maintain their own distinctive value structures. Thus, they have undertaken studies to help them better understand the values that are held by specific "target" audiences of communications. Arnheim (1944), for example, tried to understand the values of persons listening to daytime radio serials by carefully documenting the themes of these programs and the types of characters portrayed in them. One could imagine an analogous study of daytime television soap operas. In another study (Albrecht, 1956) the concern was to discover the distinctive values of different social classes by analyzing periodicals with different class readerships.

In the studies we have been considering in the last few paragraphs the focus is less on the characteristics of those who produce communications and more on how the themes contained in them reflect either comprehensive societal values or the values of specific segments of the population. We acknowledge that some considerable leaps of inference are demanded in these studies, which means that we must really weigh carefully the validity of the interpretations made. Can we know with any certainty that comic strips, for example, really do reflect the values of the larger society, or that soap operas reflect the values of a segment of persons in the society? It seems clear that in studies such as these the larger the number of independent sources showing essentially the same findings, the greater will be our faith in any interpretive assertions made.

The content analysis researches described to this point are concerned almost exclusively with the themes found in the materials studied. In a significant body of research on the *effects* of communication, the research focus is more globally on the *total process* of communication. Underlying research into the effects of communications are questions of the following sort: When are persons persuaded by communications? Do persons tend to avoid communications contrary to their preexisting attitudes? In effects-oriented research the specific analysis of content is only a part, albeit a significant part, of the total research effort.

Evaluating the Effects of Communications:
To Whom with What Effect?

One of the earliest studies designed to assess the effects of communications shows us the utility of combining content analysis with other methodological techniques. We are referring to Herbert Blumer's (1933) study of the relationship between exposure to movies and persons' conduct. A sample of persons kept diaries in which they were asked to record their attitudes, feelings, reactions, sentiments, and values concerning the themes, characters, or behaviors in the movies they watched. Researchers content-analyzed these diaries to determine how various types of persons reacted to the communications medium of movies. Blumer later conducted personal interviews with his subjects to establish still further the effects of the movies on them.

We are all familiar with the ongoing debate in the social sciences on the question of whether violence depicted in the mass media causes persons themselves to display violence and aggression. The research evidence around this question is mixed. After doing content analysis to measure the extent of violence portrayed in comic books and other media, Wertham (1972) indicates that a sample of children who had committed violent or criminal acts had more exposure to high-violence materials than a comparative sample of "normal" children. Other researchers, however, have suggested that exposure to violence and aggression usually is chosen by persons who do not, themselves, engage in such behavior. A number of studies have used content analysis as part of research to evaluate the relationship between themes in children's stories and aggressive behavior (Wolf, 1949), protest songs and the creation of countercultural attitudes (Hirsch, 1971), and newspaper editorials and the outcome of elections (Gregg, 1965; McDowell, 1965).

In the types of studies mentioned it is a major methodological problem to determine if the communications actually *cause* certain behaviors or whether they simply *reflect* persons' previously held attitudes, behaviors, or dispositions. Debate continues around this issue. In the late 1960s there were those who argued that news reports of violence in certain urban ghettos were instrumental in provoking riots in other cities, that the effect of news reports was to increase riot activities. We can surmise that if there is any relationship between news reports of riots and further rioting it is not a simple one. Perhaps the issue turns on *how* riot activity is presented in the news. The validity of this hunch could be tested by doing an analysis of the content and style of news presentations in cities with ghettos which had riots in the mid-1960s and in those that did not. Such a historical study might help to clarify the relationship between media presentations and their effects on audiences. There is a broader point to make: content analysis must play an important role in studies on the effects of communications — we have to make studies because we know they will have substantial implications for the formation of social policy.

We have reviewed and grouped studies as source oriented, audience oriented, and effects oriented; these map the general range and variety of applications for content analysis. To these categories of content analysis research we would, however, add one more. We will complete this section by briefly discussing the use of content analysis as part of structured observation of behavior.

Content Analysis and Structured Observation

A criticism frequently made of observational research is that it is difficult to discern just how and why researchers collected the data they did. We must often take it as a matter of faith that the data in a study do in fact capture the typical activities, behaviors, or events occurring in a setting. Further, as long as the rules for selecting data cannot be specified, it is virtually impossible to replicate most observational research. The use, where possible, of structured observational data recording requires researchers to specify precisely the features they will observe and the types of measurements they will make. Observational content categories have frequently been used to systematically document such features of ongoing behaviors as their duration, frequency, and effects. The behaviors observed and documented need not be only verbal. Researchers have, for example, worked out coding categories to document nonverbal and body movement behaviors (Birdwhistle, 1970) and spatial characteristics of interaction (Hall, 1963). To provide a sense of the types of variables or behaviors that might be systematically coded in observational research we turn to an example.

In a recent study (Karp and Yoels, 1975) the researchers set out to consider the processes through which both students and teachers formulate definitions of the classroom as a social setting. More directly, they sought to understand the meaning of student participation in college classrooms. Do men talk more than women? Does the frequency of student talk vary with the nature of the subject matter? How often do students disagree with the comments of their instructors? Is the nature of classroom interaction different at the beginning of class periods from the way it is at the middle or end? Does the nature of interaction change over the course of the semester? Is the sex of the teacher at all influential in the willingness of students to talk? These are some of the research questions with which they began their investigation.

In an attempt to answer some of these questions, the researchers proceeded systematically to observe behaviors in a number of classrooms over the course of a semester. A coding sheet was developed on which observers were asked to note, for every single student's verbal utterance during each class period observed, the following information:

1. The sex of the student.
2. The geographical location of the student (classrooms were divided into nine separate imaginary spatial areas).
3. The stimulus for the student's talk (was the talk a response to a teacher's question, another student's comment or question?).

In planning the study the researchers had decided that it would not be sufficient to simply document the *number* of interactions occurring; beyond that, they wanted to evaluate the *nature* of those interactions. The researchers had available to them a number of established and widely used category systems for coding the nature or content of verbal interaction. In this case they decided to make use of the coding categories developed by Robert Bales (1950) to analyze small-group interactions. Considerable observation of small-group interaction had led Bales to believe that all interactions fall into one of three classes: interactions involving positive social or emotional attitudes and feelings, interactions involving negative social or emotional feelings, and interactions explicitly related to group tasks. The elaboration of these three dimensions resulted in the construction of the following coding categories:

A. SOCIAL-EMOTIONAL AREA: POSITIVE

1. Shows solidarity.
2. Shows tension release.
3. Agrees.

B. TASK AREA: NEUTRAL

1. Gives suggestions.
2. Gives opinions.
3. Gives orientation.

4. Asks for suggestions.
5. Asks for opinions.
6. Asks for orientation.

C. SOCIAL-EMOTIONAL AREA: NEGATIVE

1. Shows antagonism.
2. Shows tension.
3. Disagrees.

Observers were asked to make fairly detailed qualitative comments on events not covered by coding categories. Included here were: special or unusual events that may have occurred in the class, the general demeanor of teachers and students, the nature of material discussed in class, nonlinguistic gestures made by teachers and students, and so on. This qualitative information was helpful to the researchers in filling out their understanding of the "objective" data collected. At the end of the data collection period, the researchers had accumulated a good deal of data indicating exactly what went on in the observed classes. At the very end of the semester they supplemented this content analysis data by having students and faculty fill out questionnaires. They were, thereby, able to examine the relationship between the *perceptions* which students and teachers had of classroom behavior and the kinds of behaviors that *actually* occurred in the classrooms.

This example of classroom observation should have served the following purposes. We should understand that content analysis need not be restricted to the study of standard communication media and may be used to record the content of behaviors in a variety of "natural" behavioral settings. Second, we should have some sense of the research problems for which structured observation might be appropriate and of the types of variables or behaviors that can be systematically tabulated. We should also appreciate the value of using content analysis in conjunction with other methodological techniques.

Our broader discussion of content analysis applications should have been sufficient to illustrate the important place of this technique among the range of methodological tools available to the social scientist. We still need to fill out the details of the picture we have been creating by describing some of the specific mechanics of the method.

CONTENT ANALYSIS: THE RESEARCH PROCESS

To this point we have broadly characterized the nature and goals of scientific content analysis and have offered some examples of the types of research where its use has proved fruitful. Such a general overview does not fully alert us, however, to the complexities of the method when actually applied to a problem. Content analysis shares in common with any other method that the manner of its application will vary somewhat with each problem studied. It is, nevertheless, possible to specify the type of decisions and judgments that will be made in the process of *any* content analysis investigation. One way to see the research process demanded by content analysis is to consider how researchers might plan and carry out a specific investigation. We will suppose, therefore, a group of researchers with a general interest in investigating changing women's roles in the United States. Since our hypothetical researchers recognize that their choice of methodological techniques must follow a clear specification of the research problem, such specification becomes their first task.

Specification of the Research Problem

Nearly any research project begins with a number of questions to answer. Our researchers begin with the question: Has the women's movement had any effect in altering images and stereotypes of the female role? From that broad question flow a number of other, more specific questions. Have there been any changes in the kinds of activities thought proper for men and women? Have there been any changes in the kinds of occupations thought appropriate for men and women? Are females today pictured in more egalitarian relationships with men than in the past?

As the researchers continue to spell out these and similar questions, they begin to consider how their focus ought to be narrowed so that they can actually begin to collect data around their questions. Let's imagine they mutually decide that one way to focus their problem would be to study changes in the kinds of gender images that children perceive. One rationale for such a choice might be that if women's roles really change, there have to be corresponding basic changes in the gender role socialization of children. The theoretical literature on socialization has convinced the researchers that gender roles are learned and deeply ingrained during childhood socialization.

Once the problem has been specified theoretically to consider only the images and stereotypes taught to young children about female roles, the attention of the researchers logically turns to the kinds of data sources that can be used to assess any changes in the content of socialization over time. We can imagine that several options could be discussed. It would be possible to consider how males and females are portrayed to children in such mass media sources as television or movies. One could, for example, do a content analysis of such children's shows as "Sesame Street" or "Mr. Rodgers" and compare them with the tapes of children's shows from several years ago.

After considering all the alternative means by which they could study socialization changes over time, the researchers decide to restrict their data source to children's books. There are several good reasons for this choice. First, as we have seen, there is considerable precedent in the sociological literature for using children's books to establish social trends (McClelland, 1961). Second, and a more pragmatic reason, children's books are easily accessible items. The researchers might also correctly believe that the use of children's books provides the opportunity for more rigorous comparative analysis than other data sources might. If they choose to, the researchers can compare books that are of a particular length; they can limit their analysis to works of fiction, and so on. Having specified their problem to this point they must begin to think how they will use the chosen data source to provide evidence relative to their guiding research question which is:

> Has the women's movement had any effect on the female stereotypes or images found in children's books?

We can see that many of the procedural decisions still to be made about sampling, category construction, the choice of units for analysis, and the mode of data presentation are contingent on the initial specification of the research problem. The first of these procedural decisions is to determine just how the children's books for analysis will be sampled.

Sampling Items

It is immediately clear to the researchers that their stated problem demands a research design allowing them to compare past and recent books. At a bare minimum, their historical problem requires two samples of books — a sample from before the beginnings of the women's movement and a sample of contemporary books. Assuming it is historically accurate that the women's movement began to emerge in the middle 1960s, the researchers could choose to sample books published each year from perhaps 1960 (four or five years prior to the emergence of the movement) to the present. If there have been any changes in sex role images, such a sampling design would allow researchers to say more surely just when these changes began to take place. If they have the money and manpower to sample materials in this way, they might be in a position to make some elegant theoretical statements concerning the length of time before a movement begins to have any discernible effect in changing the content of published materials. In order to simplify our analysis somewhat, however, we will presume that the researchers choose to compare two samples of books. One sample will be of books published in the three years immediately prior to the emergence of the women's movement. The second sample will be composed of books published in the last three years.

Even if the researchers opt for this relatively simple design, their sampling problems are not over. After all, there are literally thousands of children's books published each year. You should begin to see that sampling is, in the case of content analysis, nearly always a multistage process. Once researchers make some preliminary determination of the *universe* of materials applicable to their research problem (in our case, *all* children's books), they are still left with many more materials than are manageable. In virtually all content analysis investigations it would be literally impossible for researchers to analyze all the items applicable to their problem. Our researchers might, therefore, restrict their attention to only those *schoolbooks used in grades 1 and 2.* If asked why, they could argue that (1) children are likely to become most intimately acquainted with the books they use in school, and that (2) children in the early grades are at a formative age, an age when the content of sex role socialization will have its greatest impact.

If, after having made this decision, the researchers still feel that the universe is unmanageably large, they would likely consider analyzing only those books used in a particular area of the country, a particular city, or perhaps even a particular school district. They must recognize, however, that as they more strictly define the universe of books, they also restrict the comprehensiveness of any generalizations eventually made from their findings.

Once the universe is clearly determined there are a number of ways in which the final items for analysis might be drawn. If the total number of items is small enough the researchers would simply include them all in their final study. Our researchers, however, decide that it would be unfeasible, given resources and manpower, to analyze more than one hundred books, fifty in each of their two samples. It might be possible for the researchers to construct their two samples by choosing the one hundred books at *random.* Simple random sampling can be used, however, only if all the appropriate items that it is possible to include in the sample can be clearly identified.

Sometimes simple random sampling is not possible because one cannot identify all the elements of the universe or because such a sampling procedure does not meet the demands of the research problem. Our researchers might decide, for example, that all children's books do not have an equal influence on children because some are more widely read than others. Consequently, they would fashion a sampling procedure to put them in contact with those books likely to have greatest influence because they are the most widely circulated. Were they to make this decision they might use judges or experts to help them determine the most useful books for their research problem. They could consult with a number of primary school teachers or publishing company representatives who would be asked to submit lists of the most frequently used books. If possible, this information could be supplemented with school records of books ordered. It might even be reasonable to tabulate the books most frequently checked out of school libraries. The wisest course of all might be to use a combination of the procedures mentioned. However accomplished, we can assume that the researchers now have in hand the one hundred books that will be the basis for their analysis.

At this point, the researchers must decide which aspects of gender image they wish to measure and how that measurement shall be done. Will they consider the images portrayed in each book as a whole? Will they code the images portrayed in particular stories within each book? Will they code the images presented in the books paragraph by paragraph? Sentence by sentence? Might it be possible, indeed, to code specific words (e.g., adjectives) related to female images in the books?

There are, then, two decisions that the researchers must make at this juncture: (1) Which dimensions of female role image are they interested in assessing? Which *categories,* in other words, should guide the coding of the data? (2) What exactly ought to be the *unit for analysis* in the study (words, sentences, paragraphs, stories, the book as a whole)? In any content analysis these decisions must be made in terms of the research questions, hypotheses, and theoretical ideas guiding the study, as well as the peculiarities of the data source used. There are, however, some general methodological considerations that ought to guide both of these interrelated decisions. We can say a few words about units for analysis and then consider in some greater detail the problems of category construction.

Choosing the Unit for Analysis

In our earlier discussion of the kinds of research done employing content analysis, we saw that the specific unit of content tabulated can vary considerably. In some studies researchers will tabulate the simplest content unit constituting any communication — the *single word.* One way, for example, that our researchers studying female role images could proceed would be by coding every adjective used to describe males and females in the literature studied. They could create procedural rules for classifying each of the adjectives attached to gender. The choice of the single word or symbol as the unit of analysis has some distinctive benefits when it can be used. The primary benefit is that coders must make relatively few judgments in the classification of this unit, and, in the usual case, few inferences about the meaning of the unit. Instructions can be so explicit that virtually all decisions about proper coding are made ahead of time. Coders could be told, for example, that every time they see the adjective "aggressive" it is to be classified in category X. The researchers could even provide the coders with an exhaustive list of adjectives, with directions concerning the category into which each ought to be coded. As coders confront each adjective in the textual material, they simply consult this prepared coding list and are, therefore, relieved of any interpretive coding decisions. The use of this simplest unit has the advantage of increasing reliability.

It may be that the materials to be analyzed, the variables of interest to the researchers, the hypotheses to be tested, and the theories to be evaluated, may make the single word an inappropriate unit for analysis. Researchers may see the need to work with more comprehensive units — such as the content of sentences, paragraphs, chapters, or the entire item (a whole book, a whole film, a whole newspaper). Researchers using any of these units will set up categories to tabulate the themes, types of persons or characters, or types of behaviors represented.

We can well imagine that as researchers move to the analysis of more comprehensive units with the idea of extracting specific themes from them, the coding task becomes more complicated. Unlike the situation in which coders can simply consult a list to determine exactly how a particular word ought to be coded, the analysis of themes in sentences, paragraphs, or whole books cannot be achieved by reference to comprehensive coding rules; interpretive judgments are an integral part of these analyses.

Whatever the unit chosen, the most critical step in content analysis is the construction of the categories that will direct the coding of the content.

Category Construction

In the construction of categories the researchers indicate just how they will classify the content of the materials being investigated. If the categories are to be successful, they must bear a close relationship to the problem as originally stated. The constructed categories must faithfully reflect the major theoretical concepts on which the study is based.

Procedurally, researchers normally begin to construct coding categories by exhaustively listing all aspects or dimensions of the phenomenon being investigated. In our research example, the types of behaviors, themes, ideas, or symbols on this preliminary, tentative listing might include: power in interaction, personality characteristics, expressed occupational aspirations, leisure time activities, sexual divisions of labor, types of children's play activities, the number of males and females appearing in the items, the type of dress of male and female characters, and the like.

As the researchers continue to list the dimensions of gender role image, they will find it necessary to specify subdivisions within each broad category they propose. For example, the researchers could elaborate the interactional power dimension mentioned above by distinguishing whether females when in interaction with males are pictured in *subordinate, egalitarian,* or *superordinate* power positions. As the researchers continue to refine their categories, they will likely consider at the same time the procedural rules that will guide the classification of unit contents into one or another of the proposed categories. Coders could, for example, be provided rules of the following sort for classifying each instance of male/female power interaction:

1. Each time a female is pictured interacting with a male, classify the female as in a subordinate power position if she is asking the male for advice of any kind.
2. If the male and female are pictured as talking approximately the same amount and neither is giving advice to the other, classify this as an instance of an egalitarian role relationship.
3. If the male is asking the female for advice, classify this as an instance of the female in a superordinate power position.

Researchers also frequently find it useful to imagine just how their collected data will eventually be arranged in tabular form. If in their final report the researchers were to have a section on "changing images of female/male power relations" (see Table 11.1) and if the principles for constructing categories are well laid out, clear and unambiguous, those persons coding content data will achieve a high degree of consistency or reliability.

TABLE 11.1 Changing Images of Female/Male Power Relations

Female Role Position	Pre-movement Books (N = 50)		Current Books (N = 50)	
Subordinate	No. of cases	%	No. of cases	%
Egalitarian	No. of cases	%	No. of cases	%
Superordinate	No. of cases	%	No. of cases	%
	Total No.	100%	Total No.	100%

Before finally committing themselves to particular coding categories, researchers will normally conduct a pretest of the categories. They will ask a number of persons to independently code the same body of data. If they find that there is little consistency in the classification of the data, they will have to rework the categories. Researchers typically find it useful to put coders through a short training program on the use of the categories. Coding reliability must be high if we are to have any faith in the accuracy of the final data tabulations.

Second, it should be apparent that every single case of male/female interaction noted in the books studied will fit into one of the categories proposed. Categories are *exhaustive* when every specimen of data or every case under investigation will fit into at least one of the categories developed. Categories are exhaustive as long as there do not appear cases where it is impossible to classify the data. It is plain, then, that categories must be reconstructed if it becomes apparent that certain types of data necessary for testing research hypotheses cannot be coded into existing categories.

In many research cases it is, in actual practice, often difficult to create categories that are completely exhaustive. Unexpected or idiosyncratic units will turn up which do not clearly fit into one of the categories developed at the outset of the study. In much the same way, the criterion of mutual exclusivity is often harder to maintain in practice than to state in theory. To the extent that any symbolic communication will allow for a number of interpretations, it could potentially fit into more than one coding category. The safest assertion to make is that high reliability in any content analysis study is dependent on the production of clear, rule-guided categories.

We can see that the fewer the number of decisions, interpretations, or judgments coders must make as they classify data, the greater will be the overall reliability of the study. This general rule has implications for the number of categories researchers will wish to use in their studies. The coding task will generally become more complicated as the number of categories increases. Theoretically, the number of categories used in a study is limitless.

In the example we have been using, the researchers simply classified male/female interactions into one of three power categories — female subordinate, female equal, female superordinate. They might decide, however, that it would be theoretically useful not only to know the power positions most frequently experienced by females, but also the particular *contexts* of these relations. Are females shown more frequently in subordinate positions when in the work world than when engaged in leisure activities? And, in male/female interactions in leisure activities, are females more often subordinate in sports than in parlor games? And so on. They might, therefore, choose to elaborate their categories to include this "context" variable. By doing so, they will be able to make many more comparisons of different features of the data in their final analysis. In sum, as the number of categories used in a study increases, researchers provide themselves the opportunity for more extensive analysis of their data, but may do so at the expense of the accuracy or reliability of the data coded.

To this point we have been assuming that researchers using content analysis are concerned only with tabulating *how often* or *how frequently* themes appear in a given communication. There are, however, occasions when researchers will see it as theoretically appropriate to determine as well the *intensity* or *degree* of a theme or variable in the communications studied. We will look at a brief example to illustrate how the decision to measure the intensity of variables in content analysis necessarily complicates the coding task.

Perhaps our sex-role researchers come to feel that an important theme for analysis in the children's books is females' *expression of dissatisfaction* with their expected roles. Certainly one coding task will be to identify and tabulate each instance where a female is shown expressing dissatisfaction. Beyond that, however, the researchers come to believe that their final analysis of the data will benefit if they know the intensity of the dissatisfaction females are shown to express.

Once the decision is made to create a dissatisfaction scale, the researchers must at least double the number of judgments that coders must make as they seek to classify the contents of a unit. The coder must first decide whether the theme of dissatisfaction is present or not. Once the theme is determined to be present, the coder must employ another set of rules to rate the degree of its existence. Coders may, for example, be provided rules for placing instances of expressed dissatisfaction into *ordinal* categories (e.g., high dissatisfaction, medium dissatisfaction, or low dissatisfaction).

Our examples around the issue of intensity are intended to establish the idea that content analysis need not be limited to the simple tabulation of word or theme frequencies. It is possible to develop more sophisticated measures, but there is a cost in doing so. As the number of categories and coding rules increases, the analysis of data becomes much more time consuming, the number of interpretive judgments we ask coders to make increases substantially, and there may be a consequent decrease in coding reliability.

Once researchers have defined their problem, decided on their unit for analysis, created coding categories, and made explicit the rules for classifying data, they will have completed the major technical steps for their investigation. By now we can sense that the actual tabulation of data is likely to be a laborious, tedious process. A significant number of classification errors inevitably result simply because coding is often a fatiguing job. The problem of fatigue and boredom is greater, of course, with larger samples of items for analysis. In some cases, the number of items for analysis makes hand tabulation of data nearly impossible. In those cases researchers might find it possible to let a computer handle the coding job. As social scientists increasingly use the computer, there have been serious efforts made to create computer programs designed explicitly for certain types of content analysis. We can consider briefly the kinds of content analyses where computer technology is likely to facilitate the research process.

COMPUTER-ASSISTED CONTENT ANALYSIS

We suggested earlier that as the unit of analysis becomes larger and more comprehensive, coders must make a greater number of interpretive judgments about the meaning of the content before it can be assigned to one or another category. Human beings can recognize meanings by reading complete phrases, sentences, or paragraphs in a text. As we read textual material we do not split up a sentence or paragraph into its component parts. We do not separate out nouns, adjectives, and the like. Rather, we consider the communications read as a whole, as a gestalt, as a single meaningful picture. Human beings are, in other words, capable of high levels of symbolic abstraction. In studies where researchers must make subtle decisions about thematic meaning in a communication, computers have relatively limited use.

Computers will, however, perform with unerring accuracy any coding task in which the classification rules are absolutely unambiguous. Such was the case, we recall, in a study to determine the disputed authorship of several of the unsigned Federalist papers (Mosteller and Wallace, 1964). The researchers first looked at the known writings of the three authors — Hamilton, Madison, and Jay — and compiled a tabulation of the frequency with which each of the authors used some 265 key words. They then programmed a computer to tabulate the frequencies of these words in the twelve papers of unknown authorship. The data clearly suggest Madison as the author of those papers. In studies such as Mosteller's, where coding judgments about the specific meaning of items is not demanded, computers can dramatically facilitate the research process. This is most usually so in studies where the single word is seen as the most appropriate unit for analysis.

The first widely used computer programs for content analysis were those developed by Philip Stone (1966) and his colleagues. The General Inquirer system provides a set of computer procedures for tabulating a variety of textual characteristics. This ever-expanding system has been adapted to meet the needs of a variety of specific research problems. Special purpose programs have been created to study achievement themes, cross-cultural folk tale themes and class-related language themes in written materials.

These programs are capable of "reading" a communication word by word, comparing each word to categories of words specified by the researcher. The total set of words specified by the researcher as applicable to the particular research is often referred to as the *dictionary*. Each word included is called a *tag word* or *tag*. The computer is programmed to identify tag words and to place them into preestablished theoretical categories. It is not unusual for variations of the General Inquirer program to include several thousand tag words and eighty or more categories. After the computer has read all the materials, it will print out such information as a list of tag words and the frequency with which each appears, the proportion of sentences in the text containing tag words, and graphs indicating the number of tag words appearing in each category used in the study.

One of the difficulties in any content analysis of word items is that words *will* have different meanings in different contexts. Think about the nuances of word meaning in such expressions as "time flies like an arrow." In response to this problem, recent work has been directed at creating programs that allow the computer to distinguish between alternative meanings for the same word, on the basis of the context in which the word is used. By instructing the computer to look at the way words appear in pairs or clustered together, we can have it make more sophisticated meaning distinctions as it places words into theoretical categories. Even with these advances, however, we cannot yet rely on the computer to make sophisticated judgments. Because of the symbolic intricacy of language, coding validity remains a substantial problem. This is not to suggest that manual coding eliminates validity problems, but that direct contact with the data makes it easier to evaluate the tone and inflection of materials which are so crucial to assessing intended meaning.

Although the computer will eliminate coding error stemming from fatigue or boredom, it cannot altogether eliminate the need for highly routinized work. Researchers must prepare the text as demanded by the particular computer program used, which entails the transfer of textual information to computer cards. They must be careful, as well, not to use existing computer programs simply because they are available. If, because of the nature of the communications to be analyzed or their particular theoretical ideas, none of the established dictionaries or theoretical categories satisfies the researchers' needs, they will have to create their own computer program. The creation of new dictionaries and coding categories can itself be time consuming. But if the researchers work with ill-conceived research problems or categories inapplicable to their theoretical concerns, the computer will only function to rapidly tabulate a large volume of insignificant data.

In sum, the computer can be an enormously valuable tool for social scientists who wish to analyze a large volume of written communication. By saving researchers the countless hours ordinarily involved in manual data coding, rating, and tallying, machine data processing makes possible content analysis projects that would have been unthinkable only a few years ago. As more social scientists come to see the potential of computers for facilitating the coding of content data, we would expect a continued growth of standard computer programs based on frequently used theoretical categories in the social sciences. We would, however, emphasize again that the computer is only a tool. It is, moreover, a valueless tool without the sound theoretical reasoning of the social scientist who must, after all, choose sociologically meaningful problems, determine the materials to be used for analysis, construct categories that reflect the theoretical issues at hand, and finally make sense of the collected data.

CONCLUSION

We have examined in this chapter some of the central methodological characteristics of content analysis and the types of problems where it is profitably used. We have seen that the primary intent of content analysis is to uncover *themes* in communication sources; themes that are representative of a whole culture, a specific group of persons, or the life of an individual. In some studies the discovery of these themes may be accomplished through the tabulation of specific words. In other studies researchers may find it necessary to ascertain the themes in sentences, paragraphs, or in some cases the entire essay or book. Regardless of the specific *unit of analysis* employed, the underlying goal of the research remains constant — to find a logic in the themes uncovered such that the characteristics of authors or their audiences may be better understood.

We have seen that the capacity to realize this central goal rests on the adequacy of the *categories* developed for the classification of data. Categories reflect the major theoretical concepts considered central to an understanding of the phenomena under investigation. The validity of judgments eventually made about the values, motives, beliefs, or ideologies of individuals, specific populations, or whole societies will depend on the adequacy of the theoretical categories generated at the outset of the study.

We should also comprehend one of the most significant strengths of content analysis: it is a thoroughly *unobtrusive* method. Nearly all the methods employed by social scientists necessitate a direct involvement with persons. This is certainly so in survey, experimental, or participant observation research. But content analysis, which makes use of available materials, eliminates a source of troublesome bias that threatens our research whenever the subjects of investigation are directly questioned or observed. We do not have to bother with the potential response biases of subjects who are influenced by the presence of an investigator or the knowledge that they are participating in a study. In this respect, content analysis may serve to complement the findings of the more obtrusive methods discussed elsewhere in this book.

The authors would advocate, as they have time and again, that various methods be used in conjunction with each other. While content analysis may serve as the central method in an investigation, it can also be used to test preliminary ideas, hypotheses, hunches, or theories prior to a more complete investigation. By conducting a pilot study through the content analysis of a few selected communication sources, researchers may generate hypotheses and discover important variables. The findings of such initial research may then importantly guide further research where perhaps survey research or participant observation become the primary data collection methods. Although content analysis is a powerful tool for evaluating personal or social values, researchers will often want to employ intensive interviewing, survey research, or direct observation to check the validity of inferences made from the communication sources used in a study. This is most especially true where the specific goal of the research is to evaluate the *effects* of communications.

Content analysis is, in short, an adaptable research method. It is an economical and time-efficient procedure. It sometimes becomes the central technique in historical research concerned either with a particular period or with trends over time. Content analysis also makes possible a variety of cross-cultural studies that would likely be unfeasible using other methods. In addition, because of the availability of data sources and (as shown in our illustrative hypothetical example) the relative simplicity of the mechanics involved, students with little research experience can easily make use of the method. For these reasons, content analysis will often prove to be a useful research strategy when our interests lead us to inquire into the values, ideologies, sentiments or beliefs motivating behavior in a society.

EXERCISES

1. Reread the section of this chapter on structured observation and then construct coding categories so that you may gather data to accept or reject the following hypotheses:
   a. There is no difference in male and female participation in college classrooms.
   b. The area of the classroom in which a student sits is unrelated to the likelihood of his or her participation in class.
You may offer a preliminary test of these hypotheses by randomly choosing two or three classes at your college and observing them for a week. To increase the sample size of observed meetings of the classes, it is possible for a number of students in your class to operate as a research team with each member observing a couple of meetings. If you choose to work as a group it will be important to discuss just how the coding will be done so as to ensure a high intercoder reliability. After the data relative to these two hypotheses have been tabulated, try to offer some explanation of the findings.

2. Do different communications sources "make" news? Answer this question by comparing coverage in a "national" newspaper to that in a "local" newspaper on any political, social, or economic event that has recently been in the news. It will probably be best to restrict your content analysis to one week's reporting and analysis of the event in the respective newspapers. Decide on the features of the coverage you will document (e.g., column space devoted to the event, the kinds of details reported, the position taken by the paper on the event, etc.). Be sure to include in your brief report some *description* of the categories constructed for analyzing the reports and the *unit of analysis* used. Speculate from your collected data on the values of the audiences served by the two newspapers. If you expected a difference in coverage between the papers but found none, explain why this happened.

3. We reported in this chapter that Barcus (1961) studied the themes, types of stories, and types of characters pictured in Sunday comic strips. This study was done for the years 1900 to 1959. During that period he noted an

increase in violence and romance themes. We might ask whether there has been a significant change in the content of comics since 1959. After constructing appropriate categories (you may want to read Barcus' study in this regard) do an analysis of the comic strips in any major Sunday paper for the last six months. Does your study indicate that there may have been shifts in the content of the comics since 1959?

4. Write a brief essay indicating what you consider to be some of the validity problems involved in trying to assess the values of communicators or their audiences using the method of content analysis. How could content analysis be used in conjunction with other methods to increase the validity of the research findings?

5. Compare content analysis and any other method you have read about in this book in terms of the potential sources of bias which are avoided using content analysis. It would probably be easiest to make this comparison by choosing a relatively unstructured technique such as participant observation. What would be the *disadvantages* of using content analysis instead of the method with which you are comparing it?

6. Imagine that you wanted to conduct a study with the purpose of discovering the typical values of persons in different social classes in the United States. Assuming that you chose to do a content analysis study to assess class values, indicate the kinds of problems you would likely face in *sampling items* for the study.

SUGGESTED READINGS

Readings about the Method

Carney, Thomas F.
1972   *Content Analysis: A Technique for Systematic Inference from Communications.* Winnipeg, Canada: University of Manitoba Press.

Written for the beginning student, Carney's is a highly readable text on content analysis. In it he provides full illustrations of the issues and problems typically faced in the use of the method.

Cartwright, Dorian
1953   "Analysis of qualitative material." In *Research Methods in the Behavioral Sciences,* ed. Leon Festinger and Daniel Katz. New York: Holt, Rinehart & Winston.

Cartwright's essay is more critical than most concerning the use of content analysis. While not denying the utility of the method, he is concerned that many content analysis studies are substantively unimportant since they are preoccupied with the mere counting of items or themes. Cartwright disagrees with the idea that content analysis can be used only to describe the manifest content of communication. His criticism points to the central place of "meaning" in the analysis of communication content.

Holsti, Ole
1968   "Content analysis." In *The Handbook of Social Psychology,* ed. Gardner Lindzey and Elliot Aronson. Reading, Mass.: Addison-Wesley.

In a relatively short space Holsti succeeds in defining content analysis and describing its several uses; he also offers several reasonably detailed examples of actual research done using the method. Particularly useful is his discussion of many possible content analysis research designs. The reader will also find discussion of some of the recent advances in the use of content analysis.

1969   *Content Analysis for the Social Sciences and the Humanities.* Reading, Mass.: Addison-Wesley.

This is a comprehensive review of the major uses of content analysis in the various social sciences and humanities. It is especially useful because it contains an extended treatment of each of the stages or steps in a content analysis study discussed in this chapter. In addition, Holsti offers several examples of the kinds of categories that have been constructed in various studies, which may be used as models for any researcher about to conduct his or her own study. There is also a complete discussion of the uses of the computer in content analysis research.

Pool, Ithiel de Sola, ed.
1959   *Trends in Content Analysis.* Urbana: University of Illinois Press.

In this series of essays a number of distinctive problems involved in content analysis are discussed. Of particular importance are the questions concerning the types of errors likely to be made by human coders who must often use common sense judgments in trying to ascertain the meanings transmitted in communications of all sorts. We cannot assume that all coders are using the same criteria in assessing the meaning of communications studied. Pool suggests that researchers must learn more about how human beings interpret messages. The implication of much of the writing in this volume is that techniques must be developed for going beyond the manifest content of communication.

Stone, Philip et al.
1966   *The General Inquirer: A Computer Approach to Content Analysis in the Behavioral Sciences.* Cambridge, Mass.: The M.I.T. Press.

As mentioned in this chapter, Stone and his colleagues developed and refined computer programs for conducting content analysis studies. In this very important book, two central goals are met. First, the authors present the logic and techniques developed for computer content analysis. Second, they present a series of studies illustrating the value of computer techniques in extracting thematic data from communications sources. This book presents the most sophisticated treatment available of the potential and limits of computer technology for conducting content analysis studies.

Readings Illustrating the Method

Berger, Arthur A.
1973   *The Comic Stripped American: What Dick Tracy, Blondie, Daddy War-bucks and Charlie Brown Tell Us About Ourselves.* Baltimore: Penguin Books.

In an intriguing use of content analysis, Berger gauges changing American values by probing the themes found in comic strips over three generations. As the subject matter suggests, it is fun to read.

Birdwhistle, Ray L.
1970   *Kinesics and Context: Essays on Body Motion Communication.* Philadelphia: University of Pennsylvania Press.

Most studies of communication have centered on written or verbal communication. A growing area of interest in the social sciences is nonverbal, gestural communications. Kinesics is the label that has come to be attached to the study of gestural communication. In this book, the author not only illustrates the importance of such study, but develops as well a system for coding nonverbal communications.

Levin, J., and James L. Spates
1971   "Hippie values: an analysis of the underground press." In *Mass Culture Revisited*, ed. Bernard Rosenberg and David M. White. New York: Van Nostrand Reinhold.

An interesting example of content analysis which compares the values of conventional society with those central to the hippie movement of the mid-1960s. To assess hippie values the researchers chose to analyze a sample of underground press periodicals known to have wide circulation. From these periodicals they chose a subsample of nonfiction articles; they then selected a comparable sample of nonfiction articles from the *Reader's Digest*.

Lewis, Lionel S., and Dennis Brissett
1969   "Sex as work." In *Social Problems: Persistent Challenges*, eds. Edward C. McDonagh and Jon E. Simpson. New York: Holt, Rinehart & Winston.

Major social changes are occurring in American society. As the society becomes less production oriented and more consumption oriented, persons have increasing leisure time. Yet, the authors argue, Americans are so deeply imbued with the Protestant work ethic that they consider even their leisure as a job; even play is becoming work in mass society. In this article, the authors extend this broad theoretical notion to a particular leisure time activity — sex. A content analysis of marriage manuals reveals that sexual activity is presented as a kind of work in which certain techniques must be mastered to ensure success.

McClelland, David
1961   *The Achieving Society.* New York: Free Press.

McClelland's research on achievement values in different societies is a classic content analysis study. Even a quick reading of this fairly lengthy book will illustrate the utility of content analysis for historical and cross-cultural analyses. Especially impressive is the ingenuity of the researcher in bringing to bear a variety of data sources to test particular hypotheses.

McGinnis, Joe
1970   *The Selling of the President, 1968.* New York: Trident Press.

In this provocative study of the political control of information, the author discusses the central place of the mass media in creating an image of political candidates. A significant portion of this book describes the relationship between television "spot" commercials and the motives of political strategists.

REFERENCES

Albrecht, Milton C.
1956   "Does literature reflect common values?" *American Sociological Review* 21 (December):722–729.

Allen, Frederick
1922   "Newspapers and the truth." *Atlantic Monthly* 129 (January):44–54.

Arnheim, Rudolf
1944   "The world of the daytime serial." In *Radio Research: 1942–1943,* ed. Paul F. Lazarsfeld and Frank N. Stanton. New York: Duell, Sloan & Pearce.

Bales, Robert F.
1950   *Interaction Process Analysis.* Reading, Mass.: Addison-Wesley.

Barcus, Francis E.
1961   "A content analysis of trends in Sunday comics, 1900–1959." *Journalism Quarterly* 38 (summer):171–180.

Berelson, Bernard
1952   *Content Analysis in Communication Research.* Glencoe, Ill.: Free Press.

Birdwhistle, Ray
1970   *Kinesics and Context.* Philadelphia: University of Pennsylvania Press.

Blumberg, Nathan B.
1971   "The 'orthodox' media under fire: Chicago and the free press." In *Mass Culture Revisited,* ed. Bernard Rosenberg and David M. White. New York: Van Nostrand Reinhold.

Blumer, Herbert
1933   *Movies and Conduct.* New York: Macmillan.

Bradburn, Norman N., and David E. Berlew
1961   "Need for achievement and English economic growth." *Economic Development and Cultural Change* 10 (October):8–20.

Davis, Fred
1967   "Why all of us may be hippies someday." *Trans-action* 5 (December): 10–18.

De Fleur, Melvin L.
1964   "Occupational roles as portrayed on television." *Public Opinion Quarterly* 28 (spring):57–74.

Dornbusch, Sanford M., and Lauren C. Hickman
1959   "Other-directedness in consumer-goods advertising: a test of Riesman's historical theory." *Social Forces* 38 (December):99–102.

Gregg, James E.
1965   "Newspaper editorial endorsements and California elections, 1948–1962." *Journalism Quarterly* 42 (winter):532–538.

Hall, Edward
1963   "A system for the notation of proxemic behavior." *American Anthropologist* 65 (October):1003–1026.

Hirsch, Paul M.
1971   "Sociological approaches to the pop music phenomenon." *American Behavioral Scientist* 14 (January/February):371–388.

Holsti, Ole R.
1969   *Content Analysis for the Social Sciences and Humanities.* Reading, Mass.: Addison-Wesley.

Karp, David A., and William C. Yoels
1975   "The nature of classroom interaction: some observations on the meaning of student participation." Paper read at the 70th Annual Meeting of the American Sociological Association, August 25–29, 1975, San Francisco.

Lewis, Howard
1960   "The Cuban revolt story: AP, UPI, and three papers." *Journalism Quarterly* 37 (winter):573–578.

McClelland, David C.
1961   *The Achieving Society.* New York: Free Press.

McDowell, James L.
1965 "The role of newspapers in Illinois' at large election." *Journalism Quarterly* 42 (summer):281–284.

Mosteller, Frederick, and David L. Wallace
1964 *Inference and Disputed Authorship: The Federalist.* Reading, Mass.: Addison-Wesley.

Ogilvie, Daniel M.; Philip J. Stone; and Edwin S. Schneidman
1966 "Some characteristics of genuine versus simulated suicide notes." In *The General Inquirer: A Computer Approach to Content Analysis in the Behavioral Sciences,* ed. Philip Stone et al. Cambridge, Mass.: The M.I.T. Press.

Osgood, Charles E., and Evelyn B. Walker
1959 "Motivation and language behavior: a content analysis of suicide notes." *Journal of Abnormal and Social Psychology* 59 (July):58–67.

Otto, Herbert A.
1963 "Sex and violence on the American newsstand." *Journalism Quarterly* 40 (spring):19–26.

Paige, Jeffrey M.
1966 "Letters from Jenny: an approach to the clinical analysis of personality structure by computer." In *The General Inquirer: A Computer Approach to Content Analysis in the Behavioral Sciences,* ed. Philip Stone et al. Cambridge, Mass.: The M.I.T. Press.

Riesman, David; Nathan Glazer; and Reuel Denney
1950 *The Lonely Crowd.* New Haven: Yale University Press.

Sebald, Hans
1962 "Studying national character through comparative content analysis." *Social Forces* 40 (June):318–322.

Seider, Maynard S.
1974 "American big business ideology: a content analysis of executive speeches." *American Sociological Review* 39 (December):802–815.

Stone, Philip, et al.
1966 *The General Inquirer: A Computer Approach to Content Analysis in the Behavioral Sciences.* Cambridge, Mass.: The M.I.T. Press.

Wayne, Ivor
1956 "American and Soviet themes and values: a content analysis of pictures in popular magazines." *Public Opinion Quarterly* 20 (spring):314–320.

Wertham, Frederic
1972 *Seduction of the Innocent.* Port Washington, N.Y.: Keumkat Press.

Wolf, Bernard
1949   "Uncle Remus and the malevolent rabbit." *Commentary* 8 (July 31):31–
34.

Wolfenstein, Martha, and Nathan Leites
1950   *Movies: A Psychological Study*. New York: Free Press.

Aggregate Data Analysis

Sociology has been variously defined. Many of those definitions stress the sociologist's concern with understanding the factors that influence *individuals'* behaviors. Our introductory textbooks, for example, tell us that sociology is the scientific study of social interaction; that sociology is the study of how individuals' behaviors are affected by their membership in social groups, and so on. In much sociological research individuals constitute the *unit for analysis,* and many of the methodologies we have discussed (e.g., survey research, experimental research, participant observation) are often employed to gather data on individuals so that we might understand their attitudes, beliefs, and values — in short, the motives underlying their behaviors. When we want to understand why people vote as they do, exhibit prejudice, engage in criminal behavior, and the like, we often proceed by interviewing or observing an appropriate sample of persons. We try to show the distinctive characteristics of people who engage in these behaviors.

It is a mistake, however, to believe that individuals are always the focus of sociological analysis. Equally often sociologists want to understand the nature, character, and dynamics of *social structures.* We frequently wish to compare institutions on some attribute. Social scientists sometimes take as their unit for analysis such *organizations* as universities, business corporations, prisons, or hospitals. As we shall see, much sociological research is concerned with *geographical* or areal groupings of persons. Many studies are devoted to a comparison of neighborhoods, towns, cities, states, areas of a country, or whole countries. We might, for example, be interested in comparing rates of suicide in various countries. While it is true that individuals are responsible for taking their own lives, the focus of our research need not be on the particular or separate motives, beliefs, or personal life conditions of the individuals who end their lives. Rather, our research may be directed at understanding the characteristics of societies where, relatively speaking, large or small numbers of persons commit suicide. It is clear that there are a great many research problems for which data on individuals is used primarily to arrive at a comprehensive characterization of social structures.

The procedure of combining, summating, or *aggregating* information on individuals to produce an overall group score should not be unfamiliar to us. College administrators may boast in their public relations literature that students' average Scholastic Aptitude Test score is over 600. This one score is used to characterize the whole student body and is produced by combining data on each student in the school. In much the same way, we make judgments about society's condition and the quality of our own lives on the basis of "official statistics" computed by aggregating data on individuals. These statistics, we should note, are often the basis for the creation of social policy.

Some persons are willing to measure the morality of a society in terms of suicide statistics, divorce rates, or rates of church attendance. Politicians promise us that if elected they will institute programs to reduce crime rates in our major cities. We weigh our economic futures by monitoring unemployment rates. Ecologists and environmentalists ask us to consider seriously the implications of population growth rates. Comparisons are often made between cities, counties, states, and nations in terms of their rates of mental illness, juvenile delinquency, infant mortality, literacy, average income, and migration.

To see why the comparison of information on individuals is inappropriate for certain research problems, we should consider a recent study (Hibbs, 1973) in which the researcher sought to compare the degree or extent of political violence in different nations. This researcher was not intent on explaining why specific individuals committed acts of political violence. Instead he wanted to know "What produces differences across nations in the magnitude of domestic violence?" His goal was to compare over one hundred nations in terms of their respective *rates* of political violence. Among other things, one might want to know whether rates of violence are different in nations with different political, economic, or religious structures. In other words, the anticipated product of the research was some better comprehension of the relationship between social structural dimensions and violence. In trying to establish this connection it would have done the researcher little good to collect and examine data on specific individuals in each of the countries. The study was accomplished by computing, for a twenty-year period, a measure of political violence for each of the 108 countries in the study sample. Here the measure was produced from available statistical data on such events as the number of riots, assassinations, and antigovernment demonstrations in each country during the designated time period.

Whenever we combine information on the behaviors, attitudes, or other attributes of individuals to statistically represent some social unit comprising those persons, we are employing aggregated data. These social units or groupings, we have suggested, will vary in size and comprehensiveness. For example, researchers could study the same phenomenon at progressively higher levels of aggregation: they might study how rates of mental illness vary in different city neighborhoods, then combine the data on individuals from neighborhoods so they could examine mental illness rates in somewhat larger city areas. The aggregate data on different city areas could be further combined to look at rates for whole cities. The researchers could continue to aggregate data into ever more comprehensive groupings; they could raise the level of aggregate analysis to examine, in turn, rates of mental illness in counties, states, and areas of the country. As a logical extension of this aggregating process, researchers could compare countries in their mental illness rates.

Our goal in this chapter is to discuss some of the methodological issues raised when a certain type of data — aggregate data — is used in research studies. Among the questions that will occupy our attention are the following: How do researchers decide on the appropriate unit of analysis in their studies? How closely do the rates reflected in aggregate data approximate the true rates of the phenomenon studied? Do crime rates, for example, really tell us how much criminal activity actually exists? Very importantly, we will want to inquire whether we can ever make statements about individuals from aggregate data. If we find, for example, that rates of delinquency are highest in areas where the divorce rate is highest, can we then infer that family disorganization causes *specific persons* to engage in delinquent behaviors? Under what conditions might it be misleading to characterize an institution, for example, by summing up the characteristics of persons composing it? Are there situations, in other words, where the whole is more than, less than, or at least different from the sum of its parts? Are there any differences in the nature of the information obtained as we move from one level of aggregation to another?

These are some of the questions we want to answer as we consider the applications of aggregate analysis in the next section of this chapter.

APPLICATIONS OF AGGREGATE DATA

Aggregate analysis is not restricted to one or a few areas of sociological inquiry. Those studying such diverse subject matters as deviance, stratification, race relations, urban life, large-scale organizations, occupations and professions, and mass communications will frequently formulate research problems that require aggregate data analysis. But there are certain topics for investigation where aggregate analysis is nearly always necessary. All demographic analyses of population trends, for example, rely on official statistics already aggregated. A good deal of research in urban sociology makes use of census data collected periodically by the federal government. As might be expected criminologists must rely heavily on available crime statistics. Recently social scientists have made considerable progress in developing indicators for evaluating the "social well-being" of nations. In this research aggregate statistics are used for assessing changes in such social rates as poverty, public safety, health, and employment.

Because of the extraordinary range of issues calling for the use of aggregate data, we must be selective in our discussion of its applications. To create reasonable boundaries for our discussion, we have employed two central criteria in choosing areas for coverage. We have chosen areas (1) that make extensive if not exclusive use of aggregate data, and (2) that help us highlight the methodological problems in the use of aggregate data. Using these criteria we have chosen to organize our discussion of aggregate data applications by covering, in order, research relying on census materials, crime statistics research, research devoted to the development of social indicators, and research where the goal is to forecast future social trends.

Using Census Materials to Study Geographical Social Groupings

Suppose we had the idea that there have been major changes in the structure and composition of American cities over the past fifty years. We have a theory that suggests that the growth of suburbs has affected the age, ethnic, racial, and income characteristics of city dwellers. We want to show that large cities are increasingly inhabited by younger, lower income minority groups, especially blacks. Consider the kind of data we need to establish the validity of our contention. We need data on the attributes of persons in each major city collected periodically and regularly over a long period of time. Aggregate census statistics are indispensable to social scientists because they contain precisely the kind of *demographic* data often used to characterize the population attributes of distinctive territorial groupings of persons.

We began this example by talking about one geographical level of aggregation — cities. The data available in census reports refer, as well, to other territorial groupings; some less and some more comprehensive than the city unit. For example, census report statistics are compiled for areas which in some instances include less than 100 households. This geographical unit is called the *census block*. Traditionally, however, social scientists have made greater use of aggregate census data reported for a somewhat broader areal unit called the *census tract*. Although bigger than the census block, the census tract is still a relatively small area constituted by a population of between 3000 and 6000 persons. Each city is broken up into a number of census tracts. Although there is certainly an arbitrary component to the specification of census tract areas, they are reasonably uniform in terms of population numbers and the size of the area covered. As noted earlier, however, social scientists sometimes want to make comparisons between geographically defined social structures larger than census blocks, census tracts, or cities. Census data can be obtained to characterize counties, states, areas of the country and the country as a whole. Moreover, nearly all nations maintain census records and this makes it possible to engage in cross-cultural comparisons.

The population characteristics mentioned earlier (age, race, ethnicity, and income) are, in addition, only a few among the variety of data collected and reported in census statistics. Among other aggregate population characteristics reported for each of the territorial levels mentioned are the following: place of birth, occupational level, educational attainment, marital status, and family size.

Without the data contained in census reports much sociological investigation, especially research in urban sociology, would be impossible. On a simple descriptive level we could not, for example, determine with any accuracy how different groups (ethnic, racial, class, and so on) are distributed geographically throughout cities. We could not determine urban population growth and decline rates. We could not easily assess income differentials between city groups. Nor could we specify the relationships between such variables as population growth and economic development, or residential location and occupational status. Also, many of the comparisons social scientists make between larger population groupings such as states, areas of countries, or countries would be impossible without available aggregate data. As an example of the important type of research relying on the aggregate data provided in census reports we will examine Karl and Alma Taeuber's (1966) study of patterns of racial residential segregation in American cities, one of our most difficult social problems.

In their research titled *Negroes in Cities,* Taeuber and Taeuber make wide-ranging use of census data to investigate various aspects of residential segregation in United States metropolitan areas, focusing on the period from 1940 through 1960. On the basis of census data for each metropolitan area, the researchers computed an index of residential segregation with the following logic:

Suppose that a person's race made absolutely no difference in determining where he chose to live or where he was allowed to live. If this were so, we would expect that no area of a city would be all black or all white. If, for example, blacks constituted 25 percent of a city we would expect that in each city block examined, blacks would constitute

25 percent of the population. If the total percentage of blacks in a city were 50 percent, we would likewise expect that in any given city area one out of every two households would be black.

These assumptions would hold only if there were absolutely no residential segregation. Were this situation to obtain in a city, the segregation index would be zero. The segregation index would be 100, of course, if each block examined were all black or all white. Using census materials to compute a segregation index for 207 cities, the Taeubers (1966:2) were able to show convincingly that "A high degree of residential segregation is universal in American cities." For all cities examined, the lowest index was 60.4 and the highest was 98.1, with half the cities having values above 87.8, and one fourth above 91.7.[1]

It is not possible in a short review to represent adequately all the findings in this study. We should know, however, that we can find in the Taeubers' research: (1) comparisons in residential segregation between areas of the country; (2) statistics on *changes* in segregation rates for cities and areas of the country between 1940 and 1960, (3) data on the economic and social characteristics of black residential areas, (4) analysis of the factors involved in the flight of whites as blacks move into an area, and, (5) data describing the economic characteristics of blacks in racially mixed census tracts.

The wide-ranging information reported in this study is valuable for two related reasons. First, the descriptive aggregate rates of segregation for separate cities and areas of the country allow us to see exactly the parameters of the problems we face. The data presented in this study certainly laid to rest, for example, the stereotype held by many that segregation is primarily a Southern problem. Second, it is only by comprehensively understanding the kinds of patterns uncovered in research of this sort that we can begin to formulate intelligent social policy. Assuming that we can agree on the value of integration, we must know just how and why city neighborhoods do change or remain stably mixed racially before we can begin to create the kind of change we want. The Taeubers' study, briefly as we examined it, shows the significance of certain kinds of analyses that could not be done without the available aggregate data provided by the census.

We realize the value of such available aggregate sources as the census, but we must also recognize the limitations and methodological problems involved in the use of such "official" statistics. We must consider the types of errors that potentially creep into the aggregate statistics with which we often work. First, there may be *errors of coverage* in census-like aggregate data. Inevitably enumeration errors will be made in

---

[1] It is of interest to note that as long as race is correlated with income, it would be possible for there to be differences in the distribution of the races even if there were no racial discrimination in the allocation of residence. However, the evidence to date indicates that economic factors "cannot account for more than a small portion of observed levels of racial residential segregation." (Taeuber and Taeuber, 1966:2)

the original collection of data from individuals. Some persons are invariably missed and therefore not represented in the aggregate figures compiled, and some persons may be counted twice. (Those who work frequently with census materials suggest that coverage errors result in undercounts much more often than overcounts.)

It is important to know that the census data, collected every ten years, is obtained using self-administered questionnaires delivered through the mail or by enumerators (interviewers) hired to conduct personal interviews. As would be the case in evaluating the quality of any data collected via questionnaire, we should expect that there will be unavoidable *classification errors*. We know that respondents will lie about certain issues. Persons may want to "look good" in their own eyes and in the eyes of the interviewer and consequently give false information about such items as their education, income, and occupational levels. Common sense would lead us to expect that the direction of the error will be toward the higher education, income, and occupational categories. It is always possible, further, that persons will incorrectly understand the questions asked by census enumerators or that those collecting the data will themselves make systematic classification errors. There will also inevitably be a number of errors made in the final processing, tabulating, or aggregating of the data collected on millions of persons.

There are still other problems that the researcher using census data may face. As indicated in our review of the Taeubers' research, investigators frequently want to compare changes over time in particular areal units. We might be interested, for example, in how the income distributions for particular towns have varied over a fifty-year period. Unfortunately, town boundaries may expand during the ten years intervening between census tabulations, making the desired comparison difficult. For those researchers who wish to make cross-cultural comparisons using census data there will be other problems: certain types of data collected in one country may not be collected in another; data for certain countries may be incomplete; there may be special cultural factors in a society which induce persons to misrepresent themselves; ideological factors might affect the way that statistics are reported; the categories used for classifying persons (e.g., the categories for education or income) will vary from country to country and again hinder comparative analysis.[2]

Some of the types of problems we have been discussing with reference to census data are more strongly highlighted when we consider other "official" statistics that sociologists frequently employ in their research. Primarily in order to extend our comments on the possible errors contaminating available aggregate data — errors which, in turn, may lead

---

[2] For a discussion of some of the problems encountered by those who engage in comparative research using aggregate data, see the section on Aggregate Analysis, pp. 364–367 in Chapter 13 (Comparative Research Methods).

us to false conclusions and inferences — we shall consider briefly some of the methodological dilemmas of those who rely on official crime statistics.

Estimated Rates and True Rates: The Case of
Crime Statistics

Of all the aggregate data available to social scientists, official crime rate statistics are among the most unreliable. While the problems in the use of crime statistics may be especially severe, they are nevertheless the types of problems that must be evaluated when we use any aggregate data previously prepared by others. We need to know that because of a variety of errors in the compilation of any data, there will always be a discrepancy between the *reported rate* of some phenomenon and the *true rate*. We would do well to consider just how great this discrepancy is likely to be in the data we use.

In the case of criminal behavior we know that there are many more crimes committed than appear in official statistics. For example, crime statistics do not accurately reflect the commission of such crimes as rape that are rarely reported by victims. In other words, the number of crimes known to the police is always substantially smaller than the number actually committed. Of equal importance in making us suspicious about the validity of crime statistics is the knowledge that the tabulation of crime rates varies with local police policies, court policies, and public opinion. If the statistical data presented has not been compiled in a uniform fashion (that is, according to the same rules or criteria) comparative analysis of rates in different jurisdictions is very misleading.

The criteria used to classify crimes vary widely in different geographical areas. Indeed, there is even disagreement between various jurisdictions as to the definition of "crime" itself. Crime rates vary widely because different local administrators interpret the law differently. If we were to treat the statistics at face value, we might be led to believe that there is more crime in Berkeley than in Palo Alto, when in fact the difference is simply an artifact of the methods used in compiling the statistics. If law enforcement officials begin to systematically arrest people for such crimes as vagrancy, prostitution, and speeding, where they had previously been lenient toward these crimes, it would be incorrect to conclude that there had been a substantial upsurge in the crime rate. Because of political pressure from government leaders or citizens' groups, police officials may periodically "crack down" on certain kinds of activities. On the other hand, we could imagine police officials not reporting in their records all the crimes they know occur in their areas so that it will appear that they are succeeding in keeping the crime rate down. Such biasing factors affecting the reporting and maintenance of statistics make the study of changing rates of crime very difficult. We cannot easily know whether differences from year to year in different jurisdictions represent real differences or are the result of one or a combination of the factors mentioned.

Some have argued that crime rate statistics are badly flawed because police officials differentially enforce the law. For example, there is compelling evidence that blacks are much more likely than whites to be arrested for the same behaviors; that middle or upper class youngsters are likely to be only warned by local police when engaging in behaviors that would lead to the arrest of adolescents in working class areas. In similar fashion, as pointed out by many criminologists, there are certain kinds of crimes for which persons are very unlikely to be arrested. This is perhaps most true of what Edwin Sutherland (1961) has labelled "white-collar" crimes (e.g., income tax evasion, bribery, kickback schemes).

The factors mentioned, taken together, conspire to make the validity of statistical crime rates highly questionable. It has not been our intention, however, merely to comment on one substantive area of sociological investigation. Crime statistics stand as a convenient example to raise a larger point. Whenever we use aggregate statistics already compiled by others we need to question just how and why the rates presented may badly reflect the actual volume of behaviors, events, or demographic attributes in the groupings of persons studied.

Development of Social Indicators

A nation cannot chart its own progress, change, or development by looking at the behavior or life conditions of only a few individuals. Aggregate analysis is required if we wish to develop yardsticks for evaluating the social state and well-being of a nation. Just as economists have charted trends using such economic indicators as gross national product, median family income, and unemployment rate, so too sociologists have come to see a need to develop *social indicators*.[3] One rationale for social indicators is to measure change in such social conditions as: poverty, public safety, education, health, and housing. A related rationale is to produce knowledge that will be of use in social planning and the formulation of public policy. Such information can be of help in the determination of where our money, programs, and general efforts at creating social change are most needed and ought to be concentrated. Social indicators are generally presented as time-series data; this makes it possible to chart changes over time. However, not all time-series statistics would be classified as social indicators. Typically social indicators are quantitative aggregate measures used to assess trends in various aspects of the quality of social life (Land, 1975).

[3] When social indicator data is presented, it is always in the form of aggregate data, but it is sometimes the case that the information was obtained from a nonaggregate source, such as survey research data.

The social indicators "movement" is relatively new. Some work was done in the 1930s (e.g., President's Research Committee on Social Trends, 1933), but the effort did not really get into full swing until the mid-1960s. Some who do social indicators research focus on the production of longitudinal statistics, documenting trends in various aspects of the quality of social life. Others apply these statistics to the study of social mobility, or to changes in the female occupational structure, or to changes in degree of racial segregation, and so on — that is, to studies based on social indicator trend data.

Suppose we were to ask the question, "Is the health status of the United States improving?" We might turn to a source such as *Social Indicators 1973,* which presents graphs and tables of trends of eight areas: employment, income, leisure and recreation, housing, public safety, population, and health. Given our research question, we would be particularly interested in the data for the various health indicators. Among the statistics available would be life expectancy at birth (by sex and race), death rates (by age, sex, race, and cause of death), and infant mortality rates. Also included are several indicators assessing various forms of disability and access to medical care. Some of these statistics are available for each year since the turn of the century; others for the last fifteen years or so. To answer our research question we might decide to limit ourselves to a particular aspect of health status, or we might attempt a synthesis based on all the measures.

We would like to use our discussion of social indicators as a platform for thinking about the implications of the *level of aggregation* on which we carry out our research. We have already suggested that social indicators typically represent rates for a whole nation or society. We need to ask: What information is gained or lost as the level of aggregation becomes more comprehensive? In order to deal with this question, we might best start with a concrete example. As previously mentioned, one social indicator of health at the national level of aggregation is average life expectancy. This indicator will tell us changes, up to the present, in the average life expectancy of persons at birth. Let us look at some actual data on life expectancy rates broken down by sex and race in Figure 12.1.

These data are interesting because they show some significant differences. First, they indicate that average life expectancy has generally increased continuously since 1900. We should note, also, the substantial differences between men and women and the even more startling differences between whites and nonwhites. White women can expect to live longer than white men. Similarly, nonwhite women can expect to live longer than nonwhite men. In all cases, until very recently, whites (men and women) could expect to live longer than nonwhites. Only since about 1965 has the average life expectancy of nonwhite women become greater than that of white men. As recently as 1971, white women could expect to live some 15 years longer than nonwhite men.

FIGURE 12.1 Life Expectancy at Birth by Sex and Race, 1901–1971*

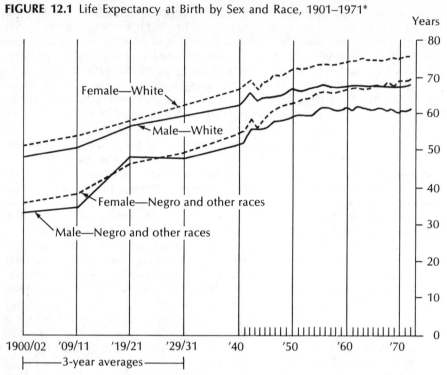

* *Source:* Executive Office of the President: Office of Management and Budget, *Social Indicators, 1973* (Washington, D.C.: U.S. Government Printing Office, 1973).

As we consider these figures representing life expectancy, there are a number of questions we might want to raise. The most basic of these questions asks what potentially important information is unavailable to us — given that the data is presented on the *national level* of aggregation. Imagine that we are administrators responsible for the allocation of monies to various health improvement programs around the country. We would say that these national figures are interesting but that they do not tell the whole story. We might comment that the national statistics do not allow us to see variations between *areas of the country* (Far West, Midwest, Northeast, etc.) in life expectancy rates. It could be that life expectancy rates are quite high in one area but relatively low in another. If we knew this to be so, we would have a better idea where to allocate available funds.

Suppose it would be possible to *disaggregate* the available data so that we could see differences between areas of the country in life expectancy rates. When we disaggregate, we take an existing unit of data and break it into finer or less comprehensive units. If we could disaggregate the national data, we would have more information because it would be possible for us to see differences between somewhat smaller "region of the country" units; differences that were "masked" in the national level data. Even now, however, we might not be altogether satisfied because separate *states* can vary widely in life expectancy rates. If we could see such variations it would further facilitate our decision making; we would give more money to programs in the states with lower life expectancy rates. Since, however, the data aggregated in the "region of the country" level does not provide us information on separate states, we ask that the data be disaggregated to this less comprehensive unit.

With the available data from the fifty states, we might have the idea that life expectancy rates will still vary for different *cities*. At this point, we have to face the fact that the data is beginning to become somewhat unwieldy. We have gone from one rate (the national level) to five or six rates (regions of the country) to fifty rates (states), and we must now recognize that disaggregation to the city level would mean looking at several hundred rates. If you were to move one step lower — to rates for *city areas* — it would become difficult to examine intelligently the many thousands of rates that would be generated.

There is an important point to be made from our example of information gained and lost as we aggregate and disaggregate data. It is that each time researchers move to a higher level of aggregation they lose information about levels immediately below. At the same time, as our prior example indicates, there is an efficiency to the statistics on higher levels of aggregation. At the national level we need deal with only one rate, at the state level it increases to fifty rates, and so forth, until it would be literally impossible to manage or interpret the extraordinary number of statistics at lower levels of aggregation.

There is, then, no easy answer to the question "At what aggregate level ought we to carry out our analyses?" We want to maximize both information and efficiency. In some cases, however, we have little choice in the matter. We simply must work at the level for which available statistics have already been aggregated. This is so, for example, when we make use of census data. Here we are constrained by the geographical units for which census data is reported. In other words, whenever we use available statistics we can always aggregate to higher levels but cannot disaggregate to levels lower than the one presented in the available data. Where researchers do have a number of options relative to level of aggregation in a study, their choice must be made in terms of the research goals and theories guiding the investigation.

Forecasting and Simulation

Social indicators, we have noted, allow researchers to evaluate changes in the condition of a nation over time from some point in the past to the present. It is, however, a somewhat different task to. adequately *forecast* future trends in a society. We know that it is important for planning purposes to estimate with some accuracy what the population will be in the United States in fifty years or more. Casual reading of newspapers also suggests the importance of knowing what our energy needs and natural resources will be in the future. We might also want to know whether welfare case loads will increase or decrease in the future or whether there will be significant changes in employment opportunities, and the like. Typically those who do social forecasting must rely on aggregate data.

Forecasting is often done by looking at aggregate trends in the factors of interest (birth rates, welfare expenditures, and so on) from some point in the past to the present. If we assume that the rates of increase or decrease we see will not change substantially, we can estimate future trends or growth. In their simplest form, forecasting models can be depicted as follows:

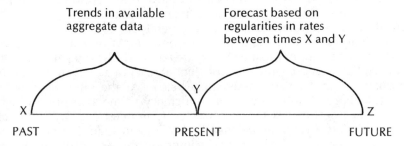

Suppose we wanted to forecast population trends in the United States. We could begin by looking at data from, let's say, 1930 to the present. Clearly we could not simply look at regular increases or decreases in birth rates; total population growth is a function of several variables, and birth rates alone would not provide enough data for us to make an adequate forecast. In order to estimate future population growth, we would have to take into account such additional factors as national *death* and *migration rates*. We might, then, begin our analysis by looking at the type of data collected by the Bureau of the Census (see Figure 12.2).

Examination of the aggregate data in Figure 12.2 reveals some of the difficulties in clearly forecasting population trends. We can see in this particular case that fertility (birth) rates do not increase or decrease with any apparent regularity. For example, there was a sharp decrease in fertility between 1968 and 1972. We wish to project population trends into the future, but we must acknowledge that these abrupt, apparently unpredictable rate changes seriously hinder clear predictions. As a consequence, *demographers* (those who study population trends) cannot make flat predictions about future population growth rates. Rather, they must

FIGURE 12.2 Estimated Births, Deaths, Net Civilian Immigration
and Net Population Growth, United States, 1930–1972*

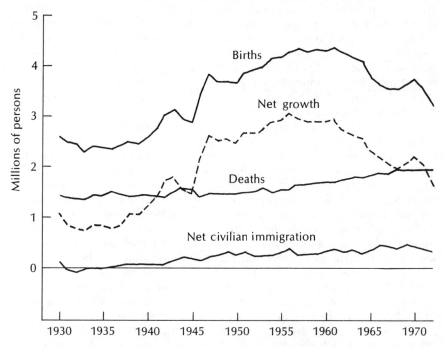

*Source: U.S. Bureau of the Census, Current Population Reports, Series
P-25, No. 499, "Estimates of the population of the United States and
components of change, 1972" (Washington, D.C.: U.S. Government
Printing Office, 1973).

talk about *ranges* of growth or decline which are based on a number of
forecasts; and each forecast is based on a different assumption about
future fertility rates. For example, the demographer will say, "If the fertility rate is 2.8 births per woman, we can expect the population to grow
this way; if the rate is 2.5 births, population growth will assume a different direction," and so forth. In other words, demographers will not make
one flat prediction, but rather will lay out a number of scenarios based
on alternative assumptions about key rates.

     While we cannot know for certain which of the several assump-
tions is correct, we can still extract important information from the kind
of research we have been describing. We might, for example, find that
for the lowest plausible estimate of future fertility, the population will
double during the next thirty years; that is, we can be sure that, at the
very least, the population will grow to a certain size within this specified
time period. Informed social planning and public policy is dependent
upon information of this kind.

In our example to this point we have been talking about some of the difficulties in forecasting trends for a single variable — population. Problems of forecasting become more formidable when researchers wish to consider the interplay of *several variables simultaneously* in predicting future social conditions. In these cases social scientists increasingly use computer technology to *simulate* future social trends. To obtain a clearer picture of how computer simulations are done, we shall consider the recent research of Donnella Meadows (1972) and her colleagues who, in the book titled *The Limits To Growth*, attempt to predict world trends in the population growth and in the use of resources.

In *The Limits To Growth*, Meadows raises no less a question than: What will happen to the world if current economic and demographic trends continue to increase at present rates? Note that the research question does not refer to a single variable but to a total social system — the world's total ecological system. The first step in this, as in any computer simulation, is to construct a *model* describing the system under investigation. Since the success of any computer simulation depends on the model constructed at the beginning of the research, we shall find it useful to look quite carefully at model construction. More particularly, we need to distinguish between static and dynamic models.

In Chapter 2 we examined the development and use of causal models in sociology. As an example we looked at Blau and Duncan's (1967) model showing the key or major variables most predictive of an individual's present occupational position. They were: father's educational achievement, father's occupational status, respondent's educational achievement, and the status of the individual's first job. We can review two major characteristics of this model:

1. The model is composed of the relatively few factors deemed most influential in describing or explaining the system, phenomenon, or events investigated.
2. The causal relationships assumed to exist among the variables constituting the model are clearly specified.

Virtually all social science models share these two characteristics. It is important to point out, however, that Blau and Duncan's model is a *static model,* which means it is one designed solely to predict events at one point in time. The success of Blau and Duncan's model is evaluated primarily on how accurately the variables named predict a person's present occupational position. The model is not designed to predict features of the stratification system in the future. It could happen, for example, that in fifty years educational achievement will be inconsequential in predicting a person's occupational position. Such potential changes in the causal influence of variables is not troublesome to Blau and Duncan, however, since their goal is only to predict an event in the present in terms of events in the past.

Where the research goal is to simulate or forecast future events, static models are not sufficient. Consider again the research problem faced by Meadows. She wanted to look at the likely condition of the world's ecological system at a number of different points in the future. The model she used had to allow her to make accurate predictions about the conditions of the ecological system in one, five, ten, twenty, thirty, fifty, or one hundred years. Clearly, her model had to be one that not only specifies the variables most influential in describing the present ecological system, but specifies as well the generic processes through which the variables in the model will continue to interact with each other over time. Models that account for the processes governing the interaction between variables in predicting certain outcomes (e.g., changes in an ecological system) are called *dynamic models*.

On the basis of aggregate data trends from 1900 to 1970 and her own theoretical reasoning, Meadows constructed a model composed of five key variables central to the world's ecological system — population, food supply, natural resources, industrial production, and pollution. Meadows then constructed a set of mathematical equations detailing the processes through which the five variables interact with each other. These equations, constructed from available aggregate data, describe a *feedback system* wherein a change in any one of the variables effects changes in the other variables which in turn modify the variable that started the change process. One of the several equations describing the dynamic interactions between the variables might, for example, detail the following feedback process, which is set in motion by a change in population growth rates:

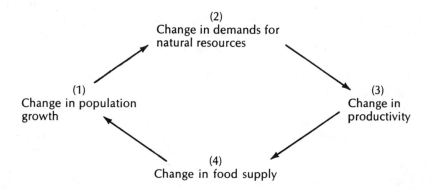

After describing mathematically how the variables have interacted with each other in the past, Meadows was prepared to simulate that same process into the future. As mentioned, the most immediate research requirement was to simulate the condition of the ecological system for different points into the future, assuming that growth rates in the key variables remain as they have in the past. The results of this simulation are quite gloomy. Meadows et al. (1972) report:

> . . . If the present growth trends in world population, industrialization, pollution, food production and resource depletion continue unchanged, the limits to growth on this planet will be reached sometime within the next hundred years. The most probable result will be a rather sudden and uncontrollable decline in population and industry .

The utility of Meadows's simulation model does not, however, end with this one prediction. We might ask, for example, what would happen to the ecological system at different points in the future if we were able to institute immediately a program to increase food production by a specified amount over its present rate. Researchers can, in other words, do any of a number of simulations by assuming a different hypothesized value or rate for the dimensions in the model. It is referred to as *sensitivity testing* each time the researchers "try out" different values or rates for a variable in the model. Through sensitivity testing researchers can produce a large number of future scenarios, each of which is generated from alternative assumptions about key rates in the parameters of the model. For this reason computer simulation models are valuable aids in designing and then testing the likely effects of alternative policies. Indeed, Meadows is able to propose from the variety of sensitivity tests done with her model just how growth rates must be reduced in order for the ecological system to reach a state of equilibrium. She advocates that social planners immediately design programs to achieve global aggregate rates compatible with the survival of the environment.

There are those who have soundly criticized the type of computer modeling we have been describing in the last few pages. One of the most basic criticisms raised suggests that because models used in computer simulation can encompass only a relatively few variables they simply are not a very good representation of reality. A critic might argue that, were a few different variables included in the models, the simulated outcomes would be radically altered. For example, we might say that one of the flaws in Meadows's model stems from the failure to include any *cultural* or *social value* variables. Certainly people's values, outlooks on the world, beliefs, and attitudes will importantly determine how they will respond to environmental changes. Since it is virtually impossible to predict just the part that such values would have in the total environmental change process, it is likewise virtually impossible to include them in a model where variables must be restricted to those with known rates and known effects. It is worth repeating that the validity of computer simulation findings must be evaluated in terms of the model used to generate them. Methodologically, then, we must insistently question whether potentially important variables have been excluded from the models used in any research.

Others have quarreled with the findings of Meadows's research because it was based only on *global aggregate* data for each of the five variables in the model. These critics suggest that if the researchers had been able to analyze data on lower aggregate levels (e.g., countries or communities), they would have produced a model that made quite different predictions. They reason that the variables named in the model interact first at *local levels* in a society and that, once these changes are seen to be occurring, there is likely to be corrective social planning at these lower aggregate levels. Should such corrective measures be taken, global failure of the ecological system, as predicted by Meadows, would not occur. The criticism recalls two points from previous discussion. First, social scientists may be constrained in their research because they must often use available aggregate data. Second, and related, the aggregate level on which data is analyzed may considerably influence the kind of information obtained and hence the conclusions reached in the research.[4]

Our goal in preceding sections was to look at some of the areas of sociological investigation where aggregate data analysis is frequently done and to ponder some of the questions, issues, and problems that

---

[4] Following the central concern of this chapter, the authors have chosen as their example of a study using simulation techniques one employing aggregate data. It would, however, be misleading for the reader to assume that all simulations depend on aggregate data or are always done to project future events, as is the case of Meadows's research. One should understand that simulations have broader applications than described in the body of this chapter. Any time we try to imitate the outcomes of a process in order to better understand, explain, or clarify the mechanisms of some phenomenon, we engage in a simulation.

Not all simulations, given this broad definition, rely on computer technology. When soldiers play "war games" during basic training, they are engaging in a simulation of the process of war. Recently social scientists have devised games to simulate some of the major components of a society. In one such game a model is created of a small community. Persons participating in this simulated society are given certain personal, social, and political goals to realize during the course of the game. While the model on which the game is based is certainly a simplification of society (any model is a simplification), it is nevertheless possible to learn about the basic processes of social organization using the model. Simulations in which human beings are the essential interacting components are called *man-model* simulations.

A second major type of simulation has been called *man-machine* simulation. A simple example of a man-machine simulation would be one in which a computer has been programmed to play chess against a person. Man-machine simulations have been used to play out complex international diplomacy scenarios based on historical data fed into the computer. Programmed with appropriate historical data, the computer can print out likely responses of foreign governments to various diplomatic positions taken by an individual representing the United States. Man-machine simulations can be used to train persons for situations too costly or dangerous for them to actually experience. Man-machine simulations may also be used to test the viability of different strategies for solving practical problems.

Finally, there are *machine* simulations where the whole process of interest to researchers is simulated by the computer. The Meadows study discussed in this chapter is representative of this third type of simulation. As one further point of clarification, computer simulations need not focus on only world or global processes, as in Meadows's research. It is certainly possible to use computers to simulate the process through which such small systems as social groups operate.

researchers who work with aggregate data will often face. We have seen that researchers must worry about the errors in the available aggregate data they use. In some cases they will have good reason to believe that aggregate rates are poor estimates of true rates. Researchers must also be certain that the data describing each of the units they compare has been collected according to the same criteria. In addition, they must know how the level of their aggregate analysis may influence the interpretations they eventually make from collected data.

Even if we could assume an ideal set of research conditions, where none of these problems existed, where researchers had perfect data, it would still be possible to commit certain logical errors in making inferences from aggregate data. Methodologists have pointed out a number of logical fallacies that researchers might make as they try to interpret the meaning of their data. In the next section we will consider the two most common of these fallacies: the ecological fallacy and the atomistic fallacy.

FALLACIES IN THE INTERPRETATION OF AGGREGATE DATA

In previous pages we have spent some considerable time examining the different levels on which investigators may carry out their analyses. These levels range from unaggregated data on individuals — the case where we make comparisons between scores or measures of individuals directly, without combining those scores — to aggregated data on as comprehensive a level as the country or nation. Nearly all cases where researchers commit logical errors in the interpretation of their data occur when they conduct their study on one level of aggregation and from the data collected try to make statements about phenomena at a different level. The most common of these fallacies has come to be called the ecological fallacy. We shall consider it first.

The Ecological Fallacy

In 1950 a sociologist named W. S. Robinson wrote a landmark paper in which he indicated that social scientists had long made the mistake when working with aggregate data of assuming that the relationships uncovered in their studies could allow them to make inferences about individuals. That is, Robinson argued that it was illegitimate for researchers to shift levels in their studies — to conduct their studies on one level and then make interpretations about the elements on another level.

In order to make clear the nature of the error involved in ecological fallacies (or as some have put it, *aggregative fallacies*) we can consider a simple example. Although our example does not involve the aggregation of individuals per se it will serve our purposes. Suppose that a jury is deciding a case and after much deliberation reports to the judge that they cannot as a group decide the guilt or innocence of the defendant. The jury is hung; the jury *as a group* is undecided. Although the jury is composed of 12 individuals we can make reference to the group as a whole (this is essentially what we do when we aggregate data). We can say that the jury is undecided.

Now to the important point. Can we move from our statement that the jury is undecided to the statement that *individual jurors* are undecided? Certainly not! Indeed, it may very well be that none of the twelve jurors is undecided; they are simply individually decided in different directions. The conceptual, logical point to be made here is that *one cannot properly make inferences about individuals in groups on the basis of data about the group as a whole.* To do so is to commit the aggregative or ecological fallacy. We can proceed from our simple example to somewhat more complicated data.

Suppose that a group of researchers are interested in seeing if there is any relationship between crime rates in areas and the racial composition of those areas. The researchers decide to use census data in order to establish any relationship that might exist between these two variables. It is important to note that they will be using aggregate group-level data in their analysis. They will not be collecting data from specific individuals. Rather, they will be relying on aggregate data already available. Since the census data is readily available, we shall assume that they choose to examine the aggregate data for census tracts and then to look at crime rates in those same tracts. We shall assume, further, that the researchers would like to see, most particularly, if there is any relationship between the percentage of blacks in a census area and the crime rate. After examining the appropriate figures, the researchers display their findings as in Figure 12.3.

An examination of this data shows a clear pattern. There is a positive correlation between the percentage of black persons in an area and the crime rate: as the percentage of black persons increases, there is a general corresponding increase in the amount of crime. Now, remember that the data represented in Figure 12.3 is aggregated, group, or ecological data. We want to ask whether it is appropriate for these researchers to now say, on the basis of this data, that black *persons* are much more likely than white persons to commit crimes. Again, certainly not! For the same reason that we cannot say anything about the individual jurors in our previous example, we cannot say anything about the propensity for crime of individual black persons. It could be, for example, that as the percentage of black persons in an area increases, the whites still remaining in the areas are more and more marginal or alienated; and that it is these relatively few alienated white persons who are com-

FIGURE 12.3 Relationship between Race and Crime
in a Hypothetical City, 1976–1977

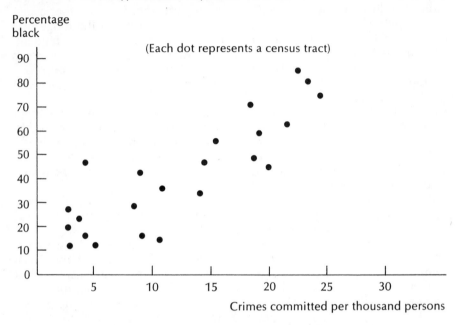

mitting most of the crime in the heavily black areas. Or to use the kind
of extreme example offered by Galtung (1967), what if the crimes committed are assaults on blacks by whites or even the lynchings of blacks?
In other words, it could be that blacks are not committing the crimes at
all but that the crimes are performed against them and that the percentage of crimes depends on the high availability of blacks.

Given the same logic presented here, we cannot say that because
there is, for example, a high correlation between the percentage of
divorced persons in an area and rates of juvenile delinquency that family
disorganization is the cause of delinquency. In the cases we have mentioned, it might immediately seem reasonable to make inferences about
individuals from aggregate data, but there is a grave danger in doing so.
We commit the ecological fallacy whenever we incorrectly assume that
properties correlated on one level of aggregation will be correlated in
the same way at lower levels of analysis.

The most important idea that the ecological fallacy alerts us to
is that the level on which we conduct our analysis must correspond to
the level of the units referred to in our hypotheses and at issue in our
theories. If the conceptual model focuses on the differences between
individuals, we must be certain that we use individual-level data. If we
are certain that the data level used in a study corresponds to the units

of analysis referred to in our hypotheses and theoretical constructs, we can be confident we have avoided the so-called ecological fallacy.

The Atomistic Fallacy

We have been discussing the possible inferential flaws in making statements about individuals on the basis of group-level data (the ecological fallacy). We must acknowledge that it is possible to commit the ecological fallacy in reverse — to incorrectly make statements about groups on the basis of data from individuals. When we try to test hypotheses about groups when we have only individual-level data, we risk committing what has been called the atomistic fallacy.

Suppose we had in mind the hypothesis that there is a relationship between rates of residential mobility in cities and rates of mental illness. More specifically, we believe that the higher the rates of residential mobility, the higher will be the mental illness rates. Please note that this hypothesis refers to the characteristics of cities as social systems. *It is not a hypothesis about differences between individuals.* Consider now the inferential error we would make if we were to mistakenly test this group-level hypothesis with individual-level data.

We might begin the research by collecting data on individuals. We could do this by getting the names of all persons in the subject city who were committed to mental hospitals within the last year. We might then interview these persons or check records to determine how many times they had moved (a measure of residential mobility) during perhaps the five years previous to entering the hospital. We might find that the persons studied move very infrequently and therefore we conclude that our original hypothesis — that high rates of residential mobility will be strongly related to mental illness rates — is incorrect. We will have rejected a hypothesis about spatial groupings or structural units by examining data from individuals. Will we have properly rejected our original hypothesis or will we have committed a logical error of inference?

It could be that the persons who become mentally ill in cities are precisely those who are left behind when their friends move out of the immediate neighborhood. There is, in other words, a *structural effect* operating. The likelihood of persons becoming mentally ill is not a function of what they themselves do, but of what is happening around them. Indeed, then, it could be that there *is* quite a strong relationship between rates of residential mobility in cities and rates of mental illness which has not been seen because our researcher looked only at individual-level data. The researcher has simply assumed that what the individuals studied do is sufficient data on which to characterize the social groupings of which they are a part.

Whether we commit the ecological or atomistic fallacy, the underlying reason for the mistake remains the same: we have mixed our levels of analysis. We have used data on one level to test hypotheses about a different level. We have, in both cases, committed what Galtung (1967) calls "the fallacy of the wrong level."

CONCLUSION

In this chapter we have been learning why social researchers wishing to study the attributes or characteristics of social structure must be knowledgeable about the problems associated with the use of aggregate data. In some respects we have extended the methodological discussions of other chapters in this book because social scientists doing historical research, comparative international research, evaluation research, content analysis, and research using institutional records will frequently be collecting and interpreting aggregate data. Many of the research problems investigated using these respective methodologies demand that data on individuals be combined to produce rates describing larger social groupings of persons.

Our strategy in this chapter has been to study four reasonably well-defined areas of sociological investigation where aggregate data is normally used. We have discussed research using census materials, crime statistics research, research concerned with developing social indicators, and social forecasting research. We have become acquainted with these areas of investigation while also pondering some of the methodological issues raised whenever we employ aggregate data. We can briefly recount some of these issues here.

Investigators must continually recognize the types of errors that potentially contaminate the data sources they use. Our analysis of such official data sources as the census and crime reports alerts us to some of the difficulties encountered whenever researchers use available statistical data. We have noted that errors of coverage, classification errors, and processing errors will combine to reduce the accuracy and validity of any findings based on such data. In addition, there may be a variety of ideological, cultural, or personal interest factors that also reduce the accuracy of official statistics. Because of the errors likely to be made in the compilation and presentation of census-like aggregate data, there will ordinarily be a discrepancy between the rates reflected in the data itself and the true parameters of the social groupings we study. We must recognize that aggregate statistics offer us only an estimate of the group characteristics of interest in our researchers. If we know the likely nature of these errors, we can take that knowledge into consideration as we interpret our findings.

In our treatment of social indicators we pointed out that the level of aggregation on which we carry out our analysis affects the type of information we obtain. We can see that because social scientists frequently must conduct their investigations on the aggregate level for which data are available, potentially important information about differences between units at lower levels of aggregation will be unavailable to them. We saw that this was an issue for critics of Meadows's simulation model. Detractors of her research maintain that she may very well have been led to incorrect conclusions because of the level of aggregate data used in simulating future trends. Whenever possible we must choose the aggregate level most consistent with the goals and theoretical ideas motivating our research.

Finally, in the most recent section of this chapter, we detailed the major kinds of inferential fallacies that researchers must avoid committing when interpreting their data. We must be certain not to make inferences about individuals based on group-level data (the ecological fallacy) or inferences about social structural units based on individual-level data (the atomistic fallacy).

These are the major kinds of issues that researchers must consider as they study aggregations of individuals. As is so in any research effort, the better we know the flaws or biases in the data used to explain phenomena, the better we will be able to evaluate the quality of the conclusions produced in our work.

EXERCISES

1. Using the most recent census data in your school or public library, construct an *index of segregation* for the city in which you live or the city closest to you. As an aid in creating your index you may want to read the appendix in Taeuber and Taeuber's (1966) book *Negroes in Cities*. This appendix is titled "The Measurement of Residential Segregation."

Describe in some detail the data used and the steps taken in the construction of your index. Following our discussion in this chapter, briefly outline some of the errors in census data that may affect the validity of your index.

2. Working alone or with another student in your class, collect data to show if there is any association between the percentage of population that is black in cities and the crime rates in cities. Collect data for both variables on ten cities of your choice. The percentage of black persons in these cities can be determined using available census materials. An overall crime rate for the same cities can be obtained from the most recent edition of the *Uniform Crime Reports for the United States*. Arrange your data graphically, as for the hypothetical study cited on page 338 in this chapter.

What trends are you able to note in your data? Is there a positive relationship between the two variables (i.e., does the crime rate increase as the percentage of black persons in the population increases)? If you do find a positive relationship can you draw the inference that black persons are more likely to commit crimes than white persons? Why? Why not?

3. Suppose that you would like to study the ways in which your college has changed or failed to change over the last twenty years. You might, for example, be interested in examining one or more of the following variables: average college board scores of entering freshmen, the proportion of persons majoring in the natural sciences, the winning percentage of the school football team, or the percentage of seniors graduating with honors. What other variables interest you?

Choose two variables for which you can obtain data for each of the last twenty years. After constructing tables to present your collected data, try to offer an explanation of any changes discovered.

4. Suppose you had in mind the hypothesis that individuals who come from broken homes are more likely to commit delinquent acts than individuals who come from "stable" homes. Could you test this hypothesis by comparing delinquency rates in city areas with high and low divorce rates? Why not? Explain the kind of fallacy you might be committing if you use the suggested data. What kind of data would you need to test your hypothesis?

5. Suppose you get into a discussion with someone who points out that the average life expectancy rate in the United States as of 1970 is 70.8 years. Further, imagine the person uses this national-level social indicator to argue that all Americans experience very good health. Would you accept his or her judgment based on this one national-level statistic? In what ways might differences between segments of the American population in life expectancy be "masked" at the national level of aggregation? What additional information can be gained by disaggregating, if possible, this national-level data? What would be the advantages and disadvantages of looking at data for a number of different aggregate levels?

6. Reread the section of this chapter on social forecasting and simulation and then briefly respond to each of the following questions:
   a. Distinguish between static and dynamic models.
   b. Indicate why simulations must use dynamic models.
   c. Describe the potential importance of sensitivity testing for the creation of social policy.
   d. Indicate why social scientists cannot forecast social trends with perfect accuracy.

SUGGESTED READINGS

Readings about the Method

Dogan, Mattei, and Stein Rokkan, eds.
1969   *Social Ecology.* Cambridge, Mass.: The M.I.T. Press.

In this book of essays various aspects of inference from aggregate data are discussed. Part I of the book is especially useful as it includes essays on the ecological fallacy. These essays carry the analysis of inference from aggregate data beyond what is found in most introductory methods books. The essays should be read by the student who wishes to acquire a more sophisticated understanding of the issues involved in ecological and atomistic fallacies.

Hannan, Michael T.
1971   *Aggregation and Disaggregation in Sociology.* Lexington, Mass.: D. C. Heath (Lexington Books).

> This book is written at a fairly sophisticated level. A major focus of the book is on assessing the effects of changes in levels of aggregation on parameter estimates in linear causal analysis (path analysis and multiple regression are examples of linear causal analysis). The author considers the problem of attempting to make inferences from the level of aggregation at which the data was collected to some other level. This includes efforts to make inferences from lower to higher levels (aggregation) as well as from higher to lower levels (disaggregation).

Land, Kenneth C. and Seymour Spilerman, eds.
1975   *Social Indicator Models.* New York: Russell Sage.

> Of particular interest is the introductory essay by Land which is general in nature and covers such topics as: rationales for social indicators (social policy, social change, and social reporting), defining characteristics of social indicators, types of indicators and social indicator models, and the content of social indicators. The rest of the essays in the book cover a very diverse range of topics. In some the focus is clearly methodological; in others the focus is on empirical analysis using social indicators data. The essays are classified into two categories: (1) replication models and (2) longitudinal models and dynamic models. Replication models are constructed using data from repeated cross-sectional sample surveys. Longitudinal studies are based on repeated observations of the same units (typically individuals).

Peterson, William
1975   *Population.* New York: Macmillan.

> This is a basic textbook in demographic population analysis. In this book Peterson shows how demographers relate population phenomena to sociological, historical, and economic variables. It is a very useful reference book, particularly Chapter 2, "Basic Demographic Concepts and Data," in which the author discusses the most frequently used aggregate data sources used in population studies and the types of errors found in those data sources.

Raser, John R.
1969   *Simulation and Society.* Boston, Mass.: Allyn & Bacon.

> Raser's book is a readable, nontechnical introduction to simulation and gaming techniques. In this work the author shows the utility of simula-

tion techniques in a number of social science disciplines. Very importantly, he demonstrates how simulation can be used as a means for developing and testing social science theories.

Riley, Matilda White
1963   *Sociological Research: A Case Approach.* New York: Harcourt, Brace & World.

In Chapter 12 of this textbook, "Special Problems of Sociological Analysis," some of the major problems of aggregate data analysis are reviewed. Further, studies are presented indicating the value of conducting research on both individual and aggregate levels of analysis.

Robinson, W. S.
1950   "Ecological correlations and the behavior of individuals." *American Sociological Review* 15 (June):351–357.

In this classic article the nature of the ecological fallacy is described. It is not difficult to follow Robinson's argument and the data presented show that it is fallacious to assume that properties associated at the group level are also associated at the individual level.

Wilcox, Leslie D., et al., eds.
1972   *Social Indicators and Social Monitoring: An Annotated Bibliography.* San Francisco: Jossey-Bass.

This volume contains an annotated bibliography of more than 600 books, articles, and papers relating to social indicators and social monitoring. The book is introduced by an historical overview of the social indicators movement, starting with the commission initiated by President Hoover in 1929 which published its findings four years later in *Recent Social Trends*. Of particular interest in this essay is the discussion of the various criticisms which have been made of the social indicators movement and the discussion of current social indicator activity. The annotated references are classified into the following categories: definition, conceptual, general theory, methodology, policy and planning, application, criticism, and state of the art.

Readings Illustrating the Method

Davis, Kingsley
1965   "The urbanization of the human population." *Scientific American* 213 (September):41–53.

This study of world urbanization places a heavy reliance on the official governmental statistics of countries around the world (especially on national censuses). Davis uses aggregate data on urbanization in a number of fascinating ways throughout the article. He presents the degree of urbanization for the major regions of the world and charts the historical development of urbanization in Europe. Finally, he considers the urbanization of today's underdeveloped societies. Davis then contrasts the causes of city growth in the developed and the underdeveloped societies.

Duncan, Otis Dudley
1957   "Community size and the rural-urban continuum." In *Cities and Society,* ed. Paul K. Hatt and Albert Reiss. New York: Free Press.

One of the longstanding issues in urban sociology has been to understand just how urban areas differ from nonurban areas. Using community size as the major independent variable in this study, Duncan employs census data to show how community size is associated with a number of population characteristics. Community size is shown to be related to such variables as age distribution, occupational levels, fertility rates, percentage of females employed in the labor force, and sex. This study shows the importance of census materials, for studies like Duncan's could not be done were they not available.

Faris, E. L., and H. Warren Dunham
1939   *Mental Disorder in Urban Areas.* Chicago: University of Chicago Press.

Faris and Dunham's is a classic study in urban ecology. They show in their research that mental illness rates consistently vary in different geographical areas of the city. More directly, they are able to show that there is a steady decline in mental illness rates as one moves toward the periphery of the city. One of the most significant features of this research is that the authors also carry out an individual level of analysis. They do this to determine whether rates of mental breakdown are, in fact, a function of the structural characteristics of the city or a function of the personal attributes of individuals living in different city areas. This work clearly shows the value of conducting research on both group and individual levels of analysis.

Forrester, Jay W.
1969   *Urban Dynamics.* Cambridge, Mass.: The M.I.T. Press.

In this book, Jay Forrester, a leading figure in the development of simulation models for social science research, creates a model to represent the growth process of an urban area through its first 250 years of life. At what point in a city's history will it reach a point of stable equilibrium? At what point will unemployment rates increase to a dangerous level? These are some of the questions Forrester tries to answer using simulation techniques.

Jackman, Robert W.
1975   *Politics and Social Equality: A Comparative Analysis.* New York: John Wiley.

Jackman presents a causal model of cross-national variations in the degree of within-nation social equality as measured by three indicators: one is an index of social insurance program experience, another is an index of social welfare based on health and nutrition indicators, and the third is a measure of inequality in the distribution of income. The study is based on aggregate data from sixty countries drawn primarily from the *World Handbook of Political and Social Indicators.* The study begins with an examination of the effects of level of economic development on various indicators of social equality. These results are combined into a relatively simple path model which is elaborated upon in each subsequent chapter; the procedures for an incremental approach to causal model construction are clearly presented.

Maris, Ronald W.
1969   *Social Forces in Urban Suicide.* Homewood, Ill.: Dorsey.

In this study Maris follows a long sociological tradition attempting to show that the causes of apparently private, individual behaviors can be found in social structures. In this case, Maris tries to test Durkheim's early theory that suicide can be understood as a product of the failure of social regulations and social integration. Chapters 4 through 6 of this book are especially useful. In these chapters Maris describes his methodology and then presents data on the relationships between suicide and such variables as sex, age, race, marital status, and time of year.

Miller, Herman P.
1971   *Rich Man, Poor Man.* New York: Crowell.

This book is about the distribution of income in the United States. The material is presented in a most readable fashion. Some comparisons are made with other countries; for example, there is a discussion of the time the average worker must work to earn enough to buy a meal in the United States and comparisons are made with eight other countries. The data used are drawn from a variety of government publications, particularly those of the Department of Labor and the Bureau of the Census. The following are chapter titles which should give some idea of the content of the book: America's Fight with Poverty, The Rich and the Very-Rich, The Cash Value of Education, It's the Job That Counts, and Where Do You Fit in the Income Picture?

Taeuber, Karl E., and Alma F. Taeuber
1966   *Negroes in Cities: Residential Segregation and Neighborhood Change.* Chicago: Aldine.

The book is a study of trends in the degree of residential segregation in American cities. The Taeubers present trends in the degree of residential segregation for 109 cities between 1940 and 1960. They also present trends for a smaller number of cities between 1910 and 1950. Census data as to the racial composition of each city block are used to construct a segregation index for the city. These index scores are used extensively throughout the book. One of the major findings of the study is that "whether a city is a metropolitan center or a suburb; whether it is in the North or in the South; whether the Negro population is large or small — in every case, white and Negro households are highly segregated from each other." They also conclude that economic factors cannot account for more than a small portion of residential segregation.

REFERENCES

Blau, Peter, and Otis Dudley Duncan
1967   *The American Occupational Structure.* New York: John Wiley.

Executive Office of the President: Office of Management and Budget
1973   *Social Indicators, 1973.* Washington, D.C.: U.S. Government Printing Office.

Galtung, Johan
1967   *Theory and Methods of Social Research.* New York: Columbia University Press.

Hibbs, Douglas A., Jr.
1973   *Mass Political Violence: A Cross-National Causal Analysis.* New York: John Wiley.

Land, Kenneth C.
1975   "Social indicator models: an overview." In *Social Indicator Models,* ed. Kenneth C. Land and Seymour Spilerman. New York: Russell Sage.

Meadows, Donnella H., et al.
1972   *The Limits to Growth.* New York: Universe Books.

President's Research Committee on Social Trends
1933   *Recent Social Trends.* New York: McGraw-Hill.

Robinson, W. S.
1950   "Ecological correlations and the behavior of individuals." *American Sociological Review* 15 (June):351–357.

Sutherland, Edwin
1961   *White Collar Crime.* New York: Holt, Rinehart & Winston.

Taeuber, Karl E., and Alma F. Taeuber
1966   *Negroes in Cities: Residential Segregation and Neighborhood Change.* Chicago: Aldine.

U.S. Bureau of the Census
1973   *Current Population Reports,* Series P-25, No. 499, "Estimates of the population of the United States and components of change, 1972." Washington, D.C.: U.S. Government Printing Office.

Comparative Research Methods

It is taken for granted by many social scientists that a major goal of our collective enterprise is to make universalistic generalizations about social structure and social behavior. In view of this goal it is ironic to note that most social research is confined to one particular society. Studies that seek to compare societies are rare, which means that much of our research "knowledge" is culture specific; and generalization to other societies based on this research may be invalid.

Despite the limited extent to which the comparative method is used today, the approach does have a long history. Herodotus (495–424 B.C.) was one of the first to use systematic observation across societies as a basis for generalizing about human behavior. Many of the topics he considered in his *Nine Books of History* would today be classified as anthropology, political science, or sociology. For example, at one point he compares the Egyptians with the Lacedaemonians with respect to interaction between young men and their elders. In both societies when they meet on the street, the young men give way to their elders by stepping aside; and when an elder comes into the room the young men rise from their seats. In the *Peloponnesian War* Thucydides (460–400 B.C.) makes a number of cross-societal comparisons. For example, he points out that Sparta controlled its allies by establishing oligarchies to rule them; in contrast, Athens tended to focus on exacting tribute from its allies. Aristotle (384–322 B.C.) collected and analyzed data on 158 political constitutions. His concern with cross-societal similarities and differences in governments, and particularly in constitutions, is extensively documented in the *Politeia*.[1]

While there is evidence of comparative analysis in the writing of Herodotus, Thucydides, and Aristotle, the comparative method can be traced most directly to the work of Herbert Spencer and other nineteenth-century evolutionists. The evolutionists viewed societies as passing through a series of stages. For this reason evidence from existing primitive societies could be used to make inferences about what more advanced societies were like at earlier stages of their evolution. Karl Marx also drew heavily on comparative historical data. One example is his discussion of the various stages or epochs characterized by differences in the "modes of production," ranging from primitive communism, to ancient society (slavery), to feudal society (serfdom), and finally to modern capitalism (wage labor).

After the First World War there was a strong reaction against the evolutionist perspective and one of the consequences of this reaction was a movement away from cross-cultural analysis. The revival of the method can be traced to the work of George Murdock (1937) who was interested in the relationship between kinship structure and other aspects of culture. He based his analysis on a sample of 230 societies (predominantly primitive) drawn from around the world. The study done by Whiting and Child to which we will shortly turn is an outgrowth of Murdock's approach to comparative analysis.

In a study conducted in Kansas City, Sears and Wise (1950) found a positive relationship between age of weaning (the age at which the infant ceases to be breast fed) and the degree of emotional disturbance the infant displays in response to the weaning. Most of the infants in their sample of 80 were weaned between zero and seven months. They found that as the age of weaning increased there was a tendency for the infant to show more emotional disturbance. However, such a finding is quite inconsistent with Blackwood's (1935) report that among the Kurtatchi in the Solomon Islands mothers do not wean their children until they are over three years old, and these children show no signs of emotional disturbance. Presented with these seemingly inconsistent results, we might decide to search for a possible explanation. Do the results for the Kurtatchi represent a single exception to the general trend established by Sears and Wise, or is there some more systematic way to account for the Kurtatchi?

One way to address ourselves to this question is to examine the relationship between these two variables for a large number of very diverse societies. Whiting and Child (1953) did just this. They originally considered some 75 societies and found that the relevant data was available for 37 of them. Their results are presented along with the results from Sears and Wise in Figure 13.1. The data points from the Kansas City

---

[1] This historical summary draws upon Warwick and Osherson (1973:3–6).

FIGURE 13.1 Relation between Age at Onset of Weaning and Amount
of Emotional Disturbance Shown by Child. Comparable Data
from 80 Individual Children from Kansas City (Sears and
Wise, 1950) and from 37 Societies (Whiting and Child, 1953).
Source: (Whiting, 1968:695, Figure 1).

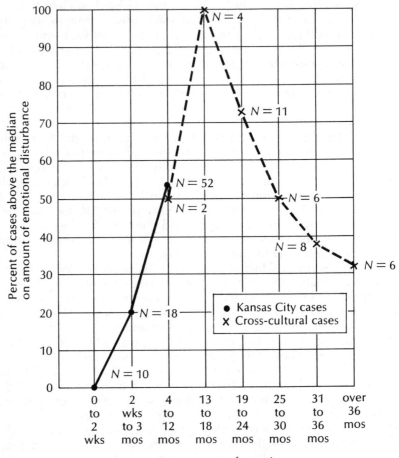

sample are connected by solid lines and the data from the 37 societies
studied by Whiting and Child are connected by dashed lines.

Before placing too much faith in these results we would want to
take a very careful look at the way in which the concept of emotional
disturbance has been measured in the Kansas City study as well as in the
37 societies Whiting and Child considered. But for the present we shall
assume that they were able to define and measure emotional disturbance
in a way that we would find acceptable and we shall focus on the actual

results. One interpretation of this data is that there is a tendency for the extent of emotional disturbance to increase as age of weaning increases from zero up to approximately 18 months and then to steadily decline from that point to at least age three. This data does not by itself tell us why the relationship is curvilinear (V-shaped) rather than linear, but it does suggest that the result for the Kurtatchi is more than a single exception or statistical fluctuation.

This example illustrates in a very dramatic way how cross-cultural analysis can be used to extend and to qualify the results that would be obtained from a study in one society. In the United States, weaning tends to occur at a very early age. To find out how the level of emotional disturbance varies with age of weaning for those weaned at two and three years of age, we would have to use cross-cultural evidence.

In some societies it is not unusual for children to be weaned at age three; in the United States this would be characterized as very deviant. In the unlikely event that we were interested in the relationship between late weaning and emotional disturbance in a cultural setting that considered late weaning highly deviant, we might want to consider the few cases of late weaning we could find in the United States. But if we wanted to consider the relationship between these same two variables in a society for which late weaning was culturally acceptable, we would have to turn to cross-cultural data.

The example we have just considered illustrates one of the most fundamental strengths of the comparative method — *it allows us to extend the range on a variable of theoretical interest beyond that which is possible in a study based on only one society.* We now turn to a brief overview of some other strengths of the comparative method. As we shall see, for many research questions comparative analysis proves to be not only useful, but essential.

One of the most noteworthy strengths of the comparative method is that *it can be used to test the generalizability of a finding based on data from one society.* It is not at all uncommon for sociological propositions to be stated as if they could be generalized to all societies, but rarely have such propositions actually been put to the test cross-culturally. We might want to ask, for example, whether the Oedipal complex is a universal phenomenon or whether it tends to be restricted to a small group of Western societies.

In most Western societies the father role includes both being the mother's lover and being the child's disciplinarian. It is reasonable to argue that for most of Freud's patients the mother's lover and the child's disciplinarian were the same person. This suggests two possible explanations for any hostility boys might show toward their fathers. One is that the boy resents his father because the father is the mother's lover and therefore the boy cannot become the mother's lover (the Oedipal theory). The other explanation is that the boy resents his father because the father is the disciplinarian. These alternative theories cannot be adequately tested in a society in which both of these roles are filled by one person. One way we can test these alternative theories is to consider comparative data from societies in which the roles are separated. Malinowski (1927) found that among the Trobriands the mother's brother acts as the disciplinarian. In this society hostility tended to be directed toward the disciplinarian rather than toward the mother's lover, casting doubt on Freud's Oedipal theory. We would want to consider evidence from other societies in which the roles of mother's lover and son's disciplinarian are separated before coming to a firm conclusion with respect to the generalizability of Freud's Oedipal theory, but the logic of the analysis should be evident from this example.

We know from our discussion in earlier chapters that replication is a fundamental aspect of the scientific enterprise. Studies are most typically replicated in the same society, but it is often of great value to be able to replicate a finding across several societies. When we turn to comparative data to test the generalizability of a finding based on one society, we can argue that the original finding has been replicated if the result for the first society holds up for the other societies we consider. A strength of the comparative method is that *it can be used to replicate findings based on one society or a small number of similar societies.*

A particularly clear illustration of the use of cross-societal comparisons for replication is the Inkeles and Smith (1974) study of the process by which people move from a traditional to a modern orientation in a developing nation. The researchers interviewed industrial workers, peasants, and urban nonindustrial workers in each of six developing nations. Basically the same questions were asked in each country. Many of the questions were designed to measure "individual modernity" as reflected in respondents' values, beliefs, attitudes, and behavior. Other questions were used to assess degree of exposure to a variety of modernizing institutions such as the factory, the school, the mass media, and so on. They found a consistent trend across all six societies for those who are most exposed to these modernizing institutions to be the most modern in their outlook.

The Inkeles and Smith study illustrates the use of the comparative method for the purpose of replication in two different ways. Prior to their study a great deal of work had been done showing a relationship between certain institutions found in industrial nations (e.g., factories, schools) and the attitudes of people living in these nations. One sense in which the Inkeles and Smith study is a replication is that it represents an effort to replicate for *developing* nations the relationship between several of these institutions and the attitudes of those in contact with them. A second sense in which the study is a replication is that the study design is the same in each of the six countries considered so that each country can be used as an independent test or replication of the theories being considered.

When we use comparative data to test the generalizability of a finding based on one society, we sometimes find that the result for the original society will hold up in some societies, but not in others. If we can find some characteristic which differentiates those societies for which the original relationship holds up from those for which it does not, we can say that we have specified the conditions under which the original relationship exists. This points to another strength of the comparative method: *the specification of the conditions under which a finding based on one society holds up in other societies.*

This use of the comparative method is illustrated by the Lipset et al. (1954) study of voter participation in the United States and in various European cities. The study focused on the participation of the working class relative to that of the middle class. The researchers found a higher rate of turnout for middle class voters than for working class voters in the United States. This pattern held up in Britain, but was reversed in some Austrian and German cities. When they looked more closely at these latter cities, the researchers found that the labor movement there had created a network for indoctrination of workers; such networks were less developed in Britain and the United States. The Lipset research illustrates what is referred to as "specification," which is the identification of the condition under which the relationship originally found for one country holds true for others and the condition under which it fails to hold true.

For some purposes it is useful to make comparisons between societies that are in many respects similar. For other purposes it is useful to select societies that are as diverse as possible. When our objective is to argue for the generalizability of a relationship between two variables, the case is strongest when it can be shown to hold up across a very diverse range of societies.

Nadel (1952) selected two very similar societies which exist side by side for a study of beliefs about witchcraft. The Nupe believe that witches are female; in contrast, the Gwari believe that witches may be of either sex. Nadel's strategy of society selection illustrates the alternative in which the researcher selects societies to compare which have minimal differences between them. In this way it is easier to narrow down the set of differences between these societies which might be relevant to an explanation of why in one society they believe witches are female and in the other they believe witches may be of either sex.

Another strength of the comparative method is that *it allows us to empirically test theories which specify societal-level characteristics as variables.* If a theory specifies that the political structure or the economic structure of a country has a causal impact on the way in which income and wealth are distributed, we run into problems attempting to verify the theory on the basis of data from that one country. We find that it is not possible to assess the impact of a variable such as economic structure which is a constant for that country. But if we compare the distribution of wealth in several societies that have different economic structures, we will be in a position to draw some conclusions about the impact of economic structure on the distribution of wealth. More generally, what we learn is that it is not possible to get a quantitative estimate of the impact of a societal-level characteristic on the basis of data from just one society. But if we base our study on several societies and select these societies in such a way that there is variation in the societal-level characteristic of interest to us, it is possible to estimate the impact of this characteristic.

This use of comparative data is well illustrated in the work of Robert Jackman (1975), who was interested in constructing a model to account for, among other things, income inequality. Among the variables of interest to him were strength of socialist parties, strength of unions, and degree of freedom of the press. By basing his study on data from sixty countries, he was able to make some quantitative estimates of the causal impact of these societal-level characteristics on the extent of income inequality within a nation. However, since he did not include any communist nations in his sample, he was not in a position to estimate the causal impact on income inequality of a nation's being communist (or capitalist).

In the preceding paragraphs we have examined a variety of reasons for doing comparative research. We have found that for some research questions the use of comparative data is helpful, although not essential; and for other research questions no adequate answer can be obtained without a consideration of comparative data. It should be clear by this point that there are a number of very strong reasons for doing comparative analysis. In view of these arguments we might ask why such a small fraction of social research is based on comparative data. One reason is that there are a variety of obstacles facing those who seek to do comparative research. Many of them turn out to be the same as those we face when doing research in one society, but in the context of comparative research they turn out to be even more problematic. In the section that follows we will look more closely at this issue in the context of our discussion of examples illustrating the range of research methods which can be used comparatively.

APPLICATIONS OF COMPARATIVE RESEARCH

Most of the research methods we have considered in the preceding chapters can be used comparatively, but some are used more extensively than others. For example, a great deal of comparative research has been done using survey research methods, but comparative experimental studies are still quite rare. In this section we discuss in some detail the three most extensively used methods in comparative research — ethnographic research, survey research, and aggregate data analysis. We shall also look briefly at three others (experimental research, content analysis, and historical analysis). There are two major objectives for this section: (1) to illustrate by example some ways in which each of these six research methods has been used comparatively; (2) to outline some of the problems that must be dealt with by those seeking to use the specified method in a comparative context. Some of the problems considered are unique to a specific method; others tend to appear in one form or another in all forms of comparative research.

Ethnographic Research

While some comparative studies using observational methods have been carried out by sociologists, most of this work has been done by anthropologists. Typically an anthropologist goes to live with a tribe (e.g., the Kurtatchi in the Solomon Islands) for a year or two and then writes a book (referred to as an *ethnography*) based on this *ethnographic research* which describes how the society is organized, its kinship system, its language, religious beliefs, and the like.

Is such ethnographic research an example of comparative research if it is based on only one society? While the ethnographic report typically describes only one society, there is a sense in which it is comparative. The anthropologist is almost always from a different society and consequently there will often be some explicit and always many implicit contrasts with that society. We can raise a similar question about much of the sociological research carried out in a single foreign country (such studies are often referred to as *area studies*). For example, suppose an American sociologist decides to study the status of women in Senegal. The study itself will typically contain few if any explicit contrasts between Senegal and the United States, but the choice of issues for emphasis will unavoidably be based on a number of implicit contrasts with the United States. We do not seek to resolve the debate as to whether ethnographic reports and other single-society area studies should be considered examples of comparative research. Some unquestionably fit the label better than do others. However, when data from several area studies or several ethnographic studies are used in one study, the product is unquestionably an example of comparative research.

One of the most widely used sources of comparative ethnographic data is the Human Relations Area Files (HRAF) which were started in 1938 by George Murdock. These files do contain data from some observational studies conducted by sociologists (typically community studies carried out by sociologists from the country in which the community is located), but most of the data is drawn from the ethnographic research of anthropologists. The data base for the HRAF files is observational ethnographic reports prepared for more than two hundred societies around the world. In the HRAF files these ethnographies have been photocopied, taken apart, and filed into a set of categories which is described in the *Outline of Cultural Materials* (Murdock et al., 1971); there are over seven hundred such categories, including: infant feeding, childbirth, independence training, cosmology, and suicide. A single page from an ethnography may be filed in more than one place if it contains information relevant to more than one topic.[2]

Numerous studies have been based on this data. One example is the study by Whiting and Child (1953) of the relationship between personality and various aspects of child training. That study considered a number of hypotheses derived from psychoanalytic theory relating to fixations. For example, one theory is that a child can develop an oral fixation as a result of certain types of socialization practices relating to nursing and weaning. A person is said to have an oral fixation if various behaviors which involve eating, drinking, smoking, and the like have greater importance than is usual for people who have not undergone this same socialization experience. The study we cited earlier of the relationship between age of weaning and emotional disturbance is one part of this larger study.

The HRAF files have proven a valuable source of data for cross-cultural research. In view of the importance of the HRAF files as a data source for comparative studies based on ethnographic data, it is of interest to consider a few of the major problems which those who choose to work with this data source must face.

One of the most common problems is that the researcher's categories do not correspond to those categories by which the ethnographic data have been classified. If we are lucky it is possible to find the relevant material by looking under two or three existing categories or by shifting to a more general category. But there are always some issues for which the standard categories are inappropriate. In such instances we run the risk of missing information which is actually available in the file, but elusive using the standard categories.

Another issue that all users of the HRAF files must face is the selection of a unit of analysis. In some of the material the report describes a nation, in others a tribe or society, but by far the most common are ethnographic reports on a specific community within a tribe or society. This fairly small unit of analysis reflects the emphasis in the ethnographic work which anthropologists have done over the past century. For example, the Kwoma is a tribe numbering approximately nine hundred in central New Guinea. It is divided into four subtribes. Each of these is in turn divided into several units referred to as "sibs" and each sib is further divided into hamlets. In his book, *Becoming a Kwoma,* Whiting (1941) actually reports on one hamlet; he did not conduct a systematic analysis of all those who call themselves Kwoma. The anthropologist will generally be explicit as to whether a hamlet or a society is being studied, but

---

[2] Many universities have the HRAF files available on microfilm; a smaller number have actual photocopies of the files available.

the researcher using the HRAF files must track down such information so as to ensure consistency, or equivalence, in the level of the cases studied.[3]

One of the most difficult issues which plague those who choose to use the HRAF files is sampling. The major problem is in deciding which communities, tribes, societies, or cultures are sufficiently distinct as to represent independent observations. There is considerable debate among anthropologists over the criteria for defining a society or a culture; we could not hope in this brief discussion to present, let alone resolve, the debate. One of the reasons there is so much disagreement is that in many instances there is considerable overlap between tribes with respect to language and other aspects of culture. This diffusion of language and culture makes it more reasonable to talk about criteria for measuring degree of independence between societies than to look for criteria for complete independence. This problem of lack of independence between units is referred to as *Galton's problem* in honor of Sir Francis Galton who in 1889 was the first to raise the issue. The issue is important because it raises the possibility that what appears to be a large number of societies in which the researcher's hypothesis is supported may turn out to be duplicate observations on what would more appropriately be considered one society. To date there has been no fully adequate mechanism for solving Galton's problem. However, several methods have been proposed which do deal with the problem. We will briefly consider two.

One proposal has been to use Murdock's *Ethnographic Atlas* which divides the world into six major regions: Africa, the Circum-Mediterranean, East Eurasia, the Insular Pacific, North America, and South America. The cultures in each of these six regions are in turn grouped into ten culture areas. This yields a total of sixty sets of cultures that are reasonably independent of one another. However, as Whiting (1968:704) points out, a major limitation of this approach is that we would never end up with a sample of more than sixty cases (out of more than two hundred in the HRAF files).

Another approach is to use the criterion of linguistic relatedness. To assess linguistic relatedness, the researcher considers a set of two hundred common terms (e.g., sun, moon, water) for which all cultures have words. Then using a technique referred to as *glotto-chronology* (or *lexico-statistics*) estimates are made of how long it has been since two languages split off from a common language. The fewer words the two languages have in common (i.e., words which are cognates), the longer it has been since the split occurred. Thus in constructing our sample for the HRAF we could use as one criterion that no two societies be included which derived from the same common language within the last 1000

---

[3] The issue of consistency in the level of the unit of analysis is sometimes solved by restricting the study to nation-states. But even this strategy has its problems. Some nation-states have a population of less than 100 thousand persons and for many purposes would be more equivalent to one state in a larger nation such as the United States.

years. Fortunately, the analysis has already been done for us and this world linguistic sample includes some 136 cases (Whiting, 1968:705–706).

We now turn to some problems that are relevant not only to studies based on the HRAF files, but also to comparative studies based on other ethnographic data as well. One such problem is that each ethnographer selects different aspects of a society to focus on. Often an issue of relevance to the hypothesis we want to test will not have been commented on one way or the other and the case will have to be excluded from our sample for lack of adequate data. Even if the issue has been considered, we cannot be sure that differences in emphasis given to the issue in different societies reflect true differences rather than selectivity on the part of the anthropologists involved.

Another problem common to most ethnographic data is that it depends heavily on the observations, judgments, and interpretations of the small number of anthropologists (often only one) conducting the study. It is a common practice among anthropologists to develop a certain territoriality about the group they have studied. The same anthropologist may return to study a community several times over the years, but it is uncommon for another anthropologist to study exactly the same community. As is illustrated in the example which follows, when independent studies are made of a single community, the observations and conclusions can be quite inconsistent.

In 1930, Robert Redfield published *Tepoztlan: A Mexican Village,* which was based on his personal observations in that village. In his report he stressed the positive aspects of "folk" as opposed to "modern" life in the community. For example, he observed a great deal of harmony and cooperation among the people. Oscar Lewis (1951) went to the same community and gave his description of their lives in *Life in a Mexican Village*. He drew an almost totally opposite portrait, including reports of discord among the village members and a description of interpersonal relationships more characteristic of the negative stereotype of the city dweller who even fears the neighbors next door.

By this point, we can see that there are a variety of methodological problems and potential pitfalls awaiting those who choose to work with the HRAF files. However, these problems are minor when contrasted with those which would be involved if we were to try to collect the relevant data for 25, 50, or 75 societies each time we sought to carry out a comprehensive comparative ethnographic study. More to the point, the existence of these data files makes possible the testing of a variety of hypotheses which would be quite unfeasible without them.

Ethnographic data in the form of the HRAF files have been available for *secondary analysis* (i.e., analysis of data collected by others and for different purposes) since the late 1930s. More recently a number of repositories have also been established for survey data. One of the largest, the Roper Public Opinion Center, has on hand data from over one thousand survey research studies conducted in more than sixty countries around the world. While such repositories (referred to as *data banks*) can be very useful to those interested in the secondary analysis of survey research data, there are again a set of problems which the user must confront. But it is most appropriate to review these problems after discussing the use of survey research as a method for *primary data collection*.

Survey Research

Since survey research is used more extensively by sociologists than is any other methodological approach, it should not surprise us to find that much comparative social research, particularly research carried out by sociologists, is based on survey data. One of the most ambitious comparative survey research studies to date was carried out under the direction of Inkeles and Smith (1974). As will be recalled from the brief description given earlier in the chapter, it was a study of the process by which people undergo change from a traditional to a modern orientation in their beliefs, values, and attitudes. The researchers hypothesized that similar processes would be involved in any developing nation; with that in mind they selected six different countries. One of the questions of particular interest to them was whether there is a fairly coherent syndrome which can be meaningfully referred to as "modern man" across countries or whether the various hypothesized components of such a syndrome are unrelated. One of the major conclusions of this study of almost six thousand respondents from Argentina, Chile, India, Israel, Nigeria, and Bangladesh is that it *is* possible to develop a composite measure of "individual modernity" which can be applied cross-culturally.

We now turn to some of the methodological problems that confront those who seek to carry out comparative survey research studies. Of particular importance are problems relating to conceptual equivalence, measurement equivalence, sampling, and interviewing. We will look at each in turn.

The *issue of conceptual equivalence* is central to all cross-societal research: the concepts used must be meaningful in all the societies being compared. Some concepts — such as unemployment, bureaucracy, and civil service — have meaning in some societies, but not in others. Obviously we cannot attempt a comparison between one society in which a concept does have meaning and another in which it does not. But often sociologists find themselves working with such concepts as individual modernity, achievement motivation, fatalism, and alienation; with these concepts it is more difficult to say with certainty that the concept has no meaning in this or that society. We are much more likely to conclude that a concept such as achievement motivation has a very different meaning in two given societies or to conclude that it is much less important in one of those societies than to conclude that in one it has no meaning at all. This would be the case when the goals toward which achievement motivation was directed were widely divergent, perhaps antithetical, in the societies being compared. The same comparison is true of, say, alienation. We must know each society well in order to comprehend the forms that alienation takes. We must then determine a uniquely appropriate way to define and measure alienation in each of these societies.

Equivalence in definition of concepts can be very difficult to deal with. We know that it is possible there will be some variation from one society to another with respect to the specific components of a concept. It does not make sense to use a concept which has not been adjusted to take into consideration cultural context, but we can never be sure that the adjustment has been done in such a way that the resulting measure is equivalent across the societies being compared.

The *problem of measurement equivalence* that is, the problem of operationalizing theoretical concepts in such a way that the resulting measures are comparable across all societies being considered, must be confronted by all who engage in comparative research. For example, suppose our theory calls for a measure of upper class membership. Clearly the criteria for upper class membership vary from one society to another. The variety of possible criteria makes the task of constructing equivalent measures difficult. Let us assume for the sake of the present discussion that one criterion that is important for each of the societies being considered is family assets. We select one society and determine that the most appropriate lower limit for upper class membership is family assets in excess of $10,000. For that society only one percent of the population is classified as upper class. Now suppose we want to construct an equivalent measure of upper class membership for a second society which is at a substantially higher level of economic development. If we again used the figure of $10,000, it would result in twenty percent of the population being classified as upper class in this second society. If alternatively we propose a different criterion, such as $50,000, we would again restrict the upper class to one percent of the population. But in effect we are shaping the criterion for upper class membership: we are making it financial elitism rather than, say, what some given amount of money can buy, or how long the money has been in the family, and so on.

So far we have considered only an assets criterion for upper class membership. The task becomes even more complicated as we attempt to introduce other criteria such as occupation, education, and annual income. Our goal is simply to obtain a measure of upper class membership which is equivalent across each of the societies being considered. But in the process we must confront choices between alternative dimensions of equivalence. We can get more equivalence in one respect, but at a cost of reduced equivalence in another. For this reason irrespective of how careful we are in constructing our measure of upper class membership, we will be vulnerable to the criticism that our indicator shows a distinct lack of comparability in at least some respects.

While the problem of measurement equivalence is one that will never be entirely resolved, a number of techniques have been developed which are of some use in dealing with the problem. For example, suppose we want to measure a concept such as fatalism for respondents in each of several countries. Typically we would start with an English version of the questionnaire and then translate it into each of the local languages needed. But how can we be sure that we have not lost something important in the translation? One strategy which has been developed for dealing with this problem is *back translation*. First we have one bilingual person translate the questionnaire from English into the language of the society we are considering. Then we have a second bilingual person who has no knowledge of the original English version translate the previously translated questionnaire back into English. Then the original version and the back translated version can be compared. When there are major discrepancies, the question is rewritten and the process is repeated.

We now turn to a way of dealing with measurement equivalence which is sometimes used when the goal is to obtain equivalent measures of an abstract psychological concept such as alienation. Typically alienation is measured using an index constructed by combining the answers for several individual attitudinal questions. The sociologist often writes a set of general questions that do not make any reference to a specific cultural context, assuming that if the question is sufficiently abstract, then the resulting measure will be equivalent across cultures. A criticism which can be made of such measures is that many respondents either do not understand these abstract questions or interpret them in ways that the researcher has not anticipated. One way to deal with this criticism is to base our measure instead on questions that are very concrete and have been tailored to each cultural context; that is, the concrete situation described will differ from one society to another so as to take into consideration cultural variation. But we will still be faced with the criticism that these questions may not yield a measure which is in all ways comparable across each of the societies being considered.

One way to deal with both of these criticisms is to combine the two approaches. That is, for each society being considered we write two types of questions. One set attempts to measure the concept of interest, in this case alienation, in very general terms. Our objective with this set is to write questions which are sufficiently abstract to be free of specific cultural content. The second set of questions prepared for each society attempts to assess the same concept, but in more concrete terms specific to that society.

Now comes the hard part. After the data has been collected, a subset of the more abstract questions which are consistently highly intercorrelated for each of the societies is selected from the original set of abstract questions. These questions are then combined to form a single overall measure referred to as an index or scale. Next we correlate the culture-specific questions with this index. Those culture-specific questions that correlate highly with this index are then selected out. This new smaller set of the culture-specific questions and the questions used to construct the index of abstract questions are now used to construct a final combined index; that is, an index composed of both the abstract questions and the highly correlated culture-specific questions.

The quality of a survey research study depends in large measure on the *quality of the sampling*. For this reason efforts to obtain equivalent samples receive considerable attention in comparative studies. Few countries have the experienced survey research organizations available in the United States. For this reason it is not uncommon for there to be considerable variability in the quality of the sampling, depending on which country a study is carried out in; this is particularly true if the studies have been set up independently by different investigators.

There are a variety of ways in which sampling comes up in the context of comparative survey research studies. One is in the selection of countries to be included in the study. Given the expense of a survey research study, it is unusual for studies to include more than five or six countries if primary data is being collected; studies based on the secondary analysis of data collected by others can extend the number of countries considered. It is not uncommon for the researcher's prior contacts to have some bearing on the final selection of countries, a fact which has obvious implications for the representatives of the countries selected. With awareness of cost considerations, the researcher sometimes restricts the study to a specific community or region of each country being studied; representative national samples are typically much more expensive to carry out. Another factor that can influence the quality of the sample is the nonresponse rate, which can vary considerably from one society to another.

Interviewing is another area in which problems may arise in comparative survey research. The pollster or interviewer is not an ordinary part of a person's life in most societies. The interview situation is a strange and frightening experience for many people. When this is compounded by differences in dress, status, and manner (and possibly in native language) between the interviewer and interviewee, the validity of the results obtained can be seriously questioned. The interviewer is often a stranger and is sometimes suspected of being a government agent. When there are fears of the interviewer being a government investigator, we can expect less than candid responses on a number of issues — such as political alienation, degree of support for the government, and personal income.

For a variety of reasons it is often necessary to conduct an interview in the presence of a third party. Women, for example, require a chaperone in some societies. The presence of a third party can be positive in the sense that the person may help keep the respondent honest or help the respondent to remember required information, but the impact is more typically to reduce the validity of responses given. For example, the presence of others may force the respondent to give culturally approved answers; it may also keep the respondent from openly discussing more personal matters.

A final factor that can affect the interview situation is "courtesy bias." This occurs when respondents provide information they feel will please the interviewer or perhaps is befitting to people of their status. There is some evidence that the direction of courtesy bias differs from country to country. It has been observed that Japanese humility has resulted in an understatement of personal achievement, class position, and income level; while in other countries, respondents have exaggerated their wealth and social position in response to survey questions (Mitchell, 1968).

Earlier we mentioned that there exist a number of repositories, referred to as data banks, which have on file data from survey research studies conducted in countries around the world. As was the case with the Human Relations Area Files, these data banks make possible the testing of a variety of hypotheses which would otherwise be quite unfeasible. They make comparative survey research data available to many who could not otherwise afford to obtain it.

However, there are a special set of problems which must be dealt with by those who seek to carry out a secondary analysis of the data obtainable from these data banks. One problem is that there is typically a lack of documentation with respect to the various sources of irregularity in the study, particularly in the area of sampling. The quality of the data varies considerably from one data set (study) to another, but it is often quite difficult to assess the quality of the data on the basis of the information provided.

Another set of problems relates to the issue of measurement equivalence. Typically the researcher will be attempting to compare the result for several countries, each of which measures a concept such as alienation in a somewhat different way. There are even serious problems of equivalence with respect to such variables as occupation and income. In the case of foreign language questionnaires, we are occasionally able to check an English version of the questions to verify that the same questions have been asked; but we know from our earlier discussion that it is dangerous to assume nothing was lost or changed in the process of translation into the relevant local language.

These are only some of the problems we must deal with if we choose to engage in secondary analysis of comparative survey data. Briefly, some of the others are: variation in the training of interviewers, and in the quality of the supervision of interviewers; variation in nonresponse rates and in ways of dealing with nonresponse; and specific national events which may have produced a temporary shift of opinion on certain issues.

The problems the survey researcher must face in the context of cross-national research are in most cases extensions of related problems that occur when a survey research study is carried out in the context of one society. But it should be evident by this point that the problems are typically exacerbated in the context of comparative research. Much the same argument can be made with respect to the use of national-level aggregate statistics, a topic to which we now turn. One reason is that many of these statistics are based on survey data and thus are subject to many of the same sources of bias.

Aggregate Analysis

Aggregate analysis can be carried out at a variety of levels of aggregation.[4] In the present discussion we are concerned with data for which the unit of aggregation is the nation. One of the major sources of such aggregate data is the various publications of the United Nations, such as the *Demographic Yearbook* and the *Statistical Yearbook*. There are also a number of social science programs that were set up to collect various types of aggregate statistics and organize them in a form permitting comparisons between nations. The National Bureau of Economic Research and the Cowles Commission are examples of two such long-standing programs in the field of economics. They collect data on national income, economic development, and economic stability. Similar programs have been established in other fields. The Yale Political Data Program gathers, analyzes, and critically evaluates aggregate statistical data from many nations on social conditions related to political development and change. Much of this information has been published in the *World Handbook of Political and Social Indicators* (Taylor and Hudson, 1972) and other similar volumes.

Our social theories sometimes specify *structural characteristics of nations* as causal factors: the political structure (e.g., representative democracy vs. totalitarianism) or the economic structure (e.g., capitalism vs. communism) are acknowledged to be important determinants of a range of social phenomena within a nation; but such factors cannot be used as variables in an analysis based on one country because they do not vary for one country. However, when we shift to the nation as the unit of analysis, such factors can be included as variables as long as there are differences between some of the nations considered with respect to these characteristics. Note that these variables are not based on aggregate data but they can be used along with other variables that are so based (e.g., infant mortality rate, percent literate, percent over age 65) when the country is the unit of analysis. In recent years a number of very interesting studies have been carried out which combine variables based on national-

---

[4] As we recall from the discussion in Chapter 12, aggregate data at one level, such as the nation, is obtained by combining data for units from a lower level of aggregation, such as the state or the individual.

level aggregate statistics with variables that measure structural characteristics of the nation. We now turn to one such example.

In Harold Wilensky's (1975) study, *The Welfare State and Equality,* the major dependent variable is "social welfare effort," which is measured by the ratio of government expenditures for various social security programs (using a rather broad definition of social security) to the Gross National Product (GNP). Wilensky was able to obtain data for his key variables, some of which were based on national-level aggregate data and others of which were national-level structural variables, for sixty countries. One question of particular interest to Wilensky was the relevance of the political structure of a country to the level of social welfare effort. For each of the sixty countries considered, he classified the political system into one of the following four categories: liberal democratic (e.g., United States, Sweden), totalitarian (e.g., Poland, USSR), authoritarian oligarchic (e.g., Taiwan, Honduras), and authoritarian populist (e.g., Mexico, Iraq).

On the basis of a cross-sectional analysis (that is, at one point in time) of this comparative data, Wilensky concluded that political structure has little impact on the level of social security effort. In another part of his analysis he reported that ideology of the elite and the proportion of the GNP spent on defense have little impact on social security effort. A major conclusion of his study is that level of economic development as measured by GNP per capita has a strong indirect effect on social security effort. These findings are consistent with the thesis that modern societies are converging toward a common form of post-industrial welfare state which is independent of variation in political system.

In a related study, Robert Jackman (1975) selected several indicators of social inequality as his major dependent variables. One is a measure of income inequality. Another is a composite index of social welfare based on a variety of health and nutrition indicators. As in the Wilensky study, Jackman considered sixty countries; again some of the variables are based on national-level aggregate data while others are based on structural characteristics of the country. One of the more interesting conclusions in Jackman's study is that high rates of population growth and high rates of economic growth tend to increase the amount of inequality in a society. A variety of other topics have also been investigated by means of techniques similar to those used by Wilensky and Jackman: for example, mass political violence (Hibbs, 1973) and economic development (Adelman and Morris, 1967, 1973).

An attractive aspect of comparative aggregate analysis is that the data can generally be obtained easily; it is often as close as the nearest major library. While the cost of obtaining primary data of this sort would be prohibitive, the cost of available secondary data is usually nominal. In recent years the number of countries for which this data is available has been increasing, as has the quality and comprehensiveness of the data. In view of this trend it is likely that the frequency with which studies are based on such data will continue to increase. For this reason, among others, it is important that we keep in mind some of the potential *pitfalls* of using this data.

The United Nations, which is the major source for much of the data, has very little control over the quality of the data provided by member nations. For some countries the data are quite reliable, but for others they are quite poor.[5] To further complicate matters, there is generally little documentation with which we could judge the quality of the data for individual countries. In general there is a tendency for the quality of the data to rise with the level of economic development. Since the collection and evaluation of such data is expensive and requires skilled personnel, the more industrialized countries are better equipped to support such ventures.

One of the most serious problems with this data is that the categories used in collecting data vary from one country to another. There is little uniformity in the definition of such basic concepts as unemployment, family size, family income, literacy, and cause of death. Take, for example, the definition of literacy. Most nations define literacy as the ability to read and write, but some countries define it simply as the ability to write. There is also considerable variation in the minimal level of reading and writing required of those classified as literate. Another factor in literacy rates is the section of the population for which literacy is determined; most countries base estimates on the population over age 15, but some countries select a different age criterion.

As a second example we can consider statistics on cause of death. Often, one death could be classified under any of several possible categories. Death is sometimes due to a variety of factors; in such situations the selection of the one primary cause can be quite misleading. Suicide is one cause of death for which the definition varies from one country to another. Even when the definition is the same for two or more countries there is a potential lack of comparability in the statistics due to variation in willingness to use the category of suicide; there are often other categories, such as drug overdose or automobile accident, under which a death might alternatively be classified.

Another source of error in statistics provided to the U.N. and other international organizations is *distortion of data for political purposes*. For example, a country might decide to slant the economic figures in a favorable direction so that it appears more stable economically than it actually is. This might be done for a variety of purposes, one of which would be to attract foreign investment capital. There are often internal political reasons for distorting data. For example, representation in the

---

[5] When a regional office is faced with a demand for data which it is incapable of collecting, it may find ingenious ways of fabricating the desired information.

national assembly may be based on population estimates provided by a national census. Such data sometimes gets intentionally inflated for certain regions of the country in an effort to obtain more seats in the assembly for those regions.

The aggregate data provided to the U.N. by member nations is not collected with the idea of social research in mind.[6] The researcher who attempts to use secondary data collected for entirely different purposes runs the risk of attempting to make the data into something they are not. There is a fine line between the creative use and the misuse of such data. It is common for the researcher to find that *the exact data called for by theory just are not available.* One response is to select one or more available variables as indicators or proxies for the variable of actual theoretical interest. If the proxy selected is too different from the theoretical variable, the results obtained will be useless. Another related problem is that some researchers start with the variables for which aggregate data are available and then attempt to construct a theory that justifies using these variables. The result is all too often a very lame theory and a study completely devoid of theoretical merit.

Historical Analysis, Content Analysis, and Experimentation

So far we have discussed three categories of comparative analysis (ethnographic, survey, and aggregate). While these approaches account for a very substantial proportion of the comparative studies that have been done in recent years, other techniques — such as historical analysis, content analysis, and experimental approaches — are also used extensively. The three examples we now turn to illustrate some of these alternative approaches.

In *Regulating the Poor,* Piven and Cloward (1971) argue that relief-giving is a mechanism for controlling the poor. They point out that relief rolls are expanded during periods of civil disorder so as to contain this disorder and restore order; they are then contracted when the threat of civil disorder subsides, thus assuring an adequate supply of low-wage labor. To document their thesis Piven and Cloward draw on historical materials from sixteenth-century England and France as well as more recent historical materials from the United States. These comparative historical data lend credibility to the claim that the use of relief as a mechanism of social control is not confined to the contemporary United States.

---

[6] Governments have many reasons for collecting aggregate statistics. Planning for the future, assessing the needs of the population, and administering existing governmental programs are just a few of the reasons. Data which satisfies these needs do not always have relevance for social science research.

In *The Achieving Society,* David McClelland (1961) argues that there is a positive relationship between the level of achievement motivation that existed in 1925 and the rate of economic expansion during the following twenty-five years. His measure of achievement motivation was based on a content analysis of a sample of children's stories that appeared in books available in 1925. He was able to obtain this data for twenty-three countries. As hypothesized, he did find a positive relationship between the level of achievement motivation and the rate of economic growth.

Stanley Milgram (1961) was interested in an experimental investigation of differences between countries with respect to conformity behavior. He adapted for the purpose Solomon Asch's (1952) now-classic study of conformity behavior in small groups. In the original experiment a group of six students is shown several lines of different lengths. Each student is then asked to make a judgment as to the relative length of these lines. The group is set up so that several of the students who are actually confederates of the experimenter would speak first and give what was clearly an incorrect answer. Asch found that in response to this group pressure a very high percentage of the experimental subjects conformed to the obviously incorrect judgments of others.

In Milgram's adaptation, subjects made judgments as to the length of auditory signals (tones). The other members of the listening group were simulated rather than actually being present; that is, the experimental subject went into one booth and was led to believe that the people he heard talking over his earphones were in the other booths, but in reality he was only hearing their voices on a tape recording. Milgram conducted his experiment in both Oslo and Paris. He ran several variations on the basic design but in all of them he consistently found: (1) a tendency for a substantial percentage of the subjects to conform to the group pressure — a replication of Asch's findings, and (2) a consistent trend for the Norwegian subjects to conform more frequently than the French subjects.

When we use historical methods, content analysis, or experimentation comparatively, there are a variety of methodological issues and problems with which we must deal. In addition to the problems which are unique to each of these approaches, there are other problems common to all research methods that are used comparatively: the definition of the unit of analysis, sample selection, conceptual equivalence, and measurement equivalence. One of the debates in the comparative literature asks whether it is meaningful to refer to the "comparative method" or whether it is more appropriate to refer to "the comparative application of other research methods" such as survey research or experimentation. The authors feel that to the extent there is a common set of problems with which all who engage in comparative research must deal, a case can be made for the study of something called the comparative method. At the beginning of the chapter we outlined several strong arguments in support of comparative research. Because all these arguments pertain to a variety of methodological approaches, they lend further support to the conclusion that the comparative method can be viewed as something in and of itself.

Ethical Considerations

Several ethical issues arise in the context of comparative research. One set of ethical considerations relates to the sponsorship, and anticipated application, of the research results. This is well illustrated by the example of Project Camelot, a multimillion dollar project sponsored by the Department of Defense some years ago. In the most general terms the objective of the study was to study social change in developing nations. Because of the sums of money involved, many social scientists were more than willing to avoid explicit questions as to what the Department of Defense was really interested in finding out. In retrospect it seems clear that a major objective was to obtain information about political unrest (more explicitly, communist-influenced peasant movements) in Third World nations. It is clear that there would have been little interest in a study of the conditions under which revolutionary developments might be a positive force. The prevailing counterinsurgency policy of the Defense Department was founded less on the best interests of the nations under scrutiny than on the much-touted need to defend our own nation from encroachments of communism among our neighbors, near or far. One small part of the study was to be carried out in Chile by an investigator who lied about the source of his funding. When he was found out, there was a reaction of extreme outrage which led to the entire project being canceled.

Another set of ethical considerations relates to collaboration with local researchers in the host country. Such collaboration can be invaluable for a variety of reasons, but there has been an unfortunate tendency for at least some researchers from the United States to use their associates in other countries as assistants in their own research projects rather than as colleagues working on a joint endeavor. The problems with this attitude are well summarized by Kelman (1968:81):

> Many of us have assumed, implicitly and without questioning, that the other society is simply there for us to research upon it, and that we can take what we wish from it as long as we pay the fair market price. In the process, we have too often displayed a lack of respect for the values of the society, the sensitivities of its members, the dignity of our respondents, and the personal and professional aspirations of our colleagues. Such an attitude simply will not do.

CONCLUSION

Some research questions cannot be answered except on the basis of comparative analysis. To say that comparative research is useful is to understate the case; comparative research is indispensable to the sociological enterprise. However, there are a host of potential pitfalls which await the unsuspecting and even the experienced researcher who engages in comparative analysis. Many of these are the same problems we must deal with when doing research in one society; but as we have seen, they typically get magnified in the context of comparative analysis.

One such problem is selecting an appropriate unit of analysis (e.g., nation-state, society, culture, or community) and defining it in such a way that the units selected are equivalent. In ethnographic research the definition of a "society" or a "culture" often turns out to be problematic. Even when we work with nation-states, questions can be raised about the appropriateness of including in the same analysis large nations such as India and small nations such as Tonga.

There are a variety of sampling-related problems that must be dealt with in comparative research. To begin with there is the selection of countries or societies. Some studies are based on only two societies while others are based on more than one hundred. The smaller the number of societies considered, the greater the chance that our findings will characterize the specific societies selected rather than societies throughout the world. The selection of societies is only the first of many sampling issues we must consider in comparative research. After selecting the countries, we must then decide whether to attempt a representative national sample, a regional sample, a community sample, or possibly a sample of a specified segment of the community (such as those who work in factories).

In all comparative studies we must deal with the issue of conceptual equivalence. Concepts such as "organized crime" make good sense in some societies, and no sense at all in others. Efforts to increase equivalence of concepts by adjusting them so as to take into consideration cultural context typically require a trade-off; that is, we can get increased equivalence in one respect at a cost of decreased equivalence in another.

Closely related to the problem of conceptual equivalence is the problem of measurement equivalence. When the definition of our concepts is adjusted to take into consideration variation in cultural context, there must be a corresponding adjustment in our measures of these concepts. There are no simple formulas to ensure measurement equivalence across societies, but a variety of techniques such as back translation have been developed to help somewhat in dealing with the problem. As with conceptual equivalence, we typically find that when measurement equivalence is increased in certain respects, it is decreased in others.

Comparative research is often based on secondary analysis. The use of published ethnographic reports, the content analysis of children's readers, the use of survey data obtained from one of the data banks, the use of aggregate statistical data put out by the U.N., and the use of published historical accounts are all examples of secondary analysis.

There are a number of methodological problems that must be dealt with by all who engage in secondary analysis. One problem is that the data has been collected for some other purpose. A risk we run when attempting to use such data is that the indicators we select to measure our theoretical concepts will not be adequate, and the results obtained using these measures will not be valid. A related risk we run is of tailoring our study to the available data. One criticism of this practice is that the resulting study is typically of little or no theoretical value. Another criticism is that it can be a source of ideological bias. If elites decide that data will be published on one phenomenon and not on another, this becomes a mechanism for controlling the kinds of issues that get researched.

Secondary data is available only for certain countries. Since the most comprehensive and accurate statistical data tends to be available for the more industrial nations, data availability tends to bias our sample selection in favor of the richer nations. This bias in turn has implications for any generalizations we may wish to make.

The researcher who wants to carry out a secondary analysis typically finds little or no documentation of the quality of the available data. As a general rule the data for richer countries tends to be of better quality, but this does not help us in making judgments about specific countries.

The issues of conceptual equivalence and measurement equivalence are particularly problematic in secondary analysis. The researcher working with secondary data has fewer options available for ensuring equivalence than does the researcher who is collecting primary data. For example, a technique such as back translation can be used when primary survey data is being collected, but it is not available to those engaged in secondary analysis of survey data.

If we are going to engage in comparative research in the face of so many threats to the validity of our results, we must have some good reasons for doing so, and there are some very good ones.

If we have a theoretical interest in the relationship between two variables over the full possible range for each variable (e.g., the relationship between emotional disturbance and age of weaning), there is often no alternative to a comparative study. For many variables of interest to us there is a rather constricted range within one society and even when a few people can be found who fall outside that range, it may not be wise to use them; for example, a people who are willing to be in one respect deviant (e.g., weaning their children at age four in the United States) are likely to be unrepresentative of that society in a variety of other ways.

If we have a theoretical interest in the extent to which a relationship or a phenomenon is characteristic of all human societies, we must again turn to comparative analysis. If we are to put a hypothesis about some universalistic phenomenon to the test, we must use data from other societies to check that hypothesis. For example, if our hypothesis is that the Oedipal complex is a universalistic phenomenon, we must look for relevant evidence in a variety of societies and not confine our attempts at replication to societies which are in many ways similar to Freud's turn-of-the-century Austria.

When our goal is to examine the impact on one variable of another variable that is a constant for a given society, there is no choice but to carry out a comparative analysis. It is common for arguments to be made about the causal impact of a nation's economic structure on a variety of phenomena within that nation. To test the hypothesis that there is a more unequal distribution of income in capitalist countries than in communist countries, we must carry out a comparative analysis which includes both capitalist and communist countries.

Sometimes we begin with a research question that asks for an explanation of a difference between two societies. For example, our research question might ask why the witches in one society are female while those in another are male. Whenever we start with a research question which asks us to account for a difference between societies, the analysis called for is necessarily comparative.

EXERCISES

1. Together with another student in class, develop a research question for comparative international research that you would approach by the survey method in two countries of your own choosing. Think of a few survey questions that would not be equivalent if they were asked in these two countries. How would you try to correct this situation?

2. Select two or three anthropological monographs that have sections on child rearing, marriage practices, or any other topic which you are interested in. Reading just those sections which deal with the topic you are investigating, compare the reports in terms of the degree of comprehensiveness and completeness. In what way do the practices between these societies differ? How are they similar? Are there any social phenomena which are discussed in only one of the reports? Can you conclusively determine that their absence in the other report(s) is not due to the failure of the observer to either record or observe their occurrence? What reasons can you give to support your answer?

3. Using one of the publications of aggregate international statistics mentioned in the text, such as the *Demographic Yearbook of the U.N.*, select a small

sample of societies (5 to 10). Choose an abstract characteristic such as industrialization or modernization and select a series of indicators for that dimension, i.e., statistics on production, gross national product, type of industry, and distribution of the work force. Are statistics available on every indicator you selected for each society in your sample? How do these societies compare with one another on each of the selected indicators? What can be said about each society in terms of the overall problem being explored? What solution can you offer to include the societies which did not have information available on every indicator in your comparative analysis?

4. As a class project, work together in groups of five to compose a questionnaire on some general topic to be administered cross-culturally. Select a topic that is broad and has universal reference such as attitudes toward education, marriage practices, or rural vs. urban life. The questionnaire should be short and written in a format that will make it easily administered to persons from other countries. Administer the questionnaire to a sample of native-born students and foreign students. What are the results? Were the questions equally relevant to both groups of students? Were there any difficulties experienced in administering the questionnaire? Were some questions embarrassing to the foreign students? Why?

5. Consider a research area of interest that you would like to pursue by comparative international research. What countries would you examine? Why? What type of comparative approach would you use to study this problem? What factors would be important to consider in selecting a particular approach?

6. In "The Urbanization of the Human Population," Kingsley Davis (see "Suggested Readings") empirically approaches the concept of urbanization by considering the percentage of the total population which is concentrated in urban settlements as a measurement of the level of urbanization in the country. How adequate do you think the percentage of people living in urban settlements is as a measurement of urbanization? Is it a good measure for comparative purposes? Are there other aspects to urbanization which should be taken into consideration? If there are, how would you tap these dimensions?

7. Discuss the ways in which sponsorship may affect a comparative international research project in terms of the goals, scope, issues investigated, and objectivity in interpreting and reporting the results. How might knowing that the sponsor is the government affect the respondent's answers in a totalitarian country? What are the advantages of sponsorship? Are there certain types of research efforts that require some form of sponsorship if they are to be performed at all?

8. One ethical and political consideration connected with comparative international research is the issue of exploitation in collaborative research efforts. The chapter has pointed to the exploitation of researchers from other countries as one example of this. What other kinds of potential exploitation can you think of in comparative international research? What would you do about them? What other ethical and political problems can you foresee arising in comparative international research? What would you do to avoid these problems?

SUGGESTED READINGS

Readings about the Method

Amer, Michael, and Allen D. Grimshaw, eds.
1973   Comparative Social Research: Methodological Problems and Strategies.
New York: John Wiley.

> The volume is based on papers presented at a conference on compara-
> tive sociology in 1971. The papers consider a range of very diverse sub-
> jects. Of particular interest are the first two chapters, which are written
> by the editors and are much more general in nature. Among the issues
> considered in the first chapter are: the definition of comparative sociol-
> ogy, how comparative sociology differs from "area" sociology, and the
> benefits of comparative analysis. The second chapter reviews what Amer
> considers the major methodological issues which face those who do
> comparative research.

Brislin, Richard W.; Walter J. Lonner; and Robert M. Thorndike
1973   Cross-Cultural Research Methods. New York: John Wiley.

> This monograph discusses a number of issues of particular interest to
> psychologists doing cross-cultural research. Some of the issues consid-
> ered are: a working definition of cross-cultural psychology, questionnaire
> wording, translation, survey methods, the conduct of experiments, and
> the cross-cultural use of psychological tests. It also includes a discussion
> of a variety of multivariate statistical techniques such as factor analysis,
> multiple regression, and discriminant function analysis.

Holt, Robert T., and John E. Turner, eds.
1970   The Methodology of Comparative Research. New York: Free Press.

> The articles in this anthology emphasize a variety of issues of particular
> interest to comparative political scientists. The first chapter is very gen-
> eral; other chapters consider more specific topics. Among the issues
> considered in the first chapter are: the question of what comparative
> politics is, the control of background factors by randomization, control
> of background factors by specification, non-culture-bound concepts and
> operational definitions, and problems of comparability in sampling.

Kelman, Herbert C.
1968   A Time to Speak: On Human Values and Social Research. San Francisco:
Jossey-Bass.

> The ethical and political considerations involved in doing research in
> general are discussed very well in this book. Of particular interest are
> Kelman's observations on the ethical and political implications of doing

foreign research (especially in developing countries). There are important discussions of Project Camelot, the problem of conducting foreign research that is untainted by national governmental influence, and the temptation on the part of foreign researchers to exploit the countries in which they conduct their work. In all of these discussions, Kelman argues forcefully and humanely for comparative international research with a truly international tone.

Marsh, Robert M.
1967   *Comparative Sociology.* New York: Harcourt, Brace & World.

> This book begins with a consideration of the theoretical and methodological schools of thought regarding comparative international research. It then turns to its main emphasis, which is a codification of ninety comparative studies. The topics of these studies include family structure, bureaucracy, stratification, and cultural values. Propositions from the studies are extracted and codified. Finally, a special section of the book is devoted to a discussion of problems of methodology involved in comparative international research. The book contains a very extensive bibliography.

Przeworski, Adam, and Henry Teune
1970   *The Logic of Comparative Social Inquiry.* New York: John Wiley.

> This is a very theoretical book about comparative research. One of the arguments made in the book is that the goal of comparative analysis is to substitute the names of variables for the names of societies in our explanation. For example, we may report that there is a difference between two countries with respect to some phenomenon. This is fine as a first step, but we must then turn to an analysis of what it is about the countries which can be used to account for the difference found. The book considers issues relating to measurement and to criteria for establishing equivalence in some detail.

Warwick, Donald P., and Samuel Osherson, eds.
1973   *Comparative Research Methods.* Englewood Cliffs, N.J.: Prentice-Hall.

> This edited collection of articles focuses much of its attention on various aspects of equivalence in comparative research. There are three sections of the book which deal with equivalence. They relate to conceptual equivalence, equivalence of measurement, and linguistic equivalence. A final, lengthy section of the book contains articles that discuss the relative merits of survey research and participant observation for comparative international research.

Whiting, John W. M.
1968   "Methods and problems in cross-cultural research." In *Handbook of Social Psychology.* 2d ed., ed. Gardner Lindzey and Elliot Aronson. Reading, Mass.: Addison-Wesley.

This article is a very well-written introduction to the anthropological literature on cross-cultural research. The discussion is somewhat focused on the tradition started by George Murdock; much of Whiting's own work is very much in this tradition. Some of the issues considered are: advantages of the cross-cultural method, the definition of a case, sampling, and transcultural definitions of variables.

Readings Illustrating the Method

Almond, Gabriel, and Sidney Verba
1963   *The Civic Culture: Political Attitudes and Democracy in Five Nations.* Princeton, N.J.: Princeton University Press.

This is a comparative international survey conducted in the United States, Great Britain, Germany, Italy, and Mexico. The focus was on what conditions encourage the development and maintenance of democracy in the political system of a country. The selected countries were chosen because of their differing routes to democracy. The research was based on approximately one thousand representative interviews conducted by native interviewers in each of the countries.

Barthel, Diane L.
1975   "The rise of a female professional elite: the case of Senegal." *African Studies Review* 18 (December):1–17.

This area study asks why, if colonialism had certain pernicious effects on women's status in Africa, did certain Senegalese women manage to rise in education and occupation, eventually to form a female professional elite? One hundred women working in the professions were interviewed and asked questions regarding their family background, education, and job history, among others. As is often the case with area studies, explicit comparisons with other societies are not made, but the reader who is familiar with American society can be expected to draw parallels between the status of women in the United States and the status of women in Senegal.

Davis, Kingsley
1965   "The urbanization of the human population." *Scientific American* 213 (September):41–53.

This study of world urbanization places a heavy reliance on the official governmental statistics of countries around the world (especially national censuses). Davis uses aggregate data on urbanization in a number of fascinating ways throughout the article. He presents the degree of urbanization for the major regions of the world and charts the historical development of urbanization in Europe. Finally, Davis examines the urbanization of today's underdeveloped societies, contrasting the causes of city growth in the developed and the underdeveloped societies.

Inkeles, Alex
1960   "The relation of status to experience, perception, and value." *American Journal of Sociology* 66 (July):1–31.

This study finds that perceptions, attitudes, and values are systematically ordered in modern societies. The proportion of respondents holding a particular view may be distinctive for a given country, but within all modern societies the order or structure of response is the same. This order is specified by occupation, income, and education. The author concludes that the findings support the theory that the standard institutional environment of modern society induces standard patterns of response, despite the countervailing effects of persisting traditional patterns of culture.

Inkeles, Alex, and David H. Smith
1974   *Becoming Modern: Individual Change in Six Developing Countries.* Cambridge, Mass.: Harvard University Press.

This book explores how individual people change their personalities from traditional to modern ones. The basic comparative data for the study was gathered by interviewers from approximately six thousand people in the developing countries of Argentina, Chile, India, Israel, Nigeria, and Bangladesh. Among the variables examined for their impact on individual modernization were education, exposure to an urban environment, and employment in a factory setting.

Jackman, Robert W.
1975   *Politics and Social Equality: A Comparative Analysis.* New York: John Wiley.

The author presents a causal model of cross-national variations in the degree of within-nation social equality as measured by three indicators: one is an index of social insurance program experience, another is an index of social welfare based on health and nutrition indicators, and the third is a measure of inequality in the distribution of income. The study is based on aggregate data from sixty countries drawn primarily from the *World Handbook of Political and Social Indicators.* The study begins with an examination of the effects of level of economic development on various indicators of social equality. These results are combined into a relatively simple path model which is elaborated on in each subsequent chapter; the procedures for an incremental approach to causal model construction are clearly presented.

Myrdal, Gunnar
1968   *Asian Drama: An Inquiry into the Poverty of Nations.* Vols. 1–3. New York: Twentieth Century Fund.

This piece of comparative international research represents a massive effort. South Asian underdeveloped countries were examined over a long period of time through a variety of data collection techniques (which included surveys and official governmental statistics). The broad range of topics covered include political problems, such as how to deal with independence; economic dilemmas, such as how to rationally plan the economy; and trends in population growth and composition.

Williamson, John B.
1970 "Subjective efficacy and ideal family size as predictors of favorability toward birth control." *Demography* 7 (August):329–339.

The study is based on samples of male factory workers in five developing nations. The focus of the study is on the question of whether subjective efficacy and ideal family size function more as independent determinants or more as intervening variables. Overall these psychological variables function more as independent determinants than as intervening variables, but in some samples these two functions are equally important.

REFERENCES

Adelman, Irma, and Cynthia Taft Morris
1967 *Society Politics and Economic Development.* Baltimore: Johns Hopkins Press.
1973 *Economic Growth and Social Equity in Developing Countries.* Stanford: Stanford University Press.

Asch, Solomon
1952 *Social Psychology.* Englewood Cliffs, N.J.: Prentice-Hall.

Blackwood, B.
1935 *Both Sides of Buka Passage.* Oxford: Clarendon Press.

Hibbs, Douglas A., Jr.
1973 *Mass Political Violence: A Cross-National Causal Analysis.* New York: John Wiley.

Inkeles, Alex, and David H. Smith
1974 *Becoming Modern.* Cambridge, Mass.: Harvard University Press.

Jackman, Robert W.
1975 *Politics and Social Equality: A Comparative Analysis.* New York: John Wiley.

Kelman, Herbert C.
1968 *A Time to Speak: On Human Values and Social Research.* San Francisco: Jossey-Bass.

Lewis, Oscar
1951 *Life in a Mexican Village.* Urbana: University of Illinois Press.

Lipset, Seymour M., et al.
1954   "The psychology of voting: an analysis of political behavior." In *Handbook of Social Psychology*, ed. Gardner Lindzey. Reading, Mass.: Addison-Wesley.

Malinowski, Bronislaw
1927   *The Father in Primitive Psychology.* New York: Norton.

McClelland, David C.
1961   *The Achieving Society.* New York: Free Press.

Milgram, Stanley
1961   "Nationality and conformity." *Scientific American* 205 (December):45–51.

Mitchell, Robert E.
1968   "Survey materials collected in developing countries: obstacles to comparison." In *Comparative Research Across Cultures and Nations,* ed. Stein Rokkan. The Hague: Mouton.

Murdock, George P.
1937   "Correlations of matrilineal and patrilinear institutions." In *Studies in the Science of Society,* ed. George P. Murdock. New Haven: Yale University Press.

Murdock, George P., et al.
1971   *Outline of Cultural Materials.* 4th rev. ed. New Haven: Human Relations Area Files.

Nadel, Siegfried F.
1952   "Witchcraft in four African societies." *American Anthropologist* 54 (January):18–29.

Piven, Frances Fox, and Richard A. Cloward
1971   *Regulating the Poor.* New York: Random House (Vintage).

Redfield, Robert
1930   *Tepoztlan: A Mexican Village.* Chicago: University of Chicago Press.

Sears, Robert R., and George W. Wise
1950   "Relation of cup feeding in infancy to thumbsucking and the oral drive." *American Journal of Orthopsychiatry* 20 (January):123–138.

Taylor, Charles L., and Michael C. Hudson
1972   *World Handbook of Political and Social Indicators.* New Haven: Yale University Press.

Warwick, Donald P., and Samuel Osherson, eds.
1973   *Comparative Research Methods.* Englewood Cliffs, N.J.: Prentice-Hall.

Whiting, John W. M.
1941   *Becoming a Kwoma.* New Haven: Yale University Press.

1968   "Methods and problems in cross-cultural research." In *Handbook of Social Psychology*. 2d ed., ed. Gardner Lindzey and Elliot Aronson. Reading, Mass.: Addison-Wesley.

Whiting, John W. M., and Irvin L. Child
1953   *Child Training and Personality: A Cross-Cultural Study*. New Haven: Yale University Press.

Wilensky, Harold L.
1975   *The Welfare State and Equality*. Berkeley: University of California Press.

Evaluation Research

CHAPTER FOURTEEN

A group of citizens, The Committee on Civil Rights in East Manhattan, decided to launch a program to investigate, and then to reduce, discrimination against blacks in restaurants surrounding the United Nations building. To arrive at a baseline measure of the amount of discrimination, C.C.R.E.M. sent survey teams of blacks and whites into the same sample of restaurants. After leaving the restaurants, members of each team answered questionnaires designed to evaluate differences in the treatment they had received. As a result of this evaluation of the amount of discrimination, C.C.R.E.M. had facts that showed that forty percent of the black teams had indeed experienced treatment inferior to that of their white counterparts (Selltiz, 1955).

The next step taken by C.C.R.E.M. was to design an action program to address the problem of how to reduce discrimination. The program agreed upon involved a two-part approach to solving the problem: (1) contacting people who ran the restaurants to get pledges of equal treatment; (2) notifying the news media about the questionnaire findings of forty percent discrimination and about the restaurants' subsequent pledges of equal treatment.

After implementing its action program, C.C.R.E.M. wanted to know how effective it was in solving the problem. To gain this knowledge it reevaluated the previously sampled restaurants by again having teams visit them and fill out questionnaires that measured discriminatory treatment. This second set of questionnaires revealed that in only sixteen percent of the restaurants was the black team given treatment clearly inferior to that of the white team. Comparing the amount of discrimination found in the survey conducted before the program (42 percent) with that found afterwards (16 percent), the Committee concluded that its program was of value in creating change toward the equal treatment of blacks.

The C.C.R.E.M. experience is of interest to us because it contains three elements which, when occurring together, define a problem-solving effort as evaluation research. The first element necessary for our definition is that the effort occur in a *real world setting*. In accordance with this requisite, C.C.R.E.M. conducted its project in restaurants surrounding the United Nations building. In evaluation research the focus is on practical applied problems which may or may not be relevant to the more general theoretical issues which often concern academic social researchers.

The second element of importance is that evaluation research involves a *program design aimed at improving the life situation* of a specified group of people. Again, the C.C.R.E.M. project, with its program of contacts with restaurants and the news media, was set up to effect reduced discrimination toward blacks, a goal seen as an improvement in the life situation of blacks.

Finally, the third element necessary for our definition is that provisions be made for an *evaluation* of the program's success. In the instance of C.C.R.E.M., the evaluation was a comparison of the amount of discrimination before its program with the amount occurring afterward. Because discrimination was reduced, the Committee evaluated its program as a success.

Putting the preceding three elements together, we have a conceptual definition of evaluation research. *Evaluation research is an investigation conducted in a real world setting to evaluate whether a program designed to improve the life of a specific group of people has in fact achieved this goal.* It assesses a program's effectiveness by comparing its goals with its actual accomplishments. The findings of this comparison are then used to make a decision about the value of the program, and perhaps how to change it in the future.

Evaluation research done by social scientists has the aim of establishing how successful a particular program is in achieving its goal of improving the condition of some group of people. Both the public and private sectors of American society have attempted to eliminate some negative condition or create some positive condition which affects the lives of people by instituting various programs. The federal government, for example, initiated a wide variety of programs during the 1960s which had the goal of eventually eliminating poverty. Similar examples can be cited in the areas of corrections, mental health, and population control. The basic purpose of evaluation research is to answer the question of whether or not such improvement-oriented programs achieve what they set out to achieve. The results of evaluation research can be used in decision making that affects social policy: Which programs should be changed and in what way? Which programs should be eliminated?

We might well ask how evaluation research differs, if at all, from nonevaluation research. One difference between the two relates to an accusation sometimes made against one or another social research project — that it seems to have little relevance to the "real" social world. In other words, some social research is of little interest except to other social scientists. Since evaluation research is used for decision making about programs designed to deal with social problems or about the delivery of various social services, it is less susceptible to this criticism. The more abstract social research that is carried out in the halls of academe certainly has a role to play in the ultimate resolution of societal problems; but our point here is that evaluation research can be thought of as applied research that more immediately and concretely seeks such solutions.

A point in common for both evaluation and nonevaluation research is that the same basic steps of the research process must be followed. It should be emphasized, however, that there are special problems associated with the attempt to do rigorous research in the evaluation context. There may be resistance to evaluation research by the administrators of programs who fear that negative findings might terminate their programs. Or there may be difficulty in getting a representative sample if those not sampled are thereby deprived of gaining something positive from the program. We shall consider these issues in some depth, but it is best to begin by considering the overall research process involved in an evaluation study.

EVALUATION RESEARCH PROCESS

In the discussion which follows we shall examine a general outline of how evaluation research is done. In actual practice there are usually some deviations from the process as described here. It would be wisest to think of the following as a checklist of important points to consider rather than as a fixed list to be replicated at all costs. The first stage in the process is the formulation of the problem, which includes identifying it and focusing in on it. The formulation stage also includes the designation of a program which has the purpose of either ameliorating or eliminating the selected problem. A second broad research phase in the evaluation process is the development of a research design for determining the effectiveness of the program. The final stage involves the implementation of the research design and the preparation of research results for decision making.

Formulation of the Problem

Social researchers who do evaluation research are usually in the position of being hired by an organization (examples are community groups, private and public service agencies, state and federal governments). The organization is either sponsoring or contemplating the sponsorship of a program designed to deal with some problem, and usually the problem has already been defined before the researcher arrives on the scene. The organization may have decided to do something about the problem of unequal education or the problem of juvenile delinquency. The fact that the general problem is already chosen by the organization is to be expected. What would be optimal, however, is for the concerned organization to contact the evaluation researchers before the general problem is narrowed down, the goals of the program are established, and the program is specified. Many times this is not the case, and the organization does not contact the researchers until after its program has been put into operation. This means that the researchers must do catch-up research, in the sense that they have to reconstruct what the objectives of the program are. Sometimes this leads to a situation where the evaluation researcher has to make an educated guess at what decision makers *really* want to find out from evaluation research.

Let us assume that the ideal situation exists: the evaluation researcher is consulted from the inception of the evaluation research process. The first aim should be to narrow down the general problem of interest in such a way that a program can be planned. If the general problem of interest is discrimination against women, the researcher must decide what kind of discrimination to focus on — discrimination in jobs? discrimination in education? Suppose that discrimination in jobs is settled on. Once again, what kind of job discrimination — discrimination in employment? discrimination in job promotion? It is through such questioning that a concrete and manageable problem area is eventually pinned down.

Another aspect of the narrowing down process is that a careful inquiry should be made about the perceived cause of the problem which is eventually to be dealt with by the program of the organization. Assume that a large corporation has decided it wants to devise a program to deal with discrimination against women in job promotions. Does the organization see the problem as caused by prejudiced behavior on the part of male administrators in the business world or, possibly, by undesirable behavior on the part of employed women? It is precisely this kind of focusing which is needed at the outset of the research in order for the researcher to be able to decide whether or not the research is desirable from a personal and ethical point of view. If the answer is that the problem is being articulated in an unethical (e.g., racist or sexist) manner, the researcher can decide to discontinue work with the organization that is sponsoring the research. In the present example, let us presume that the organization and the evaluation researcher decide to pursue the problem of discrimination against women in job promotions in terms of the prejudiced behavior of businessmen.

Once the general problem area is narrowed down in the above manner, the researchers can specify a program and clarify its purposes. There are usually many different kinds of programs they could establish to attain a goal. One possibility in the case we have discussed might be a series of consciousness-raising seminars aimed at diminishing the prejudiced behavior of businessmen in the area of job promotions for women. It is, of course, important to spell out the purposes of any program in detail. Suchman (1967:39–41) provides a guideline of questions which should be considered:

1. *What* is the nature of the content of the objective? Are we interested in changing knowledge, attitudes, or behavior? Are we concerned with producing exposure, awareness, interest, or action?
2. *Who* is the target of the program? At which groups in the population is the program aimed?
3. *When* is the desired change to take place? Are we seeking an immediate effect or are we gradually building toward some postponed effect?
4. Are the objectives *unitary* or *multiple*? Is the program aimed at a single change or at a series of changes?

How would these considerations shape the contemplated program of consciousness-raising seminars mentioned in the preceding paragraph?

1. The nature of the objective is to diminish the prejudiced behavior of businessmen in the area of job promotions for women. Any seminar program would most likely seek to inform businessmen of certain facts about the condition of contemporary women in America and the ways in which institutional sexism operates. This would hopefully lead to a reduction of prejudiced attitudes about women who work. The final goal would be for the businessmen to change in attitudes and to reduce prejudiced behavior with respect to job promotions for women.

2. The target of the program would be male administrators in the business world who make decisions about job promotions for women. But which ones? The decision might ultimately be reached to concentrate on one or two large branches of the corporation sponsoring the research.

3. The question of timing of the changes might be handled by agreeing that the desired timing of the change is both for the short term and for the long run. For example, some significantly different behavior in the area of job promotions might be expected for businessmen who had been exposed to consciousness-raising seminars over a period of six

months to a year. More dramatic changes would probably be expected over a longer period of time.

4. The changes created by any program are rarely unitary. We have already agreed that any program would most likely have the purpose of changing knowledge, attitudes, and behavior about job discrimination toward women. It is also likely that such a program would not be solely concerned with changes in the area of job promotions. There would also be interest in diminishing discriminatory behavior toward women in the day-to-day work process. Furthermore, it should be pointed out that thought should be given to both intended and unintended objectives of any program.

If the questions about the purposes and goals of a program are answered in these ways, the problem still remains of clearly specifying a program. There are many possible programs. One might be a program consisting of a series of seminars on discrimination against women in the major institutional sectors of American life (education, religion, the family system, the economic structure, and the political institution). A teaching team comprising a psychologist, a sociologist, an American historian, and an economist who have special knowledge in the area of women's studies could be contracted to organize and lead the seminars. There would be many practical issues to work out if such a program were implemented. For example, where would the businessmen be selected from for the program? How would their cooperation be gained? One possibility might be to approach business enterprises directly and seek their co-sponsorship of the seminars.

It should be clear that the formulation of the problem is a critical phase in the evaluation research process. Many commentators on evaluation research have noted that when researchers are not careful at this initial stage, they have planned some social programs with unclear goals, a failing that consequently makes evaluation research almost impossible to carry out.

Research Design

Assuming that the issues involved in the formulation of the problem are handled well, the task of the evaluation researcher will be to develop a research design that tests the effectiveness of the specified program. The research design is essentially the plan of attack or game plan which the researcher spells out in detail before the research commences. The basic questions of research design are in most respects the same for both evaluation and nonevaluation research. What we shall consider here is the particular relevance of some of these broad issues for evaluation research.

There are many possible overall research approaches that we can employ for evaluating the effectiveness of a program. The ideal approach would generally be a controlled experiment. However, before examining this approach, we should set the stage by considering other possible approaches whose deficiencies the controlled experiment corrects.

One possible approach is to study a group of people from the target population after it has been exposed to a program that had been developed to cause change. This approach is called the *one-shot study*. In the hypothetical example discussed previously, a group of businessmen who attended the seminars on the condition of women in America would be studied to see if in fact their knowledge, attitudes, and behavior toward women had changed in a nondiscriminatory direction. There are some obvious difficulties with this approach. One problem is that there is no baseline measurement; that is, there is no measurement of the knowledge, attitudes, and behavior of the businessmen toward women before their exposure to the seminars. What are the findings of such a study to be compared with? One way out of this dilemma is to ask the participants of programs, after the fact, about their prior knowledge, attitudes, and behavior. One of the many potential sources of error here is the inaccuracy generated by fallibilities of human memory.

Another possible approach is to study a group of people both before and after exposure to a particular program. This circumvents the difficulty just mentioned with respect to the one-shot study. *Before-and-after studies,* however, suffer from another potential problem. Suppose that positive findings (change in the direction that the program is aiming) emerge from such a study. These findings could be explained by things other than the experience of participating in a given program. Returning to our hypothetical example, a group of businessmen could show changes in the direction of nondiscrimination toward women. We could ask whether these findings can be explained by things other than their experience in the seminars. Other changes could have been occurring in their lives which produced the same effect of not being as prejudiced and discriminatory toward women. Some for example, may have had their consciousnesses raised through people they had met who were strong feminists. What is needed to avoid this difficulty is some means of taking such "other changes" into account. (It should be apparent that the one-shot study also suffers from this deficiency.) The *controlled experiment* provides such a check and is, therefore, considered to be the ideal research approach for evaluation research.

There are many different kinds of controlled experiments. The simplest kind for evaluation research is set up in the following way. We select a number of people from the target population (when possible, we would want to use probability sampling). Our goal is to create two groups as nearly alike as possible. The usual way to do this is through the random assignment of one half of the selected people to one group and the other half to the second group (the technical term for this process is *randomization*). The key aspect to experimentation is that one

TABLE 14.1 A Comparison in Research Design for the One-Shot Study, the Before-and-After Study, and the Controlled Experiment

	A Before Measurement	Exposure to Program	An After Measurement
The One-Shot Study			
Experimental Group	No	Yes	Yes
Control Group	No	No	No
The Before-and-After Study			
Experimental Group	Yes	Yes	Yes
Control Group	No	No	No
The Controlled Experiment			
Experimental Group	Yes	Yes	Yes
Control Group	Yes	No	Yes

group, the experimental group, participates in the program under consideration while the second group, the control group, does not.[1]

Measurements of the desired goals and outcomes of the program are made both before and after the program is conducted to see if the program produces its desired changes. This is done for both the experimental group and the control group. The measurements should show no difference between the two groups before the program commences. If, however, the program is effective, the "after" measurements should show that the experimental group has experienced a change in the desired direction which is significantly greater than any change registered for the control group. The "after" measurement for the control group is the means by which we take into account any of the "other changes" related to the desired outcome of the program which may be occurring for both the experimental and control groups. If we subtract the change experienced by the control group from the change evidenced in the experimental group, the result is a measure of the program's impact. In Table 14.1 a comparison is made of the one-shot study, the before-and-after study, and the controlled experiment.

It should be clear at this point that an experiment is clearly superior to either a one-shot study or a before-and-after study. The control

---

[1] For a more detailed discussion of experimental designs, see Chapter 9. "Experimental Research." In that chapter we describe the *true experiment* in which subjects are randomly assigned to either the control or the experimental group. We also discuss the *quasi experiment* in which a control group is used, but without random assignment of subjects. Both the true experiment and the quasi experiment are forms of what we refer to in this chapter as the *controlled experiment*.

group in an experiment eliminates the possible interpretation that "other changes" are not accounted for in the one-shot and before-and-after approaches. The "before" measurement in an experiment provides the baseline that is lacking in the one-shot study. With all these advantages, why is it that experiments are used less frequently in evaluation research than either of the other two research approaches? The answer is that there are a number of problems involved in experimental evaluation research.

A general source of resistance to using the controlled experiment in evaluation research is that the research on the effectiveness of a particular program is often considered to be secondary to the program itself; the prime concern of the organization sponsoring the program and the administrators implementing it is the successful operation of the program itself, not the evaluation research. This means that the more ideal conditions under which an experiment can be conducted in a laboratory usually cannot be duplicated in the process of carrying out a program. For example, most administrators of social programs are reluctant to allow a research approach which makes it possible for *any* members of the target population to be excluded from the services of the program. But the random assignment of people from the target population to experimental and control groups requires this exclusion.

One possible solution to this dilemma is to compare groups of persons who have self-selected themselves into one group which participates in a social program voluntarily and another group of those who have decided not to participate. If the two groups are similar in important background variables, and if differences emerge between them after the program is completed, there is some justification in attributing the differences to the impact of the program. Even if both these conditions are satisfied, there is still the gnawing question of whether or not the selectivity involved has operated in such a way as to make the two groups actually nonequivalent. However, the utilization of somewhat nonequivalent groups is better than having no comparison group at all.

Another possible solution to this dilemma is to shift the emphasis from testing the effectiveness of one program to examining the effectiveness of alternative programs. What is involved here is a variation of the simple controlled experiment wherein different groups are exposed to different programs. The issue of control groups not having the opportunity to share in the benefits of a program disappears, as should some of the resistance of program administrators. An example of this solution to our hypothetical research situation might be to compare the relative merits of three types of consciousness-raising seminars. Note that a pure control group (participating in no program) is not included in this research approach. If a pure control group is added to the groups which are exposed to different programs, some of the resistance to "experimentation" will reappear.

A third potential solution to the difficulties involved in employing the controlled experiment in evaluation research is the most obvious: randomly assign members of the target population to the experimental and control groups in such a way that it will not meet with resistance. If, for example, there are not enough funds to allow all interested people in the target population to participate in a program, a random basis for selection may be possible. The sponsoring organization may be promised that persons who are not selected initially may be able to participate in a program at a later time. In the meantime, these persons can function as a control group for the people who are selected first. It should be apparent that such situations do not always occur. The evaluation researcher is usually forced to accept some form of compromise with the desired goal of a controlled experiment.

While the controlled experiment is the ideal model for evaluation research, other research approaches can be quite appropriate, depending on the goals of the particular evaluation endeavor. Rossi (1972), for example, ranks the possible evaluation research approaches from soft to hard in the following way: program administrators' narrative reports concerning the program (least desired); program audits based on the qualitative judgments of outside observers; correlational designs in which statistical controls are used; quasi experiments with impure control groups; and controlled experiments (most desired). Rossi argues that the softer research approaches can be validly used to see if a particular program creates a *large* impact. If softer approaches do not reveal such an impact, it is unlikely that a harder approach will; but if significant results do show up in research using the softer approaches, it is appropriate to pursue evaluation by a harder approach. It is here that the closest approximation to the controlled experiment should be made.

Plans for Data Collection, Sampling, and Measurement

Aside from the question of general research approach, the research design or plan of attack for evaluation research includes plans for data collection, sampling, and measurement.

The main point to be made about data collection sources for evaluation research is that there is a very wide range from which to choose. The following is one list that Weiss (1972:53) has proposed:

> ... Interviews, questionnaires, observation, ratings (by peers, staff, experts), psychometric tests (of attitudes, values, personality, preferences, norms, beliefs), institutional records, government statistics, tests (of information, interpretation, skills, application of knowledge), projective tests, situational tests (presenting the respondent with simulated life situations), diary records, physical evidence, clinical examinations, financial records, and documents (minutes of board meetings, newspaper accounts of policy actions, transcripts of trials).

Some of these sources overlap with one another. Nevertheless, this list presents the evaluation researcher with many alternatives. The selection of a combination of data sources may be appropriate for a given evaluation study. There is usually a connection between the general research approach and the data source. If one wishes to approximate a controlled experiment, for example, the usual data sources are observation, interviews, and questionnaires.

We have already briefly considered some sampling plans for evaluation research. Probability sampling plans are generally preferred for selecting people from the target population, but they are often not possible in evaluation research. It is more likely that a sample will be composed of self-selected volunteers. In such cases, allowances and corrections must be made for the possible bias in the sample.

Some other difficulties frequently connected with samples in evaluation research are illustrated by the income maintenance experiment sponsored by OEO, the federal Office of Economic Opportunity (Kershaw, 1972). The purpose of this study was to examine what effects an income subsidy would have on the attitudes and behavior of low-income families. One problem encountered in the research was the pressure of local community groups on the sample selection process. When the experimental group to be studied is going to receive something beneficial, such as an income subsidy, the pressure on sample selection is self-explanatory. One way for the evaluation researcher to deal with this problem is to stress the scientific demands of the evaluation research process. Another potential difficulty is the attrition of members from the groups being studied; this is a problem because it can result in the loss of representativeness of the groups under study. It can be very hard to keep persons in the control group interested in an experiment that runs several months or years, as was the case with the income maintenance experiment.

The basic object of measurement in evaluation (as in nonevaluation) research is to develop measures of variables which validly and reliably reflect what we are trying to measure. It is very important for a program to have clear and explicitly specified goals if it is to permit valid and reliable measurement. Furthermore, if this condition is not satisfied, critics can argue that it was not the program itself that succeeded (or failed) but rather the invalid measurement that produced the results.

Implementation of Research Design

So far we have discussed the way in which the evaluation research process *should* move through the stages of problem formulation and construction of a research design. Suffice it to say that the realities of the evaluation research setting often make it difficult to realize those ideals.

We have seen that the effectiveness of a program is often considered by administrators and program personnel to be secondary to the implementation of the program. There are obvious conflicts between the two goals. One example of such a conflict is what has been referred to as the "shifting program," a term that describes a program that is not executed in a perfectly predictable manner. As a program is being carried out, the strategies for dealing with the problem area may change as a result of the decisions of program administrators. Or program personnel may change through the resignation of staff members. Or program participants may drop out during the program; and other participants may join the program while it is in progress. How is the evaluation researcher supposed to deal with such difficulties and still adequately evaluate how successful a program is in attaining its objectives? Some concrete suggestions for dealing with these issues are (Weiss, 1972:98):

1. Take frequent periodic measures of program effect (for example, monthly assessments in programs of education, training, therapy), rather than limiting collection of outcome data to one point in time.
2. Encourage a clear transition from one program approach to another. If changes are going to be made, try to see that A is done for a set period, then B, then C.
3. Clarify the assumptions and procedures of each phase and classify them systematically.
4. Keep careful records of the persons who participated in each phase. Rather than lumping all participants together, analyze outcomes in terms of the phase(s) of the program in which each person participated.

Another problem in the stage of executing an evaluation research design is that researchers and program personnel are not in a naturally cooperative situation. One area of difference between the two relates to the scientific versus practical objectives of an evaluation study. The researcher is at least somewhat concerned with the relationship of the study's findings to the growth of knowledge in a particular academic discipline (Will this research contribute to the long-run development of understanding in this field?). Program personnel, on the other hand, have a more nuts-and-bolts attitude toward the program. In a similar vein, there are personality differences between the two. The researcher is likely to be detached and analytical — a person who is interested in ideas and abstractions. Program personnel may be more sensitive to the issue of servicing people's needs right now (Rodman and Kolodny, 1965). Closely associated with these personality differences are the differences in the respective roles. Program personnel are usually committed to the program strategies currently in use while the researcher is in the position of asking how effective these strategies are. Indeed, evaluation researchers are probably always viewed as suspicious, often as a threat. The program personnel see the researcher as taking time and money from the program while offering a possibly unfavorable report in return. Furthermore, the program personnel may perceive the researcher as judging their work, competence, and personalities.

What solutions are there to these problems? One solution is to involve the program personnel in the evaluation research process. This will enable them to better understand the nature of the research and to reduce their uneasiness about why so many questions must be asked. A further benefit of personnel involvement should be that they become more committed to the research if they contribute to its implementation. A different, and more traditional, solution to relational problems between the evaluation researcher and program personnel is to clarify role definitions and lines of authority. This solution entails spelling out the role expectations of both prior to the beginning of the program so that both know who makes which decisions and what channels of appeal exist.

One way of dealing with the fears and suspicions of program personnel is to design an evaluation in which the focus is on providing feedback as the program progresses. Here the focus is on providing suggestions for improvement along the way rather than on one final pro or con judgment. One advantage of such a focus is that program personnel can see the benefits to the program and get some evidence that the research is of use along the way. That is, the evaluator is dealing with a series of separate short-term programs rather than one longer term program. Another advantage is that the results are more likely to be put to use. A disadvantage is that such a process may make an overall pro or con judgment all but impossible because there have been so many changes in the program along the way.

There are many other problems in the stage of executing an evaluation research design. One obvious difficulty is deciding who should know about the program and about the research in the community where they are being conducted. It is important to get community leaders and experts on one's side in order to initiate and successfully carry out evaluation research. Of course, one cannot always predict what obstacles will lie in the path of implementing a research design. One such dilemma was experienced in the income maintenance study we were looking at previously when the U.S. Senate made a request for information from the study while the research was still going on (Kershaw, 1972). Obviously, the public release of information regarding a study before it is over can have the effect of biasing results or of bringing the study to a premature conclusion.

Utilization of Results for Decision Making

Ideally, the results of evaluating research are used in the process of decision making regarding social policy. Such research is of potential help in determining how effective a proposed program is. However, there are some crucial obstacles to the fulfillment of this goal. One can be a negative reaction to evaluation research on the part of the organization responsible for the program under consideration. The negative reaction could take the form of either resistance to negative findings or the illegitimate usage of evaluation research. Another obstacle to the proper utilization of evaluation research results is that a researcher may fail to see his or her responsibility for encouraging decision makers to employ the results of research as a basis for policy formation.

In regard to the illegitimate usage of evaluation research, Suchman (1967:143) points out that an organization which is responsible for a particular social program can attempt to use evaluation research in the following ways:

1. *Eye-wash:* an attempt to justify a weak or bad program by deliberately selecting only those aspects that "look good." The objective of the evaluation is limited to those parts of the program evaluation that appear successful.
2. *White-wash:* an attempt to cover up program failure or errors by avoiding any objective appraisal. A favorite device here is to solicit "testimonials" which divert attention from the failure.
3. *Posture:* an attempt to use evaluation as a "gesture" of objectivity and to assume the pose of "scientific" research. This "looks good" to the public and is a sign of "professional" status.
4. *Postponement:* an attempt to delay needed action by pretending to seek the "facts." Evaluative research takes time and, hopefully, the storm will blow over by the time the study is completed.

What is common to all these techniques is the effort by an organization to manipulate evaluation research for its own vested interests. Evaluation researchers must always be on their guard against the possibility of being coopted as a "servant of power." They must be concerned about the possibility of cooptation from their first contact with a particular evaluation research situation until the entire research process is completed. If it appears that any of the manipulative possibilities suggested above are being planned or executed, the researcher should attempt to correct the situation or disassociate himself from the specific research enterprise.

Another possible negative reaction to the results of evaluation research is that the organization whose social program has been found lacking can disregard negative findings. Let us consider the following list of rationalizations of negative findings used by professionals in the field of corrections (Ward and Kassebaum, 1972:302):

The therapeutic relationships examined or the impact of the program is "too subtle to measure with statistics."

"The presence of outsiders disturbs the normal conduct of the program or the group or the session."

"Even though they may come back to prison, they are better or happier or more emotionally stable people for having participated in the program."

"The effects of the program can only be measured in the long run, not just during the first six months or year after release."

"The program or the technique is OK but it is not designed for this particular individual."

"The reason that the program failed is that it wasn't extensive enough or long enough or applied by the right people."

"The program is worth it if it saved one man."

It is probably sensible to expect such rationalizations from people and organizations whose programs are subjected to criticism as a result of evaluation research. One commonly offered solution to this problem is for evaluation researchers to shift their attention away from determining whether or not a specific social program should be totally accepted or totally rejected. Rather, evaluation research is much more likely to be well received and face less resistance if its concern is to examine the relative merits of different programs sponsored by the same organization or if its emphasis is to examine possible modifications in any given program. An example of research that conforms to these expectations is the evaluation done on the Sesame Street television show for children. Different presentations of the program were shown to a sample of children; the program was changed on the basis of the children's reactions to the various presentations (McDill, McDill, and Sprehe, 1972).

Another obstacle to the proper utilization in decision making of results from evaluation research is the role perception of the evaluation researcher. Most researchers are primarily oriented to the academic community for acceptance of their efforts. Furthermore, rewards are more frequently reaped via publication than through taking extra time to carefully interpret the research results for decision makers. In addition, evaluation researchers are often encouraged by those who hire them to say nothing or to stay uninvolved in the utilization of results.

A conservative interpretation of the canon of objectivity can lead one to the position that researchers should not become involved in advocating any particular use of their research findings. This interpretation is often employed. The authors take the position that the researcher should take an active role in pressing for the constructive application of research findings after the research is completed.

CONCLUSION

Evaluation research tries to establish how successful a program of action is in achieving its goal of dealing with a particular program. Such research is used for decision making about programs in a wide variety of areas: corrections, mental health, population control, and juvenile delinquency, to name only a few.

In the stage of formulating the problem and articulating a program to deal with that problem, the evaluation researcher should ideally be included from the very outset. But this is typically not the case. Two other points about problem formulation can be made: (1) it is crucial to narrow down the problem of interest to a fairly specific level and (2) it is important to carry out a detailed inquiry about the perceived causes of the problem. Both points are essential if we are to develop a specific program which addresses itself properly to the problem at hand. Such inquiry is important if we are to spell out clearly the objectives and target of a program. If we deal well with these issues, we can specify an effective program much more easily.

The next stage in the research process is for the evaluation researcher to form a research design that can determine the effectiveness of the program. A basic issue here is the general research approach to be used. The ideal model is the controlled experiment; however, approximations to this approach (the one-shot, the before-and-after approaches) are more frequently used because of the difficulty in trying to implement a controlled experiment in the evaluation research context. One problem with the controlled experiment is that administrators of programs are understandably reluctant to allow a research approach that automatically deprives some members of the target population from gaining the benefits and services of a program. One way to deal with this objection is to experiment with different programs. It is also important to keep in mind that controlled experiments are not always necessary for good evaluation research.

The third stage in the evaluation research process is the implementation of the research design. A general problem here is that program personnel often consider the evaluation research secondary to the successful operation of the program itself, an attitude that can lead to conflict between the evaluation researcher and the program personnel. One possible example of this conflict is the "shifting program," in which different strategies for dealing with the problem area may be developed as the program is in operation. The evaluation researcher must take precautions to avoid this problem. Another conflict area is the intrinsic difference in role between the evaluation researcher and program personnel, which sometimes results in the program personnel perceiving the evaluation researcher as a threat. One way of alleviating this situation is to involve program personnel in the research process.

The final stage of the evaluation research process is the utilization of research results for decision making. A potential problem at this stage is that organizations whose programs are evaluated have a tendency to reject negative conclusions drawn from research. A solution to this possibility is to frame evaluation research in a less threatening way.

One approach is to focus on a comparison of the relative merits of several different programs sponsored by the same organization. Another is to design the evaluation in such a way that the focus is on providing continuous feedback that can be used to improve the long-run success of the program. Here the focus is on making suggestions for improving the program rather than on making a final overall assessment of the program's impact. Researchers should try to disassociate themselves from attempts at coopted research (for example, eye-wash or whitewash research). Furthermore, researchers should take an active role in pressing for the constructive usage of findings from evaluation research. The possible uses of research findings should be communicated to those who are in a position to implement decisions. There is evidence that an increasing number of evaluation researchers are redefining their role in this way.

There are many difficulties involved in trying to carry out rigorous evaluation research. Few evaluation studies actually meet the ideal guidelines set up for them. A number of reasons can be cited as causes of this situation: inadequate funding, lack of cooperation from program personnel during the implementation of research, and so on. Another possible reason is the relatively low status assigned to applied research by the academic profession. The authors feel that a shift from this bias is in order. Evaluation research should be perceived as an important avenue for making the knowledge of the social sciences relevant to the solution of societal problems; and social scientists should be encouraged to devote more attention to it.

EXERCISES

1. By yourself or with another student, choose a group known to be subject to discrimination. Design a project which will both reduce the discrimination and measure its reduction. As part of your design, set up control and experimental groups, and tell how you would actually select people to be in those groups. Also, elaborate on how the design you have chosen would control for outside events which you feel could be confused with the real results. Claire Selltiz's article, "The Use of Survey Methods in a Citizens' Campaign Against Discrimination," should prove useful for this project.

2. James Coleman's controversial study, *The Equality of Educational Opportunity*, indicated that racial and ethnic minorities' average achievement scores were significantly lower than those of whites. It further stated that achievement scores were directly influenced by the students' social and cultural background. Part of the definition of evaluation research, discussed in an earlier part of this chapter, indicated that it involves a program designed to improve the lot of people. Can you imagine how Coleman's evaluation research findings could be

used in a harmful way? Who is responsible for preventing its misuse? How could its misuse be prevented?

3. Suppose you were given the assignment of helping your professor study the effects of desegregated schooling on student achievement. During the process of the study, certain social events occurred, some students dropped out of school, you were unable to randomly select those students to be studied, and the students who were studied were aware they were being studied. Taking this tough but realistic situation as a given, how would you advise your professor about the way to establish that the extraneous variables mentioned above did not influence your measurement of students' achievement? What steps may be taken, if any, to ensure that the achievement that did occur would be generalizable to similar attempts at desegregation? To get ideas as to how to answer this question, see Campbell and Stanley's *Experimental and Quasi-Experimental Designs for Research* (see Suggested Readings for full information on this work).

4. Consider an established program located in your college or residential community which has the goal of improving the human condition in some way. Assess the effectiveness of the program by any means of your own choosing as long as it takes less than two hours to collect the data.

5. After exercise number four is completed, each student in the class should be asked to contact one other student in the class. If it is possible, this should be done in a random fashion. Once the identities of the student pairs (dyads) are established, the students should inform one another of the programs which they evaluated for exercise number four. Discussion should cease at this point. Then, each student should do exercise number four for the program chosen by the other student in the dyad. When this is accomplished, the two students should compare their evaluation research experiences.

6. Work with another student on this question. Consider various problems currently of significance in the American society. Settle on one problem you both will work on independently. Each should develop a program addressed to the problem. Discuss the advantages and disadvantages of the programs which the two of you have arrived at.

7. You and your partner from question number six are now faced with the problem of making research design decisions about how you would evaluate your programs. Make these decisions. Be sure to discuss whether or not the option of using a research approach that compares the effectiveness of your two programs makes the most sense.

8. Assume that you were hired to evaluate the programs on which you collected data for questions four and five. Do you see any possibility of your findings being manipulated by the organization responsible for the program under consideration? How would you try to combat the possible negative utilization of your findings?

9. Evaluation research has the aim of establishing how successful a particular program is in achieving its goals. Is it conceivable that evaluation research can be used in harmful ways? What strategies can prevent such misuse?

SUGGESTED READINGS

Readings about the Method

Campbell, Donald, and Julian C. Stanley
1963 *Experimental and Quasi-Experimental Designs for Research.* Chicago: Rand McNally.

> This book presents one of the best coverages of experimental designs available. Five types of research approaches are examined in detail: pre-experimental designs, true experimental designs, quasi-experimental designs, correlational designs, and ex post facto designs. The major emphasis is placed on the true experimental designs. This work is obviously somewhat complex but well worth the time and effort required.

Moursund, Janet
1973 *Evaluation: An Introduction to Research Design.* Monterey, Calif.: Brooks/Cole.

> This is a good general introduction to the field of evaluation research for the beginning student in research methods. The major attention is given to questions regarding the research design to be selected for evaluation research. What type of research design should be employed? What kinds of data should be collected? How should the data be analyzed? Interesting sections also appear on how a research project should be directed and on the function of the computer in research.

Rossi, Peter, and Walter Williams, eds.
1972 *Evaluating Social Programs.* New York: Seminar Press.

> This book contains excellent discussions of evaluation research that has been carried out on social programs in the areas of compensatory education, manpower training, and income maintenance. Rossi, Williams, and others also devote their attention to theoretical discussions of the many problems involved in carrying out effective evaluation research. Some of these discussions are quite technical. A final section of the book contains discussions of the role of the university and the federal government in supplying and demanding evaluation research.

Suchman, Edward
1967 *Evaluative Research.* New York: Russell Sage.

> A very sound and sophisticated treatment of all the key methodological issues in evaluation research is presented in this now-classic book. One indication of its prestige is the extent to which the book is referred to by other discussions of evaluation research. The presentation by Suchman tends to be somewhat formal and abstract but it is well worth the needed

attention by those who are interested in evaluation research. The book is particularly good on the possible types of research designs for evaluation research and on the difficulties that can emerge in the relationships between researchers and those whose programs are evaluated.

Weiss, Carol
1972   *Evaluation Research.* Englewood Cliffs, N.J.: Prentice-Hall.

This is a good, sophisticated introduction to evaluation research which does not succumb to the temptation of using excessively technical jargon. The heart of the text is concerned with how one would design a piece of evaluation research. All the crucial design issues are handled well. Also, the beginning and end of this text have good, thoughtful discussions of the ethical issues involved in evaluation research.

Weiss, Carol, ed.
1972   *Evaluating Action Programs: Readings in Social Action and Education.* Boston: Allyn & Bacon.

This is a collection of readings by prominent people in the field of evaluation research. The topics of discussion include: kinds of evaluation research, the issue of experimentation in evaluation research, organizational resistance to evaluation research, and the effectiveness of evaluation research. There is a healthy mixture of theoretical discussion on these issues and actual examples of evaluation research which have been carried out. Weiss provides an excellent bibliography on various issues in evaluation research and good illustrations of evaluation studies.

Readings Illustrating the Method

Deutsch, Morton, and Mary Collins
1951   *Interracial Housing: A Psychological Evaluation of a Social Experiment.* University of Minnesota Press.

This study examines the impact of an integrated, interracial housing project in the New York metropolitan area. In particular, the emphasis is on whether or not the integrated project encourages closer contact and improved relationships between blacks and whites. In order to test this idea, interviews were conducted with members of both the integrated project and another project in the area which had a segregated housing policy.

Goodwin, Leonard
1972   *Do the Poor Want to Work?* Washington, D.C.: The Brookings Institution.

This work represents an extensive exploration and comparison of the attitudes towards work held by welfare families and people who participate in federal work-training programs with the attitudes towards work held by middle-class families. Goodwin finds that there are no differences between the poor and nonpoor with respect to their desire to work and succeed in the world of work. This leads to Goodwin's suggestion that welfare policy should not be articulated with the goal of punishing those on welfare for not working.

Pechman, Joseph, and P. Michael Timpane
1975   *Work Incentives and Income Guarantees.* Washington, D.C.: The Brookings Institution.

This work analyzes the negative income tax experiment that was carried out in New Jersey and Pennsylvania between 1968 and 1972. A close look is given to the impact of income guarantees on the behavior of the people who participated in the program. The results of this research have important implications for potential policy decisions regarding the welfare system in the United States.

Powers, Edwin, and Helen Witmer
1951   *An Experiment in the Prevention of Delinquency: The Cambridge-Somerville Youth Study.* New York: Columbia University Press.

This is a long-term experimental study which had the aim of examining the effect on the prevention of delinquency of a counseling relationship between a social worker and a young predelinquent person. In order to test the effectiveness of "the wise and friendly counsel" of a social worker, two matched groups of young boys from the Cambridge-Somerville (Mass.) area were created. Both groups had an equal number of boys thought to be predelinquent. One group of boys was assigned to a number of social workers. The other group was not assigned to any social workers. After a number of years, the two groups were compared with respect to the development of delinquency.

Rist, Ray
1970   "Student social class and teacher expectations: the self-fulfilling prophecy in ghetto education." *Harvard Educational Review* 40 (August):411–451.

Many studies have shown that minority students achieve less than other students. Rist's research evaluated *how* this phenomenon developed. Rist discovered that teachers grouped students, according to their social class, into groups expected to fail or succeed. By the time the student who was expected to fail reached the higher grades, his academic achievement began to match his various teachers' expectations. On the basis of his evaluation, Rist was able to recommend that systems of education not permit differential treatment of students.

Selltiz, Claire
1955   "The use of survey methods in a citizens' campaign against discrimination." *Human Organization* 14 (fall):19–25.

This article describes the attempt to reduce discriminatory public practices toward blacks through a program sponsored by a citizens' group. The program aimed at eliminating discrimination in restaurants by informing the owners of restaurants about the degree to which discrimination existed in their establishments. The owners were then asked to sign a pledge that they would give equal treatment to blacks. A before-and-after evaluation study was carried out on a number of restaurants by having teams of blacks and whites dine at selected restaurants and record how they were treated.

Vanecko, James
1969　"Community mobilization and institutional change: the influence of the community action program in large cities." *Social Science Quarterly* 50 (December):609–630.

This is an evaluation study of the Community Action Program sponsored by the U.S. Office of Economic Opportunity. Vanecko analyzes data from fifty large U.S. cities which shows that community action agencies which stress the mobilization of the poor and community organization are more effective than agencies geared toward the delivery of employment, welfare, and educational services.

Williamson, John B., et al.
1975　*Strategies Against Poverty in America.* New York: John Wiley (Halsted).

The authors systematically evaluate the gamut of antipoverty programs instituted in the United States between the 1930s and the end of the 1960s. Six general categories of strategies are considered: income-in-kind, income, manpower, education, economic development, and organization. The various strategies within each of these approaches are rated using a set of twenty-six criteria such as: proportion of the poor who benefit, impact on the distribution of income, and extent to which recipients of the programs are stigmatized. Particular attention is given to a number of proposals for a negative income tax, a form of guaranteed income.

REFERENCES

Kershaw, David
1972　"Issues in income maintenance experimentation." In *Evaluating Social Programs*, ed. Peter Rossi and Walter Williams. New York: Seminar Press.

McDill, Edward L.; Mary S. McDill; and J. Timothy Sprehe
1972　"Evaluation in practice: compensatory education." In *Evaluating Social Programs*, ed. Peter Rossi and Walter Williams. New York: Seminar Press.

Rodman, Hyman, and Ralph Kolodny
1965   "Organizational strains in the researcher-practitioner relationship." In *Applied Sociology,* ed. Alvin Gouldner and S. M. Miller. New York: Free Press.

Rossi, Peter H.
1972   "Testing for success and failure in social action." In *Evaluating Social Programs,* ed. Peter H. Rossi and Walter Williams. New York: Seminar Press.

Selltiz, Claire
1955   "The uses of survey methods in a citizens' campaign against discrimination." *Human Organization* 14 (fall):19–25.

Suchman, Edward
1967   *Evaluative Research.* New York: Russell Sage.

Ward, David, and Gene Kassebaum
1972   "On biting the hand that feeds: some implications of sociological evaluations of correctional effectiveness." In *Evaluating Action Programs,* ed. Carol Weiss. Boston: Allyn & Bacon.

Weiss, Carol
1972   *Evaluation Research.* Englewood Cliffs, N.J.: Prentice-Hall.

Quantitative Analysis

All phases of the research process are potentially problematic. A few key decisions unwisely made at any stage of the process can substantially reduce the value of the entire research effort. One of the most challenging phases of the research process is the analysis of the data. If the data is quantitative, statistical procedures are essential to analyze, summarize, and present the results. Even social scientists who do not actually conduct quantitative research find they need to make use of the published findings of quantitative studies, and familiarity with the issues and concepts of quantitative analysis is necessary just to follow the presentation of results in such studies. A thorough understanding of these statistical procedures, including their limitations and the assumptions that underlie them, is essential if we are to be in a position to critically evaluate the results of such studies. The goal of the present chapter is to present a nontechnical overview of the most basic techniques, concepts, and issues involved in the analysis of quantitative data.

A distinction is often made between descriptive research and explanatory research. In *descriptive research* the focus is on describing the sample or the population from which the sample was drawn. In *explanatory research* the focus is on examination of the causal interrelationships among variables. Descriptive research is often done as the first part of a study which also includes explanatory analysis.

DESCRIPTIVE RESEARCH

As a class project each of the fifty students in a course on research methods at Easy College has interviewed twenty people in a nearby community, for a total sample of one thousand respondents. They were careful to use a sampling procedure that provides a representative sample of the community. The survey covers opinions on a variety of issues including gun control, socialism, and abortion. It also includes a number of background questions such as age, sex, race, income, and education. The task of collecting the data has been completed, but the job of analyzing it and preparing a report summarizing the findings of the study remains. How should the students go about it?

They consider a variety of alternatives and finally decide on a two-stage procedure. First each student goes over his or her interviews and selects a few of the most representative responses to each question. Then the student uses these responses to prepare an individual interviewer report which he or she submits to a committee selected by the class; the committee is responsible for stage two — preparing a final report. The class agrees on this procedure and work begins. The interviewer reports are prepared and submitted to the committee, and the committee goes through the interview, topic by topic, putting together a composite summary based on the responses submitted. The class is confident that the composite describes the opinions of typical members of the community and also says something about the opinions of those who did not give typical responses.

However, as the report is nearing completion, a member of the committee notices that there seem to be some systematic differences between interviewers with respect to which responses were selected as being representative. She points out that for the question on socialism there is a tendency for the students who are active in Young Americans for Freedom (a conservative political organization) to select responses that are very different from those selected by the students who are active in the Young Socialist Alliance. A systematic difference is inexplicable, given the random sampling procedure used in the selection of respondents. She asks the interviewers involved about how they selected what they considered representative responses and finds that there is a tendency to select from among those respondents considered most well informed. When she pushes further she finds that those considered most well informed tend to be those who agree with the interviewer.

This finding opens up the possibility of serious bias in the analysis procedure being used. Not only is the procedure vulnerable to bias on the ideological questions, but it might well be biased on other types of questions in ways that would be more difficult to detect. Clearly an alternative procedure for summarizing the findings is called for. After the

TABLE 15.1 A Computation of Marginals

"Should admitted socialists be allowed to teach at Easy College?"		
Yes	700	70%
No	300	30%
Total	1000	100%

problem is called to everyone's attention, the class decides that the optimal analysis form is to tabulate the responses of all one thousand respondents for each question. They decide that, given the large body of data to be summarized and given the potential bias in efforts to select "representative" responses, it is best to use a quantitative approach. In other words, they decide to carry out a descriptive statistical analysis of the data.

As a first step in such an analysis it is useful to compute a set of marginals for the data. The *marginals* are a listing of the *frequency* of each response and the *percentage* of the sample in each response category for each question in the survey. The marginals for a question on socialism are presented in Table 15.1. We see that 700 respondents, or 70 percent, of the sample believe that an admitted socialist should be allowed to teach at Easy College.

Although a set of marginals is useful for summarizing the responses of a large sample of respondents, we are sometimes interested in producing an even more concise summary of the data. For this purpose *measures of central tendency* and *measures of variability* are useful. We will consider measures of central tendency first.

Measures of Central Tendency

Measures of central tendency are used to say something about the average or typical respondent in the sample. The actual measure used depends on the level of measurement that is appropriate for the characteristic being considered. We recall from our discussion in Chapter 3 that we can distinguish between the nominal, ordinal, interval, and ratio levels of measurement.

For a *nominal-level variable* such as sex, race, or religion we must be able to classify all our respondents into a set of categories that are mutually exclusive and exhaustive. That is, it must be possible to find a category that each respondent in the sample will fit into (the categories must be exhaustive) and no respondent can fit into more than one of the categories (the categories must be mutually exclusive).

An *ordinal-level variable* shares the properties of a nominal-level

TABLE 15.2 The Mode as a Measure of Central Tendency

Religion			
Protestant	600	60%	(Mode)
Catholic	300	30%	
Jewish	100	10%	
Total	1000	100%	

variable (i.e., the categories are mutually exclusive and exhaustive) but has the additional property that the categories can be ranked, put into an order, such as high to low. Each category represents more of the dimension being considered than the next lower category, but we are not able to measure the distance between categories. We can say that respondents in category A are higher than those in category B who in turn are higher than those in category C, but we cannot say how much higher those in one category are than those in an another.

An *interval-level variable* has all the properties of an ordinal-level variable but has in addition the capacity to measure the distance between categories. An example is temperature, measured in Fahrenheit degrees. A *ratio-level variable* has all the properties of an interval-level variable and in addition has a zero point that represents the absence of whatever the variable measures (e.g., age, income, or years of education). For most research purposes in sociology the distinction between the interval and the ratio level of measurement is not made. Typically a variable that achieves the interval level of measurement also achieves the ratio level, but it is often referred to as an interval-level variable because that is all that is needed for the purposes of most statistical procedures.

For a nominal-level variable, such as religion, the only measure of central tendency available is the mode. The *mode* is the category with the greatest number of respondents in it. In Table 15.2 the mode is the Protestant category; this category is the mode because there are more respondents in this category than in any other single category. It is not necessary that the mode contain a majority of the respondents.

The data presented in Table 15.2 can also be summarized graphically. In Figure 15.1 this same data is presented in the form of a *bar*

FIGURE 15.1 Bar Graph for Data in Table 15.2

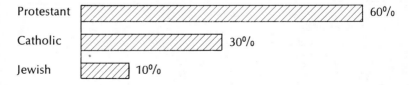

FIGURE 15.2 Pie Diagram for the Data in Table 15.2

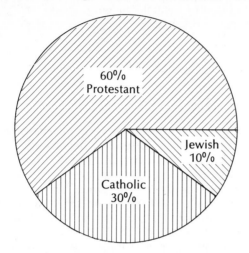

graph; in Figure 15.2 it is presented in the form of a *pie diagram.* These graphs do not tell a different story; rather, they are alternative ways to present exactly the same data.

Sometimes respondents are asked to indicate whether they agree strongly, agree slightly, disagree slightly, or disagree strongly with a statement such as, "The private ownership of hand guns should be made illegal." The results for such a question are presented in Table 15.3. This is an ordinal-level variable; that is, it makes sense to view the response categories as constituting an ordered set of alternatives ranging from strong agreement to strong disagreement.

For variables that reach the ordinal level of measurement it is appropriate to consider another measure of central tendency referred to as the median. The *median* is the category in which the middle observation falls. For example, for the following set of numbers (1, 5, 7, 17, 20) the median is 7 because this is the observation that falls in the middle of the distribution; half of the cases fall above the median and half of the

TABLE 15.3 Example of an Ordinal-Level Variable

"The private ownership of hand guns should be made illegal."		
Agree strongly	400	40%
Agree slightly	250	25%
Disagree slightly	150	15%
Disagree strongly	200	20%
Total	1000	100%

cases fall below the median. For the data in Table 15.3 we would start at either end of the distribution and count to the 500th person; this person would fall in the "agree slightly" category, which therefore becomes the median for the variable. Note that for ordinal-level data it is still possible to use the mode, which in this case would be the "agree strongly" category, but the median is for most purposes more useful as a measure of central tendency because it takes into consideration the ordering of the response categories.

For interval-level and ratio-level variables the *mean* can be used as a measure of central tendency. The mean is simply the sum of the observations divided by the total number of observations; for the set of numbers cited earlier (1, 5, 7, 17, 20) the mean would be 10. The mean is often used with such variables as income, years of schooling completed, and age.

When a variable has a large number of categories, it is often useful to categorize (consolidate the categories of) the variable prior to presenting the appropriate marginals in a table. This is particularly true with many ratio-level variables such as income. Were we to use a separate category for each different income value given, we might end up with a table which had several hundred (or possibly a thousand) categories. A table with a large number of categories can be very inconvenient to work with. One possible categorization of the income variable is presented in Table 15.4.

When we take a ratio-level variable such as income and categorize it as we have done in Table 15.4, what level of measurement can we appropriately assume for the resulting variable? In going from the un-categorized income data to the categories presented in this table, we have lost information. What was a ratio-level variable is now an ordinal-level variable. Why? Because the difference in income between respondents in adjacent income categories in Table 15.4 may be $2, $30, $400, or $5000. Whenever an interval-level or ratio-level variable is categorized into ranges, the resulting variable drops to an ordinal-level of measurement. For example, the readers of our report would have only the cate-

TABLE 15.4 A Categorization of the Income Variable

Income		
$ 0–$ 5,000	50	5%
$ 5,001–$10,000	300	30%
$10,001–$15,000	400	40%
$15,001–$20,000	200	20%
$20,001 and over	50	5%
Total	1000	100%

gorized data and would not be in a position to compute a mean on the basis of the data presented in Table 15.4. We have lost information in the sense that the uncategorized data gave us an estimate of each respondent's income to the nearest dollar, whereas the categorized data rounds off these estimates to the nearest $5000. The result is a loss of precision in our income variable.

For interval- and ratio-level variables it is always possible to compute the median and the mode as well as the mean. The mode is rarely used with interval- and ratio-level data; but the median is used, particularly when the researcher wants to de-emphasize a few extreme observations. The mean can be strongly influenced by even one observation at an extremely high or low value; this makes the measure less stable than the median. For example, for the following set of numbers (1, 5, 7, 17, 170) the mean is 100 and the median is 7. If we have reason to believe that there might be some error in the one extremely high observation or for some other reason want to de-emphasize its impact on our assessment of the typical or average observation, then we would use the median rather than the mean.

The measures of central tendency we have considered can be used to describe the typical or average respondent, but such measures tell us nothing about the dispersion (variability) in our data. We can get some idea of this variability from marginals (e.g., Tables 15.1–15.4), but we often want a more concise way to summarize this variability. For this purpose we use what are referred to as *measures of variability*; these same measures are also referred to as *measures of dispersion*.

Measures of Variability

There are no generally accepted measures of variability for either nominal- or ordinal-level variables. In this section we shall be considering the range, standard deviation, and variance, each of which is a measure of variability appropriate to use with either interval- or ratio-level data.

The *range* is the simplest measure of variability; it is equal to the difference between the largest and the smallest observation in the sample. If in our sample of 1000 respondents the lowest reported income is $1,500 and the highest reported income is $76,500, then the range would be $75,000. The main advantage of this measure is that it is easy to compute and easy to understand. A disadvantage is that it is a very unstable measure of variability because it can be substantially influenced by just one extreme observation. Since the measure is based on only two observations, much of the information in our data is not being used.

The *standard deviation* is the most frequently used measure of variability in descriptive analysis; it is based on the square of the deviation of each observation from the mean. The formula for the standard deviation is:

$$\text{Standard Deviation} = s = \sqrt{\frac{\Sigma(X_i - \bar{X})^2}{N}}$$

That is, it is equal to the square root of the mean of the sum of the squared deviations of each observation from the sample mean. See Table 15.5 for the meaning of X_i, $\bar{X}$, and N; the table also presents a simple example of the computation of the standard deviation for a small number of observations.

The squaring of the deviations in the computation of the standard deviation gives emphasis to the larger deviations from the mean. To check

TABLE 15.5 The Computation of the Standard Deviation

The following computations give the standard deviation for the five observations of the variable X: 0, 50, 100, 150, 200.

Observed Value (X_i)	Deviation from Sample Mean $(X_i - \bar{X})$*	Square of Deviation from Sample Mean $(X_i - \bar{X})^2$
0	−100	10,000
50	− 50	2,500
100	0	0
150	50	2,500
200	100	10,000

N = sample size = 5

$$*\bar{X} = \text{mean} = \frac{\Sigma X_i}{N} = \frac{(0 + 50 + 100 + 150 + 200)}{5} = 100$$

$$\text{Standard Deviation} = s = \sqrt{\frac{\Sigma(X_i - \bar{X})^2}{N}}$$

$$= \sqrt{\frac{(10{,}000 + 2{,}500 + 0 + 2{,}500 + 10{,}000)}{5}}$$

$$= \sqrt{5000}$$

$$= 70.71$$

* The symbol "X_i" is used to refer to the observations for the variable X. In this case $X_1 = 0$, $X_2 = 50$, $X_3 = 100$, $X_4 = 150$, $X_5 = 200$. The symbol "$\bar{X}$" is used to refer to the mean of the observations for the variable X. In this case, it is the mean of X_1, X_2, X_3, X_4, and X_5. The symbol N refers to the number of observations the mean is based on. In this case, N = 5. The symbol "ΣX_i" is used to indicate that we are to sum the observations of the variable X for all values of the subscript "i". In this case we sum X_1, X_2, X_3, X_4, and X_5.

this point, compare the relative magnitudes of the values in the $(X_i - \bar{X})$ column and do the same for the values in the $(X_i - \bar{X})^2$ column. A small standard deviation indicates that the observations tend to cluster very close to the mean; a large standard deviation indicates that there is a great deal of dispersion in the data, with relatively few observations falling close to the mean. When the standard deviation is small, the mean gives a fairly accurate description of most respondents in the sample; but when the standard deviation is large, the mean may give an accurate description of only those few respondents who are close to the sample mean.

One reason that the standard deviation is so frequently used as a measure of dispersion is that it has a very special relationship to the *normal curve*. The normal curve is the bell-shaped curve illustrated in Figure 15.3 which can be used to describe the distribution of many variables. When plotted, some variables, such as the S.A.T. (Scholastic Aptitude

FIGURE 15.3 Percentages of Observations within Various Standard
Deviation Units of the Mean for the Normal Curve

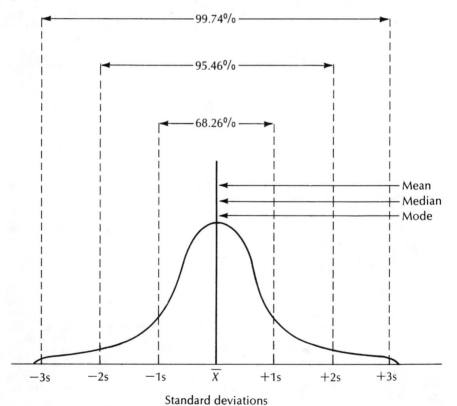

Test), closely approximate a normal curve; other variables, such as years of education, at least fairly well approximate the normal curve. What is still more important is the tendency for the *sampling distribution* of the mean to be normally distributed even when the variable itself is not at all normally distributed. If we draw a very large number of simple random samples of the same size from the same population and if we compute the mean for each of these samples, we find that the resulting set of means (referred to as the *sampling distribution* of the mean) is normally distributed. The mean for this set of means approximates the population mean, but some of the individual samples overestimate the population mean and some underestimate it. For example, age is not a normally distributed variable. However, if we were to draw a large number of samples of the same size from the same population and then to compute the mean age for each of these samples, we would find that this sample of means would be normally distributed. It is this property of sampling distributions (of means and of other statistics too) which underlies much sampling theory and significance-testing theory.

One of the characteristics of the normal curve which makes it so useful is that we can specify the proportion of the observations which will fall a given distance from the middle of the curve. As we see in Figure 15.3, for the normal curve approximately two-thirds (68 percent) of the observations will fall within one standard deviation of the mean, approximately 95 percent of the observations will fall within two standard deviations of the mean, and approximately 99 percent of the observations will fall within three standard deviations of the mean. If, for example, we know that the mean for a sample is 100 and that the standard deviation is 71, then we would expect 68 percent of the observations to fall between 29 (100 − 71) and 171 (100 + 71); we would expect 95 percent of the observations to fall between −42 (100 − (2 × 71)) and 242 (100 + (2 × 71)). This property of the normal curve (and of variables and statistics which we can assume are normally distributed) allows us to estimate how likely it would be to find a deviation from the mean of a given magnitude as a result of chance alone. Another noteworthy property of the normal distribution, which we can see in Figure 15.3, is that the mean, median, and mode all take on the same value.

We recall that the formula for the computation of the standard deviation requires that we take the square root as the last step. We might wonder why we should bother to take the square root. It turns out that there is another measure of variability referred to as the *variance* which is equal to the square of the standard deviation. As we can see from the following formula, it is the measure we get when we do not take the square root:

$$\text{Variance} = s^2 = \frac{\Sigma(X_i - \bar{X})^2}{N}$$

The standard deviation is used more extensively than the variance in descriptive analysis because of its special relationship to the normal curve. As we shall see later in the chapter, the variance is used more extensively in explanatory research; it plays an important role in the interpretation of such statistical techniques as correlation and regression. It is also used extensively in tests of statistical significance.

Up to this point we have considered a variety of techniques for describing the characteristics of a sample and summarizing the opinions of those in the sample. Marginals provide a great deal of descriptive information, but for some purposes it is useful to summarize this information more concisely, using measures of central tendency and measures of variability. Such measures give us some idea of what the typical or average respondent is like and how similar to this respondent others in the sample tend to be.

The descriptive analysis we have been considering so far considers only one variable at a time, and for this reason it is often referred to as *univariate analysis.* Many studies do not attempt to go beyond univariate descriptive analysis. However, when the goal of our study is to say something about why people hold the opinions that they do, it is necessary to engage in what is referred to as *explanatory analysis.* Explanatory analysis typically calls for examination of the relationship between two variables (*bivariate analysis*) or more than two variables (*multivariate analysis*).

EXPLANATORY RESEARCH

In descriptive research there is no effort to assess the causal impact of one variable on another; in explanatory research this effort is the focus of the analysis. The simplest form of explanatory analysis involves consideration of the relationship between two variables, one of which can be viewed as having some causal effect on the other. We refer to the variable being affected as the *dependent variable.* The variable we see as the cause of this effect is the *independent variable.*

Although the distinction is often made between explanatory research and descriptive research as if there is never any problem in classifying a particular study as one or the other, in practice studies do exist for which the distinction is difficult to make. It is sometimes hard to determine whether the researcher is presenting a causal analysis or simply some descriptive statistics. To illustrate this point let us consider the data presented in Tables 15.6–15.8.

In Table 15.6 the actual number of observations in each *cell* of the table is specified. You will note that *row* (across) and *column* (down) totals are also given. In the total sample of 1000 respondents, we see that 100 are Jewish; and of these 100, 25 are in the low-income category ($15,000 and under) and 75 are in the high income category ($15,001 and over). For certain purposes we want to be able to compare the proportion

TABLE 15.6 An Example of Cell Frequencies

	Religion		
Income	Jewish	Christian	Total
Low $0–$15,000	25	725	750
High $15,001 and over	75	175	250
Total	100	900	1000

of the Jewish respondents in the low-income category with the proportion of Christian respondents in the same category, but this is generally difficult to do on the basis of the raw cell frequencies alone. From a casual observation of the cell frequencies in Table 15.6 we can tell that there is a tendency for the Jewish respondents to be in the high-income category and for the Christian respondents to be in the low-income category; but we cannot say with any precision how great this difference is. The comparison is easier if we translate the frequencies into percentages as is done in Table 15.7; we now see that 25 percent of the Jews in comparison to 81 percent of the Christians are in the low-income category. It is a common procedure in table construction to put both the raw frequencies and the percentage figures in the same table as is illustrated in Table 15.8.

The question at hand is whether to classify the information presented in Table 15.8 as descriptive analysis or explanatory analysis. Before making this decision we would want to take a close look at the textual treatment of this table which appears in the research report. If the researcher is just attempting to make a descriptive statement about the sample of respondents by cross-classifying income by religion, then we would classify the effort as an example of descriptive analysis. If, on the other hand, the researcher attempts to argue that religion is a cause of,

TABLE 15.7 An Example of Cell Percentages

	Religion		
Income	Jewish	Christian	Total
Low $0–$15,000	25%	81%	75%
High $15,001 and over	75%	19%	25%
Total	100%	100%	100%

TABLE 15.8 A Contingency Table Presenting Cell Frequencies and Cell Percentages

	Religion		
Income	Jewish	Christian	Total
Low $0–$15,000	25% (25)	81% (725)	75% (750)
High $15,001 and over	75% (75)	19% (175)	25% (250)
Total	100% (100)	100% (900)	100% (1000)

or can be used to explain the level of respondents' income, then we would classify the effort as an example of explanatory analysis.

The tables formed by cross-classifying the sample by the categories of at least two variables are referred to as *contingency tables,* or alternatively the procedure is referred to as *cross-tabulation.* The simplest possible contingency table is formed by cross-classifying two variables, each of which has been dichotomized. A dichotomized variable has two categories. If a variable has more than two categories (as in the case of the religion variable in Table 15.2), it can be made into a dichotomy by combining categories; for example, the Catholics and Protestants can be combined into a new category called Christians as we have done in Table 15.6. Table 15.8 is an example of such a contingency table, and as we can see it has four *cells.* As we saw earlier, when interval-level or ratio-level variables are recoded into ordinal categories, information is lost. The more categories used for each variable, the less the amount of information lost. For example, by categorizing as we have done in Table 15.4 we lose the information needed to compute the sample mean. When we further reduce the number of categories, as in Table 15.8, we cannot even say what percent of respondents have incomes above $20,000 (this is a statement we could make on the basis of the information in Table 15.4). It is possible to construct tables with a very large number of cells; but if the number gets too large, the table becomes awkward to use and difficult to read. It is unusual to find contingency tables with more than 25 cells.

You will recall that the univariate information presented in Table 15.4 is referred to as an example of *marginals.* This term is used because the same data is presented in the margins (for row totals or for column totals) of a contingency table such as Table 15.8. For example, we can use the data for row totals in Table 15.8 to construct a univariate marginals table for a dichotomized version of the income variable. The resulting table is similar to Table 15.4, but there are now two rather than five income categories. As practice, we should try doing the same for the religion variable in Table 15.8, relating it to the marginals data in Table 15.2.

It is possible to construct tables using any combination of nominal-, ordinal-, interval-, or ratio-level variables. But with interval- and ratio-level variables it will almost always be necessary to combine categories; and for nominal- and ordinal-level variables it will sometimes be necessary to combine categories. You will note that in Table 15.8 both the income variable (as used in Table 15.4) and the religion variable (as used in Table 15.2) have been recoded so that each is a dichotomy.

So far we have considered only contingency tables that present the relationship between two variables at a time; such tables are referred to as *two-way tables* or as *bivariate tables*. A great deal of explanatory research calls for an analysis of what happens to the relationship between two variables when we take into consideration a third variable. When we introduce a third variable, the resulting classification can be presented as a series of two-way tables (often referred to as *subtables*), one for each category of this third variable; or alternatively the results can be presented in one three-variable table. Such tables are also referred to as *three-way tables*. Table 15.9 presents the two-variable relationship between birth rate and stork count. Table 15.10 is an example of the corresponding three-variable table in which population density has been added as a *control variable*. We refer to the process of introducing a third variable as *controlling* for the variable because the result is a series of subtables for which the third variable is held constant (i.e., controlled). The control variable takes on different values for each subtable, but for any given subtable the value of the control variable does not change. For example, in Table 15.10 the control variable is population density. It takes on the same value for all the observations in the left-hand subtable (rural) and it takes on the same value for all the observations in the right-

TABLE 15.9 The Bivariate Relationship Between Birth Rate and Stork Count

		Stork Count	
		High	Low
	High	82% (82)	18% (18)
Birth Rate	Low	18% (18)	82% (82)
	Total	100% (100)	100% (100)

TABLE 15.10 The Relationship between Birth Rate and Stork Count Controlling for Population Density: an Example of Explanation

		Population Density			
		Rural Counties		Urban Counties	
		Stork Count		Stork Count	
		High	Low	High	Low
Birth Rate	High	90% (81)	90% (9)	10% (1)	10% (9)
	Low	10% (9)	10% (1)	90% (9)	90% (81)
	Total	100% (90)	100% (10)	100% (10)	100% (90)

hand subtable (urban). It should be clear from an examination of Table 15.10 that it would also have been possible to present these same results in the form of two separate subtables, one for rural counties and one for urban counties. The elaboration paradigm, which we shall discuss in the next section, outlines a set of procedures for analyzing the relationship in a two-variable table by introducing a third variable.

The Elaboration Paradigm

The *elaboration paradigm* is a set of procedures for analyzing causal relationships in three-way tables. Much of the early work on the paradigm was done by Paul Lazarsfeld and his name is still strongly identified with it.[1] Elaboration involves an analysis of what happens to the relationship between two variables when a third variable is *controlled.* There are three major categories of elaboration: *explanation, interpretation,* and *specification.* We will first consider explanation.

Suppose we have decided to do a study of the relationship between birth rate and stork count for the two hundred counties in Nacirema. We have been presented with the data in Table 15.9 which shows a strong positive relationship between birth rate and stork count. We see that 82 percent of the counties with high stork counts have high birth rates and only 18 percent of the counties with low stork counts have high birth rates. We suspect the relationship is spurious because we do

[1] For an early treatment of the work, see Kendall and Lazarsfeld (1950). For more recent extensions of the paradigm see Hyman (1955) and Rosenberg (1968).

not believe that storks cause births, or that births cause storks. To demonstrate that the relationship is *spurious* we must show that it can be accounted for in terms of some other variable which is (1) *causally prior to* both birth rate and stork count, and (2) *related to* both birth rate and stork count. If we are successful in locating a control variable that meets these two conditions and also makes the original relationship disappear, we will have carried out a form of elaboration referred to as *explanation*.

We try a variety of alternative *test factors* (alternatively referred to as *control variables*) in an effort to show that the relationship between birth rate and stork count is spurious. Eventually we hit on the idea of controlling for population density as measured by an urban/rural dichotomy. Our argument is that the population density is causally prior both to stork count (there are more storks in an area because it is rural) and to birth rate (birth rate tends to be higher in rural areas). We can see from Table 15.10 that when this test variable is introduced, that is, when population density is controlled for, the original relationship disappears. We call the relationship between the two original variables within each category of the test variable a *partial*. Thus in Table 15.10 there is no relationship between the original two variables for either of the partials. In the rural areas birth rates are high in 90 percent of the counties with high stork counts and in 90 percent of the counties with low stork counts. Similarly, in urban areas birth rates are low in 90 percent of the counties with low stork counts and in 90 percent of the counties with high stork counts.

We know that to qualify as an example of explanation the test factor must be both causally prior to and related to each of the original variables. We should be able to construct the tables needed to determine whether or not the test factor is related to both the original variables by using the data presented in Table 15.10. We construct one table relating population density to birth rate and another table relating population density to stork count. When we do this, we find that the condition is met: there is a strong relationship in both of these tables. The form of elaboration illustrated in Table 15.10 is referred to as *explanation* because the test factor has explained the apparent relationship between birth rate and stork count which we started with.

We now turn to a second form of elaboration referred to as *interpretation*. Here the goal is to make the relationship between the two variables in the original table disappear by introducing a third variable that can be viewed as causally intervening between these two variables. In Figure 15.4, we see models that illustrate the distinction between the form of elaboration we call explanation and the form we call interpretation. In the case of *explanation* the control variable X_3 is causally prior to both variable X_1 and variable X_2 of the original relationship. In the case of *interpretation* the control variable X_3 is causally prior to variable X_2 but it is *not* causally prior to variable X_1. That is, variable X_3 is causally affected by variable X_1 and in turn has a causal effect on variable X_2.

FIGURE 15.4 Models Illustrating the Distinction between Explanation and Interpretation

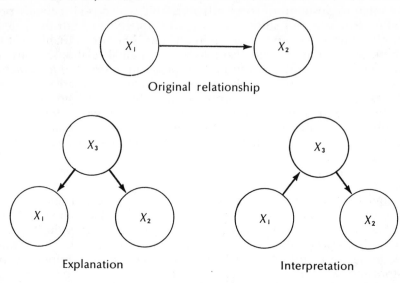

Another way to say it is that variable X_3 is an *intervening variable* between variable X_1 and variable X_2.

For a concrete example of interpretation we return to the hypothetical opinion survey we have been considering. Suppose we have classified the respondents by the size of birthplace into towns (places with a population of under 50,000) and cities (places with a population of 50,000 or over). The data presented in Table 15.11 shows a strong relationship between size of birthplace and opinion on the abortion issue: those who were born in cities are much more likely to support abortion. Some 82 percent of those born in cities support abortion, in contrast to only 18 percent of those born in towns.

TABLE 15.11 The Bivariate Relationship between Abortion Attitude and Size of Birth Place

		Size of Birthplace	
		Town	City
"Should it be possible for a woman to obtain an abortion on demand?"	No	82% (410)	18% (90)
	Yes	18% (90)	82% (410)
	Total	100% (500)	100% (500)

As part of an explanatory analysis of this relationship it would be relevant to look for other variables which might intervene between size of birthplace and attitude toward abortion. One hypothesis we might be interested in investigating is that political ideology intervenes between size of birthplace and attitude toward abortion. The argument would be that people born in towns are more likely than those born in cities to be politically conservative and that those who are politically conservative are more likely than liberals to oppose abortion. Data relevant to this hypothesis is presented in Table 15.12. We see that when political ideology is controlled, the original relationship between size of birthplace and attitude toward abortion disappears. Among conservatives there is no relationship (10 percent of those born in cities support abortion and 10 percent of those born in towns support abortion); among liberals there is no relationship either (90 percent of those born in cities and 90 percent of those born in towns support abortion). The ideology variable can easily be viewed as being causally prior to the variable measuring attitude toward abortion, but there is no way to conceive of ideology as being causally prior to size of birthplace. On the basis of this data we can argue that political ideology is an intervening variable between size of birthplace and attitude toward abortion and in this sense it provides an *interpretation* of the original relationship.

Using the data presented in Table 15.12, we should be able to construct the tables needed to demonstrate that the test factor is related to both of the original variables. We should construct one table that relates ideology to attitude toward abortion and another table that relates ideology to size of birthplace. We would find that there is a strong relationship in both these tables.

TABLE 15.12 The Relationship between Abortion Attitude and Size of Birthplace Controlling for Political Ideology: an Example of Interpretation

		Political Ideology			
		Conservative		Liberal	
		Size of Birthplace		Size of Birthplace	
		Town	City	Town	City
"Should it be possible for a woman to obtain an abortion on demand?"	No	90% (405)	90% (45)	10% (5)	10% (45)
	Yes	10% (45)	10% (5)	90% (45)	90% (405)
	Total	100% (450)	100% (50)	100% (50)	100% (450)

So far we have considered types of elaboration in which the objective has been to find a test factor that makes the relationship in the original table disappear. We now turn to a third form of elaboration referred to as *specification* in which the objective is not to reduce the original relationship, but rather to specify the conditions under which the relationship between the two variables in the original table is stronger or weaker. In a pure case of specification, the test factor introduced is unrelated to one of the two variables in the original relationship. This criterion can be used to distinguish specification from the other forms of elaboration we have considered, both of which require that the test variable be related to each of the variables in the original relationship.

However, more typically there will be at least some relationship between the test factor used in specification and both of the original variables. In view of this, the distinction between specification and other forms of elaboration is often based on the way in which the relationship changes in the partial tables. If all the partial tables show relationships that are very weak relative to the relationship in the original table, then we are likely to classify the result as a case of explanation or interpretation. If on the other hand the original relationship is substantially stronger in one of the partial tables than in another, we would classify the result as an example of specification. The specification category includes a variety of quite different outcomes. It is possible for the relationship in one of the subtables to disappear and for that in another to remain quite strong. The relationship may decrease in one of the partials and increase in another. It is even possible for the relationship to be positive in one of the partials and negative in the other; that is, conservatives may show more opposition to abortion than liberals in one partial table and show more support for abortion than liberals in another partial table.

Suppose that in our analysis of the relationship indicated in Table 15.11 we introduce region of birthplace as a test factor. If the results were to turn out as indicated in Table 15.13, we would classify the outcome as an example of *specification*. That is, the original relationship in Table 15.11 between size of birthplace and attitude toward abortion disappears for the partial corresponding to the Southern region, but it becomes even stronger for other regions of the country. This example illustrates what is referred to as a pure case of specification, in that the test factor is completely unrelated to one of the two variables in the original table. By constructing the table for the relationship between region of birthplace and attitude toward abortion, we should be able to show that 50 percent of those born in the South support abortion and 50 percent of those born in other regions support abortion; in short, there is no relationship between region of birth and attitude toward abortion.

The elaboration paradigm has been extended in a variety of ways since its original formulation. One such extension suggested by Rosenberg (1968:88–89) has been the consideration of *suppressor variables*.

TABLE 15.13 The Relationship between Abortion Attitude and Size of Birthplace Controlling for Region of Birthplace: an Example of Specification

		Region of Birthplace			
		South		Other Regions	
		Size of Birthplace		Size of Birthplace	
		Town	City	Town	City
"Should it be possible for a woman to	No	50% (90)	50% (90)	100% (320)	0% (0)
obtain an abortion on demand?"	Yes	50% (90)	50% (90)	0% (0)	100% (320)
	Total	100% (180)	100% (180)	100% (320)	100% (320)

Consider the case in which we find no relationship between the two variables in the original table, but we suspect that under at least some conditions these two variables are related. Suppose we try several test factors and eventually hit on one that results in a substantial relationship between the two variables in one or more of the partial tables. This test factor is referred to as a suppressor variable because unless it is controlled it masks or suppresses the relationhip between the two original variables.

In Table 15.13 we find no relationship between *size of birthplace* and *attitude toward abortion* for those respondents born in the South. We might be interested in doing an analysis of these 360 respondents born in the South (the left-hand partial table in Table 15.13) to determine whether some factor is suppressing the relationship between size of birthplace and attitude toward abortion. Suppose we try a variety of test factors and eventually hit on the variable *percent black,* a variable that classifies the community of birth as either high or low in percent black population. The results are as indicated in Table 15.14. Here we find a strong positive relationship between size of birthplace and attitude toward abortion for those born in communities with a high percentage of blacks and a strong negative relationship between size of birthplace and support for abortion for those born in communities with a low percentage of blacks. In this example, the variable assessing percent black in community of birth would be classified as a *suppressor variable,* because unless it is controlled it masks the relationship between size of birthplace and attitude toward abortion.

The data we have presented in our discussion of various forms of elaboration (Table 15.9–15.14) is highly idealized. In actual research the outcome is never so close to the pure types. However, if we understand

TABLE 15.14 A Three-way Table Illustrating the Effect of Introducing a Suppressor Variable

		Percent Black in Community of Birth for Respondents Born in South			
		High		Low	
		Size of Birthplace		*Size of Birthplace*	
		Town	City	Town	City
"Should it be possible for a woman to obtain an abortion on demand?"	No	100% (90)	0% (0)	0% (0)	100% (90)
	Yes	0% (0)	100% (90)	100% (90)	0% (0)
	Total	100% (90)	100% (90)	100% (90)	100% (90)

the logic behind the various types of elaboration we have considered, then we should find it fairly easy to correctly classify examples of elaboration as they occur in actual research. The most fundamental point to keep in mind when doing elaboration analysis is that the interpretation of results is influenced by what we find in the partial tables as well as by the causal relationship between the control variable and the variables in the original table.

We have considered the simplest form of elaboration, in which the researcher is working with variables that have only two categories. The same logic can be extended to include variables with more than two categories. However, when the number of categories gets large, the interpretation process gets more difficult. This is particularly true when we consider test factors with a large number of categories or if we consider more than one test factor at a time. When we want to control for several variables simultaneously (rather than one at a time) and when we want to work with control variables with many categories, tables analysis can become very difficult. In these situations it is more appropriate to use such statistical techniques as *partial correlation* or *multiple regression* which we will turn to shortly.

Correlation Analysis

Suppose that we are interested in measuring the relationship between verbal S.A.T. (Scholastic Aptitude Test) scores prior to college entrance and grade point average for the one thousand seniors who have just graduated from Easy College. It would be possible to categorize each of these variables and then summarize the relationship in tabular form, but much information would be lost in the process of categorizing these variables. A preferable alternative, which would give us a more precise estimate of the actual relationship, would be to compute the correlation coefficient between these two variables using the uncategorized data.[2]

The *correlation coefficient* (alternatively referred to as the *Pearson correlation* or the *product-moment correlation*) is a statistic appropriate for use with interval-level or ratio-level data. It is typically designated by "*r*". The values of *r* range from 1.00 (for a perfect positive relationship) to .00 (when there is no relationship) to −1.00 (for a perfect negative relationship). In Figure 15.5 we present several scattergrams which illustrate alternative possible relationships between variables *X* and *Y*. A *scattergram* is constructed by plotting a point corresponding to the *X* and *Y* values for each unit in the sample. We now turn to a brief interpretation of the scattergrams in Figure 15.5:

a. The data for this scattergram illustrates a moderately strong positive correlation which would be approximately .60. You will note that in this scattergram, as in the others, the *X* values increase from left to right, that is, from L (low) to H (high); and the *Y* values increase from bottom to top. As with all positive correlations there is a tendency for the *Y* values to increase as the *X* values increase.

b. Here all the data points fall along a straight line; this is what would happen where there is a perfect positive correlation between *X* and *Y* (*r* = 1.00). The correlation is "perfect" only in the sense that it represents the upper limit for the correlation coefficient. In actual social research applications we do not get correlations of 1.00 unless we have somehow managed to correlate a variable with itself.

c. Here we have no relationship between *X* and *Y* (*r* = .00).

d. Here we have a weak positive correlation (*r* = .20) between *X* and *Y*.

e. Here we have a very strong positive correlation (*r* = .90).

f. Here we have a perfect negative correlation (*r* = −1.00). Note that for a negative correlation *Y* decreases as *X* increases.

g. Here we have a strong negative correlation (*r* = −.90). An example of a negative correlation would be the relationship between cigarette consumption (*X*) and life expectancy (*Y*). As cigarette consumption *increases,* life expectancy *decreases.* (In reality the correlation between these two variables is undoubtedly weaker than −.90).

h. Here we have a strong nonlinear relationship between *X* and *Y* (*r* = .00). It is not appropriate to use the correlation coefficient to summarize a nonlinear relationship such as this. The low correlation masks the evidence that there is a strong nonlinear relationship between *X* and *Y*.

---

[2] The formula used to compute a Pearson correlation coefficient can be found in any introductory statistics text.

FIGURE 15.5 Scattergrams for Alternative Correlations between *X* and *Y*

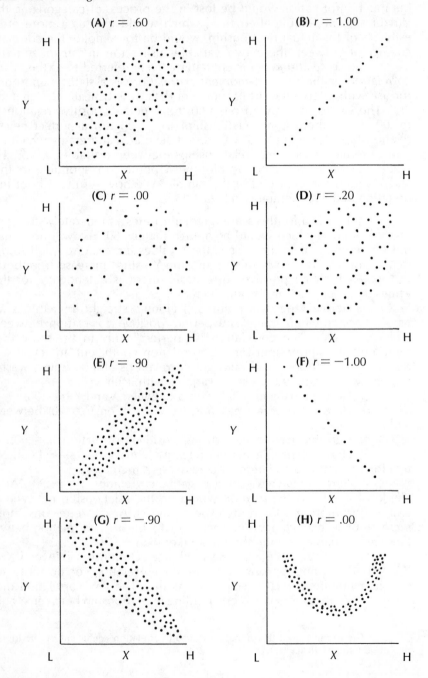

Measures of Association

A *measure of association* is a statistic that summarizes the relationship between two variables. The correlation coefficient is the most frequently used measure of association, but there are also several measures of association used to measure the degree of association in contingency tables. A *positive association* exists between two variables when there is a tendency for those who score high on one of the variables to score high on the other and for those who score low on one to score low on the other (Figure 15.5E). When there is a *negative association* between two variables, there is a tendency for those who score high on one to score low on the other (Figure 15.5G).[3] If there is a *strong* positive association between X and Y (Figure 15.5E), the Y scores for those who score high on X will tend to be considerably higher than the Y scores for those who score low on X. If there is a *weak* positive association between X and Y (Figure 15.5D), the Y scores for those who score high on X will tend to be a little higher than the Y scores for those who score low on X.

Some measures of association range from .00 (indicating no association between the two variables) to 1.00 (indicating a perfect association between the two variables).[4] Such measures do *not* distinguish between positive and negative relationships. Other measures of association are similar to the correlation coefficient in that the values run from 1.00 (for a perfect positive association) to .00 (indicating no association) to −1.00 (for a perfect negative association). For example, there are a variety of correlation coefficients showing positive and negative relationships which are appropriate for use with ordinal-level data (in contrast to the Pearson correlation, which is supposed to be used with interval- and ratio-level data, even though in actual practice it is often used with ordinal-level data); they are often referred to as *rank-order correlations* or *nonparametric correlations*.

For use in table analysis there are some measures of association available which have the same range as the correlation coefficient and others which take on maximum values of less than 1.00. In some instances the maximum value that the measure can take is influenced by the number of categories for each of the variables used to construct the table, that is, by the number of rows and columns in the table. Such measures tend to be less useful than those which take on a maximum value of 1.00 regardless of the number of categories for the variables involved.

While the gamma statistic (a measure of association frequently used in table analysis) and the correlation coefficient take on identical

---

[3] If we assume that a "yes" response on the abortion question indicates more of the dimension "favorability toward abortion," then we can say the association in the left-hand partial in Table 15.14 is positive.

[4] For example, the phi coefficient (which is described in any introductory statistics text).

values when there is no association (.00), a perfect positive association (1.00), or a perfect negative association (−1.00), they tend to take on different values when there is a nonzero association which is not a perfect association, a condition that includes virtually all associations that occur in actual research applications. In general for these intermediate values the actual numerical value describing the relationship will depend on the measure of association used. For this reason it is not legitimate to compare the relationship in one table as measured by one measure of association with that in another table indicated by a different measure of association. This incompatibility sometimes produces difficulties when we attempt to compare the findings of different studies in which alternative measures of association have been used. In making comparative statements about the strength of the relationship in one table relative to that in another, it generally does not matter which of the several appropriate measures is used as long as the same measure is used consistently; the alternative measures will with rare exceptions give the same relative rankings. For example, if the association in Table X is stronger than the association in Table Y which uses the gamma statistic, we would expect to find the same relative ranking of the associations in Tables X and Y for other measures of association.

For most measures of association there is no specific interpretation for nonzero values not equal to 1.00 or −1.00. The correlation coefficient is a noteworthy exception. We can recall from our earlier discussion that the variance is a measure of the variability which is equal to the square of the standard deviation. Variance can be viewed as the scatter around the sample mean. If all respondents have the same value (this value would then by definition become the sample mean) there is no variance to account for. To the extent that the actual values vary around the mean there is scatter or variability to be accounted for. The square of the correlation coefficient is a measure of the proportion of the scatter in Y values that can be accounted for by knowing the X values. When there is a perfect correlation between X and Y, we are able to explain all the scatter in Y knowing the X values; this is illustrated in Figures 15.5B and 15.5F. If we square the correlation coefficient (e.g., if $r = .50$, $r^2 = .25$), the result is called *the proportion of the variance accounted for,* which we often convert to *percent of variance explained* by multiplying by 100. The amount of variance accounted for ranges from 0 percent (when $r = .00$) to 100 percent (when $r = \pm 1.00$); if $r = .50$, then we have accounted for 25 percent of the variance ($25 = .50^2 \times 100$).

Partial Correlation

So far we have discussed the correlation coefficient as a measure of association between two variables. There is also a multivariate form of correlation referred to as partial correlation which can be used to carry out an analysis of correlation data which is in many ways similar to the contingency table elaboration analysis discussed earlier. The *partial correlation* between variable X_1 and variable X_2 controlling for X_3 is designated symbolically as "$r_{12.3}$" and conceptually it can be thought of as the mean of the correlations between X_1 and X_2 for each of the scattergrams that would result if a separate scattergram were plotted between X_1 and X_2 for each value of X_3. It is a measure of the average correlation between X_1 and X_2 when X_3 is controlled.[5] It has the same range and interpretation in terms of explained variance as does the two-variable (Pearson) correlation.

Suppose we are presented with a zero-order correlation between X_1 and X_2 which we suspect is spurious. To check for this possibility, we introduce several control variables that are causally prior to both X_1 and X_2. Eventually we hit on a causally prior control variable X_3 for which the partial correlation drops to zero (or nearly zero). In so doing we have demonstrated that the original relationship was spurious.

To be more concrete, suppose we are doing a study in which the census tract is the unit of analysis (a census tract, we recall, is an area made up of a cluster of blocks which includes approximately 3,000 residents). Suppose that we find a high correlation ($r_{12} = .60$) between our measure of *delinquency rate* (X_2) and *percent broken homes* (X_1). If we suspect that this correlation is spurious, we might attempt to locate a causally prior control variable that can account for this relationship. Suppose we eventually hit on the variable *percent poor* (X_3). When X_3 is controlled for, the partial correlation turns out to be very close to zero ($r_{12.3} = .05$). On the basis of this evidence, we would conclude that the original correlation ($r_{12.} = .60$) was spurious. This outcome is illustrated in Figure 15.6B. It should be clear that there is a very close parallel between what we have done here and our earlier discussion of the form of contingency table elaboration referred to as *explanation*.

Suppose we are presented with a strong correlation ($r_{42} = .60$) between the variable *percent black* (X_4) and delinquency rate (X_2). As part of our analysis of this relationship, we might decide to search for possible variables which intervene between percent black and delinquency rate. Suppose we eventually try the variable *percent poor* (X_3) and find that when this variable is controlled, the partial correlation is much below the original correlation. With such results we would conclude that the percent poor is an intervening variable between percent black and delinquency rate. This outcome is illustrated in Figure 15.6D. The parallel

---

[5] The formula for the computation of the partial correlation coefficient can be found in any introductory statistics text. The partial correlation is more precisely conceptualized as the *weighted* mean of the correlations between X_1 and X_2 for the scattergrams corresponding to each of the values of the control variable X_3. If there are a small number of observations for some values of X_3 and a large number for others, this must be taken into consideration by weighting each of the correlations by the number of observations it is based on.

FIGURE 15.6 Models Illustrating Alternative Interpretations
of Partial Correlation Results

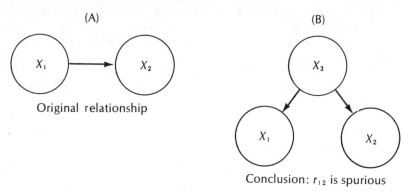

(A)

$X_1 \longrightarrow X_2$

Original relationship

(B)

X_3

X_1 X_2

Conclusion: r_{12} is spurious

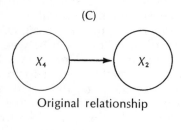

(C)

$X_4 \longrightarrow X_2$

Original relationship

$X_1 =$ Percent Broken Homes
$X_2 =$ Delinquency Rate
$X_3 =$ Percent Poor
$X_4 =$ Percent Black

(D)

X_3

X_4 X_2

Conclusion: X_3 is an
intervening variable

between this example and the form of contingency table elaboration
referred to as *interpretation* should be evident.

In our discussion so far we have considered only examples in
which we introduce one control variable. It is possible to control for
several variables simultaneously using higher order partial correlations.
Thus we can compute the partial correlation between X_1 and X_2 controlling for X_3, X_4, X_5, X_6 ($r_{12.3456}$). In partial correlation analysis, the Pearson
correlation is often referred to as the *zero-order correlation* to distinguish
it from a *first-order partial correlation* (e.g., $r_{12.3}$), a *second-order partial
correlation* (e.g., $r_{12.34}$), and other *higher order partial correlations* — in
which the order of the partial correlation corresponds to the number of
variables being controlled.

An advantage of partial correlation as a statistical technique relative to contingency table analysis is that the controlling operation is based

on statistical adjustments of the scores for the original two variables rather than on the construction of physically separated subtables as is the case in contingency table analysis. Partial correlation is very useful when the investigator wants to control simultaneously for several factors, particularly if the sample is relatively small. In contrast, attempts to control for several variables simultaneously in contingency table analysis become awkward because some of the partial tables end up with few if any respondents.

However, this advantage of partial correlation analysis also has its costs. A major disadvantage is the *loss of information* about variation in the strength of the relationship between the original two variables for the various categories of the control variable. The strength of the relationship may fluctuate considerably for the different categories of the control variable. If we were to construct separate scattergrams (and compile separate zero-order correlations) for the same data we would be able to see this fluctuation. But with partial correlation analysis all we get is one summary number which averages the relationship for the various sub-categories. If these fluctuations are of no interest to us or if there is very little fluctuation in the strength of the relationship for the various categories of the control variable, then this loss of information is not a major problem. It is of interest to note that the contingency table alternative to partial correlation also involves a loss of information — albeit in a different form; that is, information is lost when interval-level variables are recoded into a relatively small number of categories for tabular analysis.

When there is a high positive correlation between two variables, we know that persons who are high on one dimension will tend to be high on the other, but it is not possible to use correlation information to make a precise prediction of scores on one variable on the basis of information about the scores on another. The appropriate technique for statistical prediction is linear regression.

Regression Analysis

Linear regression is a statistical procedure used to estimate the amount of change in a dependent variable which can be expected for a given change in an independent variable. We shall begin by considering *simple regression* which involves one dependent variable and one independent variable (or *predictor*). We shall then consider multiple regression which involves one dependent variable and two or more predictors.

We recall from elementary algebra that the equation for a straight line is:

$$Y = a + bX.$$

In Figure 15.7 we illustrate the interpretation of the constants a and b in this equation. We find that a is the value Y takes when X is equal to zero.

FIGURE 15.7 The Equation for a Straight Line

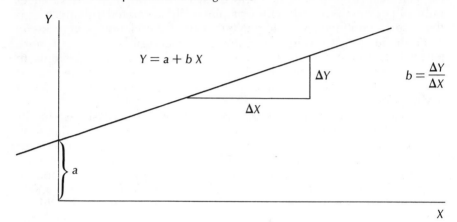

It is referred to as the Y intercept because it is the value of Y at the point where the straight line crosses the Y-axis. The constant b is equal to the slope of this line. The slope is the rate at which Y changes divided by the rate at which X changes. If we move an arbitrary distance along the line described by this equation, recording the amount that Y has changed (call it ΔY) and the amount X has changed (call it ΔX) and then divide the change in Y by the change in X, the result is the slope of the line (i.e., $b = \Delta Y / \Delta X$).

In this example from elementary algebra, the Y values refer to points along the straight line defined by the equation: $Y = a + bX$. There is no concern with or mention of any Y values that do not fall on this line. For any arbitrary value of X we can find the corresponding Y value that satisfies the equation by locating that Y value on the straight line which falls directly over the specified X value (i.e., we would determine that point at which a line constructed perpendicular to the X-axis from the specified X value intersects the straight line given by the equation: $Y = a + bX$).

Simple regression is a procedure for fitting a straight line to a set of points in a scattergram as illustrated in Figure 15.8. The regression line is that line through the set of points for which the sum of the squares of the deviations from the line are a minimum. These deviations are shown in Figure 15.8. For any line other than the regression line through the same set of points, the sum of the squares of the deviations is greater.

The major distinction between the equation for the regression line and the corresponding equation for a straight line from elementary algebra is that the values of Y for regression rarely fall along the actual regression line, but the values of Y for the elementary algebra example always fall along the line. However, by constructing a vertical line from each observed Y value to the regression line, as illustrated in Figure 15.8, we

FIGURE 15.8 Fitting a Least Squares Regression Line to a Set
of Points in a Scattergram

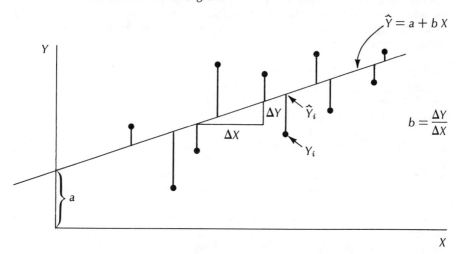

can locate a set of $\hat{Y}$ (called Y − predicted) values which do fall along
the regression line. Thus the equation for the regression line becomes:

$$\hat{Y} = a + bX.$$

Suppose that Y is annual income and that X is years of education.
In simple regression the slope (b) is referred to as the *regression coefficient*. If the regression coefficient has a value of 500, we would estimate
that for a one-year increase in level of education there will be a $500
increase in annual income. More generally, the regression coefficient
gives the number of units of change in Y (in whatever units Y is measured
in) that can be expected for a one-unit change in X (in whatever units X
is measured in).

In regression analysis it is important to distinguish between the
actual Y values that do not fall on the regression line and the corresponding $\hat{Y}$ values that we would estimate on the basis of knowledge about a
given respondent's X value. The discrepancy between the actual Y value
and the estimated $\hat{Y}$ value represents prediction error. When the Y values
tend to cluster very close to the regression line, Y and $\hat{Y}$ values will be
very similar and the error in prediction will be low. But when the Y values
tend to deviate markedly from the regression line, the Y and $\hat{Y}$ values
will be quite different and the error in prediction will be high.

Multiple regression is an extension of simple regression; instead
of one predictor we include two or more predictors in a single regression
equation. For example, when there are four predictors, the equation is
as follows:

$$\hat{Y} = a + b_1X_1 + b_2 X_2 + b_3X_3 + b_4X_4.$$

The *b* values in multiple regression are referred to as *partial regression coefficients*.[6] These coefficients give the change in the dependent variable (in whatever units the dependent variable is measured in) that we would estimate for a one-unit change in the specified predictor (in whatever units the predictor is measured in).

The *multiple correlation coefficient* (designated symbolically as "*R*") is used to summarize the accuracy of our prediction equation.[7] It is equal to the Pearson correlation between *Y* and the $\hat{Y}$ values. As we recall, the difference between *Y* and $\hat{Y}$ represents error in our prediction. If we have selected a set of predictors that yield accurate estimates of *Y*, then the difference between *Y* and $\hat{Y}$ values will be small and the multiple correlation will be high. If, on the other hand, we have selected a set of predictors that yield poor estimates of *Y*, then the difference between *Y* and $\hat{Y}$ values will tend to be larger and the multiple correlation will be low. The multiple correlation ranges from .00 (when the independent variables in no way help predict *Y*) to 1.00 (when the independent variables predict *Y* with complete accuracy). The multiple correlation coefficient squared (R^2) gives the proportion of the variance in the dependent variable which is accounted for by the set of predictors included in the regression equation. For example, if $R = .50$, then $R^2 = .25$ and we would conclude that the predictors being considered account for 25 percent of the variance in the dependent variable.

Let us return to the example mentioned earlier, in which the goal is to predict the grade point average for the one thousand seniors who have just graduated from Easy College. Suppose we decide to use the following four predictors: high school grade point average (X_1), father's education (X_2), verbal S.A.T. (Scholastic Aptitude Test) score (X_3), and father's occupational status (X_4). These variables are all measured in different units; consequently, we cannot make direct comparisons among these partial regression coefficients (b_1, b_2, b_3, and b_4) to determine their relative strength as predictors of grade point average.

Fortunately there is a way to deal with this problem. It calls for computing *standardized partial regression coefficients* (these coefficients

---

[6] The *b* values are referred to as partial regression coefficients because they are estimates of the change in the dependent variable that is estimated for a one-unit change in a specified predictor after we statistically control for the effects of the other predictors in the equation.

[7] The subscripted version of the multiple correlation coefficient is designated symbolically as "$R_{1.2345}$" where the subscript 1 refers to the dependent variable X_1 and the subscripts 2,3,4, and 5 refer to the predictors X_2, X_3, X_4, and X_5. There will be as many numbers following the period in the subscript as there are predictors. Note that the notation system has been changed here so that the dependent variable referred to in the text as *Y* is referred to here as X_1. For the subscripted multiple correlation coefficient, as for several other multivariate statistics (e.g., the partial correlation coefficient), the notation is simpler if we refer to our variables as X_1, X_2, X_3 and so on, rather than as *Y*, X_1 and X_2.

are commonly referred to as *beta weights*) for each of these predictors. The beta weight is a partial regression coefficient which has been adjusted in such a way that the unit of measure does not influence its value. The way this is done is that all units are changed to standard deviation units. Thus, when a beta weight equals .50, our interpretation is that there will be a .50 standard deviation change in the dependent variable (grade point average) for a one standard deviation change in the specified predictor. Since each of the coefficients is now stated in standard deviation units, it is possible to compare the relative strength of each predictor.

The statistic referred to earlier as the *partial regression coefficient* is also referred to as the *unstandardized partial regression coefficient*. As we recall, this statistic indicates how many units the dependent variable is estimated to change (in whatever units it is measured in) for a one-unit change in the independent variable (in whatever units it is measured in). For this reason the units in which the variables are measured makes a difference. For example, if income were one of our predictors, we would have a choice of units for measuring income. We might decide on cents, dollars, or thousands of dollars. Depending on which of these three units we selected, we would get a different unstandardized partial regression coefficient for income. However, the standardized partial regression coefficient is not influenced by the unit of measurement and would be the same for each of these three alternatives.

Path Analysis

Now that we have considered multiple regression, it is appropriate to elaborate on the description of path analysis presented in our earlier discussion of causal modeling in Chapter 2. Path analysis can be viewed as a procedure for presenting the results of a series of multiple regressions or alternatively as a procedure for doing causal modeling with multiple regression. To clarify this point let us return to the model of the process of stratification which we considered in Chapter 2. In this chapter it is reproduced in Figures 15.9 and 15.10.

In Figure 15.9 we have presented a preliminary model of the process of stratification. This model includes four predictors and the respondent's present occupation, which is the main dependent variable. The arrows in the model specify a seemingly plausible causal order among these variables — prior to looking at our data. The selection of predictors and the assumed causal ordering among these predictors is based on our theory, past research, and common sense. We assume at this point that father's education and father's occupation influence respondent's education, and that all three in turn influence respondent's first job, and that all four in turn influence present occupation. We can use this preliminary causal model to set up a series of multiple regression equations. For the model we are considering, three separate multiple regression equations

FIGURE 15.9 A Preliminary Model of the Process of Stratification

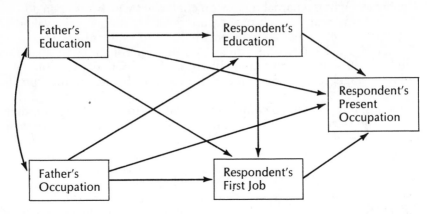

would be specified, one for each variable in the model which is used as a dependent variable. (Any variable which has a straight arrow coming into it is being used as a dependent variable.) For one of these equations, respondent's present occupation would be the dependent variable and it would be predicted by the other four variables in the model, all of which are causally prior. In a second equation respondent's first job would be the dependent variable and it would be predicted by the three variables in the model, which are causally prior to it. Finally, in a third equation respondent's education would be the dependent variable and it would be predicted by the two variables that are causally prior to it.

As the first stage in our path analysis we carry out the calculations for each of these regressions. From these calculations we get a series of *beta weights* which in path analysis are referred to as *path coefficients*. The three regression equations which we have described yield beta weights for each of the paths in the preliminary model.[8]

If some of the beta weights in the preliminary model turn out to be small, we drop them and compute a new set of beta weights based on a revised multiple regression equation. For the preliminary model presented in Figure 15.9, we shall assume that the paths from father's education to respondent's first job and to respondent's present occupation were both low. For this reason they were dropped and a new set of beta weights were computed for the final model presented in Figure 15.10. For this example, the revised multiple regression equation which has respondent's first job as the dependent variable will include respondent's education and father's occupation as predictors, but it will *not* include

[8] You will note that *father's education* and *father's occupation* are connected by a curved arrow with a head at both ends of the arrow. Here we are not attempting to estimate causal effects. The number along this curved arrow is a correlation coefficient not a beta weight. Such curved arrows are used to connect those variables in the model which are used only as independent variables.

FIGURE 15.10 A Final Model of the Process of Stratification*

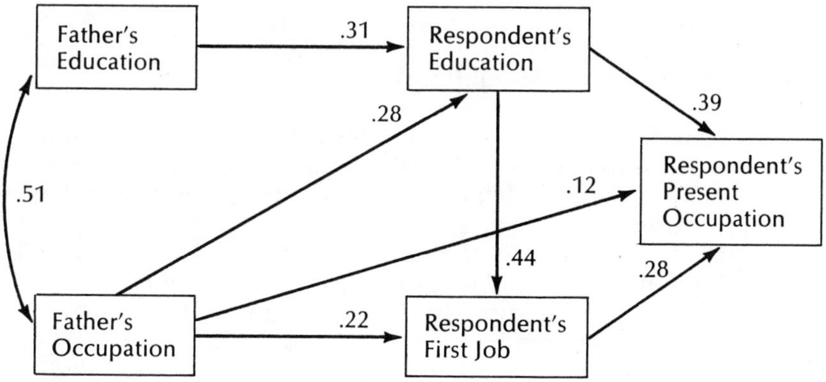

* Adapted from Peter Blau and Otis Dudley Duncan, *The American Occupational Structure* (New York: John Wiley, 1967), p. 170. We have excluded the residual paths.

father's education, a predictor which did appear in the preliminary model. The path coefficients presented in Figure 15.9 are the beta weights from this second set of regressions. To illustrate the interpretation of one of the path coefficients, we can say that for a one-standard-deviation increase in father's education we would estimate a .31 (or approximately one-third of a) standard deviation increase in respondent's education.

We have specified that if the beta weight for a path in a preliminary model is small, the path is eliminated from the final model. Generally the decision as to whether to drop a path is based on the level of statistical significance of the beta weight. Testing for statistical significance is one aspect of statistical inference more generally.

STATISTICAL INFERENCE

In quantitative research we are rarely interested in our sample per se. Rather we are interested in making generalizations about the larger population from which the sample was drawn, on the basis of what we know about the sample. When our goal is simply to describe the characteristics of the sample or to describe the relationship between variables for the sample, we engage in descriptive statistical analysis. But when our goal is to infer certain characteristics of the population on the basis of characteristics of the sample or to make inferences about the relationship between variables in the population on the basis of information about the relationship between these same variables in the sample, we engage in *statistical inference*. Tests of statistical significance are often used as a basis for statistical inference.

Tests of Statistical Significance

Significance tests are used extensively in both descriptive and explanatory research. One of the most common uses of significance tests is as an aid in deciding whether to infer on the basis of the relationship between two variables in a sample that there is a relationship between these same two variables in the population from which the sample was drawn. Returning to the survey of residents in the community neighboring Easy College, let us suppose that the sample estimate of the mean income for Jewish respondents is $17,437 and that the sample estimate of the mean income for Christian respondents is $14,321. On the basis of this evidence we know that there is a difference in mean income between the Jews and Christians for the sample, but we are probably more interested in knowing whether we can infer from this that there is a tendency in the community as a whole for Jews to have higher incomes than Christians.

We can recall from our discussion of *sampling distributions* earlier in the chapter that estimates based on a sample rarely correspond to the exact value for the population. Probability theory assures us that there will be *sampling error* in our estimates of the mean; that is, sample estimates will fluctuate around the true population value. Since some sample estimates will be too high and others will be too low, we do not know whether our estimate of $17,437 is above or below the actual mean income of Jews in the community. It is even possible that the mean income for Christians is higher than the mean income for Jews in the community. This would be the case if, owing to *sampling error* (the deviation of the mean for our sample from the true population mean), the sample estimate for Jewish respondents overstates the actual income for Jews in the community by $2,000 (so that the actual mean income in the community is $15,437) and the sample estimate for Christian respondents understates the actual income of Christians in the community by $3,000 (so that the actual mean income in the community is $17,321).

Suppose that prior to looking at our data we have the hypothesis that in the community the mean income for Jews is higher than the mean income for Christians. How might we test this research hypothesis? As a first step we might compute the mean income for Jews ($17,437) and Christians ($14,321) in our sample. However, our research hypothesis refers to the community, not to our sample from the community. One way to address ourselves to this research hypothesis is to determine whether a difference in mean income as great as that found in our sample could be expected on account of sampling error (chance) alone — if in the community the mean income for Jews were actually exactly equal to that for Christians. More generally, whenever we want to test the hypothesis that one group is different than another, the way we go about it is to ask whether the difference found in the sample could be expected on the basis of chance alone. To this end we formulate what is referred to as a null hypothesis. Our null hypothesis in this case is that in the community the mean income of Jews is equal to the mean income of Christians.

Tests of significance always call for the formulation of a null hypothesis. Typically the *null hypothesis* states that there is no relationship in the population between the variables of interest. Along with the null hypothesis we always formulate a *research hypothesis.* In the preceding example we specified a *directional research hypothesis,* that is, that the mean income of Jews is higher than the mean income of Christians. However, sometimes we do not specify a direction in our research hypothesis. An alternative *nondirectional research hypothesis* appropriate to the example would be that the mean income for Jews is not equal to that for Christians: Note that the income for Jews could be either higher or lower than that for Christians and still be consistent with this nondirectional research hypothesis. When our research hypothesis is *directional* we use what is referred to as a *one-tailed test of significance.* When our research hypothesis is *nondirectional* we use a *two-tailed test of significance.*[9]

When carrying out a significance test, we always specify a significance level. It is a common practice to select in advance one of the conventional significance levels, such as .05, .01, or .001. These significance levels refer to there being a chance of 5 in 100, 1 in 100, and 1 in 1000 respectively of getting a relationship as strong as that in our sample due to chance (sampling error) when there is no relationship between the variables in the population. If for example, we select the .05 level, this says that we are going to classify the difference in means as statistically significant if the chance that the difference is due to sampling error alone is less than 5 in 100. Suppose we carry out a test of significance on the difference between the mean income of Jews and Christians for our sample. If the difference is significant at the .05 level, we refer to the relationship as being statistically significant: that is, we reject the null hypothesis that the incomes of Jews and Christians are equal for the community. But in so doing we realize that we are taking a 5 percent chance of being wrong. We realize that there are 5 chances in 100 that a difference as great as that found in our sample could have been due to sampling error alone if in the community the mean income were exactly equal for Jews and Christians. Even though we have decided to classify the difference in income as statistically significant, it is still pos-

[9] The rationale for the names "one-tailed" and "two-tailed" tests of significance is too technical for the present treatment, but a full discussion of the issue can be found in any introductory statistics text.

sible that the incomes for Jews and Christians in the community are equal.

What if we had carried out a test of significance and found that we were not able to reject the null hypothesis that the mean incomes for Jews and Christians are exactly equal (to the nearest penny)? Does this mean that we accept the null hypothesis and conclude that the incomes are exactly identical? No, we do not. There is a difference between failing to reject the null hypothesis and actually accepting the null hypothesis. It is very unlikely that the mean income for Jews will be exactly equal to the mean income for Christians to the nearest penny, even if we have failed to reject the null hypothesis. There is an important distinction between the conclusion that the difference in means found in our sample *could be due to chance* (sampling error) alone if the population means were exactly equal and the conclusion that the population means are exactly identical.

A test of significance is a procedure for deciding how likely it is that the relationship we have found in the sample (in this case the difference in income between Jews and Christians) can be accounted for in terms of sampling error when there is actually no relationship between variables in the population. *A test of significance cannot be used to prove that there actually is a relationship in the population, or to prove that there actually is no relationship in the population; it can be used only to indicate how likely we would be to get the relationship we find in the sample if there were no relationship in the population.*

The test of significance which we use when we are interested in comparing the means for two samples or two categories of the same sample, as in the case of a comparison of the mean income of Jews with the mean income for Christians, is the *t-test*. The null hypothesis for a t-test is that the population means are equal, in this case that the means for the Christians and Jews are equal. When we want to compare the means for more than two groups in the same test of significance, we use the *F-test*. The null hypothesis for the F-test is that the means for all the groups being compared are equal (e.g., the means for the Catholics, Protestants, and Jews). The research hypothesis for the F-test is that the means are not equal; there is no (one-tailed) directional option when more than two groups are being considered.

Tests of significance are often used in contingency tables analysis. The most widely used test of significance with contingency tables when at least one of the variables concerned is of nominal level is *chi-square*. The null hypothesis for the chi-square test is that there is no relationship between the two variables in the table; that is, the respondents are distributed among the table cells as would be expected by chance.[10]

---

[10] The null hypothesis in this case does not assert that the frequency in each cell of the table will be equal. Instead the frequency that would be expected in each cell of the table by chance is calculated on the basis of the marginals for the two variables used to construct the table. The row and column totals for a table typically give these marginals. For example, suppose that we look only at the row and column totals in Table

The Pearson correlation coefficient can be tested for statistical significance. The null hypothesis here is that the correlation between the two variables in the population is zero. If we have grounds for predicting the direction of the correlation, we choose an alternative research hypothesis that states that there is a positive correlation between the variables (or states that there is a negative correlation, depending on the direction of the relationship we are predicting) and we use a one-tailed test. If we do not have a prior hypothesis as to the direction of the correlation, the alternative research hypothesis states that in the population the correlation between the two variables is not equal to zero and we use a two-tailed test. In this case if the correlation proves to be statistically significant, we accept the research hypothesis that the correlation in the population is not zero. Note that the significance test does not say the correlation in the population is equal to the correlation for the sample. In fact, it says nothing about the actual strength of the correlation in the population. More generally, the strength of a correlation and the statistical significance of a correlation are conceptually independent. In general, for a given sample size, correlations that are statistically significant will tend to be larger than correlations that are not. But with a large enough sample, a weak correlation will be statistically significant; and with a small enough sample, a strong correlation will not be statistically significant.

The reason that the same strength correlation is more likely to be classified as statistically significant if it is based on a larger sample is that there is less sampling error for a large sample. For example, if we were to draw a sample of size 5 to estimate the mean income for a community, our estimate would tend to be less accurate than if it were based on a sample of size 500. In general, a sample statistic based on a larger sample will more closely approximate the corresponding population parameter than will the same statistic based on a smaller sample. Thus a nonzero correlation based on a large sample is less likely to be due to chance than the same correlation based on a smaller sample. The same logic applies to all measures of association. For a given strength of association, the larger the sample size, the more likely it is that the association will prove to be statistically significant.

The Misuse of Tests of Significance

There has been a great deal of debate among sociologists over the use of tests of significance. Of particular concern is the evidence

---

15.6. On the basis of this information would we expect the same frequency in each cell of the table? No, we would not. There are more low-income respondents (750) than high-income respondents (250) and more Christian respondents (900) than Jewish respondents (100); thus we would expect that even if there were no relationship between income and religion, there would be a larger number of respondents in the low-income Christian cell than in other cells.

that such tests are frequently used in situations for which the requirements underlying the test have not been met. Some argue that the problem has been exacerbated by pressure from journal editors and reviewers who encourage the use of such tests (so that the results will seem more scientific?) despite the violation of the assumptions that underlie them. Others argue that tests of significance do have their use even when the assumptions that underlie them are not completely satisfied.

All tests of significance assume we have a probability sample and most assume a simple random sample. But it is not uncommon to find tests that assume a simple random sample being used with a sample that is not even a remote approximation to a simple random sample. Most social research is based on cluster, quota, or accidental samples, which are rather poor approximations to a simple random sample. With such samples the sampling error is much greater than in a simple random sample which can lead to inflated estimates of statistical significance.

A related problem is the use of tests of significance when the researcher is working with the entire population. Suppose we are working with state-level data and we find a correlation of .30 between median income and level of state educational expenditures. Suppose also that we are working with data for all 50 states. In such a situation our sample (N = 50) is the population, and so it is inappropriate to compute a test of statistical significance. If the correlation between these variables is .30, then .30 is the correlation in the population and it is meaningless to compute a test of significance to test the null hypothesis that in the population the correlation is zero.[11] In short, if we already have the population there is no need to make the inferences that tests of significance are designed to help us make.

It is not uncommon for a researcher to use a test of significance to make generalizations beyond the population from which the sample was drawn. Suppose we have a simple random sample of the seniors at Easy College and we find that the Jews in the sample are more likely to support gun control than the Catholics. If this difference turns out to be statistically significant, we can generalize to the seniors at Easy College. It might seem plausible that a similar trend would hold for seniors at other colleges, or for all college students, or for the adult population in general; but we have no grounds for making such a generalization on the basis of the data we have.

Statistical significance is often confused with *substantive significance*. It is fairly common for a researcher to suggest that a finding is important because it is statistically significant. While it is generally reasonable to discount findings that are *not* statistically significant, statistical significance per se does not make a relationship important. We can often find statistically significant relationships between variables that are caus-

[11] See Winch and Campbell (1969) for an alternative perspective on this issue.

ally unrelated (e.g., the relationship between birth rates and stork counts), variables that are alternative measures of the same thing (e.g., the relationship between age and year of birth), and variables that are sociologically uninteresting (e.g., the relationship between weight and waist measurement). There can also be relationships based on very large samples which are statistically significant but so weak as to be substantively unimportant. And finally, a correlation can be very close to zero (even .01) and still be statistically significant if the sample size is large enough.

Another misuse of significance tests is illustrated by researchers who compute a very large number of statistical tests and then prepare research reports based on those relationships which are statistically significant. Such researchers are capitalizing on sampling error and may prepare an entire report around a set of correlations that could not be replicated. Suppose a researcher computes 1000 correlation coefficients and tests each for statistical significance. Even if all of these correlations in the population are zero, we would expect on the basis of sampling error that 50 (or 5 out of every 100) of these correlations would be significant at the .05 level. Thus if the researcher looks through the 1000 correlations and bases the report on the 50 or so that are statistically significant, the findings reported run a risk of being highly unreliable. Most of these correlations will have been due to sampling error alone. For this reason it will not be possible to replicate the findings of the study.

There are different tests of significance for different types of data. Some tests are appropriate for nominal-level data, some are appropriate for ordinal-level data, and still others are appropriate for interval- and ratio-level data. A common error is to use a test of significance appropriate for interval-level data when the data is actually only ordinal level. This generally occurs when the researcher has computed a measure of association which assumes interval level data on data that is actually ordinal level. One of the most common examples of this error is the computation of a test of significance for a Pearson correlation between two ordinal-level variables.

CONCLUSION

We began with a discussion of descriptive research, pointing out that the objective is simply to describe characteristics of the sample or characteristics of the population from which the sample was drawn. Descriptive research can also involve consideration of the relationship between variables. In this context we sometimes use tests of significance as an aid in making inferences, on the basis of the sample, about the population.

In explanatory research we do not stop with the conclusion that there is a relationship between two variables: we go on to ask *why* there is a relationship. We attempt to explore the causal relationship between two variables by introducing various control variables. Explanatory analysis can be carried out using contingency tables, partial correlation, multiple regression, and path analysis. We often find it convenient to present the results of such analysis in the form of causal models.

In much explanatory analysis we make extensive use of causal language; for example, we make frequent reference to the "effect" of one variable on another. It is important to keep in mind that we are working with statistical estimates of such effects based on rather simplified models of the social world. There are procedures for estimating the accuracy of sample estimates of population characteristics. Thus we can say something about the accuracy with which our beta weight for education estimates the corresponding population beta weight. But we have no way of estimating how accurately this beta weight captures the true causal effect of education on income. Our estimates are usually based on data collected at one point in time which provides a static picture of the world, the causal interrelationship among variables may be quite different some five, ten, or fifty years into the future. We might, for example, find that the "effect" of education on income will decline in the future as more and more people get college educations.

We can discuss the distinction between the strength of a relationship and the statistical significance of a relationship. We know that if the sample size is sufficiently large even a weak association will be statistically significant, and if the sample size is sufficiently small even a strong association will not be statistically significant. This chapter has concluded with a discussion of the ways in which tests of significance are misused. We have seen that they are frequently used in situations where the underlying assumptions are not met. One of the most common violations is the assumption that the sample is a simple random sample, which it seldom is.

EXERCISES

1. On the basis of the data presented in Tables 15.11 and 15.12, would you conclude that the original relationship between size of birthplace and attitude toward abortion was spurious? Why?

2. In Table 15.1 we note that the modal category includes 60 percent of the sample. Is it possible for the modal category to include less than 50 percent of the sample? What is the smallest percentage of the sample that a category can include and still be classified as the mode?

3. Construct a contingency table with 45 observations in each row and in each column so that the value of the gamma statistic would be:

    a.   1.00
    b.   .00
    c. −1.00

You do not need to know the formula for the computation of gamma to construct these contingency tables.

4. The argument is made that an advantage of partial correlation over multivariate contingency table analysis is that partial correlation can be used when we want to control several variables simultaneously and have a relatively small sample size. Why is partial correlation more useful in such situations?

5. Why does the multiple correlation coefficient never take on negative values? (Hint: plot a set of Y and $\hat{Y}$ values for a simple regression in which there is a very high positive association between X and Y, and do the same for the simple regression in which there is a very high negative association between X and Y.)

6. For the following set of numbers compute the mean, median, and mode: 5, 10, 6, 5, 10, 5, 10, 1, 5, 10, 10.

7. There is a partial correlation equivalent of *explanation* as the term is used in contingency table elaboration analysis. There is also a partial correlation equivalent of *interpretation*. Is there a partial correlation equivalent of *specification*? Why?

8. Select any recent issue of the *American Sociological Review* and attempt to locate an article in it which you believe uses a test of statistical significance improperly. Indicate why you believe this.

9. Using the data presented in Table 15.10, construct the tables you would need to show that the test factor is related to both of the variables in the original table (Table 15.9).

10. Using the data presented in Table 15.12, construct the tables you would need to show that the test factor is related to both of the variables in the original table (Table 15.11).

SUGGESTED READINGS

Amos, Jimmy R.; Foster L. Brown; and Oscar G. Mink
1965   *Statistical Concepts.* New York: Harper & Row.

> This is a very basic introduction to descriptive statistics in a programmed learning format. Although the author's claim that the book can be completed in four and one-half hours may be an underestimate, the book is one of the shortest introductions to statistical concepts available. Among the topics considered are measures of central tendency, the normal curve, measures of variability, the standard score, the correlation coefficient, reliability and validity, inferential statistics, and regression.

Anderson, Theodore R., and Morris Zelditch, Jr.
1975   *A Basic Course in Statistics with Sociological Applications.* 3d ed. New York: Holt, Rinehart & Winston.

A good introduction to descriptive and inductive statistics written for the undergraduate sociology major. The first part of the book deals with univariate analysis including such topics as univariate table construction, measures of central tendency, measures of dispersion, and the normal curve. The second part focuses on relationships between two or more variables including such topics as the bivariate table, measures of association, the principle of least squares, and multiple regression. The third part is an introduction to statistical inference.

Blalock, Herbert M., Jr.
1972   *Social Statistics.* 2d ed. New York: McGraw-Hill.

A very useful, but more advanced, introduction to statistical analysis for sociologists. It includes the same material covered in the more elementary texts, but in addition considers advanced topics such as two-way analysis of variance, intraclass correlation, nonlinear correlation and regression, dummy variable analysis, analysis of covariance, and tests of significance for correlation coefficients. It also includes a thorough chapter on sampling.

Campbell, Stephen K.
1974   *Flaws and Fallacies in Statistical Thinking.* Englewood Cliffs, N.J.: Prentice-Hall.

This book is longer than but in many ways similar to the Huff book (see below). It includes a number of cartoons; unfortunately, several are quite sexist. The objective of the book is to sensitize the reader to the various ways in which statistics are used, in the mass media and other popular sources, to mislead the audience. This is particularly the case with statistical analysis presented in advertisements.

Huck, Schuyler W.; William H. Cormier; and William G. Bounds, Jr.
1974   *Reading Statistics and Research.* New York: Harper & Row.

The focus of this book is on learning to understand and critically evaluate statistically oriented articles and research reports, but its value for a sociological audience is limited because the applications are often drawn from psychology. The book starts with a very competent discussion of the typical format of a journal article. The second part of the book considers one-way analysis of variance, factorial analyses of variance, analysis of variance with repeated measures, analysis of covariance, multiple correlation, and discriminant function analysis. The last section deals with research design and includes such topics as pseudo-experimental designs, true experimental designs, and quasi-experimental designs.

Huff, Darrell
1954   *How to Lie with Statistics.* New York: Norton.

A very simple introduction to descriptive statistics with many cartoons. This book is appropriate for use during the first weeks of an undergraduate course in social statistics. It is written for a lay audience. Like Campbell, Huff alerts his audience to the deceptive uses of statistics in the mass media. Considered are sampling bias, the well-chosen average, and making small differences or changes appear large.

McCollough, Celeste
1974   *Introduction to Statistical Analysis.* New York: McGraw-Hill.

An introduction to descriptive and inductive statistics which combines aspects of the standard textbook format with the programmed learning approach. Correlation analysis, regression analysis, one-way analysis of variance, the chi-square test, measures of dispersion, measures of central tendency, and conditional probability are considered.

Morrison, Denton E., and Ramon E. Henkel
1969   "Significance tests reconsidered." *American Sociologist* 4 (May):131–140.

An easy introduction to the significance test that argues against its use. The article describes tests of statistical significance. It then reviews the most frequent misuses of such tests, especially the use of nonprobability samples and treating the population rather than a sample from a population. They also point to the frequent confusion of statistical significance with substantive significance. One of the most valuable aspects of the article is a content analysis of the major sociological journals over a twenty-year period citing the proportion of quantitative articles in which tests of statistical significance have been misused.

Rosenberg, Morris
1968   *The Logic of Survey Analysis.* New York: Basic Books.

This is a book-length treatment of the issues considered in the section of this chapter on the elaboration paradigm. It deals with the use of contingency tables in the analysis of survey research data. The book comes directly out of the Lazarsfeld tradition.

Winch, Robert F., and Donald T. Campbell
1969   "Proof? No. Evidence? Yes. The significance of tests of significance." *American Sociologist* 4 (May): 140–143.

A defense of the use of tests of significance, this article can be read as a reply to the Morrison and Henkel article. One of the important arguments made is that tests of significance often can be used to exclude certain relationships from further consideration. While the violation of various assumptions associated with tests of significance may inflate significance levels and lead to the invalid conclusion that a specified relationship is statistically significant, if the relationship turns out not to be statistically significant we have little ground for attempting to account for it. The authors also make an interesting argument in support of the use of tests of significance when the researcher is working with an entire population rather than a probability sample from that population.

REFERENCES

Hyman, Herbert
1955   *Survey Design and Analysis.* Glencoe: Free Press.

Kendall, Patricia L., and Paul F. Lazarsfeld
1950   "Problems of survey analysis." In *Continuities in Social Research: Studies in the Scope and Method of The American Soldier,* ed. Robert K. Merton and Paul F. Lazarsfeld. Glencoe: Free Press.

Rosenberg, Morris
1968   *The Logic of Survey Analysis.* New York: Basic Books.

Winch, Robert F., and Donald T. Campbell
1969   "Proof? No. Evidence? Yes. The significance of tests of significance." *American Sociologist* 4 (May):140–143.

The Value and Limits
of Social Science Knowledge

EPILOGUE

By now we have spent many weeks reading about social research methodology. We have been examining a non-technical presentation of the general issues involved in the use of any research method — issues such as sampling, bias, reliability, validity, and measurement. We have also looked at some of the more specific issues and problems of concern to those who seek to use a particular method of data collection or data analysis.

Most students begin the study of social research methodology with a "What's-so-important-about-methodology-anyway?" attitude. In each chapter we have attempted to find the answers to this question. In our first chapter we examined the goals that most frequently motivate social research: the production of information that can be used in the formulation of social policy, as a form of social criticism, to bring about social change, to satisfy the researcher's intellectual curiosity, to test the validity of social theories, and so on. Examples in each succeeding chapter have demonstrated how specific methodological procedures can be used to facilitate the realization of these goals.

To this point in our study, the first priority has been to acquaint ourselves with the mechanics of the various methods discussed in Part Two of the book. Having accomplished that task, we can now appropriately step back and consider a more general issue: the significance of rigorous methodological procedures for producing important knowledge that can matter in our lives.

One way to think about the various methods we have described and analyzed is as "inventions." Each method is designed to collect certain types of data about the social world. Each lends itself more to one set of research issues than to another; each has its own strengths and weaknesses. That social scientists have seen the need to invent the number of methods covered in this volume is partial confirmation of our earlier judgment that social life is an enormously complicated affair. We cannot use the same tools to investigate historical trends in a society as we would use to ascertain contemporary attitudes and beliefs. Our grasp of basic processes of social interaction depends on modes of inquiry different from those we would use to compare social values cross-culturally. Observational techniques do us little good if our research goal is to forecast world population trends.

In short, the methods with which we are now acquainted vary along a number of dimensions. Some methods are best employed to study persons in their "natural" settings; others allow researchers to exert maximum control over variables extraneous to their immediate research interests. If we wish to assess attitudes, we choose certain methods; but if we wish to directly catalogue persons' behaviors, we need other methods. The methods described vary in degree of obtrusiveness. Some, such as survey research, are highly obtrusive; others, such as content analysis, are unobtrusive. One method lets us systematically study large numbers of persons, while another best helps to capture the flavor of behavior in small groups. We choose our methods according to whether we seek breadth or depth in our investigation. Some methods provide quantitative renderings of social phenomena and others yield more qualitative images. We can test a priori hypotheses with certain methods. Others are better suited to the discovery of theoretical explanations.

The differences mentioned are revealing. They substantiate the idea that we cannot adopt uniform procedures to deal with the quite varied problems that are legitimately part of sociological investigation. But it would be a mistake to underscore only how and why social scientific methods differ from one another. While it is certainly true that the method chosen must fit the theoretical questions, and fit the distinctive goals of the research, and fit the available data sources, it is also true that all research methods are employed to realize a common end — providing complete, honest, reliable, valid, objective descriptions or explanations of social phenomena.

Researchers want to say at the conclusion of their investigation: "We have employed every safeguard feasible to ensure that our findings are correct." As bodies of procedural rules, social science methodologies are designed to cause researchers to continually ask themselves: "What might we do to be even more certain of our findings?" Our knowledge of methodologies, then, serves to make us critical of the accuracy and validity of sociological reports. We should now be equipped to look at any piece of research and quarrel with it, to question its possible errors, and to ask how the research might have been more convincingly done. We will want to ask the following sort of questions about the research that we read: Have the researchers employed the method(s) most appropriate to their research problem? Have proper sampling procedures been used? Have necessary steps been taken to reduce as far as possible bias and error in the findings? To what extent might the researchers' own assumptions, ideologies, or interests have colored the findings offered? Have the researchers taken care to use the most precise measurement procedures feasible? Is there any question about the validity of the presented findings? Might the researchers have shown greater sensitivity to the ethical issues raised by their research? Are statements of cause and effect warranted by the data collected and the methods used? Have researchers remained true to their data in making their interpretations and inferences? And so on.

We can agree that study of this textbook has increased our sophistication about methods of social research. We now feel we can carry out our own research and critically evaluate the quality of others' research. But many fellow readers will not pursue careers in the social sciences. Does this mean that their knowledge of methodology will be of no value to them? To the contrary, we would say that the methodological criteria used to evaluate social science research equip them to critically consider the wide range of assertions about social life that all of us read and hear nearly daily. Our knowledge of the obstacles to a sure understanding of social phenomena should enable us to evaluate the generalizations about social life offered in the mass media, in literature, and in daily conversation.

As scientists seeking after truth, we are not happy with explanations of events or situations that rely on hunches, guesswork, or casual observation. However, we must acknowledge the falseness of any assertion that methodological scrupulousness will easily and inevitably yield unquestionable, universal, or unalterable findings about social life. There are, it is fair to say, limits to sociological knowledge. We must be candid about these limits and consider briefly why absolute knowledge or truth about social life is impossible. It is important to stress the idea of *absolute* knowledge: absolute knowledge about something implies that, once it is acquired, there will be nothing left to learn. We need to recognize that we can know certain things only partially; that knowledge can be a matter of degree; that knowledge useful at one point in time may be inapplicable at another. An example will make this point clear.

What does it mean when we speak of "knowing" someone? Certainly it does not suggest that we know absolutely everything there is to know about a person, that there is nothing we don't know. Our knowledge of persons may be a function of the type of relationships we have with them. Persons may show different sides of themselves in different social situations. There may, in other words, be aspects of persons that we will never learn. We also realize that persons change and that what we previously knew about them is not altogether helpful in explaining their present behaviors. And since persons are always changing (getting older, taking new jobs, getting married, and the like) we recognize there are always new things to be learned about them.

Social scientists who endeavor to know or explain how a society works face a distinctive task. A society, like an individual, is multifaceted and will look different to us depending on the angle from which we view it. We cannot hope to incorporate into one explanation every aspect of social life (although some have tried). Most importantly, society is always changing. In some cases the change may be so rapid that our prior knowledge no longer applies. Whether rapid or slow, however, social change ensures that there will always be new things to learn about social life — that we will need to continually amend, specify, or enlarge upon our already acquired knowledge.

Many essays have been written comparing the social sciences with the natural sciences. The conclusions drawn from the comparison nearly always place the social sciences in a negative light, stressing the relative failure of the social sciences to surely explain and predict phenomena. The comparison seems, on the face of it, a legitimate one. Why have the natural sciences been able to produce apparently more certain findings? Why is natural scientific knowledge cumulative while social scientists continue to argue the validity of theoretical propositions produced, in some cases, two centuries earlier? Why haven't social scientists produced laws about society as natural scientists have done for the physical world? How is it that social scientists seem unable to predict events any distance into the future? Natural scientists, it might be pointed out, can predict certain phenomena (e.g., eclipses) years in advance.

Invidious comparisons can be made between the nature of natural and social scientific discoveries. The discovery of DNA's molecular structure is a convenient example. After reading Watson and Crick's findings, scientists uniformly agreed that the researchers had discovered the structure of DNA. There was no question but that one of the mysteries of life itself had been solved. Scientists did not say "perhaps this is the structure of DNA" or that Watson and Crick's description of the DNA molecule "seems plausible" or that their data "generally seem to confirm" their picture of the structure as correct. In comparison, social scientists can rarely establish the incontrovertible truth of their findings or interpretations.

Social science critics are correct in these assertions. Social scientific knowledge does not have a high cumulativeness to it. Social scientists are not easily able to make accurate predictions about social life in the future; many events take them by surprise. How many social scientists accurately forecast the civil rights activity of the early 1960s, the urban riots of the mid-1960s, the antiwar movement of the late 1960s, or the women's rights activity of the 1970s? Social scientists frequently seem to be in the business of trying to explain why something happened after its occurrence.

It is also true, to a much greater extent than among natural scientists, that social scientists disagree about the theories used to explain a body of data. A casual search will find frequent debates in the sociological literature about the causes of deviance, poverty, prejudice, and so forth. One can, as well, easily find studies whose findings directly contradict one another, or studies where the same variables are measured in thoroughly different ways.

We must, however, ask whether these criticisms are misplaced. Should social scientists faced with a comparison of natural and social scientific achievements apologetically bow their heads and merely promise to try harder in the future? Certainly progress can be made in further refining their methodological techniques. However, it would be appropriate for social scientists to point out that the social world and the physical world are really two quite different kinds of subjects. The structure of a DNA molecule remains constant, but that simply is not true of social structures. It may be appropriate for natural scientists to ask whether they have discovered absolute truths, but it would be unwise to ask whether social truths are absolute. To make the simple comparison suggested on the last couple of pages misses a most obvious and telling point: Human beings are continuously in the process of rearranging their social worlds. We simply do not respond in completely predictable ways to the situations in which we find ourselves. Unlike atoms, molecules, or stable elements of the physical universe, people think, construct meanings, and interpret the behaviors of others. Individuals possess a certain "plasticity" that allows them to respond creatively to their environments. The meanings of events, persons, objects, and institutions can change over time. Values and attitudes change. Behaviors once thought taboo become incorporated into our repertoire of legitimate or conventional behaviors. We create new social forms if they seem better able to meet our needs. We participate in unpredictable fads of our own making. In short, human activity and hence the social world is continually in a state of process, a state of production. It is human beings' unparalleled capacity for adaptation that makes any generalization produced by social scientists time-specific.

It is for these reasons that social scientists face a special task. We must be prepared to alter our theories as persons alter their views and perceptions of the world. The emergence of certain types of leaders, the outbreak of wars, unpredicted changes in the economic structure, and the like, transform the face of society. Our theories, methods and explanations must reflect the nature of the objects with which they deal. If the world is continually changing, we must give our theoretical constructs freedom to change. Explanation, in this sense, never ends. We can and must produce good, complete contemporary explanations. We can with a high degree of certainty and accuracy say, on the basis of our carefully collected data, this is the way the world is operating now; these are persons' attitudes, beliefs, ideologies and these are the behavioral consequences of their present constructions of the world.

There is another respect in which social scientists have a novel task. It is that we are professionally obligated to question what might seem obvious and unproblematic to us as members of a society. There is a tendency for some to put down or disregard social science investigation because, they say, "it deals with what we already know anyway." Our subject matter does not have a mysterious quality to it. Social scientists write about phenomena or social processes with which we are familiar. Although it is difficult for most of us to have our own ideas, interpretations, and theories about the causes of cancer, or the physics of space travel, it is easy for us to feel expert about social life. Why shouldn't we feel as experts about society since we all do, after all, participate in it? The subject matters of social science investigation are also frequently the discussion topics around the family dinner table, at parties, in Ann Landers's columns, in popular magazines, on radio talk shows, in bars, and the like. We all have our private theories about why people commit crimes, go on welfare, consume as they do, display prejudice, resist integration, get married, have babies, get divorced, steal from bureaucracies, and engage in deviant behaviors. We all recognize, as well, that we are members of one or another social class; that our group affiliations affect our behavior; that our children are gradually inducted into the life of a society; and that the way we behave and are viewed by others will be related to our educational level, sex, age, race, religion, ethnicity, occupation, and income.

When it comes to social issues it is easy to feel that one person's opinion is every bit as valid as another's. The authors would maintain, however, that people frequently mistake general familiarity with absolutely correct knowledge.

It is important to realize that individuals are, in some measure, limited by the boundaries of their own experience. Their knowledge of social life emerges from the distinctive social positions they occupy and their realities are constrained by their own life situations. Our private understandings of social life are generated from a limited data base. The promise of the social sciences is to let us transcend our own realities so that we might be freed to view the world from unfamiliar perspectives.

A major goal of social science investigation must be precisely to question, critically examine, and frequently show the faulty character of many commonly held generalizations about social life. In Peter Berger's words, social scientists must be preoccupied with "debunking" the validity of longstanding "truisms" about social life. He says (1963:38):

> The sociological frame of reference, with its built-in procedures of look-
> ing for levels of reality other than those given in the official interpreta-

tions of society, carries with it a logical imperative to unmask the pretentions and the propaganda by which men cloak their actions with one another.

Sociologists have succeeded in showing that shorthand characterizations of the social world often do not capture the complexity involved in the processes described. The generalizations that all of us make on the basis of our own experience and observation certainly operate to help us make our individual and collective experiences more intelligible. At the same time, such generalizations are, by definition, based on only selected aspects of social reality. Therefore, a continuing task of social science investigation is to uncover those features of social life that lie hidden beneath the veneer of accepted social knowledge about the world. In some instances our investigations will cause us to thoroughly reject images or stereotypes commonly held. In other cases, our research will let us specify those images in important ways.

The methodologies used by social scientists are indispensable in enabling them to discover how our assumptions, images, stereotypes, or generalizations may blind us to the way the world is operating. Methodologies serve the function of helping us become strangers to that which is normally familiar to us. Methodologies act as safeguards in that they force us to question what we usually do not. Once we commit ourselves to systematic, dispassionate, methodologically rigorous investigation we maximize the likelihood of seeing how and why our individual understandings of the world may be dramatically incorrect. It is when we accomplish this end that sociological research fulfills the promise for which methodologies were invented.

We have been careful to broadly suggest the limits of sociological knowledge. We need not, however, be overly modest about the significance of our scientific work. Social scientific research can be profoundly liberating by letting us see how social forces shape our identities and life situations. Sociological knowledge frequently allows us to better understand how we are influenced by the institutions with which we live. Close examination of the social world informs us about the delicate balance between social order and personal freedom existing in a society. Sociological findings are liberating because they work to raise our consciousness about the constant interplay between individuals and social structures. The knowledge and insight provided by social scientists has direct implications for collective action. Those groups, in any society, oppressed socially or economically, will better be able to alter their respective situations once they correctly perceive how that oppression has been accomplished.

On a more concrete level, sociologists have successfully questioned longstanding beliefs about the poor, have demonstrated the faulty character of racial stereotypes, have uncovered the "informal" structure of bureaucratic organizations, and have caused us to better understand the behaviors and attitudes of segments of the population with whom we might rarely come into contact. When social scientists seek to explain such life constancies as the allocation, distribution, and use of power in a society, modes of social interaction, group formation, patterns of deviance, and the like, they are talking about processes that touch us all. The important point we must make is this. The clarity and insight that social scientists gain about such processes can be only as good as the data which is the basis for their explanation. Our methodologies ensure, as far as possible, that the data from which we infer our understanding of society is as correct as possible.

Why is all this important? Why must we worry so about the correctness of the data from which we draw our generalizations about social life? All decision making, all policy formulation, must proceed from some knowledge base — not just the decisions that we privately make, but also, and perhaps more importantly, the decisions often made for us. The type of schools we shall have, the character of our cities, the programs developed to eradicate prejudice, rehabilitate criminals, treat the mentally ill, and so on, must be based on some conception of how and why persons behave as they do. Social scientists proceed with the belief that we ought to avoid creating social policy with information or knowledge that is intuitive or developed with inadequate data. Is punishment a deterrent to antisocial behavior? Does the physical deterioration of an area lead to family disorganization? To what extent is education related to future occupational success? Does integration raise the academic achievement levels of minority students? Does welfare destroy people's incentive to work? Do persons learn better in classroom type X than in type Y? These are the types of questions to which sociologists can provide clear answers. These are also the kinds of questions that must be answered as we work to develop plans for creating beneficial social change in a society.

The dangers of using intuition, common sense, or what appears obvious to answer questions like those posed above are very great. Time and again enormous amounts of money and time have been invested in programs that were bound to fail because they were based on faulty knowledge. Planners, for example, have torn up areas of cities because they incorrectly believed there to be an obvious relationship between the physical appearance of an area and social disorganization. Our prison system reflects the faultiness of another "obvious" assumption — that if persons are severely punished they will cease to engage in anti-social behavior. In other words, as long as common sense is frequently shown to be neither common nor necessarily sensible, social scientists will have a crucial task to perform.

We face extraordinary problems in our society and throughout the world. Social scientific knowledge alone will not solve these problems, but we have no hope of forging solutions without a sensitive and deep understanding of how persons relate to each other in the social structures and institutions of their own making. In social science we seem to overstress such issues as objectivity, bias, reliability, and validity because these are the yardsticks against which we must judge the certainty with which we can proclaim our knowledge as correct. Social scientists, we think, must reconcile themselves to the apparently obdurate fact that they will never be able to say they fully and completely know why human beings act as they do or that their findings have a universal applicability. They can say, though, that they have honestly tried to assess the validity of their knowledge at every stage in its production.

While we ought to refuse attaching any sacred quality to the findings of social science research, we should not be led to think of our work as having small importance. The study of our behaviors, values, attitudes, beliefs and institutional arrangements is not a trivial concern. It is not an inconsequential pursuit to explore the nature and quality of social life; to assess the potentialities of persons' relations with each other and, ever more frequently, to have a hand in the creation of the world that we will leave behind us. As we do make the decisions that will shape our individual and collective futures we ought to be informed by the best knowledge possible. The methodological procedures that have occupied our attention in this book are designed precisely to produce that knowledge.

REFERENCES

Berger, Peter L.
1963   *Invitation to Sociology: A Humanistic Perspective.* Garden City, N.Y.: Doubleday.

Author Index

Adelman, Irma, 365
Albrecht, Milton C., 294
Allen, Frederick, 293
Allport, Gordon, 274
Anderson, Charles H., 268
Aristotle, 348–349
Arnheim, Rudolf, 294
Asch, Solomon, 368

Backstrom, Charles H., 120
Bales, Robert F., 291, 297
Banaka, William H., 182
Barcus, Francis E., 294
Bart, Pauline, 103
Barton, Allen, 52–53
Beard, Charles, 266
Becker, Howard S., 10, 23, 34, 91–92, 95, 166, 170, 205, 217, 274–275
Bensman, Joseph, 96
Berelson, Bernard, 288–290
Berger, Peter, 3, 8, 454–455
Berlew, David E., 294
Bernstein, Arnold, 37
Birdwhistle, Ray L., 296
Blackwood, B., 349
Blau, Peter, 49, 53, 54n, 55, 332–333
Blumberg, Nathan B., 293

Blumer, Herbert, 70, 217–218, 295
Bogdan, Robert, 274
Bonjean, Charles, 66
Bottomore, Thomas B., 37
Bradburn, Norman N., 294
Brown, Claude, 274
Burgess, Ann Wolbert, 167, 182

Campbell, Donald T., 83, 233n, 442n
Carr-Saunders, A. M., 270
Child, Irvin L., 349–350, 356
Cloward, Richard A., 37–38, 42, 278–279, 367
Coch, Lester, 247–248
Comte, Auguste, 267–268
Cressey, Paul, 199

Darwin, Charles, 9, 13, 16
Davis, Alan J., 37
Davis, James A., 121
Davis, Kingsley, 33
DeFleur, Melvin L., 292
Denzin, Norman K., 97, 166, 250
Deutscher, Irwin, 75
Dornbusch, Sanford M., 294
Duncan, Otis Dudley, 53, 54n, 55, 332–333
Durkheim, Emile, 49, 154, 261, 270–271

Subject Index

Achieving Society, The, 293, 368
Aggregate data analysis. See also Comparative research, Historical analysis
  applications of, 320–336
  census data in, 321–325
  crime statistics in, 325–326
  explanation of, 318–320
  fallacies in, 336–340
  forecasting in, 329–331
  level of aggregation in, 327–329, 334–335
  simulation in, 332–336
  social indicators in, 326–329
Applied research, 3
  evaluation research as, 383
A priori research, 15, 32
Atomistic fallacy, 339–340
Autobiography of Malcolm X, The, 274
Axiomatic theory, 42–44

Bar graphs, 407–408
Basic research, 3
Becoming a Kwoma, 356
Bias. See also Objectivity, Values of the researcher
  in analysis of data, 405
  in methods, 25–26
  and objectivity, 10–11
  of researcher, 89, 91–92
  in sampling, 122

Case study, 19, 23
Causality, 56–57, 227–228
Causal modeling, 53–57, 138
Census data. See also Demography
  in aggregate data analysis, 321–325
  compared with sample data, 126–127
  in historical analysis, 276
  and survey interviews, 133–134
Census tract, 322
Chi square, 440
Coding,
  in content analysis, 303–306
  in observational field research, 214–215
  in survey research, 152–153
Communist Manifesto, The, 268
Comparative Guide to American Colleges, 117
Comparative research,
  aggregate data analysis in, 364–367
  applications of, 354–369
  content analysis in, 368
  ethnographic research in, 355–359
  experimental research in, 368
  historical analysis in, 367